ECONOMIC & MANAGEMENT
RESEARCH

ECONOMIC & MANAGEMENT RESEARCH

EDITORS
VENTER | VAN ZYL

JANSE VAN RENSBURG | JOUBERT
PELLISSIER | STACK

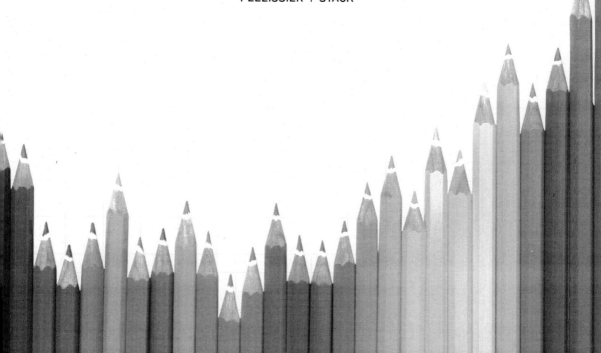

Oxford University Press is a department of the University of Oxford.

It furthers the University's objective of excellence in research, scholarship, and education by publishing worldwide. Oxford is a registered trade mark of Oxford University Press in the UK and in certain other countries.

Published in South Africa by
Oxford University Press Southern Africa (Pty) Limited

Vasco Boulevard, Goodwood, N1 City, Cape Town, South Africa, 7460 P O Box 12119, N1 City, Cape Town, South Africa, 7463

Oxford University Press Southern Africa (Pty) Ltd 2017

The moral rights of the author have been asserted.

First published 2017

All rights reserved. No part of this publication may be reproduced, stored in a retrieval system, or transmitted, in any form or by any means, without the prior permission in writing of Oxford University Press Southern Africa (Pty) Ltd, or as expressly permitted by law, by licence, or under terms agreed with the appropriate reprographic rights organisation, DALRO, The Dramatic, Artistic and Literary Rights Organisation at dalro@dalro.co.za. Enquiries concerning reproduction outside the scope of the above should be sent to the Rights Department, Oxford University Press Southern Africa (Pty) Ltd, at the above address.

You must not circulate this work in any other form and you must impose this same condition on any acquirer.

Economics and Management Research

ISBN 978 0 19 904930 1

Third impression 2018

Typeset in Utopia 10 pt on 12pt
Printed on 80gsm Bond

Acknowledgements

Publisher: Janine Loedolff
Editor: Deanne Vorster
Proofreader: Sarah Floor
Designer: Studio designers
Typesetter: Stronghold Publishing
Indexer: Lois Henderson
Cover reproduction by: Judith Cross
Printed and bound by: Print on Demand (Pty) Ltd

[Any other dedications/photos/other permissions/website links]

The authors and publisher gratefully acknowledge permission to reproduce copyright material in this book. Every effort has been made to trace copyright holders, but if any copyright infringements have been made, the publisher would be grateful for information that would enable any omissions or errors to be corrected in subsequent impressions.

Links to third party websites are provided by Oxford in good faith and for information only.

Oxford disclaims any responsibility for the materials contained in any third party website referenced in this work.

Contents in brief

Contributors		xv
Preface		xvi
Part 1	**Introduction**	**1**
1	An introduction to the philosophy and aims of business research	2
2	The research problem	31
3	The literature review	52
Part 2	**Conceptualising and environment scanning phase**	**73**
4	Research design	74
5	Qualitative research designs	99
6	Surveys as research strategy	131
7	Quantitative data analysis techniques in research	156
Part 3	**Academic literacy**	**185**
8	Writing a research proposal	186
9	Research reporting	214
10	Academic literacy	237
Index		259

Table of contents

Part 1		Introduction	1
	1	**An introduction to the philosophy and aims of business research**	2
	1.1	Introduction	3
	1.2	Approaches to business research	3
	1.2.1	Initiating research	4
	1.2.2	Choosing a topic	4
	1.2.3	Research philosophies	6
	1.2.4	Formulating a research problem	7
	1.2.5	Research purpose	7
	1.3	Research approaches	8
	1.3.1	Deductive research	8
	1.3.2	Inductive research	9
	1.4	Research designs	10
	1.4.1	Methodological approaches and research designs	11
	1.5	Research purpose and research design	14
	1.5.1	Suitability of research designs for creating business knowledge	17
	1.5.2	Research methods	17
	1.5.3	Writing up and reporting research	18
	1.6	Ethical research	18
	1.6.1	Plagiarism	18
	1.6.2	Ethical considerations in business research	18
	1.7	Business research	19
	1.7.1	Importance and purpose of business research	20
	1.7.2	Identifying problems or opportunities	21
	1.7.2.1	Diagnosing and assessing problems or opportunities	21
	1.7.2.2	Selecting and implementing a course of action	21
	1.7.2.3	Evaluating the course of action	21
	1.8	Basic and applied research	22
	1.9	Producing academic research	23
	1.10	Summary	24
Key terms and concepts			27
Test yourself questions			27
Activities			28
References			28
	2	**The research problem**	31
	2.1	Introduction	31
	2.2	The importance of formulating a research problem	32
	2.2.1	From topics to questions	33
	2.3	Developing a research problem	34
	2.3.1	Problem identification	34
	2.3.2	Problem definition	35

2.3.2.1	Step I: Understand the problem	36
2.3.2.2	Step II: Approach to the problem	37
2.3.2.3	Step III: Problem formulation	38
2.3.3	Research subproblems	38
2.3.4	Criteria for good research problem statements	39
2.4	Formulating statements of research purpose	40
2.4.1	Statement of overall purpose	40
2.4.2	Research questions	40
2.4.3	Research objectives	41
2.4.4	Hypotheses	42
2.5	Approach to the problem	44
2.5.1	The empirical unfolding of research problems	45
2.5.2	The importance of methodology	45
2.5.3	The role of theory in problem formulation	46
2.6	Summary	47
Key terms and concepts		48
Test yourself questions		48
Multiple-choice questions		48
Activities		48
Case study		49
References		50

3 The literature review 52

3.1	Introduction	52
3.2	What is a literature survey?	53
3.3	The purposes of a literature survey	53
3.4	Surveying the literature	56
3.4.1	Performing a literature survey	56
3.4.1.1	Planning your research	56
3.4.1.2	Sources of research items relevant to your research	57
3.4.1.3	Stages in the literature survey	58
3.4.1.4	When to stop reading	58
3.4.2	Record-keeping	58
3.4.2.1	Suggestions for record-keeping	58
3.4.2.2	How to record the results of your literature survey	59
3.5	The literature review	60
3.5.1	Ensuring quality in your literature review	61
3.5.1.1	Primary, secondary and general sources	61
3.5.1.2	Evaluating the quality of a literature item	61
3.5.2	Writing the literature review	63
3.5.2.1	Reproduce or review	63
3.5.2.2	The content and structure of the review	63
3.6	Summary	65
Key terms and concepts		66
Test yourself questions		66
Multiple-choice questions		66

Activities		67
Case study		68
References		70

Part 2 Conceptualising and environment scanning phase 73

4 Research design 74

4.1	Introduction	75
4.2	Practical considerations in research design	75
4.2.1	Limited resources	75
4.2.2	The required scope	76
4.2.3	Ethical considerations	76
4.2.4	Paradigmatic preferences	77
4.2.5	Access	77
4.2.6	The role of triangulation	77
4.3	Basic research approaches	78
4.3.1	Non-empirical research designs	78
4.3.1.1	Literature review	79
4.3.1.2	Conceptual studies	79
4.3.1.3	Analysis of existing data	80
4.3.2	Deductive research	81
4.3.3	Inductive research	82
4.3.4	Mixed methods research	83
4.3.4.1	Explanatory mixed methods design	83
4.3.4.2	Exploratory mixed methods design	84
4.3.4.3	Triangulation	85
4.3.4.4	Embedded mixed methods design	85
4.4	Types of research designs	86
4.4.1	Exploratory research designs	87
4.4.1.1	Historical research	87
4.4.1.2	Phenomenology	87
4.4.1.3	Ethnography	88
4.4.1.4	Grounded theory	88
4.4.1.5	Case research	88
4.4.1.6	Action research	88
4.4.2	Descriptive research designs	88
4.4.2.1	Observation studies	89
4.4.2.2	Developmental designs	89
4.4.2.3	Descriptive surveys	89
4.4.3	Causal research designs	90
4.4.3.1	True experimental designs	91
4.4.3.2	Quasi-experimental designs	92
4.4.3.3	Ex post facto studies	93
4.4.3.4	Correlational research	93
4.5	Chapter outline for this section	93
4.6	Summary	94
Key terms and concepts		95
Questions for review and critical thinking		95

Research activities		96
Case study		96
References		97

5 Qualitative research designs — 99

5.1	Introduction	99
5.2	Perspectives on qualitative research	101
5.2.1	Interpretivism	101
5.2.2	Critical theory	102
5.2.3	Critical realism	102
5.2.4	The practice turn in management research	103
5.3	Qualitative research designs	103
5.3.1	Phenomenology	104
5.3.2	Ethnography	105
5.3.3	Grounded theory	105
5.3.4	Case research	106
5.3.4.1	Single case study	107
5.3.4.2	Multiple case studies	108
5.3.5	Action research	109
5.4	Qualitative research methods	111
5.4.1	The role of the researcher in qualitative research	111
5.4.2	Sampling	112
5.4.2.1	Sampling strategies	113
5.4.2.2	Sample size in qualitative data	113
5.4.3	Data production	114
5.4.3.1	Interviews	114
5.4.3.2	Focus groups	115
5.4.4	Alternative methods for producing data	117
5.4.4.1	Participant observation	118
5.4.4.2	Direct observation	119
5.4.4.3	Documents	119
5.4.4.4	Artefacts	119
5.4.5	Qualitative data analysis and interpretation	120
5.4.5.1	Deductive and inductive approaches to qualitative data analysis	120
5.4.5.2	Types of qualitative data analysis	121
5.4.5.2.1	Content analysis	122
5.4.5.3	Conversation analysis	122
5.4.5.4	Discourse analysis	122
5.4.5.5	Narrative analysis	122
5.4.6	The process for analysing qualitative data	123
5.4.6.1	Preparing data for analysis	123
5.4.6.2	Becoming familiar with the data	123
5.4.6.3	Coding and theorising	123
5.4.6.4	Evaluating emergent understandings	124
5.4.7	Presentation of qualitative data	124
5.5	Summary	125

	Key terms and concepts		126
	Questions for review and critical thinking		127
	Research activities		127
	Case study		127
	References		128

T3 **6 Surveys as research strategy**   **131**

6.1	Introduction		131
6.2	Characteristics of surveys		132
6.3	Steps in the design of a survey		133
6.3.1	Step 1: Translating the problem statement into a set of research objectives		133
6.3.2	Step 2: Sample design		134
6.3.2.1	Probability sampling methods		135
6.3.2.2	Non-probability sampling methods		136
6.3.3	Step 3: Data collection		136
6.3.3.1	Interview-based surveys		137
6.3.3.1.1	Personal face-to-face interviews		137
6.3.3.1.2	Telephone interviews		138
6.3.3.2	Questionnaire-based surveys		139
6.3.3.2.1	Mail/postal surveys		139
6.3.3.2.2	Web-based surveys		139
6.3.3.2.3	Systematic observation		140
6.3.4	Step 4: Design of a questionnaire and other data collection instruments		141
6.3.4.1	Types of variables (i.e. attributes, behaviour, opinion)		141
6.3.4.2	Types of questions		142
6.3.4.3	Types of data		144
6.3.4.4	Scales as proxy measures for hypothetical constructs		146
6.3.4.5	Question wording and layout of the questionnaire		147
6.3.4.6	Reliability and validity		148
6.3.4.7	Importance of pilot testing to assess reliability and validity		151
6.3.5	Step 5: Data capturing, coding and editing (including imputation)		152
6.3.6	Step 6: Data analysis		152
6.3.7	Step 7: Data dissemination and documentation		152
6.4	Sources of errors in surveys		152
6.5	Summary		153
	Key terms and concepts		153
	Questions for review and critical thinking		154
	Research activities		154
	Case study		154
	References		154

T4 **7 Quantitative data analysis techniques in research**   **156**

7.1	Introduction		156
7.2	A step-wise approach to analysing your data and reporting the results		157
7.2.1	Step 1: Preparing your data for analysis		158

7.2.1.1	Selecting a suitable statistical program to analyse your data		158
7.2.1.2	Data coding		159
7.2.1.3	Database design and capturing		163
7.2.1.4	Data cleaning		164
7.2.2	Step 2: Assessing scale reliability (internal consistency reliability)		165
7.2.3	Step 3: Conducting preliminary analysis (univariate)		165
7.2.4	Step 4: Exploring relationships among variables and comparing groups (bivariate and multivariate)		172
7.2.4.1	Exploring relationships among variables		173
7.2.4.1.1	Correlation analysis		173
7.2.4.1.2	Regression analysis		174
7.2.4.1.3	Exploratory factor analysis		175
7.2.4.1.4	Confirmatory factor analysis		176
7.2.4.1.5	Structural equation modelling		176
7.2.4.2	Comparing groups		177
7.2.4.2.1	Chi-square test for independence		177
7.2.4.2.2	Two independent-samples test		178
7.2.4.2.3	Paired-samples test		178
7.2.4.2.4	Multiple independent samples test		178
7.3	Summary		179
Key terms and concepts			180
Questions for review and critical thinking			180
Research activities			180
Case study			181
References			182

Part 3	**Academic literacy**		**185**
8	**Writing a research proposal**		**186**
8.1	Introduction		187
8.2	What is a research proposal?		188
8.3	The purpose of a research proposal		188
8.4	Preparing to write your proposal		189
8.5	The structure and content of the research proposal		191
8.5.1	Guidelines for a research proposal		191
8.5.1.1	Title page		192
8.5.1.2	Introduction		192
8.5.1.3	Review of the literature		193
8.5.1.4	The research question or hypothesis		193
8.5.1.5	The purpose and goals of the research		193
8.5.1.6	The research method and design		195
8.5.1.7	Ethical clearance		195
8.5.1.8	Other aspects of the proposal		196
8.5.1.9	Provisional outline of the chapters of the thesis		196
8.5.1.10	References		196
8.5.2	Concluding remarks		196

8.6	How to write a reseach proposal	197
8.7	Judging the proposal	198
8.7.1	Requirements of a research proposal	199
8.7.2	Defending your proposal	202
8.7.3	Weaknesses in research proposals	202
8.8	Summary	204

Key terms and concepts 205
Questions 205
Multiple-choice questions 205
Activities 207
Case study 207
References 211

9 Research reporting 214

9.1	Introduction	215
9.2	Planning to write the report	216
9.3	The structure and contents of the report	217
9.3.1	Title page, acknowledgements and list of contents, diagrams, figures and graphs	217
9.3.2	The abstract	218
9.3.3	The introductory chapter	218
9.3.4	The literature review	219
9.3.5	The research methodology chapter	219
9.3.6	Chapters dealing with the data collection, measurement, analysis, results and interpretation	221
9.3.7	The concluding chapter	222
9.4	How the report will be judged	223
9.4.1	Guidelines and criteria provided to examiners	223
9.4.1.1	Guidelines	223
9.4.1.2	Assessment criteria	224
9.4.2	How examiners examine a thesis in practice	225
9.5	Writing the report	227
9.5.1	Hints on writing	227
9.5.1.1	Technical aspects	227
9.5.1.2	Referencing	228
9.5.1.3	Logical argument	229
9.5.2	Other problems experienced by researchers	230
9.5.2.1	Writer's block	230
9.5.2.2	Feelings of worthlessness	230
9.5.2.3	Loneliness and isolation	230
9.6	Summary	231

Key terms and concepts 231
Questions 232
Mutiple-choice questions 232
Application questions 233

Case study		234
References		235

10 Academic literacy — 237

10.1	Introduction	238
10.2	Academic literacy	239
10.3	Structuring the writing of a research report	240
10.3.1	Using knowledge by making notes	245
10.3.2	Organising ideas in sentences, paragraphs and sections	247
10.3.3	Developing an argument	249
10.4	Referencing	249
10.4.1	Plagiarism	251
10.5	Structuring requirements of academic research writing	252
10.5.1	Language usage	252
10.5.2	Establishing a niche within a broader research territory	253
10.5.3	Linguistic structures	253
10.6	Writing the background chapters	253
10.7	Linguistic strategies	254
10.8	The Results/Findings chapter or section	254
10.9	The conclusion	254
10.10	Summary	255
Key terms and concepts		255
Questions		256
Case study		258
References		258

Index — 259

Contributors

DION VAN ZYL is Manager: Information Services in the Directorate: Information & Analysis at the University of South Africa. He holds a PhD in Marketing Management from the University of Pretoria. He has conducted statistical consultancy since 1995 for a range clients, including multi-national companies, NGO's, government departments and academia. He is a member of the Southern African Association for Institutional Research.

PEET VENTER is a professor in Strategy at the University of South Africa's Graduate School of Business Leadership, which he joined in 2001. He holds an MBA from the University of Pretoria and a Doctorate in Business Management from the University of South Africa. He has published widely in the fields of strategy and marketing and is the editor and author of a number of successful strategy and marketing textbooks.

ELIZABETH STACK is a professor in Taxation and Research Methodology at Rhodes University. She holds a DCompt from the University of South Africa. She is also a Chartered Accountant.

WILHELM VAN RENSBURG is Research Fellow at the Visual Identities in Art & Design (VIAD) research centre at the Faculty of Art, Design & Architecture (FADA), University of Johannesburg (UJ). He directed the Post-Graduate Writing Centre at the Faculty of Education for many years and, apart from editing the academic journal, Education as Change, he co-authored two books: *Finding Your Way in Academic Writing* (First Edition: 2002, Second Edition: 2012), and *Finding Your Way in Qualitative Research* (2004). He is an independent facilitator of Research Methodology training sessions and Academic Writing workshops at various Higher Education Institutions in South Africa.

PROFESSOR PIERRE JOUBERT is a consumer psychologist and researcher at the Bureau of Marketing Research at the University of South Africa. Prior to his appointment to the University of South Africa, he was a market researcher at Clover SA, and a lecturer at the University of Johannesburg.

PROFESSOR RENÉ PELLISSIER is an international academic and researcher of note. She is a member of faculty at the University of Massachusetts (USA), University of Connecticut (USA), Bath University (UK), as well as universities in Southern Africa. She holds six degrees, three in Mathematical Statistics, two in management and a doctorate in Systems Engineering. She specialises in Research, Technology and Innovation. She is the author of several books in these fields and regularly presents workshops in Research Design, Research Methodology and Innovation Strategies in Higher Education and Complexity and Innovation in the corporate environment.

Preface

When there are so many different and excellent research books available on the market, a natural question to ask would be: Why another research book? We believe that there is a need for a book that focuses on the systematic decision-making process around research, and the academic production of research. For that reason, our focus is less on the specific methods and techniques of research, and more on the research decisions that every research student has to make. This process is based on many years of research and supervision experience of the authors, and has been tried and tested with a wide range of successful Master's and Doctoral researchers. Underlying our approach to this book is the knowledge that no research book provides a comprehensive source to all types of research, and accordingly the purpose of this book is to serve as a compass to guide researchers through the research process and to point them in the right direction before they immerse themselves in the design and methodologies supported by their research decisions.

The book is divided in three sections. Chapters 1 to 3 deal with an overview of the process and the initial phases of research, where the researcher conducts a literature review and develops the research problem and purpose. Chapters 4 to 7 deal with the important aspect of research design and analysis, and in this section we have tried to focus on those qualitative and quantitative research strategies and designs most applicable to business and management research. The final section (Chapters 8 to 10) focuses on the production of actual research outputs, by way of a research proposal and a research report.

We trust that you will find this South African book a useful contribution to the research journey of your postgraduate students.

Acknowledgements

PAGE	ACKNOWLEDGEMENT
2 (opener)	Based on case study FNB 'Steve' campaign Online Available: http://www.rab.co.za/radioworks-2011/case-study-fnb-steve-campaign.html. Reprinted by permission of Ryan Till, CEO The South African Radio Advertising Bureau (RAB SA)
42 (2.4.4)	Oxford Dictionaries.com (2016) In: English Oxford Living Dictionaries [online] Available at: https://en.oxforddictionaries.com/definition/hypothesis Oxford: © 2016 Oxford University Press [Accessed 04 November 2016]. By permission of Oxford University Press.
49 (case study)	Van Schalkwyk, Riaan Dirkse. 2012. The impact of leadership practices on service quality in private higher education in South Africa. Thesis (Business Management) University of South Africa 2011. Reprinted by permission of the author
62 (table 3.1)	Unisa. Undated. Template to evaluate journal articles. Pretoria: Dept. of Business Management, University of South Africa. Reprinted by permission of the Dept.
68 (case study)	Permission was granted by the student and the supervisor to use the research proposal.
74 (opener)	Adapted from Moody, Glyn, 2012. Making the most of file-sharing: free market research and a captive audience. Techdirt, Available online at: http://www.techdirt.com/blog/?tag=market+research [Accessed 21 January 2012] and Show doing well on BitTorrent? We'll buy it. 2012. Torrentfreak, Available online at http://torrentfreak.com/show-doing-well-on-bittorrent-well-buy-it-121010/, [Accessed 21 January 2012].
76 (ethical issues)	Adapted from ESOMAR Guideline for conducting mobile market research. Available online at: http://www.esomar.org/uploads/public/knowledge-and-standards/codes-and-guidelines/ESOMAR_Guideline-for-conducting-Mobile-Market-Research.pdf [Accessed 28 October 2012].
77 (4.2.6)	Adapted from de Vos, A.S. 2004. Combined qualitative and quantitative approach. In: de Vos, AS, Strydom, H, Fouché, CB and Delport, CSL (eds). 2004. *Research at grass roots*. Third edition. Hatfield, Van Schaik. p. 362
79 (4.3.1.2)	Based on the guidelines for conceptual stage model studies by Solli-Sæther, H. and Gottschalk, P. 2010. The Modeling Process for Stage Models, *Journal of Organizational Computing and Electronic Commerce*, Vol. 20 No. 3, p. 284. Reprinted by permission of the publisher (Taylor & Francis Ltd, http://www.tandfonline.com).
96 (case study)	Tustin, DH. 2012. Practice makes perfect – simplify your marketing research skills. Unpublished. p. 5–6. Bureau of Market Research (BMR), Unisa. Reprinted by permission of Prof. D H Tustin, Bureau of Market Research (BMR), Unisa.
99 (opener)	Adapted from Jane Goodall's biography. Available online at http://www.biography.com/people/jane-goodall-9542363?page=2 [Accessed 7 March 2013]; http://www.janegoodall.org/wp-content/uploads/the-Jane-Goodall-Institute_JaneGoodall_LongBio.pdf

PAGE	ACKNOWLEDGEMENT
104 (example box)	Savage-Austin, Amy R.; Honeycutt, Andrew. Servant Leadership: A Phenomenological Study Of Practices, Experiences, Organizational Effectiveness, And Barriers. *Journal of Business & Economics Research* (JBER), [S.l.], v. 9, n. 1, Jan. 2011. ISSN 2157-8893. Available at: <http://www.cluteinstitute.com/ojs/index.php/JBER/article/view/939>. Date accessed: 16 Aug. 2016. doi:http://dx.doi.org/10.19030/jber.v9i1.939.
105 (example box)	Fitzgerald, M. 2005. Corporate Ethnography. MIT Technology Review. Available at: https://www.technologyreview.com/s/404920/corporate-ethnography/ [Accessed 19 August 2016].
108 (example box)	http://www.informaworld.com: Venter, P, Wright, A and Dibb, S. 2015. Performing market segmentation: a performative perspective. *Journal of Marketing Management*, 31 (1–2): 62–83. Copyright © Westburn Publishers Limited. Reprinted by permission of Taylor & Francis Ltd, www.tandfonline.com on behalf of Westburn Publishers Limited.
109 (example box)	McCoy, Sean Patrick. 2012. Brand alignment: developing a model for competitive advantage through a study of selected South African companies Unpublished DBL thesis, University of South Africa, Pretoria.
111 (example box)	Botha, M.J., Van der Merwe, M.E., Bester, A.B. & Albertyn, R. 2007. Entrepreneurial skill development: Participatory action research in a rural community. *Journal of Family Ecology and Consumer Sciences*, 35: 9–15. Reprinted by permission of the authors
114 (example box)	Grebe, L. 2014. Source: Grebe, Lindie. 2014. The use of strategy tools by chartered accountants in the South African mining industry. University of South Africa: Unpublished Master's dissertation. M. Phil. (Accounting Sciences) University of South Africa 2014. Reprinted by permission of the author.
120 (example box)	Williamson, Charmaine Mavis. 2013. "Strategy in the Skin": An exploration of the strategic practices of South Africa's Official Development Assistance. University of South Africa: Unpublished Doctor of Business Leadership thesis. Reprinted by permission of Charmaine Williamson.
161 (example box)	South African Advertising Research Foundation. 2009. The SAARF AMPS Living Standards Measure (LSM). [Online] Available from: http://www.saarf.co.za/AMPS/technicalreport-2009A/data%20files/Technical/21+22.pdf. Reprinted by permission of SAARF
171 (reflection box)	Velleman, P. & Wilkinson, L. 1993. Nominal, Ordinal, Interval, and Ratio Typologies are Misleading. *The American Statistician*, 47(1): 65–72. p. 65, reprinted by permission of the publisher (Taylor & Francis Ltd, http://www.tandfonline.com).
175 (example box)	Anscombe, F.J. 1973. Graphs in Statistical Analysis. *The American Statistician* 27(1):17–21, reprinted by permission of the American Statistical Association, www.amstat.org and the publisher publisher (Taylor & Francis Ltd, http://www.tandfonline.com).
186	The Shorter Oxford English Dictionary on Historical Principles prepared by William Little, H.W. Fowler & Rev. J. Coulson; edited by C. T. Onions. Third edition (1973:1689). By permission of Oxford University Press.

PAGE	ACKNOWLEDGEMENT
188–205	Various quotes from: Hofstee, E. 2009. *Constructing a good dissertation*. Johannesburg: EPE. Permission to use was granted by the author.
198	Eaves, G. N. (1984:151). Preparation of the research-grant application: Opportunities and pitfalls. *Grants Magazine*, 7, 151–157
216–230	Various quotes from: Hofstee, E. 2009. *Constructing a good dissertation*. Johannesburg: EPE. Permission to use was granted by the author.
224	Rhodes University Internal and External Examiner's Report, undated. Assessment criteria. Reprinted by permission of the Head Librarian: Technical Services Rhodes University Library Services.
234 (case study)	Stevens, Nicol Susan. 2012. Unpublished thesis, Masters M.Com. Faculty of Commerce, Accounting. An analysis of the financing mechanisms proposed for funding national health insurance in South Africa. Grahamstown: Rhodes University. Available [online] http://hdl.handle.net/10962/d1001642 Reprinted by permission of the author.
240	Weideman, A. (2003) *Academic Literacy: Prepare to Learn*. Pretoria; Van Schaik Publishers, p. ix. Reprinted by permission of Van Schaik Publishers.
241 (figure 10.2)	L. Flower & J. Hayes, "A Cognitive Process Theory of Writing" Figure 3.1: Structure of the Writing Model in College Composition and Communication, 1981 32 (4) 364–387. Copyright 1981 by the National Council of Teachers of English. Reprinted with permission.
243 (figure 10.3)	Coffin, C., Curry, M.J., Goodman, S., Hewings, A., Lillis, T.M. & Swann, J. *Teaching Academic Writing: A toolkit for higher education*. Copyright © 2003. London: Routledge p. 34. Reproduced by permission of Taylor & Francis Books UK.
244 (figure 10.4)	Haas, S. S. (2010). By writers for writers: developing a writer-centred model of the writing process (Doctoral dissertation, Aston University) Copyright © S. Haas sshaas@mac.com Reprinted by permission of Sarah Haas

PART 1

AN INTRODUCTION TO THE PHILOSOPHY AND AIMS OF BUSINESS RESEARCH

Pierre Joubert

1

AFTER STUDYING THIS CHAPTER, YOU SHOULD BE ABLE TO:

- Understand how research approaches and associated paradigms influence doing business research
- Explain the use of a particular research methodology and design
- Explain the importance of research questions and hypotheses
- Understand how research contributes to business success
- Know how to define business research
- Understand the difference between basic and applied business research

'Hi I'm Steve?' – The big idea

Realising that no one sits in their cars or homes, or works for hours in order to hear and 'get' four separate messages that the bank wants to communicate, First National Bank took to the drawing board to figure out how to communicate these messages successfully. Their turning point came in the form of the hugely successful 'Steve' radio campaign.

The challenge for financial institutions is that often the last thing people think about are banking products whilst these institutions have to build and grow their customer base. Financial institutions are also bound by terms and conditions and other industry-related compliance issues, which have to be included in advertisements.

The birth of 'Steve'

The campaign came about by turning a slice of life on its head. Most of the ideas came from customer complaints such as 'how dare a bank call me at 7:30 pm in the evening, selling me something'. The intention was to make people cry, laugh, and in some cases, to offend. The advertising agency sat down and wrote the ads, as long as they needed to be. Putting its money where its mouth is, FNB went on air in May 2011 broadcasting not 30 or 35 second ads, but 45, 60 and even 84 second ads.

> **'Ads are only as good as the results'**
>
> The advertising agency is quick to add that the tongue-in-cheek 'Steve' campaign owes its success to radio. Within two months, this no-holds-barred approach to radio advertising had resulted in more than 10 999 opened (and swiped) FNB Gold Cards, and an increased uptake of other banking products on offer. What's more, FNB also benefitted from added exposure as certain radio presenters raved about the 'Steve' character and in the process added additional airtime to the campaign. Other channels also used the topical Steve campaign as editorial content. This all contributed to making 'Steve' a household name in the financial services market.
>
> **Lessons learnt from 'Steve'**
>
> - An advertisement has to be as long as necessary to get the message across.
> - Radio allows one to reach people directly.
> - Don't let the duration of the advertisement hamper the creativity.
> - There's no such as thing as too much exposure. Listeners should hear two to three advertisements at least.
> - Advertisements have to be entertaining and topical for the listener. Everyone loves a soapie.
> - Use audible triggers by starting and ending advertisements in the same way.
>
> Source: Based on case study FNB 'Steve' campaign Online Available: http://www.rab.co.za/radioworks-2011/case-study-fnb-steve-campaign.html
> Reprinted by permission of Ryan Till, CEO, The South African Radio Advertising Bureau (RABSA)

1.1 Introduction

The study of the philosophy and the aims of **business research** is an important undertaking since it provides researchers with a fundamental understanding and frame of reference when they have to consider particular **paradigms, research approaches, research designs** and **specific techniques to** undertake either **basic or applied research**. In this chapter, we explore the conceptual nature of business research, as well as the associated research paradigms, approaches, methodologies and designs. The importance of research questions and hypotheses in engaging a particular research approach is addressed. The purpose of this book is to provide a practical research guide for business and economics students.

1.2 Approaches to business research

Literally, *research* (re-search) means 'to search again'. Persistent study and scientific investigation where the researcher takes another, more careful, look at data to discover all that is known about a subject are generally associated with research. Even though research is commonly mistaken for gathering information, documenting facts and searching for information, it involves the process of collecting, analysing, and interpreting data in order to understand a phenomenon.[1] The research process is furthermore systematic in that it occurs within established frameworks and in accordance with existing guidelines. The frameworks and guidelines provide researchers with an indication of what to include and how to perform the research, as well as the types of inferences based on the data collected.

Research can also be understood as a movement from the unknown to the known. We all possess the vital instinct of inquisitiveness so, when the unknown confronts us, we want to attain a fuller understanding of the unknown. The process we use for obtaining knowledge of the unknown can also be termed research. Research can therefore also be defined as a 'systematised effort to gain new knowledge'.[2]

The term 'research', as an academic activity, should be used in a more technical sense. Slesinger and Stephenson in the *Encyclopaedia of Social Sciences* consequently define research as 'the manipulation of things, concepts or symbols for the purpose of generalising or verifying knowledge, whether that knowledge aids in construction of new knowledge, theory or in the practice of an art'.[3] Research is, therefore, also an original contribution to the existing body of knowledge.

Research originates with at least one question about a phenomenon of interest. For example, a financial institution might ask what they should be doing differently to attract more customers and ultimately changing existing behaviour. Or, what factors might influence the retention of existing customers? Research questions, such as these, help researchers choose the appropriate approach or perspective from which to make sense of each phenomenon of interest.

Research is therefore a process, starting with a question and moving to seek a solution though the researcher's choices of methods and techniques. This process is shown in Figure 1.1 and subsequently discussed. It should, however, be noted that research is not always a neat and sequential process. While certain steps have to occur before others, researchers will often find themselves moving back and forth between the elements of the research process and constantly revisiting their research decisions.

It is also important to mention the role of the **literature review** in the research process. You will notice that we did not include the literature review as a separate step in the research process. That is simply because the critical reading of literature is an integral part of each and every step in the research process. In fact, without demonstrating a thorough understanding of the literature in your field of study, it is unlikely that you will succeed in academic research at postgraduate level. The literature review is discussed in more detail in Chapter 3.

1.2.1 Initiating research

Whether the need to conduct research springs from the need to fulfil certain course requirements, to address a business problem (or opportunity), or simply from the curiosity of the researcher, all research begins somewhere with a need or an idea. This need or idea triggers the researcher to initiate a research project. The next step in the process is to identify a research-worthy topic.

1.2.2 Choosing a topic

In some instances, the research topic may be very clear. If a business is concerned about an increasing number of customer complaints, for example, it might be very clear that the topic they need to focus on is service delivery and customer satisfaction. In academic research, researchers may not be so lucky, and it may take considerable effort to identify and refine a suitable research topic. The issue of topic choices will be addressed in Chapter 2.

CHAPTER 1 An introduction to the philosophy and aims of business research

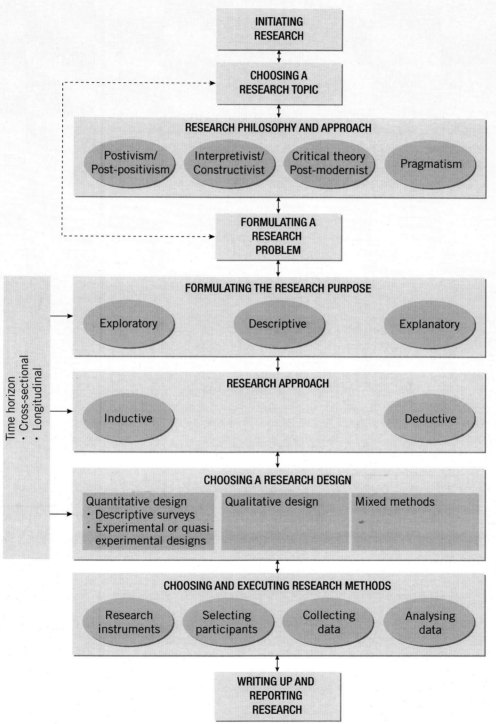

Figure 1.1 The research process

Social science paradigms form the scientific foundation for business research. These paradigms exemplify a theory of scientific enquiry and imply certain assumptions shared by an accepted group of researchers. Arbnor and Bjerke explain that these assumptions include the researcher's assumptions of reality and what science can contribute, as well as conventions relating to ethics and aesthetics.[4] Methodological approaches to business research furthermore derive from paradigms and form the basis for both the research design and selection of methods. Therefore, it is necessary to develop an understanding of both the relevant social science paradigms and methodological approaches in order to establish the basis for the selection of research designs and research methods.

1.2.3 Research philosophies

Before we discuss the different basic research philosophies or paradigms, it is important to understand what a **research paradigm** is.[5] In the first instance, the researcher may have a certain view about the nature of reality, and what can be known about it. This is referred to as **ontology**, or the ontological positon of the researcher. The relationship between the researcher and the ways in which knowledge about the reality can be discovered is the epistemological issue, and **epistemology** can accordingly be described as the study of knowledge and ways of knowing. The third and final element of the paradigm relates to the ways in which the researcher can find out about the phenomenon being studied. This is the element of **methodology**. In every research paradigm or philosophy, these three elements are aligned, as you will notice in the rest of the discussion in this section.

The dominant social science paradigms in business research are positivist/post-positivist, interpretivist/constructivist and critical theorist/post-modernist, with the fundamental difference found in the researcher's view of reality or worldview.[6] As the researcher moves from the positivist/post-positivist towards the interpretivist/constructivist to the critical theorist/post-modernist paradigms, their view of reality shifts from objective and rationalistic to subjective and relativistic, and their research objective shifts from explaining reality to understanding reality.[7]

The positivist/post-positivist sees an objective world that the researcher can model based upon knowledge, while the interpretivist/constructivist sees an inter-subjective world that the researcher can represent with a social construction of reality.[8] The critical theorist/post-modernist on the other hand sees a material world that the researcher can only attempt to know objectively by removing ideological bias.[9]

The objective view supported by positivism has led positivists to develop and rely on fixed research designs using experimental and quantitative methods in order to gather data, with the research grounded in existing knowledge. The post-positivist paradigm represents researchers who also view the world as objective but search for data that might not only be deterministic, but also probabilistic.[10] It is the inclusion of a probabilistic component that has lead post-positivists to develop and rely on mixed method designs in business research using qualitative and quantitative methods rather than a strict reliance on quantitative and experimental methods. Post-positivists therefore acknowledge their probable impact on a research study and work to maintain objectivity.

In contrast to the positivist or post-positivist paradigms, the constructivist paradigm views the world as inter-subjective, and attempts to represent the world through a social construction of reality made up of concepts and actors.[11] This means that the researcher is concerned with patterns and meanings and tries to develop an understanding of the individual's view of the world, as well as examine how objective realities are created. Constructivists, in this sense, have developed and rely heavily on flexible designs using qualitative methods for data gathering which include interviews, ethnography and textual analysis.

It is important to examine the shift in paradigm from positivist to post-positivist as it represents a fundamental change in the ultimate assumptions and beliefs of a large body of business researchers. Kuhn explains that the creation of knowledge is marked by revolutionary changes where entire views of reality are displaced by new ones due to a new discovery, leading to a shift in paradigm. In this sense, Kuhn asserts that new paradigms share two characteristics; (i) "an achievement that is sufficiently unprecedented enough to attract an enduring group of adherents away from competing modes of scientific activity", and (ii) "sufficiently open-ended to leave all sorts of problems for the redefined group of researchers and practitioners to resolve".[12] In this context, the shift in paradigm from positivist to post-positivist advances a range of mixed research designs that can be used to explain and understand complex systems where strict cause and effect relationships are difficult to determine due to the synergistic relationship of the various factors.

As an alternative to the paradigms already described, pragmatism has been making a lot of headway in economic and business studies, as it has in social research. Pragmatism is founded on the idea that researchers will use whatever works best for addressing a specific research problem, and is regarded as the philosophical basis for the emergence of mixed methods.[13] Pragmatism is therefore not rooted in a specific philosophy or approach, but uses the research problem and purpose as a point of departure and adopts whatever designs and methodologies will be the best solution to that problem. In that sense, pragmatism is similar to post-positivism. In this book, we generally adopt a pragmatic stance, suggesting that the research problem and research purpose should determine the choices researchers make. This process starts with the formulation of a research problem.

1.2.4 Formulating a research problem

The identification and formulation of a research problem is a very important step in the research process, because it influences all subsequent decisions about the research. The identification and formulation of a research problem is discussed in more detail in Chapter 2. The research problem influences, and is influenced by, the purpose of the research.

1.2.5 Research purpose

Researchers will generally have one or more of three broad research purposes, namely exploratory, descriptive or explanatory research.
- Exploratory research: The purpose of exploratory research is quite simply to explore a phenomenon with the idea of developing new insights. Exploratory research can be used on its own as research to develop new theory, or in conjunction with descriptive or explanatory research as a means for refining the research problem and hypotheses. In fact, it could be argued that any research project has an exploratory phase, ranging from informal inquiry to formal and structured projects.
- Descriptive research: Descriptive research attempts to describe a phenomenon with the purpose of developing a better understanding of the characteristics of a population.

It is often used as part of or as a precursor to explanatory research. Descriptive research typically makes use of the survey method as a means of collecting data.
- **Explanatory research:** The purpose of explanatory research is to establish the causal relationships between two or more variables. Because of the rigour required to establish causal relationships, explanatory research will often make use of experimental or quasi-experimental designs. In business and economics studies, it is almost impossible to establish the conditions for true experimental research, and researchers will often have to use quasi-experimental designs.

The relationship between research purpose and research design is touched on in section 1.5 in this chapter and discussed in more detail in Chapter 4.

The research purpose is operationalised by expressing it as research objectives, research questions or hypotheses. These operational elements of research purpose are discussed in more depth in Chapter 2.

Another important decision the researcher has to make when considering the purpose and resulting design of the research is the timeline. Research can generally be cross-sectional or longitudinal.[14] Cross-sectional research is generally a 'snapshot' of a population at a given time, and is accordingly conducted over a relatively short period of time using a sample from the population. Longitudinal studies are generally conducted over longer periods of time using the same set of subjects. The value of longitudinal studies lies in its ability to track the development of the research subject over time. Given the time and funding constraints of most research students, it is not surprising that most academic research projects will tend to be cross-sectional.

Bearing in mind the purpose of the research, a research approach will emerge, or the researcher will have to make a decision about the research approach.

1.3 Research approaches

Deductive research is more outwardly focused and **inductive** research is more inwardly focused. Research projects can also be a combination of the two approaches, in which case a mixed methods design will most likely be used. These basic approaches are discussed in more detail below. The research purpose often already suggests what type of research has to be conducted, but it is ultimately a decision made by the researcher.

1.3.1 Deductive research

Deductive reasoning is the logical process of deriving a conclusion about a specific instance based on a known general premise or something generally accepted to be true.[15] It is a top-down approach in the sense that it moves from the general to the specific. Research based on deductive reasoning will, therefore, start with a strong theoretical basis and specific proposition hypotheses. Based on observations, such as survey responses, the hypotheses can be tested and the theory supported. Once the theory has been confirmed, it can be applied to members of the population that were observed, i.e. it can be generalised. It should be mentioned that deductive research is generally dependent on rigorous scientific method in sampling and observation, and accordingly favours the positivistic or post-positivistic paradigm. Deductive research is generally only possible where the theoretical foundations in the field of study are established and known widely, in other words, where there is already some measure of certainty or at least relatively low levels of ambiguity. The process of deductive research is depicted in Figure 1.2.

The process starts with a review of previous research and existing literature, and the outcome of this review is typically a set of hypotheses, a theoretical framework or concepts, or research propositions. The research is designed in a way that enables the testing or evaluation of hypotheses, concepts or propositions, or the implementation of theoretical frameworks. The purpose is often to generalise the findings of the research to the population in which the research was conducted. This evaluation, and the extent to which findings support hypotheses or propositions (or not), lead to proposed explanations of the findings and the identification of new problems for further investigation. Thus it is clear that deductive research is more suited to fixed and quantitative research designs and testing or confirming theories than to developing new theories, and is accordingly more suited to descriptive or explanatory research.

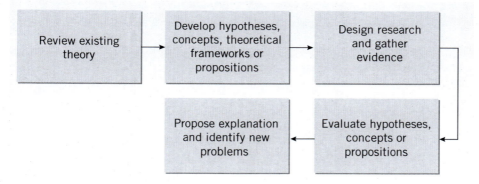

Figure 1.2 Basic deductive research design

Example box: deductive research

In 2010, three South African researchers used the well-known SERVQUAL questionnaire (a measure of service quality expectations and perception) to determine the service quality expectations of African retail banking customers. The study involved 4 035 banking customers in 10 African countries. The study found that there were significant differences in retail banking service expectations across the different countries. This study is an example of deductive research.[16]

However, not all research deals with describing a population. The purpose of research is often to explore certain phenomena and to develop new insights or theories. This is the focus of inductive research.

1.3.2 Inductive research

Inductive reasoning is the logical process of observing particular facts or occurrences and establishing a general proposition on the basis of the empirical observation.[17] It is thus the opposite of deductive research in that it moves from the specific to the general. Where research is inductive, the focus is on observing an object or phenomenon, identifying emerging patterns, and establishing a general proposition (a theory) on the basis of these empirical observations. Inductive research is often used where the theoretical foundations in the field of study are not strongly established and where there is a large degree of uncertainty and ambiguity. It may also be used simply as an alternative to deductive research, where researchers are critical of deductive research or its findings. For example, the current focus on practice-based research in management came about as a result of criticism against the prevailing rational-economic perspectives in management research that favour quantification and macro-perspectives of management, rather than a human perspective. Inductive research uses mainly flexible research designs and is strongly associated with the processes of **theory-building**. The process of inductive research is depicted in Figure 1.3.

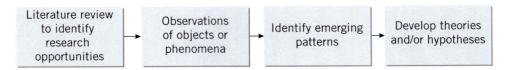

Figure 1.3 Basic inductive research design

Although the observations (using mainly qualitative methods such as in-depth interviews) are the starting point of the research process, it is usually preceded by a literature review to identify the research gaps and opportunities. The observations are usually directed at individual actors (rather than at a population) and the purpose is to identify emerging themes or patterns. The identified themes or patterns form the basis for the development of theories and hypotheses. However, the purpose of inductive research is not to confirm or to test the theories, although it should by now be apparent that inductive research may precede or be used in conjunction with deductive research.

> **Example box: inductive research**
>
> In a study on internal brand alignment, the researcher found that the extant (existing) literature on the topic was very limited. As a result, the researcher opted for a qualitative case study methodology, conducting interviews with senior and middle managers in four organisations as a means of developing a theoretical model for internal brand alignment.[18]

1.4 Research designs

The basic approaches to research discussed in the previous section and their implications for research lead us to the three common approaches to conducting business research, namely quantitative, qualitative, and mixed methods. The nature of the research question itself suggests that the researcher anticipates a data type, for instance, is numerical, verbal, or both numerical and verbal data needed? Based on this assessment, the researcher selects one of the three aforementioned approaches to conduct research. Researchers typically select a quantitative approach to respond to research questions requiring numerical data, a qualitative approach for research questions requiring verbal data, or a mixed methods approach for research questions requiring both numerical and verbal data.

The *quantitative approach* is basically deductive in nature and can be further sub-classified into *inferential, experimental* and *simulation approaches* to research. The purpose of an *inferential approach* to research is to form a database from which to infer characteristics or relationships of a population. This usually means survey research where a sample of a population is studied (questioned or observed) to determine its characteristics, and it is then inferred that the population has the same characteristics. An *experimental approach* is characterised by much greater control over the research environment and, in this case, some variables are manipulated to observe their effect on other variables (i.e. causal effect). A *simulation approach* involves the construction of an artificial environment within which relevant information and data can be generated. This permits an observation of the dynamic behaviour of a system (or its subsystem) under controlled conditions. The term 'simulation' in the context of business and social sciences applications refers to 'the operation of a numerical model that represents the structure of a dynamic process. Given the values of initial conditions, parameters and exogenous variables, a simulation is run to represent the behaviour of the process over time.'[19] The simulation approach can also be useful in building models for understanding future conditions.

The *qualitative approach* is essentially inductive and is concerned with subjective assessment of attitudes, opinions and behaviour. Research in such a situation is a function of the researcher's insights and impressions. Such an approach to research generates results either in non-quantitative form or in a form that is not subjected to rigorous quantitative analysis. Generally, the techniques of focus group interviews, projective techniques and in-depth interviews are used. All these are explained later.

Many research projects require a combination of qualitative and quantitative approaches, in which case mixed methods may be the chosen approach.

The various qualitative, quantitative and mixed methods research designs are discussed in more detail in Chapter 4.

1.4.1 Methodological approaches and research designs

Three broad methodological approaches are useful in creating business knowledge, namely the analytical approach, the systems approach, and the actors' approach. Differences between these approaches are due to the researcher's idea of reality, the impact or perceived role of the researcher and participants in the generation of knowledge, and the aim of the research. Based upon the methodological approach taken, the business researcher can develop a fixed, flexible, or mixed method research design based on quantitative and qualitative methods.[20]

The analytical approach entails that the researcher views reality as objective and consisting of the sum of its parts. The perceived role of the researcher is seen as independent and objective with researchers using this approach attempting to provide descriptions and explanations of reality that are general in nature and unqualified.[21] It is this aim of the analytical approach that leads to the use of fixed research designs and quantitative methods. As Cooper and Schindler explain, fixed designs are well suited to a study where the researcher is attempting to describe, explain or predict rather than attempting to understand or interpret.[22] In this sense, fixed designs are often viewed as theory testing designs rather than theory building designs, and are accordingly more suited to address descriptive and explanatory research. Arbnor and Bjerke support this view in clarifying that researchers adopting the analytical approach seek to explain reality through the discovery of causal relations and differences and, as a result, expand on the broader theory of reality through the addition of verified research questions and hypotheses.[23] A key benefit of the analytical approach using fixed research designs and quantitative methods is consequently the ability to build on existing theories when studying new problems. This ever growing foundation of knowledge frees the researcher to focus on the development of new knowledge without having to prove the validity of the foundation. A key weakness of the analytical approach is, however, an inability to consider that complex systems can develop where the whole is not simply the sum of its parts.

The actors' approach is, in contrast, used to describe a socially-constructed reality where the participants or actors being studied and the ensuing reality, in effect, create each other, and the knowledge generated is dependent on the individuals being studied, as well as on the researcher.[24] Researchers using this approach attempt to provide an understanding of reality that provides conceptual meaning based upon how the individuals perceive and act in their reality. It is this shift in purpose from explanation to understanding that leads to the selection of flexible research designs using qualitative methods. As Cooper and Schindler explain, flexible designs are well suited to a study where the researcher is attempting to understand or interpret rather than attempting to describe, explain, or predict.[25] In this sense, flexible designs are often viewed as theory building designs rather than theory testing designs, and are thus more exploratory in nature. Arbnor and Bjerke reinforce this by clarifying that researchers using the actors' approach seek to understand reality and describe the constantly changing relations between the actors and their reality.[26] As a result, the understanding of the interactions of the socially constructed reality is improved and communicated through the use of descriptive language. Researchers using the actors' approach can benefit from using general contributions from previous researchers as a starting point but they will need to develop their skill over time. A key benefit of the actors' approach using flexible research designs is the ability to develop new theories when studying new problems. A key weakness of the actors' approach lies in its use of descriptive language to describe reality, rather than verifiable and quantifiable facts, which can lead to misunderstandings or misinterpretations.[27]

The systems approach, in comparison to the analytical and actors' approaches, also describes an objective reality, but in this case, one that consists of a whole that is not simply the sum of its parts and where the knowledge generated is dependent on the system being observed.[28] Arbnor and Bjerke further explain that researchers using this approach are attempting to provide descriptions of reality that consist of representations of the system studied and that are less general in nature.[29] Scandura and Williams found a significant rise in the use of a systems approach and mixed methods in a review of field studies conducted from 1985 through 1997.[30] Their analysis showed this approach offered lower generality, precision and control in favour of higher contextual realism. The limitations of the summative nature of the analytical approach using quantitative methods are, as a result, becoming more apparent with a growing understanding of the complexity of society. Through the systems approach, the business researcher seeks to explain, as well as understand reality through the discovery of producer and product relations, and as a result, their view of reality is improved through the explanation and understanding of the behaviour of the systems studied. It is this dual purpose of explanation and understanding that leads to the use of mixed methods designs using a combination of quantitative and qualitative methods that can be used for developing and testing theory in a single study.[31]

Similar to the analytical approach, the systems approach using mixed research designs allows a researcher to draw analogies from the results of similar studies conducted in the past in order to develop new knowledge. A key benefit of the systems approach is that it incorporates the concept of synergy where the whole can be more than the simple sum of its components. A key weakness of the systems approach is the inability to draw simple cause and effect relationships.

From the preceding discussion it is possible to synthesise a comprehensive view of fixed, flexible and mixed methods research designs based upon their scientific foundations in the social science paradigms and methodological approaches (see Figure 1.4). Researchers following a positivist paradigm will use the analytical methodological approach and will design a fixed study using quantitative methods in order to explain an objective and rational reality. Importantly, the resulting knowledge generated with the analytical approach will be independent of the individuals involved and the observers. Conversely, researchers following a constructivist paradigm will use the actors' methodological approach and will design a flexible study using qualitative methods in order to understand a subjective and relativistic reality. In contrast to the analytical approach, the knowledge generated during the actors' approach is dependent on the individuals being studied, as well as on the observer or researcher. Researchers following a post-positivistic paradigm, however, use the systems methodological approach to explain and understand an objective and rational reality where the relevant facts might not only be deterministic, but also probabilistic. The resulting mixed methods design uses a combination of quantitative and qualitative methods, and the knowledge generated is dependent on the system being studied. The researcher, in this case, views these system as being more than simply the sum of its parts. Pragmatically, the post-positivists acknowledge the probability that their involvement could impact the study and work to maintain objectivity.

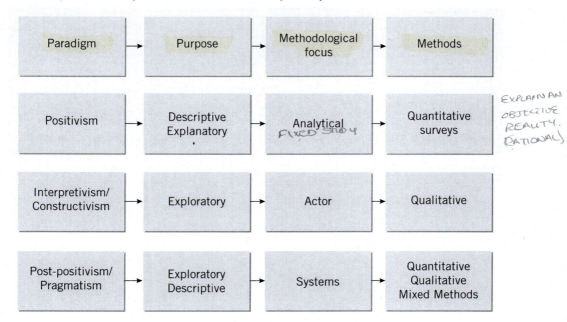

Figure 1.4 Methodological approaches and research design

Arbnor and Bjerke explain that the post-positivistic paradigm with its associated systems methodological approach and mixed methods design offers a tremendous amount of power and flexibility to the researcher when working to explain and understand the complex systems found in business today.[32] It is this power and flexibility that explains the shift towards a systems approach, making it the dominant point of view in business practice and business theory research.

With the scientific foundation of fixed, flexible and mixed method designs established, it is possible to examine the suitability of their associated quantitative and qualitative methods to the creation of business knowledge.

It seems appropriate at this juncture to explain the difference between research design, research methods and research methodology. *Research design* is described as the general plan of how the researcher will go about answering the research questions or attaining the research objectives.[33] *Research methods* may be understood as all those methods or techniques that are used for conducting research. *Research methodology* is a way to systematically solve the research problem. It involves the various steps that are generally adopted by a researcher in studying a research problem along with the logic behind them. Researchers not only need to know how to develop certain indices or tests, how to calculate the mean, the mode, the median or the standard deviation or chi-square, and how to apply particular research techniques, but they also need to know which of these methods or techniques are relevant and which are not, and what they would mean and indicate and why. Researchers therefore need to understand the assumptions underlying various techniques and they need to know the criteria by which they can decide that certain techniques and procedures will be applicable to certain problems.

All this means that it is imperative for the researcher to adopt a methodology for a particular problem. Research methodology has many dimensions and research methods constitute one part of the research methodology.

1.5 Research purpose and research design

Once the purpose of the research has been established, researchers can turn their attention to the construction of a research design using fixed, flexible or mixed methods. Researchers will create a fixed design using quantitative methods if they are attempting to describe, explain or predict, as well as precisely measure something through answering questions such as how much, how often and how many.[34] Conversely, a flexible design using quantitative methods will be created if the researcher is attempting to understand or interpret through a detailed description developed by asking and answering the why question. In this sense, Cooper and Schindler clarify that fixed designs are often viewed as theory testing designs while flexible designs are often viewed as theory building designs.[35]

Fixed designs using quantitative methods are advantageous to the researcher because of their ability to produce results that can be generalised, which means that they can go beyond individual characteristics to identify characteristics of a larger population. Also, with much of the data from fixed designs being in the form of numerical data, proven statistical techniques can be applied to data analysis which helps avoid confusion between facts and judgements. By providing separation between the researcher and the participants, fixed designs improve objectivity reducing the likelihood of researcher influence on the study. The primary weakness of fixed designs, however, is their inability to measure the complexity of individual behaviour at a deeper level.

Flexible designs using qualitative methods assist in clarifying research questions through the research process itself.[36] In this sense, flexible designs are well suited to exploring situations where the researcher does not fully understand theories or the nature of relationships and allows the researcher to develop a deeper level of understanding. This understanding is further improved through direct participation and involvement with the participants, which allows the researcher to evaluate and form insights. Further, qualitative or non-numeric data have the advantage of providing richer, fuller and more real descriptions when contrasted with quantitative data.

The primary weakness of flexible designs is the prevalent view that qualitative data are open to bias and human error during data collection and interpretation, making the process less objective. Coghlan and Brannick support this caution and highlight the need for researchers using flexible methods to minimise their impact on the research in order to maintain the highest level of objectivity possible.[37] Another weakness of flexible designs is the inability to apply proven statistical methods to data analysis, and the researcher must bear in mind that design choices regarding data analysis can affect the types of conclusions that can be drawn.[38] Robson, however, minimises the impact of these issues by explaining that it is now "respectable and acceptable in virtually all areas of social research" to use designs based upon qualitative methods.[39]

Mixed method designs offer a wide range of exciting possibilities to the researcher by combining both quantitative and qualitative methods, allowing the researcher to determine the optimal balance of objectivity, generalisability, and researcher objectivity and detachment. As an example, in order to allow triangulation of results, a researcher can use the results of a qualitative method to test the results of a quantitative method, thereby improving the range of data, as well as credibility of the study.[40] Also, to improve the credibility and statistical generalisability of qualitative studies, a researcher can organise qualitative data into numerical form through categorising and grouping, and once in this form, apply quantitative methods of data display and statistical analysis.

At a higher level of integration, a researcher can take advantage of the strengths of one type of method to offset the weaknesses of the other by applying them concurrently in order to develop a deeper understanding and better explanation of reality than would otherwise be possible. In general terms, fixed designs are better suited to exploring social structure, and flexible designs are better suited to exploring social process. By using both methods concurrently, a researcher can develop a higher fidelity view of reality that includes both social structure and process. Similarly, researchers can facilitate better interpretation by using the ability of fixed methods to establish relationships together with the ability of flexible methods to explain relationships. Researchers can therefore take advantage of fixed methods and their focus on small-scale or micro aspects of social life, as well as flexible methods and their focus on large-scale or macro aspects of social life to form a more complete and integrated view. Finally, recognising that fixed methods will have a more researcher-focused perspective and flexible methods will have a more participant-focused perspective, a mixed methods design can integrate both aspects. It is this higher level of integration of quantitative and qualitative methods that truly demonstrates the power of mixed methods designs, as well as the systems methodological approach where they originated.

From the preceding discussion, it is clear that fixed, flexible, and mixed methods research designs using quantitative and qualitative methods are all suitable for creating business knowledge. As exemplified, selection of methods including quantitative, qualitative or a combination of both is the final step in conceptualising a research study.

The researcher needs to first understand the purpose of the research and the objectives of the research design, as well as make choices based upon the relative importance of factors including objectivity, generalisability, and isolation of researcher and research subject. A fixed design using quantitative methods could, for instance, be more suitable to a researcher in search of a higher level of objectivity, generalisability, and isolation from the research subject.[41] Alternatively, if the researcher is unable to make a prediction and can only form an open-ended research question, a flexible design using qualitative methods is suitable for the study and will provide the researcher with a lower level of objectivity, generalisability, and isolation from the research subject. Mixed method designs offer a wide range of possibilities to the researcher by combining both quantitative and qualitative methods in ways that allow the strengths of one method to overcome the weaknesses of the other, allowing the researcher to determine the optimal balance of objectivity, generalisability, and detachment from the research subject. In this sense, the real strength of the mixed method design is found in designs that use both types of methods concurrently rather than simply sequentially, and it is this higher level of integration and synergy of methods that allows the researcher to develop a deeper level of explanation and understanding.

Robson cautions that regardless of the design selected, the goals of research are to produce findings that are believable, trustworthy, objective, reliable, valid, and generalisable.[42]

This discussion began with a comparative analysis of fixed, flexible, and mixed methods designs and their foundation in accepted scientific research principles. The positivist, constructivist, and post-positivistic paradigms were found to be the foundation for the fixed, flexible, and mixed research designs respectively. The analysis further showed that the knowledge generated by fixed designs can be considered independent of the individuals involved or the observers, while in flexible designs it is dependent on the individuals being studied, as well as the observer. In contrast, knowledge generated in the systems approach was found to be dependent on the system being studied. The researcher viewed the system as being more than simply the sum of its parts, and the researcher recognised and took steps to mitigate the probability that this will impact the study.

Following the comparative analysis of research designs, the suitability of qualitative and quantitative methods for the creation of relevant business knowledge was evaluated. While both methods were found to be suitable, the choice should be guided by the purpose of the study, as well as the relative importance of factors including objectivity, generalisability, and isolation of researcher and research subject. In this sense, quantitative methods will provide the researcher with a higher level of objectivity, generalisability and isolation from the research subject, while qualitative methods will provide a deeper level of understanding at the expense of a lower level of objectivity, generalisbility and isolation from the research subject. In contrast to the more rigid quantitative or qualitative methods, mixed methods designs using both quantitative and qualitative methods allow the researcher to determine the optimal balance of objectivity, generalisability and isolation from the research subject that will still allow him or her to meet the objectives of the study. The balance that is achieved through the integration of methods demonstrates the power and necessity of mixed methods designs, as well as the systems approach. Through this comparative analysis of research designs and the evaluation of research methods, this discussion supports the author's contention that mixed methods designs deserve increased recognition and acceptance, despite the historical dominance of fixed designs in the field of business research. Chapter 4 discusses research design in more detail.

1.5.1 Suitability of research designs for creating business knowledge

The suitability of fixed, flexible and mixed methods research designs using quantitative and qualitative methods for creating business knowledge can be evaluated from several perspectives. Before making the choice of design and method, the researcher must understand the purpose and objectives of the research design supporting the study.[43] As part of the design process and method selection, the researcher will also make choices about the relative importance of several factors such as objectivity, generalisability, and the relative detachment of the researcher to the research subject. McGrath summarises this dilemma by referring to certain trade-offs that all researchers must make.[44] In his view, the choice of a particular research design will require judgements concerning generalising findings, validity, precision, control of the business or behavioural variables, and realism of context. Cook and Campbell support this contention and stress the importance of the trade-off in internal, external and construct validity as critical aspects when selecting research designs and methods.[45]

Meaningful research requires a guiding statement that gives direction and purpose to the study and can be provided by either a hypothesis or a research question. This choice is guided by the researcher's ability to make a prediction about the outcome of the study before it is conducted. In basic research, the prediction is generally based on a theoretical perspective. As Robson explains, in situations where the researcher is able to make a prediction before data are gathered, a hypothesis that can be tested with a fixed design using quantitative methods is the best fit.[46] Cooper and Schindler support this view by explaining that when a statement is made about concepts or phenomena that can be observed by the researcher and can be found to be true or false using quantitative methods, it is considered a hypothesis.[47]

Conversely, in situations where the researcher is unable to make a prediction until after or during the data gathering process, a research question that can be answered with a flexible design using qualitative methods is more appropriate.[48] Cooper and Schindler support this view by explaining that it is any question that best states the objective of the research study and is not formatted to solicit a definitive answer.[49] Once posed, research questions are initially fine-tuned during a review of the literature and discussions with experts, and the process of refining the research question continues during the data-gathering phase until the question has been fully answered or a different question has presented itself as the actual core question. It is this evolving nature of research that forms the basis for the use of the term 'flexible' when describing the research design.

A powerful alternative to these two very different and potentially rigid methods of conducting research is offered by mixing hypotheses and research questions. Recognising both the advantages and limitations of each, many researchers are taking a pragmatic approach that combines both. The benefits of this approach are far reaching. For example, a single study could use a research question that is investigated using qualitative methods to develop a hypothesis that could then be tested using quantitative methods.

1.5.2 Research methods

Research methods are the specific techniques selected by the researcher for conducting the actual research. It includes techniques for developing the research instruments, selecting participants, as well as collecting and analysing data. In Chapters 5 to 7 the methods of qualitative and quantitative research are discussed in more detail.

1.5.3 Writing up and reporting research

The final step in the research process is the presentation of the research, most often in some form of research report. Academic writing skills are important in the process of producing a research report, and in this book we address the research report in Chapter 9 and academic writing skills in Chapter 10.

1.6 Ethical research

Ethical research is high on the agenda of universities all over the world, and it is more than likely that you will have to obtain ethical clearance from your university before being able to commence with your research. There are two important elements to ethics in research, namely **plagiarism** and **ethical research**.

1.6.1 Plagiarism

A writer is guilty of plagiarism where a substantial part of the research that is produced is essentially the work of others. It is important to ensure that your work can be regarded as your own, as being found guilty of plagiarism can result in detrimental consequences, such as being expelled from a university. In the ethics box below, we provide an example of what the University of South Africa regards as plagiarism. It is important to ensure that you are aware of the rules of your university around plagiarism.

> **Ethical issue: plagiarism**
>
> Plagiarism can occur when authors:
> - fail to acknowledge the source where phrases or passages are taken verbatim (word-for-word) from a published or unpublished text
> - use a summary or paraphrasing which contains the ideas of others and presents the essence of an argument without acknowledging the author of the work
> - use patch-writing, where pieces of other works, including those taken from the internet, are blended with one's own words and phrases without acknowledging the sources
> - copy a significant portion of the assignment from other sources, even when the authors are acknowledged.
>
> It is important that you familiarise yourself with the policies and requirement of your institution with regard to plagiarism and copyright protection.

1.6.2 Ethical considerations in business research

In business research, ethical research mostly means that the researcher obtains informed consent from participants. 'Informed' means that the researcher has informed the participant of the purpose and nature of the research and his or her participation, and has ensured the anonymity of participants. Participants should also be informed that they have the choice of withdrawing their participation at any time. 'Consent' generally means that the participant and his or her organisation (where applicable) have explicitly consented to be part of the research. Different universities have different policies and procedures, so you should ensure that you fully understand the processes for obtaining ethical clearance for your research project before you commence with your study.

Where research targets vulnerable groups such as under-age children, the disabled or aged, ethical guidelines will be required to ensure that special care is taken to ensure that participants are not harmed or traumatised in any way.

1.7 Business research

Business research can be defined as the application of the **scientific method** in searching for the truth about business phenomena.[50] These phenomena include, amongst others, defining business opportunities and problems, generating and evaluating alternative courses of action, and monitoring employee and organisational performance. Business research, therefore, involves more than only conducting surveys, it includes idea and theory development, problem definition, searching for and collecting information, analysing data and communicating the findings and their implications. This definition also emphasises, through reference to the scientific method, that any information generated should be accurate and objective.

This definition suggests that whatever the research approach, design or method, one thing that is furthermore important is that they all meet on the common ground of the scientific method employed by them. Experimentation as a scientific method is mostly associated with physical phenomena subjected to laboratory tests and physical control. Business policies, procedures and decisions, however, often affect human beings. One individual's behaviour differs substantially from that of another from time to time, place to place and environment to environment. Behaviour cannot be placed under absolute control, making it very difficult to employ experimentation in the practice of business. This does not, however, imply that the scientific method cannot be used in business research.

For example, the relationship between the sales revenue and the advertising budget may be apparent but it is not easy to establish which one the actual cause of effect is because both advertising and sales are interlinked. The exact magnitude of the effect of each on the other cannot be easily determined, for various other factors – economic variables, market forces, changes in fashion, tastes, temperaments, and the competitors' policies – make a substantial impact on the sales volume. However, the scientific method that empirically tests a hypothesis has a far-reaching utility value, not only for theoretical purposes, but also for practical applications and policy decisions.

The scientific method is the same whether used in social sciences, business, physical sciences or physics. The scientific method involves the pursuit of truth through systematic observation, explanation and testing and is generally based on theory and facts. It furthermore has to conform to a number of formalities and procedures resulting in the scientific method relying on enough time to verify and generalise findings. It is therefore often in conflict with management problems requiring timely solutions and decisions.

By emphasising the scientific method, this definition also suggests that business research should be structured with specified steps to be taken in a specified sequence in accordance with a well-defined set of rules. This systematic characteristic of business research does not rule out creative thinking but it certainly does reject the use of guessing and intuition in arriving at conclusions. It furthermore advocates that business research should be guided by the rules of logical reasoning, of induction and deduction to understand, explain, or predict business phenomena.

Within an organisation, a business researcher may be referred to as a marketing researcher, a marketing information manager, an organisational researcher, a director of financial and economic research, a market analyst or one of many other titles. Although business researchers are often specialised, the term *business research* encompasses all of these functional fields.

Finally, this definition of business research is limited by one's definition of *business*. Certainly, research regarding production, finance, marketing, human resources and management in for-profit organisations like British American Tobacco, Bidvest, AECI, REMGRO, Reunert and Tiger Brands can rightfully be termed business research. However, business research also includes efforts that assist non-profit organisations such as the Automobile Association of South Africa, the Desmond Tutu HIV Foundation, LoveLife South Africa, the Media Institute of Southern Africa, the Nelson Mandela Children's Fund, a school or even a ministry. Furthermore, parastatals and government structures such as the Accounting Standards Board (ASB), Agricultural Research Council (ARC), Airports Company South Africa (ACSA), Armaments Corporation of South Africa (ARMSCOR), Central Energy Fund (CEF), Competition Commission, Denel (Pty) Ltd, Human Sciences Research Council (HSRC), National Gambling Board of South Africa and the Water Research Commission (WRC) perform many functions that are similar, if not identical, to those of for-profit business organisations. While the focus is on for-profit organisations, this book explores business research as it applies to all institutions.

1.7.1 Importance and purpose of business research

The ultimate goal of business research is to supply accurate information that reduces uncertainty in managerial decision-making. Very often, decisions are made with little information due to cost considerations, insufficient time to conduct research, or management's belief that enough is already known. Business research helps decision makers shift from intuitive information gathering to systematic and objective investigation.

The primary activity of business research involves finding answers to key strategic, tactical and operational questions. For managers, the purpose of research is to provide knowledge regarding the organisation, the market, the economy, or another area of uncertainty. A financial manager may ask, 'Will the environment for long-term financing be better two years from now?' A human resource manager may ask, 'What kind of training is necessary for productive employees?' or 'What is the reason for the company's high employee turnover?' A marketing manager may ask, 'How can I monitor my retail sales and retail trade activities?' However, it is important to note that research is an aid to managerial decision-making, never a substitute for it.

The decision-making process associated with the development and implementation of key strategic, tactical and operational questions generally involves four stages:
1. Identifying problems or opportunities
2. Diagnosing and assessing problems or opportunities
3. Selecting and implementing a course of action
4. Evaluating the course of action

Business research, by supplying managers with pertinent information, may play an important role in reducing uncertainty in each of these stages.

1.7.2 Identifying problems or opportunities

Before any strategy can be developed, a business must determine where it wants to go and how it will get there. Business research can help managers plan strategies by determining the nature of situations or by identifying the existence of problems or opportunities present in the organisation or the environment within which it operates. Business research may be used as a scanning activity to provide information about what is occurring within an organisation or in the environment. The mere description of some social or economic activity may familiarise managers with organisational and environmental occurrences and help them understand a situation. Once business research indicates a problem or opportunity, managers may feel that the alternatives are clear enough to make a decision based on their experience or intuition.

1.7.2.1 Diagnosing and assessing problems or opportunities

After an organisation recognises a problem or identifies a potential opportunity, business research can help clarify the situation. Managers need to gain insight about the underlying factors causing the situation. If there is a problem, they need to specify what happened and why. If an opportunity exists, they may need to explore, refine, and quantify the opportunity. If multiple opportunities exist, research may be conducted to set priorities.

1.7.2.2 Selecting and implementing a course of action

After the alternative courses of action have been clearly identified, business research is often conducted to obtain specific information that will aid in evaluating the alternatives and in selecting the best course of action. Opportunities may be evaluated through the use of various performance criteria. For example, estimates of market potential allow managers to evaluate the revenue that will be generated by each of the possible opportunities. A good forecast supplied by business researchers is among the most useful pieces of planning information a manager can have. Of course, complete accuracy in forecasting the future is not possible, because change is constantly occurring in the business environment. Nevertheless, objective information generated by business research to forecast environmental occurrences may be the foundation for selecting a particular course of action.

Even the best plan is likely to fail if it is not properly implemented. Business research may be conducted to indicate the specific tactics required to implement a course of action.

1.7.2.3 Evaluating the course of action

After a course of action has been implemented, business research may serve as a tool to tell managers whether or not planned activities were properly executed and if they accomplished what they were expected to accomplish. In other words, managers may use evaluation research to provide feedback for evaluation and control of strategies and tactics. Evaluation research is the formal, objective measurement and appraisal of the extent to which a given activity, project, or programme has achieved its objectives. In addition to measuring the extent to which completed programmes achieved their objectives or whether continuing programmes are presently performing as projected, evaluation research may provide information about the major factors influencing the observed performance levels. In addition to for-profit organisations, non-profit organisations and governmental agencies frequently conduct evaluation research. Every year, evaluation studies are undertaken to systematically assess the effects of public programmes. For example, the South African Department of Labour has been responsible for measuring the outcomes of the Acts regulating various forms of social security and social grants. Performance-monitoring research is a specific type of evaluation research that provides feedback for the evaluation and control of recurring business activity. For example, most forms of business continuously monitor wholesale and retail activity to ensure early detection of sales declines and other anomalies. In the grocery, toiletry and confectionary retail industries, sales research may use computerised cash registers and electronic scanners at checkout counters to provide valuable market-share information to the store and brand managers interested in the retail sales volume of specific products.

1.8 Basic and applied research

Depending on the purpose, business research can also be classified as either basic research or applied research. **Basic business research** is sometimes referred to as pure or fundamental research undertaken for expanding on or creating a body of knowledge. It is conducted without a specific decision in mind, and it usually does not address the needs of a specific organisation. It is inquisitive by nature and asks fundamental questions such as:
- What makes things happen?
- Why do things happen?
- Why do people react in a particular way?

In fact, it is the source of most new theories, principles and ideas.

Basic research can be used to test the validity of a general business theory (one that applies to all businesses) or to learn more about a particular business phenomenon. For instance, a great deal of basic research addresses employee motivation, specifically trying to identify the drivers that managers can use to encourage workers to dedicate themselves to an organisation's goals. From such research, we can learn the factors that are most important to workers and how to create an environment where employees are most highly motivated. No one organisation alone can benefit from the insights gained from the research. However, management in organisations may become aware of such research and use it to design applied research studies examining questions about their own employees. In the long run, it forms the basis of applied research or the development of commercial products. Thus, the two types of research are not completely independent, as basic research often provides the foundation for applied research later on.

Applied business research is conducted to address a specific business decision for an organisation. It is the use of basic research or past theories, knowledge and methods for solving an existing problem and therefore deals with practical problems. Applied business research can be distinguished from basic research in terms of the fact that more emphasis is placed on increasing knowledge, which may or may not be used in future. For example, in the present real world situation, more emphasis is being given to applied research to solve problems arising out of, amongst others, overpopulation and scarcity of natural resources.

The opening vignette describes a situation in which FNB may have used applied research to decide how to best create heightened awareness, knowledge and usage of its products and services.

While the distinction between basic and applied is useful in describing research, there are very few aspects of research that apply only to basic or only to applied research. The focus in this book is more on applied research studies that are undertaken to answer questions about specific problems or to make decisions about particular courses of action or policies. Applied research is emphasised in this text because most students will be oriented toward the day-to-day practice of management, and most students and researchers will be exposed to short-term, problem-solving research conducted for profit or non-profit organisations.

1.9 Producing academic research

Academic researchers working on postgraduate qualifications do not work alone. They are guided by peers, mentors and supervisors, and ultimately assessed by colloquia, research committees and/or internal and external examiners. It is therefore important to understand the basic process of producing academic research before commencing on this journey. Figure 1.5 depicts the academic research production process.

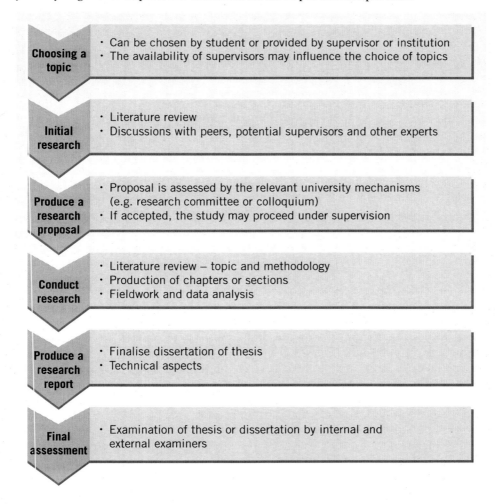

Figure 1.5 The academic research production process

The first step is to identify a suitable topic. In some instances, universities may provide certain topics, but in other instances, students may be allowed to choose and formulate their own topics. Whatever the topic, it is very important for students to select topics where adequate and capable supervision is available.

After the selection and acceptance of a suitable topic, the researcher will have to produce an acceptable **research proposal**. In this book, the research proposal is discussed in Chapter 8. The purpose of a research proposal is to convince your assessors that the research you are proposing is meaningful and of sufficient quality to meet the learning outcomes, and doable within the limitations, such as time and money. At most universities, the research proposal will be assessed by a panel of experts rather than an individual. The student may proceed with the research only after the research proposal has been accepted. The compilation of a research proposal is the result of a preliminary research process, which includes (but is not limited to) a thorough literature review and discussions with peers, potential supervisors and other experts in the field.

Once research commences, the researcher has to balance reading, writing and the execution of fieldwork. Conducting research means that the researcher reads more extensively on the topic, and also consults literature on research design, methodology and research methods as required. At the same time, the relevant sections in the research document (whether it is called a research report, mini-dissertation, dissertation or thesis) have to be produced and submitted to the supervisors for consideration and feedback. One of the most challenging elements of the process is that fieldwork (for example, a survey) has to be conducted, data has to be analysed and the findings have to be recorded in the research document.

The final step is to finalise the research document by ensuring that all the supervisor's comments have been addressed, and ensuring that the technical elements are up to the required standard. It is advisable to send the final version of the document for extensive and professional editing. After this has been done, the document is generally ready for submission to be examined and assessed by internal and external examiners.

1.10 Summary

The business research process is often presented as a linear, sequential process, with one specific step following another. In reality, this is not the case. For example, the time spent on each step varies, overlap between steps is common, some stages may be omitted, occasionally we need to backtrack, and the order sometimes changes. Nonetheless, the process remains systematic and some structure for the research process is necessary.

The book is organised to provide this structure, both within each chapter and in the order of the chapters. Each chapter begins with a set of specific learning objectives followed by a chapter vignette – a glimpse of a business research situation that provides a basis of reference for that chapter. Finally, each chapter concludes with a review of the learning objectives.

The book is organised into three parts. Part 1 is the Introduction, which includes this chapter. This chapter provided an introduction to research approaches, designs and methods, as well as introduced business research and its importance and purpose. The first three chapters of the book give students a fuller understanding of the business research environment. Part 2 provides the conceptualising and environment scanning phase of the business research process. It discusses data collection methods and introduces measurement of research constructs and questionnaire design. It describes the process involved in selecting a research sample and collecting data and explains the various approaches to analysing the data and describes methods of presentation. Part 3 looks at academic literacy.

There are six learning objectives in this chapter. After reading the chapter, you should be competent in the following areas:
1. Understand how research approaches and associated paradigms influence a researcher when doing business research: The social science research paradigms of positivism, post-positivism and constructivism form the scientific foundation for business research. These paradigms exemplify a theory of scientific enquiry and imply certain assumptions shared by an accepted group of researchers. These assumptions include the researcher's assumptions of reality and what science can contribute, as well as conventions relating to ethics and aesthetics. The quantitative, qualitative, mixed methods, analytical, systems, and actors' approaches furthermore derive from the paradigms and form the basis for both the research design and selection of specific research techniques. It is therefore necessary to develop an understanding of both the relevant social science paradigms and methodological approaches in order to establish the basis for the selection of research designs and research methods.
2. Explain the use of a particular research methodology and design: Differences between research methodologies and design are due to the researcher's idea of reality, the impact or perceived role of the researcher and participants in the generation of knowledge, and the aim of the research. Based upon the methodological approach taken, the business researcher can develop a fixed, flexible or mixed methods research design based on quantitative and qualitative methods. Researchers following a positivist paradigm will use the analytical methodological approach and will design a fixed study using quantitative methods in order to explain an objective and rational reality. The resulting knowledge generated from the analytical approach will be independent of the individuals involved and the observers. Conversely, researchers following a constructivist paradigm will use the actors' methodological approach and will design a flexible study using qualitative methods in order to understand a subjective and relativistic reality. The knowledge generated from the actors' approach is dependent on the individuals being studied, as well as on the observer or researcher. Researchers following a post-positivistic paradigm, however, use the systems methodological approach to explain and understand an objective and rational reality where the relevant facts might not only be deterministic, but also probabilistic. The resulting mixed methods design uses a combination of quantitative and qualitative methods, and the knowledge generated is dependent on the system being studied. The researcher, in this case, views the system as being more than simply the sum of its parts. With the scientific foundation of fixed, flexible and mixed method designs established, it is possible to examine the suitability of their associated quantitative and qualitative methods to the creation of business knowledge.
3. Explain the importance of research questions and hypothesis: Meaningful research requires a guiding statement that gives direction and purpose to the study and can be provided by either a hypothesis or a research question. This choice is guided by the researcher's ability to make a prediction about the outcome of the study before it

is conducted. In basic research, the prediction is generally based upon a theoretical perspective. In situations where the researcher is able to make a prediction before data are gathered, a hypothesis that can be tested with a fixed design using quantitative methods is the best fit. Conversely, in situations where the researcher is unable to make a prediction until after or during the data-gathering process, a research question that can be answered with a flexible design using qualitative methods is more appropriate. Once posed, research questions are initially fine-tuned during a review of the literature and discussions with experts, and the process of refining the research question continues during the data-gathering phase until the question has been fully answered or a different question has presented itself as the actual core question. It is this evolving nature of the research that forms the basis for the use of the term flexible when describing the research design. A powerful alternative to these two very different and potentially rigid methods of conducting research is offered by mixing hypotheses and research questions. Recognising both the advantages and limitations of each, many researchers are taking a pragmatic approach that combines both.
4. Understand how research contributes to business success: While many business decisions are based on a decision maker's intuition, this type of decision-making is typically more risky. By first researching an issue and gathering the appropriate information (from employees, customers, competitors, and the market) business decision makers can make a more informed decision. Research can, from this perspective, be viewed as the intelligence-gathering function in business. The intelligence includes information about customers, competitors, economic trends, employees, and other factors that affect business success. This intelligence assists in making decisions ranging from long-term strategic direction and planning to short-term tactical decisions.
5. Understand the difference between basic and applied business research: Applied business research seeks to facilitate managerial decision-making. It is directed toward a specific managerial decision in a particular organisation. Basic or pure research seeks to increase knowledge of theories and concepts. Both are important, but applied research is more often the topic in this text.
6. Understand how research activities can be used to address business decisions: Businesses can make more accurate decisions about dealing with problems and/or the opportunities to pursue and how to best pursue them. The chapter provides examples of studies involving several dimensions of managerial decision-making. Thus, business research is useful both in a strategic and in a tactical sense.
7. Know how to define business research: Business research can be defined as the application of the scientific method in searching for the truth about business phenomena. These phenomena include, amongst others, defining business opportunities and problems, generating and evaluating alternative courses of action, and monitoring employee and organisational performance. Business research, therefore, involves more than only conducting surveys, it includes idea and theory development, problem definition, searching for and collecting information, analysing data and communicating the findings and their implications. This definition also emphasises, through reference to the scientific method, that any information generated should be accurate and objective. It suggests that whatever the research approach, design or method, one thing that is important is that they all meet on the common ground of the scientific method employed by them.

Key terms and concepts

applied business research: use of basic research or past theories, knowledge and methods for solving an existing problem
basic business research: pure or fundamental research undertaken for expanding on or creating a body of knowledge
business research: the application of the scientific method in searching for the truth about business phenomena
cross-sectional research: a 'snapshot' of a population at a given time, conducted over a relatively short period of time using a sample from the population
deductive research: research that is more outwardly focused
epistomology: ways of knowing about reality
ethical research: the researcher obtains informed consent from participants
inductive research: research that is more inwardly focused
longitudinal research: studies generally conducted over a longer period of time using the same set of subjects
literature review: a thorough review of the literature in the chosen field of study
methodology: methods by which the researcher can find out more about the phenomenon being studied
ontology: researcher's view of the nature of reality
paradigm: a model
plagiarism: where a substantial part of the research that is produced is essentially the work of others
research approach: the type of research to be conducted
research design: general plan of how the researcher will go about answering the research questions or attaining the research objectives
research paradigm (or philosophy): researcher's dominant world view, consisting of the combination of ontology, epistemology, and methodology
research proposal: a document approved by your supervisor (and possibly the head of the department in which you are pursuing your studies) that is submitted to a research committee or a colloquium at your university for approval, before you can start your actual research
scientific method: the pursuit of truth through systematic observation, explanation and testing
theory building: the process of generating theory

Test yourself questions

1. A food processor is conducting research in an attempt to formulate the ideal cereal for the affluent, urban South African market. Is this basic or applied research? Explain.
2. Define *business research* and describe its aim.
3. Comment on the following statements:
    a. Managers are paid to take risks with decisions. Researchers are paid to reduce the risk of making those decisions.
    b. A business strategy can be no better than the information on which it is based.
    c. The purpose of research is to solve business problems.

4. Which of the following organisations are likely to use business research? Why? How?
   a. Manufacturer of breakfast cereals
   b. Manufacturer of nuts, bolts, and other fasteners
   c. A hospital
   d. A company that publishes academic textbooks
5. Identify and provide evidence of some products that have been developed with the help of business research.
6. What are research paradigms? Explain their contemporary significance.
7. Distinguish between research methods and research methodology.
8. Distinguish between inferential, experimental and simulation approaches to research.
9. Write short notes on research and scientific method.
10. 'Research is primarily concerned with fact finding, analysis and evaluation.' Do you agree with this statement? Give reasons in support of your answer.
11. It is often said that there is not much linking business research in the world of academics and business research in for-profit and not-for profit business organisations. Account for this state of affairs and give suggestions for improvement.

Activities

1. Suppose you owned a fast food store in Durban, KwaZulu-Natal. You are considering opening a second store. You are undecided on whether to locate the new store in Durban, Pietermaritzburg or Bloemfontein. Why would you decide to have some research done before making the decision? Should the research be conducted? Go to http://www.statssa.gov. Do you think any of this information would be useful in the research?
2. Search the internet for recent examples of the use of business research in making decisions about different aspects of business.
3. Search for an article illustrating an example of an applied research study involving some aspect of business. How does it differ from a basic research study also focusing on a similar aspect of business?

References

1 Leedy, P. & Ormrod, J. 2001. *Practical research: planning and design*. 7th ed. Upper Saddle River, NJ: Merrill Prentice Hall. Redman, L.V & Mory, A.V.H.
2 1923. *The romance of research*. p. 10.
3 *The Encyclopaedia of Social Sciences*. 1930. Vol. IX, MacMillan.
4 Arbnor, I. & Bjerke, B. 1997. *Methodology for creating business knowledge*. 2nd ed. Thousand Oaks, CA: Sage.
5 This discussion is based upon Guba, E.G & Lincoln, Y.S. 1994. *Competing paradigms in qualitative research*. In N. K. Denzin & Y.S. Lincoln (Eds.), Handbook of qualitative research (pp. 105-117). Thousand Oaks, CA: Sage.
6 Gephart, R. 1999. Paradigms and research methods. *Academy of Management Proceedings, Research Methods Division*. [Online] Available: http://www.liberty.edu/media/1130/LBR%20rev%2007%2013%2009.pdf [13 April 2012].

7 Arbnor, I. & Bjerke, B. 1997. *Methodology for creating business knowledge.* 2nd ed. Thousand Oaks, CA: Sage.
8 Gephart, R. 1999. Paradigms and research methods. *Academy of Management Proceedings, Research Methods Division,* [Online] Available: http://www.liberty.edu/media/1130/LBR%20rev%2007%2013%2009.pdf [13 April 2012].
9 Ibid.
10 Ibid.
11 Ibid.
12 Kuhn, T. 1996. *The structure of scientific revolutions.* Chicago, IL: The University of Chicago. p. 10.
13 Ivankova, N.V., Cresswell, J.W. & Plano Clark, V.L. *Foundations and approaches to mixed methods research.* In: Maree, K. (Ed.). 2007. *First steps in research.* Pretoria: Van Schaik.
14 Saunders, M., Lewis, P. & Thornhill, A. 2009. *Research methods for business students.* 5th ed. Essex: Pearson Education. p. 155.
15 Zikmund, W.G., Babin, B.J., Carr, J.C. & Griffin, M. 2010. *Business research methods.* 8th ed. Canada: South-Western Cengage Learning. p. 44.
16 Bick, G., Abratt, R. & Moller, D. 2010. Customer service expectations in retail banking in Africa. South African Journal of Business Management, 41(2): 13–27.
17 Zikmund, W.G, Barry J. Babin, B.J., Jon C. Carr, J.C. and Griffin, M. 2012. *Business research methods.* 9th ed. Mason, OH: Cengage Learning.
18 McCoy, S.P 2012. Brand alignment: Developing a model for competitive advantage through a study of selected South African companies. Unpublished DBL thesis, University of South Africa, Pretoria.
19 Meir, R.C., Newell, W.T. andvDaizer, H.L. 1969. *Simulation in Business and Economics.* New Jersey: Prentice Hall.
20 Arbnor, I. & Bjerke, B. 1997. *Methodology for creating business knowledge.* 2nd ed. Thousand Oaks, CA: Sage.
21 Ibid.
22 Cooper, D.R. & Schindler, P.S. 2003. *Business research methods.* 9th ed. Boston, MA: McGraw-Hill Irwin.
23 Arbnor, I. & Bjerke, B. 1997. *Methodology for creating business knowledge.* 2nd ed. Thousand Oaks, CA: Sage.
24 Ibid.
25 Cooper, D.R. & Schindler, P.S. 2003. *Business research methods.* 9th ed. Boston, MA: McGraw-Hill Irwin.
26 Arbnor, I. & Bjerke, B. 1997. *Methodology for creating business knowledge.* 2nd ed. Thousand Oaks, CA: Sage.
27 Ibid.
28 Ibid.
29 Ibid.
30 Scandura, T.A. & Williams, E.A. 2000. Research methodology in management: current practices, trends, and implications for future research. *Academy of Management Journal.* 43(6): 1248–1265.
31 Robson, C. 2002. *Real world research: a resource for social scientists and practitioner-researchers.* 2nd ed. Malden, MA: Blackwell Publishing.

32 Arbnor, I. & Bjerke, B. 1997. *Methodology for creating business knowledge*. 2nd ed. Thousand Oaks, CA: Sage.
33 Saunders et al (2009:136–137).
34 Ibid.
35 Cooper, D.R. & Schindler, P.S. 2003. *Business research methods*. 9th ed. Boston, MA: McGraw-Hill Irwin.
36 Ibid.
37 Coghlan D. and Brannick, T. 2009. *Doing Action Research in Your Own Organisation*. 3rd ed. London: Sage.
38 Moore, E.M. 2007. *The impact of leadership style on organizational effectiveness: leadership in action within United Way of America*. Unpublished thesis. Minneapolis: Capella University.
39 Robson, C. 2002. *Real world research: a resource for social scientists and practitioner-researchers*. 2nd ed. Malden, MA: Blackwell Publishing, p. 163.
40 Crossan, F. 2003. Research philosophy: Towards an understanding. *Nurse Researcher*. 11(1): 46–55.
41 Cooper, D.R. & Schindler, P.S. 2003. *Business research methods*. 9th ed. Boston, MA: McGraw-Hill Irwin.
42 Robson, C. 2002. *Real world research: a resource for social scientists and practitioner-researchers*. 2nd ed. Malden, MA: Blackwell Publishing.
43 Crossan, F. 2003. *Research philosophy: towards an understanding*. Nurse Researcher. 11(1):46–55.
44 McGrath, J. 1982. Dilemmatics: the study of research choice and dilemmas. In J.E. McGrath, J. Martin, & R.A. Kulka (Eds.), *Judgement calls in research*. Newburry Park, CA: Sage. pp. 69–102.
45 Cook, T.D. & Campbell D.T. 1976. The design and conduct of quasi-experiments and true experiments in field settings. In: Dunnette M.D. (Ed.), *Handbook of industrial and organizational psychology*. pp. 223–36. Chicago, IL: Rand McNally.
46 Robson, C. 2002. *Real world research: a resource for social scientists and practitioner-researchers*. 2nd ed. Malden, MA: Blackwell Publishing.
47 Cooper, D.R. & Schindler, P.S. 2003. *Business research methods*. 9th ed. Boston, MA: McGraw-Hill Irwin.
48 Robson, C. 2002. *Real world research: a resource for social scientists and practitioner-researchers*. 2nd ed. Malden, MA: Blackwell Publishing.
49 Cooper, D.R. & Schindler, P.S. 2003. *Business research methods*. 9th ed. Boston, MA: McGraw-Hill Irwin.
50 Zikmund, W.G., Barry J., Babin, B.J., Carr, J.C. & Griffin, M. 2012. *Business research methods*. 9th ed. Mason, OH: Cengage Learning.

THE RESEARCH PROBLEM

Pierre Joubert
Peet Venter

2

AFTER STUDYING THIS CHAPTER, YOU SHOULD BE ABLE TO:

- Explain the importance of formulating a research problem
- Identify considerations in selecting a research problem
- Identify research problems
- Define research problems
- Apply the criteria for good research problems
- Develop statements of research purpose

> **First things first**
>
> Maria is a student embarking on the great adventure of thesis research. She has read a number of articles in a business journal and has a vague idea for a topic that she could use for her master's degree thesis.
>
> She meets with her supervisor, Professor Ntuli, to discuss the topic and how she should proceed. He agrees that this topic would probably be suitable for her thesis, but that she needs to refine her idea for a topic into a research problem that is relevant and achievable. Maria is a little confused. She is just starting out on her research, but all this talk of research problems, hypotheses and units of analysis is very confusing. Where does everything fit in? And more importantly, where should she start with her research? When she asked Prof Ntuli what the first step was, he answered that she should develop a research problem statement. But what is a research problem statement, and how does one develop it? What do you do with it once you have it? Maria decides to start with first things first and to read up about research problems.

2.1 Introduction

'The formulation of the problem is often more essential than its solution.'
(Albert Einstein)

In virtually every subject area, our knowledge is incomplete and problems are waiting to be solved. These problems or questions point either to observed events that are perplexing in terms of our currently accepted ideas, or current ideas that are challenged by new questions. We can address these gaps in our knowledge and those unresolved problems by stating the underlying problem, asking relevant questions and then seeking answers through systematic research. However, it is important to realise that not all questions can be transformed into research-worthy problems and some may prove to be excessively difficult to study. In this regard, it is frequently wrongly assumed that if you read enough of the research literature in an area of interest, you will somehow magically be able to formulate problems to guide further research. The formulation of a research problem does, however, not only require extensive knowledge and insight of the subject area, but also competence and skill in applying acquired research methodology knowledge.

Although it may seem relatively simple to ask potential research questions, the process of formulating them in a meaningful way is not at all an easy task. Researchers generally only have a diffuse, even confused notion of the problem and it may take a researcher a number of years to explore, consider and conduct research before gaining clarity on the underlying problems or questions. By not spending considerable time reflecting on and thinking through the research problem, some difficulty in conceptualising the main idea, problem, question or opportunity underlying a research project is generally evident. This is partly due to it not always being possible to formulate a research problem simply, succinctly, clearly and completely.

It is important to reiterate that not all problems are suitable for scientific research because some problems simply reveal what is already known, do not lead to any new knowledge or apply statistical calculations without any appropriate interpretation. There is so much to learn and so many important questions being generated each day that researchers should look for noteworthy problems and not dwell on those that will make little, if any, contribution.

This chapter discusses the importance and benefits of problems and hypotheses in research, the criteria that good problems should conform to and various types of hypotheses. To further clarify the nature of problems and hypotheses, common errors in research problems are discussed. This is followed by a discussion of the perennial conundrum of generality and specificity of problems and hypotheses. The chapter also aims to provide a better idea of how professional researchers typically generate research problems and ideas.

2.2 The importance of formulating a research problem

The research problem is commonly accepted as the first and most crucial step in the research process. A common analogy illustrating the importance of research problems is that the formulation of a research problem is similar to identifying the destination before undertaking a journey. In the absence of a destination, it would be impossible to identify any possible route. Similarly, a research plan is impossible without a research problem. The way in which a problem is formulated moreover influences almost every step that follows in the research process, particularly the study design, sampling plan, data collection and the type of analyses. Another useful analogy is to compare the research problem to the foundation of a building. Any structural design would be dependent on the foundation. The research problem can be regarded as the foundation of a research study and, if well formulated, a consummate research study can follow.

2.2.1 From topics to questions

Researchers often experience a sense of being overwhelmed or frustrated when confronted by the array of topics that may interest them to do research on. At some point, however, one has to settle on a topic and narrow it down to a manageable scope to find the makings of a problem that could potentially guide the research. During this process, the researcher also needs to bear in mind that weeks, months or even years could be devoted to doing the research, writing it up and then expecting readers to spend their time reading the ensuing research report. This report should also continue the conversation between the researcher(s) and readers, thereby contributing to a body of knowledge and a community of researchers. In choosing a suitable research topic, the following may be factors that may shape the choice of a topic:[1]

- Personal experience, interest and first-hand knowledge.
- Ideas from your mentor, instructor or research supervisor
- A logical next step in a line of research or an industry or context that has not been addressed in research presents itself as a research opportunity in a field that interests you. For example, in many research areas, research has been conducted in the USA and Europe, but not in Africa or other developing regions, which presents researchers with a logical next step to address in their research.

It is important to note that your topic is the theoretical and practical area of focus of your study, but is not the same as the title of your study.

To do all this, researchers need to find answers to the questions and problems that the community of researchers needs solved. Perennial and currently debated problems abound in all research communities but certain problems and questions may intrigue only the researcher. At some point, the researcher will, however, have to decide whether this more private question is also of interest to others such as colleagues, other researchers or even a public who could be influenced by the research findings and implications. At this point, the aim is not just to answer a research question but to pose a problem that others also consider worth solving. There are three steps in the process of developing a research problem:[2]

1. The first step is to find out what others have done with the topic you have chosen. This implies that the researcher will need to conduct a preliminary literature review (the literature review is discussed in more detail in Chapter 3).
2. The second step is to define the **unit of analysis**. The unit of analysis specifies who or what the focus of the research is, and what you want to find out about them. It is accordingly not sufficient to specify that Human Resource Managers is the unit of analysis; you have to specify what about them you are researching. For example, the perceptions of Human Resource Managers towards the use of psychometric testing in the recruitment process may be a unit of analysis.
3. The final step is to specify what you want to achieve, in other words, what the purpose of your research is.

In this chapter we consider the formulation of the problem statement and the statement of research.

2.3 Developing a research problem

There are two aspects to developing a **research problem statement** discussed in this section. Firstly, the problem has to be identified, and this can be a challenge in its own right. After identifying the research problem, the research problem has to be formulated.

2.3.1 Problem identification

One of the most common sources of research ideas is by experiencing or becoming aware of practical problems in the field. Some researchers are directly engaged in the private or government sectors of the economy and deal with the application of economic and management sciences on a daily basis. These researchers come up with ideas based on what they experience and see happening around them. Others researchers may not directly be involved in providing and using or consuming services, goods and ideas, but work with (or survey) people who are, and in so doing, learn what needs to be better understood.

Another source for research ideas is the discipline-specific literature within economic and management and related sciences. Researchers conceptualise ideas for research by reading the literature and thinking of ways to extend or refine previous research. Some academic sources, such as academic journal articles, dissertations or theses, will often contain specific recommendations on what research problems or future research the researchers have identified as seen in the example box below.

> **Example box: future research idea**
>
> While this study focuses on the extent of strategy disclosure, future research could analyse the correlation between the extent of strategy disclosure and the profitability of the company. A further aspect of investigation could focus on whether more strategy disclosure could have a bearing on the rating of the company. It would also be interesting to assess whether the new King III would have any impact on the extent of strategy disclosure by companies with regard to their non-financial information in Annual Reports.[3]

Government agencies such as the National Research Foundation (NRF) also provide a rich source for research ideas. The NRF promotes and supports research in all fields of knowledge. It also established Centres of Excellence (CoEs), that concentrate existing capacity and resources to enable researchers to collaborate across disciplines and institutions on long-term projects that are locally relevant and internationally competitive. CoEs have become a common research-funding instrument, having already been established in several countries including Australia, Canada and the USA. The five key performance areas identified for South African CoEs at the NRF are Research/knowledge production, Education and training, Information brokerage, Networking, and Service rendering. Numerous research ideas are available within these areas and researchers are invited to tender research proposals to address the identified research problems.

Finally, many researchers conceptualise research topics on their own. It should, however, be emphasised that these ideas are influenced and shaped by the researcher's background, culture, education and experiences.

Once an idea for a study has been generated, a researcher has to consider the feasibility of doing the research. These considerations involve making trade-offs between scientific rigour and pragmatism. If researchers had unlimited resources and unbridled control over the circumstances, they would in most instances be able to do the most valuable quality research. However, these ideal circumstances seldom exist, and researchers are almost always forced to consider the best trade-offs they can find in order to realise the desired rigour.

2.3.2 Problem definition

In defining the research problem, researchers should attempt to isolate symptoms from causes. A symptom can be described as a sign or indicator that something is wrong, flawed or less than ideal. A problem, on the contrary could be the actual reasons or possible causes for the discrepancy between the current situation and the desired situation. Addressing the symptoms may not necessarily solve the problem; the real or root causes must be identified and addressed.

The research problem is consequently the researcher's paraphrasing of a practical business problem into a form that will guide the data collection effort and provide the required information to solve the problem. A clearly defined research problem should reduce the risk of collecting data that does not solve the problem. It is vitally important because other stages of the research process often depends on how the research problem has been defined. The research problem or hypothesis statement furthermore leads to the formulation of the purpose of the research. The research problem is often expressed as a research problem statement, a single sentence that provides a summary of the problem that the researcher wants to investigate. The research problem should not be confused with other statements of research, such as research objectives or research questions.

The following table provides examples of pragmatic problems and related research problems.

TABLE 2.1 PRAGMATIC AND RELATED RESEARCH PROBLEMS

Pragmatic problem	Research problem
Should a new product be introduced?	What are our customers' needs with regard to product X?
Should the advertising campaign be changed?	How effective is our current advertising campaign?
Should the price of the brand be increased?	How price-elastic is demand with regard to brand X?

Figure 2.1 provides a schematic representation of the problem definition process in research, while the example box on page 37 contains three examples of the problem statements from three different studies.

This representation of the process involved in defining a research problem includes four steps namely: understanding the problem, adopting an approach to the problem, formulating the research problem and purpose, and research design.

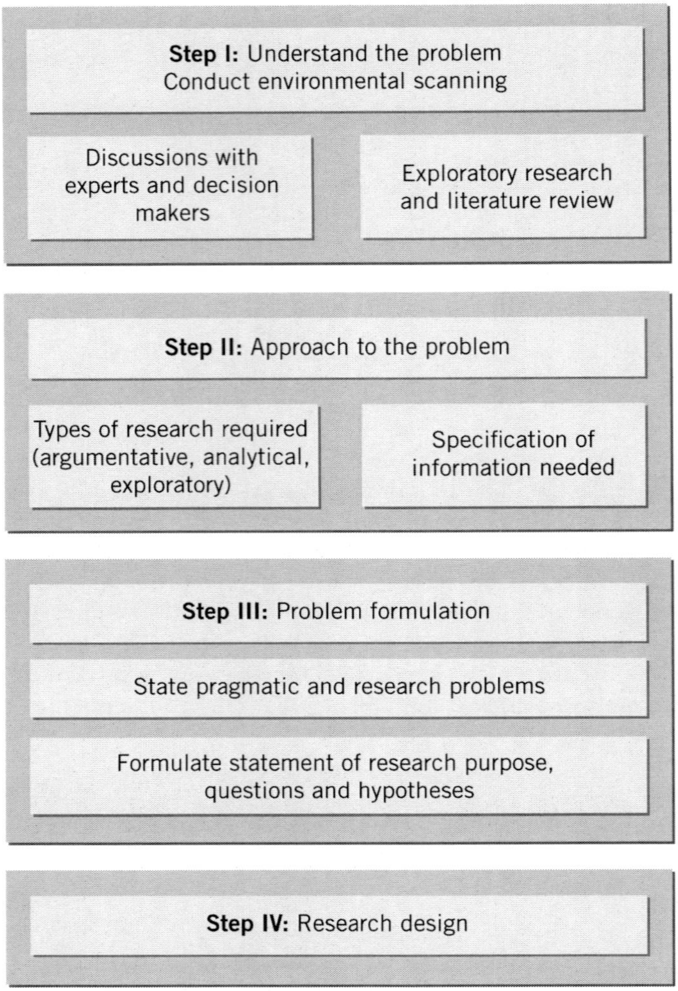

```
┌─────────────────────────────────────────────────────┐
│         Step I: Understand the problem              │
│         Conduct environmental scanning              │
│                                                     │
│   Discussions with                                  │
│   experts and decision    Exploratory research      │
│   makers                  and literature review     │
└─────────────────────────────────────────────────────┘

┌─────────────────────────────────────────────────────┐
│         Step II: Approach to the problem            │
│                                                     │
│  Types of research required                         │
│  (argumentative, analytical,   Specification of     │
│  exploratory)                  information needed   │
└─────────────────────────────────────────────────────┘

┌─────────────────────────────────────────────────────┐
│         Step III: Problem formulation               │
│                                                     │
│     State pragmatic and research problems           │
│                                                     │
│   Formulate statement of research purpose,          │
│   questions and hypotheses                          │
└─────────────────────────────────────────────────────┘

┌─────────────────────────────────────────────────────┐
│         Step IV: Research design                    │
└─────────────────────────────────────────────────────┘
```

Figure 2.1 The problem definition process

2.3.2.1 Step I: Understand the problem

Defining the problem requires a clear understanding of the context or environment within which the problem manifests itself and is framed. To this end, exploratory primary and secondary research can help to:
- clarify and better understand the problem
- understand possible causes of the problem
- determine what research data should be collected to help solve the problem.

Discussions with experts and decision makers in the field of research can also contribute to a greater understanding of the problem, and symptoms underlying the problem.

Example box: problem statements

1. This points to the problem statement of this thesis. Brand, as a concept, is adopted too narrowly by business (Schmidt & Ludlow, 2002:21) in that it focuses predominantly on brand as an external issue. There is a need to examine contemporary thinking, and to explore a framework of theory regarding brand as a means for developing competitive advantage when aligned internally and externally to the organisation in a more holistic and integrated manner.[4]
2. Most researchers including Dhumale and Sapcanin (2006), Lewison (1999), and Scott (2007) are of the view that Islamic banking actually rides on the crest of the world's renewed interest in the ideas of ethical banking. The latter view raises the following question: Is there a relationship between ethical banking and Islamic banking?[5]
3. Since the development of the UWES (Utrecht Work Engagement Scale) by Schaufeli, Salanova et al (2002), very few studies regarding engagement could be found in the literature (Maslach, Schaufeli & Leiter, 2001; Naude & Rothmann, 2004; Schaufeli et al, 2001; Schaufeli, Martinez et al, 2002; Schaufeli, Salanova et al, 2002; Storm & Rothmann, 2003). As a result, information regarding differences in engagement levels is almost non-existent. This study will be an attempt to determine differences in engagement levels of employees at a higher education institution in South Africa, and the focus will be on gender, age, job category, language group and years of service at the institution.[6]

2.3.2.2 Step II: Approach to the problem

Business researchers need to work closely with stakeholders related to the research topic to clearly establish the information needed by the decision maker to solve the problem. Academic research intentionally sets out to enhance the understanding of a phenomenon and expects to communicate what is discovered to the larger scientific community. The formulation of a research problem differs depending on whether argumentative research or analytical research is undertaken. Unlike argumentative research, which forces the researcher to take a definitive stance on a topic, analytical research poses a research question or problem that requires further investigation. This question or problem is the driving force behind analytical research and it requires that the researcher takes no stance and remain objective throughout his/her investigation of the topic.

Exploratory research is used when searching for insights into the general nature of the problem, the possible decision alternatives and relevant variables that need to be considered (research purpose). The research methods used under an exploratory research design are highly flexible, unstructured and qualitative. Literature reviews are generally mandatory in any academic research, while qualitative methods such as individual and group unstructured interviews (for example, focus groups, panels and observation) can also be used as exploratory approaches.

2.3.2.3 Step III: Problem formulation

In addition to seeking more exact confirmations of existing claims to knowledge, research has the equally important goal of generating new claims. Problem formulation is the logical first step toward this goal. The formulation of research problems also has an important social function. Researchers have to justify the demands for attention and other scarce resources that research makes. Achieving research results of consequence is perhaps the most powerful justification for such claims, but this type of justification can be offered only after the fact, and only in the event that the research is efficacious. A compelling research problem, by contrast, must marshal support in advance of research and, if it is sufficiently compelling, can even sustain that support through the sometimes fruitless periods that researchers experience.

It sometimes seems that there is little about which social scientists agree, and the most effective procedure for formulating research problems is no exception. In particular, there has been considerable debate over whether or not it is important to define problems explicitly in advance of research and to show how they are linked to prior work. Many social scientists hold that research problems should be formulated by carefully analysing as much of the relevant research literature as possible, formally stating the problem and the major hypotheses that the literature suggests, and only then collecting the data. Their intention is to give research a clear and firm justification and to encourage hypothesis testing.

This will ensure that each new study does its utmost to add in an orderly fashion to the body of knowledge. However, there are many other researchers who are equally convinced that this style of formulating problems tends to stifle questions and prevent discoveries that a more open-ended approach might stimulate. This latter group argues instead for letting problems and hypotheses emerge throughout the research process, pushed forth by new empirical observations that encourage the researcher to ask new questions and build new theories. In original research, there is less likely to be a conceptual closure to inquiry, for as the work of discovery continues and new kinds of data are conceptualised, new problems and hypotheses will emerge.

In practice the decision as to when and how research problems should be defined usually depends less upon the perceived merits of one or the other of these procedures than upon the research design selected. Methods differ in their abilities to predict the kinds, quantities, and quality of the data that may be available in any given instance.

This step also encompasses the formulation of statements of research purpose, which we discuss in more depth in section 2.4 of this chapter. The final phase in the process outlined above is to develop a research design in line with the research problem and purpose. The research design process is the focus of Chapters 4 to 7.

2.3.3 Research subproblems

Some research problems may be so complex or large that it is useful and pragmatic to divide them up into subproblems. Subproblems are an integral part of the 'main' research problem, and should not include decisions or problems that do not form a part thereof. In such cases the researcher should carefully examine the research problem and identify the sub-areas that could be investigated on their own.

Leedy and Ormrod identified four characteristics of subproblems:[7]

1. Each of the subproblems should be researchable in its own right, and is simply a logical sub-area of the larger research problem. As in the case of the research problem, it may be more direct to pose the subproblems as questions rather than as declarative statements.
2. Each subproblem must be clearly linked to the interpretation of data, meaning that the subproblem should contain some indication that data interpretation will be used in addressing it.
3. The subproblems together must make up the totality of the research problem, and should not exceed it in scope, or fail to address each of its most important subareas.
4. The subproblems should typically not exceed two to four in number. If the main problem is properly specified, there will be no need for a whole range of subproblems.

2.3.4 Criteria for good research problem statements

How do we determine whether a research problem statement is good or not? Various criteria for what constitutes good research problems have been proposed.

Problem statements should reflect the existing knowledge base of the researcher; a sense of dissatisfaction (scepticism, distrust, reservation) should be widely applicable.[8] Three criteria for good research problem statements were identified by Kerlinger:[9]

1. Problems should generally express a relationship between variables such as: Is A related to B? How are A and B related to C? How is A related to B under conditions C and D? The exceptions to this principle occur mostly in taxonomic or methodological research.
2. Problems should be stated clearly, unambiguously (and briefly) in question form. Instead of saying, for example, 'the problem is …' or 'The purpose of this study…' ask a question. Questions have the virtue of posing problems directly.
3. Problem statements should suggest possibilities of empirical testing. This implies that a problem statement that does not contain implications for testing its stated relation or relations is not a scientific problem. Certain philosophic and theological questions may be important for specific individuals but are of little or no use to a scientist. The philosophical question, 'How do we know?' is such a question. These types of questions can be called metaphysical in the sense that they are, at least as stated, beyond empirical testing possibilities and are thus 'unresearchable'.

While the research problem statement specifies the research problem, it does not fully indicate what the researcher wants to achieve with the research. In response to the research problem, the researchers can specify specific statements of research purpose. These are discussed in the next section.

2.4 Formulating statements of research purpose

There are a range of possible statements of research purpose (specifying what researchers want to achieve or test), and researchers are often confused by which options to use when. In this section, we try to provide an overview of the main types of statements of research purpose in the form of research questions, research objectives and hypotheses and some guidelines to assist researchers in choosing which options to use when.

2.4.1 Statement of overall purpose

The statement of overall purpose (or aim) is a single statement outlining what the researcher wants to achieve with the research. The overall purpose should contain the following:[10]

- An indication of *how* the research will be done. Words like 'assess', 'explore' or 'compare' all provide indications of how you are approaching the research.
- The focus of the study is clearly identified; this gives an indication of *what* you will be researching.
- The participants are described. This gives an indication of *who* will be involved in the research.
- The context is outlined, i.e. *where* the research will be conducted. This could be a geographic area and/or an industry, or even a specific organisation.

The overall statement of research purpose can be broken down into more specific research questions and/or research objectives in order to operationalise the study.

2.4.2 Research questions

The importance of having clear and unambiguous **research questions** cannot be underestimated. Many studies start off with an overarching or main research question (or overall purpose of the research), followed by a number of sub-questions or sub-objectives. Exploratory studies especially will generally have research questions rather than research objectives. There are three guidelines that can be used to determine the 'rightness' of a research question:[11]

1. The research question is not too broad, too narrow or too sensitive.
2. The research questions, if answered, will generate new insights.
3. The research question should be as simple and direct as possible. Strip away all unnecessary complexity and 'wordiness' to get to the heart of the question(s).

> **Ethical issue: look at the ethicality of your research**
>
> Your statements of research purpose should already consider the ethicality of your research. You should not include research questions or objectives that may later on raise ethical issues about your research. For example, if a vulnerable group such as children or the aged form part of your study, there are many ethical considerations around data collection, which may impact on how you develop your research purpose.

Maree and van der Westhuizen also offer some guidelines for the setting of research questions:[12]
- In any study of limited scope, there should be a limited number of research questions. Having too many research questions may be an indication of a lack of focus.
- Research questions should link directly to the overall statement of research purpose.
- They should be linked logically (e.g. question 2 can only be answered once question 1 has been answered) and together they will add up to the overall purpose or main research question.
- They are linked conceptually through key terms which appear in each question.
- They are self-explanatory, clear to an outsider and each can stand on its own as a researchable question.

The example box contains an example of a main research question and a set of sub-questions.

> **Example box**
>
> The research question to be answered in this thesis is:
> *What are the interrelationships between buyer seller exchanges and customer retention from the viewpoint of the buyer/client in the South African advertising industry?*
>
> The investigative questions to be answered in this study are:
> a) What decision process is applied when advertising agencies are appointed?
> b) Who is the buying centre for advertising agency appointments?
> c) What supplier selection criteria are used for advertising agency appointments?
> d) What are the forces that shape organisational buying behaviour for advertising agencies?[13]

In generating and refining research questions, exploratory research will be very important. This may include (but not be limited to) a preliminary literature review to ensure that the research questions address a specific need or gap in the literature, discussions with your research advisor or supervisor, and interaction with your peers or other experts through discussion or by way of applying techniques like brainstorming to generate ideas and refine questions.

Research objectives are an alternative or supplementary form of research purpose statement that can be used alongside research questions or on its own to express the purpose of the research.

2.4.3 Research objectives

To some degree, **research objectives** are more readily accepted by the scientific community as indicative of a clear focus in the research, as they tend to be more specific and goal-directed. Again, the overall purpose of the research may be broken down into a number of more specific research objectives. Objectives may also assist in clarifying and operationalising research questions. While Saunders et al argue that research questions can be written more specifically, they contend that it is the specific structure and formal language of setting research objectives that make them so useful to researchers.[14]

Ultimately the researcher should make a decision on what statements of research purpose to include. This decision is dependent on a number of issues as outlined below:
- The examining body may have certain prescriptions with regard to the use of objectives and/or questions, and you should familiarise yourself with those requirements.
- Your research supervisor or advisor may have certain preferences that need to be clarified.
- The type of research may play a role. For example, qualitative research is more exploratory in nature and research questions may be more suited to such types of studies. In other types of studies, it may make sense to include both research questions and research objectives.

Whichever approach you decide to follow, the key issue is ultimately whether the purpose of your study is as clear and unambiguous as it can be.

> **Reflection**
>
> When considering a research problem, research question or research purpose to identify possible subproblems, secondary or sub-questions and secondary or subobjectives, start with the original statement and break it down into as many separate phrases as you can. Examine each phrase to see if it should be a secondary problem, question or objective in its own right. It might also be a good time to involve your peers and to brainstorm or discuss your ideas with them and to consider their input.

2.4.4 Hypotheses

Whereas problems are interrogative statements that ask about the relationship between variables, **hypotheses** are speculative statements about the relationship between two or more variables. As a general rule, hypotheses can only be formulated where the nature of the study is quantitative and may lead to statistical data suitable for testing hypotheses.

The question as to whether scientific research can be accomplished without defining a hypothesis depends on the subject of the scientific research, as well as the nature of the scientific research. For example, while a researcher in the natural sciences will most likely use the experimental method from a more positivistic stance, a researcher in the human sciences will tend to use a mixed method from a more interpretivist stance. While an experimental approach inevitably requires identifying a hypothesis as the basis for defining an experiment to test the experimental results, the mixed methods approach can start and finish all research without ever defining a hypothesis. In the case of research in the field of natural sciences where results are based on experiments, it is quite normal and even necessary at times to define a hypothesis, because the hypothesis becomes a basis for defining the next steps. Experiments and testing of results dictate and lead the whole process of scientific research. In economic and management sciences, the hypotheses may in certain studies only emerge after the literature review has been completed.

The origin of the word 'hypothesis', according to the online version of Oxford Dictionaries, is from the Greek word *hypothesis*, and is translated as a 'supposition or proposed explanation made on the basis of limited evidence as a starting point for further investigation'.[15] The same source offers another definition used in case of philosophy:

'a proposition made as a basis for reasoning, without any assumption of its truth'.[16] A hypothesis can therefore be defined as an unproved assertion.

Very often, the hypothesis is wrongly identified as an idea or theme, or even a theory. An idea is immeasurably wider than a hypothesis and can be anything that a human brain can imagine or fabricate. A theme is much narrower than an idea and is usually related to a subject of discussion, branch of science, or research. The definition and choice of the theme is almost always known in advance. A theory is something that is already accepted and is usually based on verified hypotheses. A theory is also a source for new hypotheses that can be used to prove or disprove the same theory or other theories.

A hypothesis is a preliminary or tentative explanation of what the researcher considers the outcome of an investigation will be. It is an informed or educated guess. It indicates the expectations of the researcher regarding certain variables. It is the most specific way in which an answer to a problem can be stated. A problem is formulated in the form of a question; it serves as the basis or origin from which a hypothesis is derived.

According, solely to testing and verification, hypotheses can be divided into two groups:
1. Null hypotheses
2. Alternate or alternative hypotheses.

The alternate hypothesis states that the expected relationships and differences within the subject of research exist and that that sample observations are consequently influenced by some non-random cause. The null hypothesis negates the alternate hypothesis and assumes that anticipated relationships and differences do not exist or that sample observations result purely from chance. The null hypothesis has special meaning in cases of final verification and testing of a hypothesis, and its misuse can cause errors. It is possible to distinguish between the following types of error:
- A Type I error known as false positive
- A Type II error known as false negative.

A Type I error occurs when the null hypothesis is rejected, although this hypothesis is true. The probability of committing a Type I error is called the significance level, and is often denoted by α. A Type II error occurs when the researcher accepts a null hypothesis that is false. The probability of committing a Type II error is called Beta, and is often denoted by β. The probability of not committing a Type II error is called the power of the test. It is also important for the researcher to understand how to calculate a p-value that is calculated as part of a typical hypothesis testing. In many cases, the p-value is interpreted incorrectly. This is addressed in Chapter 7.

There is little doubt that hypotheses are important and indispensable tools of scientific research. They are firstly the working instruments of theory. Hypotheses can be deduced from theory or from other hypotheses. Hypotheses can secondly be tested and shown to be probably true or probably false. Hypotheses are thirdly tools for the advancement of knowledge because they enable scientists to indicate the probability that their presumptions and suppositions are correct or incorrect independently from the scientists' values or opinions.

Since the use of hypotheses is subject to the generation of statistical data suited to do hypothesis testing, it is clearly not suited to use in qualitative and exploratory research. However, in more inductive approaches researchers may opt to specify testable **research**

propositions. While the procedure for testing propositions is not quantitative, it still needs to be rigorously conducted by examining alternative explanations, negative examples not conforming to the pattern or identifying intervening variables. In this way, any conclusions about the relationships between variables will be well-grounded rather than speculative.

> **Reflection**
>
> In this chapter we have emphasised the importance of starting out with a well thought-out problem statement and research purpose. Can you imagine what the consequences will be if you start out on your research and your research problem statement turns out not to be feasible?

2.5 Approach to the problem

To the extent that theoretical styles and research styles are systematically linked, it may be expected that researchers will pose problems that are compatible with their own particular theoretical orientations and with the methods linked to those orientations, and ignore problems that are either theoretically or methodologically incompatible. The form in which research problems are initially posed may consequently be shaped by methodological or theoretical commitments.

It is also to be expected that researchers working in different theoretical and methodological styles will frequently disagree about the relative importance of particular research problems. For example, human ecologists and demographers who study the relationships between resources and population characteristics are often criticised by conflict theorists for ignoring concepts and variables pertaining to political power and governmental structures. Such debates will and should continue until the issues are resolved. However, the practicality of employing multiple research methods to study the same general problem has some pragmatic implications for theory. Rather than being linked to a particular theoretical style, its cherished problems and questions and its most compatible method, one might instead combine methods that would encourage or even require the integration of different theoretical perspectives to interpret the data. If hypotheses and variables that have been previously isolated each within their own theoretical systems are empirically interrelated in the same study, then conceptual linkages between different theoretical systems are more likely to follow.

The issue of when and how to formulate research problems is closely related to another issue: the relative importance of generating new theories versus the verification of existing theories. An increasing focus on interdisciplinary research has since at least the 1960s, provoked considerable controversy in the social sciences. Glaser and Strauss argued that the emphasis on verification of existing theories kept researchers from investigating new problem areas; prevented them from acknowledging the necessarily exploratory nature of much of their work, encouraged instead the inappropriate use of verification logic and rhetoric; and discouraged the development and use of systematic empirical procedures for generating, as well as testing theories.[17]

If we accept that generating theories empirically is not a substitute for empirical verification, then building theories without immediate regard for testing poses no special logical problems. However, it may complicate matters methodologically. One serious complication is that theories are often built empirically using research methods that are different from the methods required to verify them.

2.5.1 The empirical unfolding of research problems

Once a study is published, it is in many ways irrelevant whether the research problem prompted the study or instead emerged from it. With publication, the study's problem enters the public domain and becomes the responsibility not only of the study's author but of all who are professionally interested in that research area. At that point, the key issue is what to do with the problem next. Research into a problem does not end with a single study. Nor is there truly a final formulation of a problem anymore than there is a final solution. All research involves some simplification of the problem being investigated. This is unavoidable given the limitations on our resources, theories, and methods.

However, each of a discipline's separate new studies, or each phase of study in an individual's research programme, reveals new aspects of the problem by addressing issues that earlier research could not address.

The two modes of formulating research problems that we have just discussed differ in that one looks to past studies, while the other looks to ongoing work. But the two are similar in that both rely upon empirical inquiry rather than upon non-empirical procedures, such as speculation or the purely logical analysis of ideas. This means that whether research problems emerge from current research or instead derive from earlier work, research methods are directly implicated in the process. Every empirically based research problem has a methodological, as well as a substantive component, and this methodological component may equally influence our perceptions as to which particular phenomena and theories are problematic. One of the central questions to be posed, therefore, is how do the methods employed in research directly affect the formulation of research problems?

2.5.2 The importance of methodology

As research into a problem proceeds with researchers posing it in different ways, the problem unfolds to reveal new dimensions that facilitate the problem's solution. The variety of available research methods is a key element in this process in that it provides researchers with a multifaceted empirical view of the phenomena and of the theories in question. This enables researchers to formulate problems in a manner that does greater justice both to the complexity of social phenomena and to the complex implications of our theories.

However, employing a variety of methods also complicates the process of problem formulation because different types of research methods very often provide conflicting answers to the same research questions. For example, in a study by Deutscher he found the problem of attitude versus action to be complicated by the fact that experimental studies generally reported greater consistency between subjects' words and deeds than did observational field studies.[18] When such methodologically linked contradictions appear in the course of a problem's development, the suspicion is that they may derive from theoretically irrelevant characteristics of the different methods employed rather than from the substantive complexity of the problem. Inconsistent findings require reformulations of research problems.

When these inconsistencies reflect unanticipated substantive complexity, then concepts and propositions must be recast to take account of that complexity. But, although more complicated theories are sometimes necessary to achieve theoretical realism, simplicity is preferable.

When contrasting different methods' results, there are two general classes of potential research questions that emerge in particular. The first is whether quite different styles of research really study the same phenomenon in anything but name. The second is whether different variants of the same research style will yield the same results.

2.5.3 The role of theory in problem formulation

Theory plays a dual role in research. On the one hand, new theories solve research problems by accounting for unexplained phenomena and by superseding questionable older theories. On the other hand, existing theory guides researchers in formulating research problems.

The guiding role of theory in problem formulation is obvious in verification studies. But while less obvious, it is equally important in exploratory research. To a large degree, pre-existing theories define both the territory to be explored in the search for problems, and the nature of the new facts one hopes to discover. Of course, opinions differ about how explicit the theoretical background of exploratory research should be. Some recommend spelling it out in nearly as much detail as in verification research, stating exactly what existing theory leads you to expect and why. Others object to granting existing theory such a directive role and prefer instead to work with general theoretical orientations that sensitise the investigator to important but less precise categories of data. Closure in either the definition of concepts or the statement of hypotheses is avoided in favour of more open 'sensitising concepts' and the 'suspension of expectations'.

In the first view, new problems and hypotheses emerge from the confrontation between old theories and new data, much as in verification. In the second view, new problems and hypotheses emerge from the confrontation between the data and a theoretically-oriented and sensitised investigator.

If individual researchers are to be their own theoreticians, however, then each must also accept some responsibility for synthesis; otherwise, we risk inundation by idiosyncratic theories that may be firmly grounded in their authors' research but that are of problematic significance in the larger scheme of things. Verification research, which by its very nature draws upon and feeds back into a larger body of knowledge, is the conventional way in which researchers in the past assumed this responsibility.

However, today we need models of synthetic problem formulation for researchers who want instead to generate theories. We, therefore, conclude this chapter with two such models, paradigmatic pragmatism and mixing metaphors, which take into account both the role of theory and the role of method in defining research problems.

According to Kuhn, 'puzzle solving' is a characteristic of normal science. Rather than employing explicit rules that define problems and their solutions, scientists work by example, analogy or metaphor, applying exemplars from one situation to another:[19]

> ❛❛ The resultant ability to see a variety of situations as like each other … is, I think, the main thing a student acquires by doing exemplary problems … . After he has completed a certain number, which may vary from one individual to the next, he views the situations

that confront him as a scientist in the same gestalt as other members of his specialists' group. "

The legitimacy of the use of exemplars or analogies is ultimately based upon the community of practicing scientists accepting such models. For example, biological analogies have been widely accepted within sociology, whereas models from physics have not. Social physics was offered by St. Simon as an alternative label to sociology as a name for the discipline, but only a few analogies from physics are to be found in research. One such is Samuel Stouffer's gravity model (inverse square law) that relates the amount of geographical mobility between cities to the distance between them.[20]

New metaphors and new concepts suggest new variables and new methods – new questions and new data to answer them. As in the parable of the blind men and the elephant, the metaphor used to describe a phenomenon (it is like a snake said the man holding the trunk, like a tree said the one holding a leg, etc.) depends partially upon the aspect of reality one happens to get hold of. But metaphorical depiction of reality is also determined by the method of observation one uses. Hearing an elephant, one might liken it to a trumpeter swan; or tasting a juicy, rare elephant steak, one might liken it to a cow. In short, metaphors are often (some say always) used to define reality, and metaphors are in part measurement and method specific. Mixing metaphors can suggest new questions requiring new methods, and mixing methods can generate new questions leading to new metaphors.

The concept mapping method isn't the only method around that might help researchers formulate good research problems and projects. Virtually any method that's used to help individuals and groups to think more effectively would probably be useful in research problem formulation. Some of the methods that might be included in our toolkit for research formulation might be: brainstorming, brain-writing, nominal group technique, focus groups, Delphi methods, and facet theory. And then, of course, there are all the methods for identifying relevant literature and previous research work.

2.6 Summary

In this chapter, we emphasised the importance of a research problem as a logical starting point for the research process. The research problem firstly has to be identified (for example through existing literature), and secondly has to be defined (i.e. written down) in such a way that it provides a useful point of departure for the research being undertaken. In addition to stating the problem as clearly and succinctly as possible, there are also various other components of research purpose that flows from the problem statement, such as the research questions, research objectives and hypotheses. If we consider the contents of this chapter, it is clear that the proper identification of the research problem is the most crucial step in the research process. Therefore, every single aspect of the research should be measured against the problem statement and the other statements of research purpose to ensure that the research stays focused and on track.

Key terms and concepts

hypothesis: speculative statements about the relationship between two or more variables
research topic: the theoretical and contextual focus area of the research
research problem statement: the identification and formulation of the research problem to be investigated in the form of an interrogative statement that asks about the relationship between variables
research questions: the specific questions that a research study will seek to answer
research objectives: specific and goal-directed statements of research intent
research propositions: a testable research statement for non-quantitative testing
unit of analysis: specifies who or what the focus of the research is, and what you want to find out about them

Test yourself questions

1. List the characteristics of a good problem statement.
2. Explain the difference between research questions and research objectives.
3. Explain the role of theory in problem formulation.

Multiple-choice questions

Please indicate whether each of the following statements are **true** or **false**:
1. The research topic and research title is the same.
2. Defining the problem statement is the starting point of the research.
3. When conducting research, the researcher should generate as many research problems as possible.
4. Each research subproblem must be researchable in its own right.
5. Hypotheses can only be used in research projects that yield quantitative data.

Activities

Analyse the problem statement below and answer the questions that follow:
Most researchers including Dhumale and Sapcanin (2006), Lewison (1999), and Scott (2007) are of the view that Islamic banking actually rides on the crest of the world's renewed interest in the ideas of ethical banking. The latter view raises the following question: Is there a relationship between ethical banking and Islamic banking?[21]

1. Identify one subproblem statement that meets the criteria specified in section 2.3.3.
2. Identify an overall research question from the problem statement given above.
3. Identify one possible research subquestion from the main research question.

Case study[22]

The following examples are from a Master's dissertation examining the impact of leadership practices on service quality in private higher education (PHE) institutions in South Africa. Critically evaluate the problem statement and statements of research purpose as used in this dissertation. What recommendations do you have for the author, based on your analysis?

Problem statement
One of the challenges facing private higher education (PHE) institutions is an increasingly competitive, marketing oriented and highly regulated environment. In this environment, these institutions have to function, survive and compete, not only with one another, but also with HE public institutions. Hence the problem is that competition is on the increase and PHE institutions need to find new ways to compete if they wish to survive in this dynamic environment. As indicated previously, leadership appears to influence service quality, which is essential in gaining a competitive edge in this ever-evolving environment.

Research statement
Proven leadership practices will have a positive impact on service quality in a PHE institution in South Africa. This will thus impact on the competitive advantage, which, in turn, will then lead to the long-term sustainability of the institution.

Research objectives
Primary objective
The primary objective of this study was to investigate the impact of leadership practices on service quality in PHE in South Africa as a source of competitive advantage. Hence the impact of leadership (the independent variable) on service quality (the dependent variable) will be investigated.

Secondary objectives
In order to achieve the primary objective, the following secondary objectives were formulated for this study:
1. To identify service quality criteria used to evaluate the quality of service
2. To identify a leadership assessment instrument that measures leadership practices
3. To analyse students' perceptions and expectations of service quality
4. To evaluate the way in which leaders view themselves in terms of exemplary leadership
5. To evaluate the way in which the organisation views its leader in terms of exemplary leadership
6. To recommend interventions to improve leadership and service quality in a PHE provider in South Africa.

In order to address the research purpose, the student conducted a literature review of the service quality measurement and leadership fields and developed a questionnaire to measure both the perceptions of the leader and perceptions of service quality for the institutions.

Source: van Schalkwyk, Riaan Dirkse. 2012. The impact of leadership practices on service quality in private higher education in South Africa. Thesis (Business Management) University of South Africa 2011. Reprinted by permission of the author.

References

1. Salkind, N. 2012. *Exploring research (International Edition)*. 8th ed. Upper Saddle River, N.J.: Pearson Education.
2. Henning, E., Gravett, S. & Van Rensburg, W. *Finding your way in academic writing*. 2nd ed. Pretoria: Van Schaik. p. 20.
3. Padia, N. & Yasseen, Y. 2011. An examination of strategy disclosure in the annual reports of South African listed companies. *South African Journal of Business Management*. 42(3): 27–35.
4. Schmidt K. & Ludlow C. 2002: *Inclusive Branding: The Why and How of a Holistic Approach to Brands*. New York: Palgrave Macmillan.
5. Saidi, T.A. 2009. Relationship between ethical and Islamic banking systems and its business management implications. *South African Journal of Business Management*. 40(1):43–49.
6. Naudé, J.L.P. & Rothman, S. 2004. The validation of the Utrecht Work Engagement Scale for Emergency Medical Technicians in Gauteng. *South African Journal of Management Sciences*, 7(3): 459–468.
7. Leedy, P.D. & Ormrod, J.E. 2005. *Practical research* (international edition). 8th ed. Upper Saddle River, N.J.: Pearson Merrill Prentice Hall.
8. Webb, W.B. 1961. The choice of the problem. *American Psychologist*, 16: 223–227.
9. Kerlinger, F.N. 1986. *Foundations of behavioural research*. 3rd ed. Fort Worth, TX: Holt, Rinehart, and Winston.
10. Adapted from Maree, K. & Van der Westhuizen, C. 2007. Planning a research proposal. In: Maree, K (ed). 2007. *First steps in research*. Pretoria: Van Schaik. pp. 23–45.
11. Adapted from Saunders, M., Lewis, P. & Thornhill, A. 2009. *Research methods for business students*. 5th edition. Essex: Pearson Education.
12. Adapted from Maree & Van der Westhuizen (2007).
13. Jansen van Rensburg, M. 2009. The evaluation of business relationships from the buyer's perspective: antecedents to the consideration set for supplier replacement in the South African advertising industry. Unpublished Doctor of Commerce thesis, University of South Africa.
14. Saunders, M., Lewis, P. and Thornhill, A. 2009. *Research Methods for Business Students*. 5th ed. Harlow, England, FT; Pearson Education.
15. Oxford Dictionaries.com (2016) In: English Oxford Living Dictionaries [online] Available at: https://en.oxforddictionaries.com/definition/hypothesis Oxford: ©2016 Oxford University Press [Accessed 04 November 2016].
16. Hobson, A. (Ed.) 2004. *The Oxford Dictionary of Difficult Words*. Oxford University Press.
17. Glaser, B.G. & Strauss, A.L. 1967. The discovery of grounded theory: strategies for qualitative research. Chicago: Aldine Publishing Company.
18. Deutscher, I. 1966. Words and deeds: social science and social policy. *Social Problems*. (13):235–265.

19 Kuhn, T.S. 1970. *The structure of scientific revolutions.* University of Chicago Press: Chicago. pp. 35–42.
20 Brewer, J.D. & Hunter, A. *Foundations of multimethod research synthesizing styles.* London; Sage.
21 Saidi, T.A. 2008. Relationship between ethical and Islamic banking systems and its business management implications. *South African Journal of Business Management.* 40(1):43–49.
22 Dirkse van Schalkwyk, R. 2012. The impact of leadership practices on service quality in private higher education in South Africa. Unisa: Unpublished M.Com. thesis.

THE LITERATURE SURVEY

Elizabeth Stack

3

AFTER STUDYING THIS CHAPTER, YOU SHOULD BE ABLE TO:

- Understand what a literature review is
- Understand the difference between a literature survey and a literature review
- Appreciate the purposes of a literature review
- Perform a literature survey
- Write a literature review.

> From Maria's readings she has realised that carrying on a business in the form of a partnership involves a complex interaction of legal and tax principles and she would like to explore this in her research. In Maria's discussion with Professor Ntuli, he explained that she needs to carry out a literature survey. This will refine her idea for a topic into a research question that is relevant and achievable. He explains that the literature survey will equip her to write a literature review for her research proposal and the literature review chapter in her thesis.
>
> He suggests a number of electronic databases for business, legal and tax research and sends her to the library to survey the available literature. Not wanting to take up any more of Professor Ntuli's time, she hurries off to the library with a number of questions buzzing in her head. What is a database? How do you carry out a literature survey? How will it help her to formulate a research question?

3.1 Introduction

Research is seldom completely original, with the exception possibly of research in the natural sciences. Most research builds on and expands or provides a new perspective on existing knowledge. Salkind writes that "[t]oday's research is built on a foundation of hard work and dedication of past researchers and their productive efforts".[1] You therefore need to have a thorough knowledge of research that has been carried out in your field and you familiarise yourself with this body of knowledge by carrying out a literature survey. This entails reading books, journal articles, theses, reports and other material. In the past this would have meant a visit to the library to search paper-based catalogues relevant to your field of research to identify possible sources of material and then a journey through the bookshelves of the library. The advent of computers and the internet have made the task of carrying out a literature survey much easier and have provided a much richer choice of material on almost any topic.

A thorough knowledge of the literature relevant to your field of study is essential for several reasons discussed in this chapter, but particularly in order to write your research proposal and later the literature review in your thesis.

This chapter describes what is meant by a literature survey, sets out the reasons why a literature survey is conducted and provides guidance on how to carry it out. It also describes what is meant by a literature review, advises how to ensure quality in the review and provides hints on how to write it.

3.2 What is a literature survey?

Every article, paper or thesis must be positioned within the body of knowledge relating to the research topic. In order to do this, existing literature must be reviewed. The extent of the literature review depends on whether you are writing an article for a refereed journal, a paper to be presented at a conference, a research proposal or a master's or doctoral thesis. This chapter concentrates on the literature review in a thesis.

The terms **literature survey** and **literature review** are often used interchangeably, but a literature survey is simply what the name infers, a survey of what has been written on your particular topic. Once you have a clear idea of the 'body of knowledge' on your research topic, this needs to be written up in the form of a review of the literature.

3.3 The purposes of a literature survey

In identifying a field of interest and a possible topic for her research from an article that she has read, Maria has already started her literature survey. Leedy and Ormrod advise that "[a]s a way of getting your feet wet in the world of research, take some time to read articles in research journals in your own academic discipline."[2] The first reason why we read books, journals or other research material is therefore to get ideas for our research.

Professor Ntuli has also given Maria another reason for carrying out a literature survey – to narrow down her field of interest and research topic into a research question that is relevant and achievable. Welman, Kruger and Mitchell confirm that the "literature review [survey] sets the scene for a clear formulation of the research problem, hypothesis or question".[3] Maria needs to find out what research has been done in the field for another reason: to make sure that she is not duplicating the work of other researchers. An important requirement of research is that you add (however modestly) to the existing body of knowledge. In order to narrow down her topic into a research question, she must therefore find a niche or gap for her research within the greater body of knowledge on the topic. This may be an aspect of the topic that has not been researched or a theory that can be refined or tested in a different context. Welman et al suggest that "[p]revious researchers may have suggested ways of eliminating inconsistencies between their findings and those of other studies or a theory".[4] The identification of these inconsistencies, as well as areas for future research, would normally be found in the concluding chapter of a researcher's thesis or journal article. This may provide a 'gap' for your research.

A literature survey is carried out for a number of reasons in addition to narrowing down the research topic into a specific research question. The functions of a literature survey are as follows, the first three of which have been discussed above:
- to identify a research topic
- to find out what other research has been done in the field
- to refine a research topic into a specific problem that can be expressed in the form of a working hypothesis or question
- to identify a possible theoretical framework or model on which to base the research
- to identify interesting or unique research methods or techniques to use in addressing the research question
- to justify the importance of the research in the research proposal.

> **Reflection**
>
> A literature survey is therefore an exhaustive survey of the relevant literature for a specific purpose. In your case, the purpose of performing the survey of the literature is to identify the literature that is relevant to the topic of your thesis.

Researchers often set out to develop a **theory, framework** or **model** to investigate, explain or measure a particular phenomenon. Other researchers then proceed to test the theory, framework or model. During the course of your literature survey you may have identified a theory, framework or model that you can test in another research setting. Or you may have found that other researchers have pointed out inconsistencies in the results of the application of the theory, model or framework in their research or a particular aspect of a problem that has not yet been explored, and you would like to pursue this in your own research.

What is a theory, framework or model? Most research sets out to test a theory (or a theoretical framework or model) developed in earlier research or uses a theory developed in earlier research as the basis for the design of the current research. Different authors describe a theory or the development of a theory in similar ways. According to Leedy and Ormrod, "[a] theory, in the form of a verbal statement, is offered to explain the phenomenon in question."[5] Welman et al describe a theory as "a group of logical related statements that is presented as an explanation of a phenomenon";[6] and as "a system which orders concepts in a way that produces understandings and insights; ... a statement or collection of statements that specify the relationship between variables with a view to explaining phenomena ... in some or other population".[7] Bailey states that:[8]

> ❝ Explanations and predictions are provided by theories. Theories attempt to answer the why and how questions. Theorizing can be described as the process of providing explanations or predictions of ... phenomena, generally by relating the subject of interest ... to some other phenomenon. ❞

A model is simply a theory expressed in mathematical terms explaining the relationship between variables. Models are used in empirical research and particularly in research employing econometric methodologies.

Terre Blanche and Durrheim describe the *process* for the development of theories as follows:[9]

> Theories stand for truth when, through a process of falsification, incorrect theories are rejected on the basis of empirical evidence. The process, described as the hypothetico-deductive model of science, is as follows: a theory is used to develop a hypothesis (a deductive process), the hypothesis is tested empirically (observation), then the results are interpreted and the theory adjusted to fit the new facts.

Reading the research of others may also help you to develop your own theory, framework or model that you can use in your research. The literature survey may, for example, provide you with a comprehensive list of the variables relating to your field of study.

> **Example box**
>
> One researcher wanted to do research on tax avoidance and the reasons why people avoid or evade paying taxes. By carrying out an exhaustive survey of research on the subject, she was able to identify a comprehensive list of these reasons (her theoretical framework), which she incorporated into the questionnaire that she used to carry out her research. Her research filled a niche or gap as no previous research had attempted to find out whether the reasons for tax avoidance identified in previous research were relevant in a South African context and whether these reasons applied equally to the various population groups in South Africa.[10]

When you write your research proposal, you need to justify the relevance of your research – why you are doing the research – and the literature survey will assist you to do this by demonstrating what has been done by researchers who have gone before you, why they considered the problem to be important and how your research fits into the body of knowledge. Professor Ntuli's instruction to Maria to narrow down her topic to a research question that is relevant relates to identifying the niche or gap into which her research fills, but also relates to the need to justify the relevance of her research. It is necessary to indicate the relevance of your research in your research proposal and in your thesis. Your literature survey will provide evidence that leading researchers in your field have considered the problem important enough to study. Professor Ntuli has also referred to the need for Maria to demonstrate the achievability of her proposed research. This relates, amongst other things, to the scope of her research. This aspect will be discussed in Part 2.

Reading earlier research on your topic of interest may also provide you with interesting or unique ways in which to carry out your research (research methods or techniques). Research methods are discussed in Part 2.

Welman et al add a further advantage of carrying out a literature survey – they express the view that it can also provide motivation.[11] Leedy and Ormrod give additional reasons for carrying out a literature survey: it can reveal sources of data that you may not have known existed; it will increase your confidence in the topic you have chosen if other researchers have an interest in the topic and have studied it; and finally, it can help you to make sense of your findings and to relate your work to the work of other researchers.[12] Welman et al also add that the literature survey helps you to write the conclusions arrived at in your research by putting them into context.[13]

Because the literature survey provides the entire basis for your research, it is essential that it is comprehensive.

3.4 Surveying the literature

How do we perform a literature survey? Where do we start? There are two basic approaches to performing a literature survey.

The first method involves starting with a search of all the relevant **databases** at your university library and through them, other libraries. These databases are usually electronic databases, but in some instances may still be in the form of card indices. The search may also be carried out using search engines and the internet. A physical survey of available books on the library shelves may also yield further sources of relevant material. The problem with starting your literature survey in this way is that you often find so many possible sources of research material that it becomes extremely time consuming to weed them out. This is particularly the case if you use search engines and the internet. The academic value of some of the material on the internet is also questionable.

The second method entails scanning recent editions of academic journals in your discipline to find an article relating to your research interest. Once you have identified one relevant article, the bibliography (reference list) at the end of the article will provide references to other relevant material. Reviewing these references will enable you to judge their relevance and will again be the source of further bibliographies. This has a 'snowball' effect. Continuing in this way, you will soon find that authors are citing the same important sources and you will have exhausted the relevant literature. The advantage of this method is that you are able to identify the most authoritative writers in your field of interest, as they will be those most frequently cited.

Researchers will usually use a combination of the two methods.

> **Example box: the 'snowball' method**
>
> Samantha (an imaginary researcher) wants to do research on carbon taxes. She uses the search engine Google Scholar (accessed at http://scholar.google.com/) and types in the words 'carbon taxes'. She notes that 81 700 items have been identified. She tries to look at a few titles, but feels overwhelmed. She then goes online to the university library and identifies a recently completed thesis with the title 'The Use of Taxation Incentives to Reduce Greenhouse Gas Emissions – A Comparative Study'. In the reference list at the end of the thesis, she finds a number of citations that she can follow up. The 'snowball' method has worked for her.

3.4.1 Performing a literature survey

Careful planning will make the process of carrying out your literature survey more effective and efficient. Your plan should be based on your research question and the goals of your research.

3.4.1.1 Planning your research

The first step in the planning process is to formulate **key words** to use for your search and decide on the databases you will access in your search. This may initially be difficult as you may be carrying out the survey in order to formulate your research question and the goals of your research. Once you have identified a topic that you are interested in, this should give you, at least, a starting point from which to identify key words and start to plan your research.

Most writers on research methodology agree that you should start by identifying key words that relate to your research. You cannot carry out a literature survey without using key words. Identifying key words may not be an easy task. Until you have narrowed your broad research idea or topic into a clearly defined problem, question or hypothesis, you may not be able to identify all the key words. Brainstorming and discussing your topic with colleagues and your supervisor will be of great assistance. Unfortunately research is often a circular process and you may find that you identify further key words in the course of your literature survey and that you then have to go back to the beginning to broaden your search. Welman et al also caution that trying to be too specific in the key words you use for your search could limit the relevant references that you find, whereas key words that are too general may leave you swamped with references.[14] In your initial survey of the research field, it is often helpful to start off fairly broadly and then narrow down your search as you get closer to refining your topic into a clearly defined problem, question or hypothesis.

Another aspect of your planning is to decide how you are going to record the relevant literature items that you identify. This may be in the form of index cards or their equivalent in electronic form. This is discussed in more detail below. You also need to decide how you will record *how* you have carried out your search (the steps you followed and the databases you used). This is also discussed below.

Having identified the key words, the next and most important step is getting to know your subject librarian – he or she is an expert in identifying sources of research material. The librarian can also provide valuable advice and training in the use of databases, finding material on the shelves or obtaining material not available in the library by means of an inter-library loan. Many libraries provide training courses on the use of the library facilities. If such a course is available, you should take advantage of it.

3.4.1.2 Sources of research items relevant to your research

The library catalogue, which is usually online, is a valuable source of references. For example, the Rhodes University online catalogue is OPAC. References can be identified by the name of the author, the title or key words. Another source of material relevant to your research is the various subject indices, which are alphabetical lists of entries by topic or author or both. You can scan these to identify references that you want to follow up.

The next port of call is to review collections of abstracts. They provide a brief summary of the research described in the journal article and provide a quick and easy method of deciding which of the articles are relevant to your study, as well as ideas that you can use in your research. Most abstracts also include subject and author indices to help you find what you are looking for. One such abstract can be viewed in the task that is set at the end of this chapter.

The library may have a collection of CD-ROM databases. Welman et al refer to the following databases available on CD-ROM for business, management, accounting, finance, economics, etc., namely ABI/INFORM, Anbor and ECONLIT.[15] Online databases in the commercial field include:
- EBSCO Host
- Emerald Full text
- Sabinet Online
- Scopus
- LexisNexis
- E-journals A to Z via SFX
- Science Direct.

You can also use online searches, which give you simultaneous access to multiple databases enabling you to locate a greater number of relevant books, articles and reports and also allow you to do a cross-disciplinary search. You can gain access to the internet using computer software, such as Netscape Navigator and Microsoft Internet Explorer. One or more of these will be available at your university. Having gained access to the internet, there are a number of search engines that can be used, including www.yahoo.com and www.google.com (in particular Google Scholar accessed at http://scholar.google.com/). Caution must be exercised with the use of these search engines as not all the material they include is of an appropriate quality.

Some additional sources of relevant material include Government publications, such as the publications in South Africa by the National Treasury, the South African Revenue Services, the Department of Labour, the Department of Trade and Industry and Statistics South Africa. Journals also publish bibliographies and reviews of research that are a rich source of references. An example of reviews in the fields of Accounting, Economics and Taxation can be found in the *Journal of Accounting and Economics:* 'A review of tax research,'[16] and 'Empirical tax research in accounting.'[17]

3.4.1.3 Stages in the literature survey

Your literature survey will probably be carried out in two or more stages. The first stage may simply be to identify a possible topic for your research. The next stage will be directed at getting to know the most important research that has been done in the field and the theories or frameworks developed in this research, sufficient to enable you to narrow down your topic and write your research proposal (discussed in Chapter 4). The third stage is a more extensive literature survey which will provide a comprehensive reference list that you will use to write the literature review chapter (or chapters) in your thesis.

3.4.1.4 When to stop reading

When do you stop your search for relevant literature? This is a difficult question for many students to answer, but an essential one. You will find that at a certain stage your search will yield mostly repetitions of citations. That is probably a good time to stop as you will probably have exhausted the field of research.

3.4.2 Record-keeping

The literature survey is a complex and time-consuming exercise and avoiding duplication and repetition by careful documentation will make the process more efficient. Meticulous record-keeping is essential for the success of your research and will prevent much heartache and wasted time.

3.4.2.1 Suggestions for record-keeping

The following suggestions will assist you to avoid having to duplicate your work and prevent the loss of valuable information:
- Keep multiple records of all your files and databases, particularly if they are electronic.

This also applies to drafts of your research proposal and chapters of your thesis. The loss of these records can be disastrous.
- Keep a careful record of your specific searches, including key words that you have used and indices, databases and websites that you have accessed. This will prevent you from covering the same ground more than once.
- From each relevant journal article, book or other source, make careful notes of the material relevant to your research in order to create your own database. Careless or cryptic notes will mean that you may have to go back to the original source when you write your literature review. There are various ways of keeping these notes. This is discussed in more detail below.
- Keep a careful bibliographic record for each journal article, book or other record. If you don't, you will have to go back to the source. Journals or books may not be available in the library at the time you need to follow up the bibliographical record. In the case of internet references, because websites are periodically updated or changed, you should print out the internet page. This will record the date you accessed the website and the full website address. Your bibliographical record is used for in-text referencing, as well as the bibliography (or reference list) at the end of your thesis and must be meticulously accurate. Referencing is discussed in Chapter 10.

There are a number of electronic bibliographic systems that will assist you to keep track of your references, enter them, organise them and compile your bibliography. Your librarian will be able to tell you about them and provide training in how to use them. Two of the more well-known systems are EndNote (available at http://www.endnote.com) and ProCite (available at http://www.procite.com).

3.4.2.2 How to record the results of your literature survey

Each literature item that you identify as relevant to your research must be carefully recorded. Some students prefer to photocopy all relevant material and highlight the important passages. Other students make handwritten notes and use a card system. Many software programs allow you to copy material and transfer it to your electronic database, which saves time and prevents the loss of information. Whichever system you use, the basic principles remain the same:
- **Recording bibliographic details:** Whether you are photocopying abstracts, articles or extracts from books or documents, or recording the details on index cards or computer records, make sure that you record a full and accurate bibliographical record for each:
  - author(s), recording both surnames and initials
  - year of publication and the edition
  - book title, the name of the journal or the title of the document
  - journal articles, in addition to the name of the journal, also the name of the article and the volume number of the journal
  - place and name of the publisher
  - the page number(s) on which the relevant passage appears; in the case of a journal article, in addition to the particular page on which the relevant passage appears, also the beginning and ending page numbers on which the article appears; or if you are using an internet source, the full internet address and the date you accessed the internet website; also print out the pages that you are using for your research as internet websites change.

- **Extracting information from the literature item:** If you use a photocopying system, you will have photocopied the relevant extract. If you are using a handwritten card system or an electronic record, carefully note the details that you plan to use in your literature review. If you wish to quote from the literature item, place the quotation within quotation marks and record the exact page on which it appears.
- **Other relevant material:** As you progress with your research, you will often wake up in the middle of the night with ideas about your research, or while you are walking to work, or in talking to colleagues about your research. You may see something in a television programme or hear it on the radio. Record the ideas and information in detail immediately or they will be lost forever.
- **Themes:** You will find it very helpful if you can, even at this early stage, identify themes relating to each literature item. These themes may be theories, models or frameworks, lines of argument, methodologies, etc. If you are using a photocopying system, you may wish to sort your photocopies into themes, placing items relating to each theme in a file. In a card system, cards can be sorted according to themes and in an electronic system different folders can be opened for each theme. You will find this invaluable when you start writing your literature review.

You have now learned that carrying out a literature survey entails different steps.

> **Example box: steps in carrying out a literature survey**
>
> Access a search engine or an online database
> - Specify a subject area
> - Identify key words
> - Specify a time period, for example, five years
> - Select the type of publication, for example, a journal
> - Read all relevant articles, recording the sections of the article relevant to your research and full bibliographical details to enable you to insert in-text references and compile your reference list or bibliography
> - File the information electronically or in hard copy
> - Back up the information in more than one place to avoid the loss of all your hard work.

3.5 The literature review

Once you have carried out your literature survey and identified all the relevant literature, the next step is to write a review of the literature. A literature review is required in your research proposal and in your thesis. In both, the literature review is not simply a documentation of existing research.

> **Reflection**
>
> A literature review is a structured discussion from a critical and comparative perspective of the important research relevant to your research topic. For the review, you select only the literature from your survey that relates directly to your research.

The literature review sets the scene for your own research. A well-written literature review is critically important to the success of your research and is also a valuable source of information for other researchers. In the review, you demonstrate your knowledge of the field of research and the important research in the field, you use it to describe the problem that forms the basis of your research, it provides a detailed description of the theory or framework you will use in your research and it documents how you have narrowed down the broader area of research on the topic to the specific question or hypothesis (or questions and hypotheses) that forms the basis of your research.

This section of the chapter describes how you ensure quality in your literature review and provides guidelines on how to write a literature review.

3.5.1 Ensuring quality in your literature review

Your thesis will be judged by readers and most importantly, your examiners, on the basis of its quality. Right from the outset, you must take measures to ensure this. Therefore your literature review must not be based mainly on articles in the popular press and in non-accredited journals. Your research must be positioned within the greater body of research and the literature that you refer to must reflect credible evidence of this.

3.5.1.1 Primary, secondary and general sources

Journals are by far the most important source of information about a topic and should be the major reference source in your literature survey and in your literature review. Journal articles are **primary reference sources** and therefore have greater evidential value.

Salkind explains that a primary source is one that contains reports of original work and also includes scholarly books, abstracts, Government publications and statutes. He also explains that **secondary sources** provide a level once removed from the original and refer to books on specific subjects and reviews of research. He also refers to general sources such as newspapers, magazines and periodicals.[18] He cautions researchers to "[i]nclude mostly primary sources in your literature review, with some secondary sources to help make your case [but] [d]o not even think about including **general sources**".[19]

3.5.1.2 Evaluating the quality of a literature item

Although journal articles constitute the most reliable sources of prior research, the quality of journal articles is not always assured. Evaluating the quality and relevance of a journal article may not be an easy task for a novice researcher. Leedy and Ormrod state that one rough indicator of the quality of a study is whether it has been refereed (been subjected to peer review). They advise researchers to use only recent publications of books. They also warn researchers not to accept the research of others at face value, but to evaluate it.[20] When reading journal articles, you must therefore read them critically.

Welman et al provide the following guidelines to assist with evaluating the relevance and quality of the work.[21] Ask yourself:
- how recent the item is; it may have been overtaken by later research
- whether the context is central to your research question, or only marginally related to your research
- whether you have seen references to the item or the author in other relevant items – this may indicate its reliability

- whether the item supports or contradicts your arguments – in either case it can provide external validity for your study
- whether the item appears to be biased
- whether you can identify any methodological omissions in the work – it may still be relevant as it may provide a gap for your research
- whether it displays a sufficient level of precision.

The Department of Business Management at the University of South Africa uses a template designed by Johan Strydom (undated) to evaluate journal articles, which is summarised (and slightly amended) below in Table 3.1. This template will not only assist you to keep a full bibliographical record of the journal article, but will also enable you to record your assessment of its value and usefulness for your research. It serves as a brief summary of the article, and can be captured electronically or on a card in a manual system. When you read an article, you often get lost in the detail. Summarising it in this way allows you to make a more precise judgement.

Table 3.1 Template for evaluating journal articles

Bibliographical details	Title: the full title of the article is recorded
	Full bibliographical reference
	Authors: the names of all the authors are noted
	Year published
Goal and objectives	Both the overall goal and the detailed objectives are recorded
Methodology	Research methodology followed: a very brief statement of the methodology adopted
	The number of participants or respondents
	The type of sample: this relates to the sampling method used in the research
	The setting where the study was carried out: this relates to the population which was used for the research
	Methods and tools used to collect the data: these methods may be personal interviews, questionnaires, observations, etc.
	Methods of data analysis: the specific statistical tests used in the study are recorded, as well as the purpose of the tests, or in the case of qualitative research, the data analysis technique and the methods used to strengthen the reliability and validity of the conclusions
Findings	The findings are briefly summarised
Relevance to my research	How can I apply this to my research? This relates to the relevance of the article to your own research – its relevance may be related to the research question, the literature discussed in the article or the design of the research.
Evaluation	Strengths/weaknesses of the study: at this stage you are able to evaluate the article and identify the strengths and weaknesses.

Source: UNISA, Undated. Template to evaluate journal articles. Pretoria: Dept. of Business Management, University of South Africa. Reprinted by permission of the Dept.

3.5.2 Writing the literature review

You have now completed your literature survey, ensuring the quality and relevance of the literature that you will use. You now have to write the literature review. You may need to write two reviews: a review for the purpose of your research proposal and a detailed review in your thesis. This section of the chapter discusses a comprehensive literature review, but most of the discussion is also relevant for the research proposal. How to get started? Salkind advises researchers to read other literature reviews to get a feeling for what a review should look like and also refers to the fact that you will have to re-write it several times.[22]

You have carefully documented the results of your literature survey, grouping them into themes. You now need to organise the items by themes and within themes in order to support your discussion and the arguments you present.

3.5.2.1 Reproduce or review

As stated above, a literature review does not simply document previous research. It is a structured discussion from a critical and comparative perspective of the important research relevant to your research topic.

Leedy and Ormrod warn researchers not to simply reproduce the literature, but to review it. They emphasise that what *you* say about the studies you review is important. They provide three rules to follow when you write the review:[23]
1. **Evaluate the work of others:** you have already evaluated the quality of the literature you will use; you need to reflect this evaluation in your review, as certain material, though flawed, may be important and may even provide the niche for your own research.
2. **Organise the ideas you have encountered during your survey:** chronologically or by opposing views, using overviews, headings and transitional sentences (links) to do this.
3. **Synthesise:** pull together the diverse perspectives and research results into a coherent whole by comparing and contrasting the findings, showing how approaches have changed over time, describing general trends in the findings, identifying contradictory findings and suggesting possible explanations.

While reviewing the literature, you also need to tie it in with your own research. This must be the unifying theme or 'golden thread' that runs through your review.

3.5.2.2 The content and structure of the review

The literature review would usually start with an introductory paragraph. In this paragraph you refer to the goals of your research, in order to put the discussion into context. Hofstee states that in this paragraph you also comment on the scope of your literature review – what you have included and why – and how you have structured it – the order in which the themes are discussed.[24] The paragraph is usually written last, after you have written the rest of the review. The following sections then deal with the actual review of the literature.

Leedy and Ormrod advise you to start your discussion of the literature from a comprehensive (broad) perspective, like an inverted pyramid, then deal with more specific ideas and finally focus in more and more on your own problem.[25] Hofstee refers to it as a funnel.[26]

Hofstee gives the first rule of structure: to group your items by 'commonalities'.[27] You will already have identified preliminary themes for your literature items when you were surveying the literature and these should assist you to group works by common themes. You may need to read through the items at this stage to make sure that you have identified all the themes, or to group certain themes together. If you need to place a certain item under more than one theme you can do this by duplicating the item.

One of the major themes that you discuss would be the theories, models or frameworks developed and tested in earlier research. They should be discussed first in your literature review as they provide the 'big picture'. There is often a seminal work that developed a particular theory and this should be dealt with first. The research that follows can be discussed in chronological order, reflecting their relationship to the seminal work – how they developed, added to or critiqued it. In your discussion you compare and contrast the various theories.

As you discuss the theories, models or frameworks of earlier research, you gradually narrow the discussion down to those closest to your own research and explain how you have applied the theory or theories in your own research.

In the concluding paragraph you provide a brief summary of the main points of your review. Here you also indicate how your work fits into the body of knowledge relating to the problem and its original contribution and importance.

Headings and subheadings in the literature review should reflect the flow of your argument. Where a certain section presents a complex argument it is useful to summarise briefly the main points and the conclusion reached and possibly end with a sentence that links it with what is discussed in the following section. This helps the reader to follow your line of argument.

Your discussion should reflect your own thinking. Welman et al advise you to make sparing use of quotations in your review and to write in your own words.[28] A well-written literature review is therefore infused with the mind of the researcher.

The literature review, which forms part of your research proposal, should not be too long (between five and ten pages) and should summarise the main points. In a master's thesis, the literature review would not be as extensive or as wide-ranging as for a doctoral thesis. It may form part of the first chapter of the thesis, or may occupy a chapter of its own. In a doctoral thesis, the literature review is detailed and wide-ranging and occupies its own chapter, or chapters.

The type of research may determine the approach, content and even placing of the literature review. In quantitative research the purpose of the literature review is usually to develop a theoretical framework or hypotheses upfront, to be tested empirically. Qualitative research is more exploratory in nature and the purpose is accordingly to develop theoretical frameworks or hypotheses, often in the absence of a substantial body of literature. In some types of qualitative studies, such as ethnography and phenomenology, the literature review will be used to identify the theoretical lenses that will guide the research. In other types of qualitative research, such as grounded theory, the literature will be used at the end of the study to link the newly generated theory to other bodies of knowledge. Delport and Fouché suggest the following functions for a literature review in a qualitative study:[29]

- it demonstrates the underlying assumptions behind the general research questions
- it demonstrates the familiarity of the researcher with related research and the underlying intellectual traditions of the research paradigm
- it identifies gaps in previous research and demonstrates that the research will make a meaningful contribution
- it places the research within larger empirical traditions, and in that way contributes to refining the research questions.

> **Ethical issues: bias and referencing**
>
> Researchers strive to produce research that is ethical and unbiased. Just as you would not ignore data that does not support your argument, you would not select for review only the literature that supports the position that you are taking in your research and ignore the work of researchers that does not support it.
>
> Referencing is equally important in your review of the literature. Not only when you are quoting from the work of others do you need to provide a reference, but even when you are simply using their ideas.

In summary, the literature review must achieve the following goals:
- it must demonstrate your familiarity with the most important research in the field
- it must identify a theory, framework or model on which your research will be based or which your research will test
- it must indicate the gap or niche in existing research that your research aims to fill
- it must help you to justify your research – demonstrate the importance of your research.

3.6 Summary

This chapter has provided a detailed discussion of how to carry out a literature survey and write a literature review based on a detailed and comprehensive literature survey. In the process, the meaning of the terms literature 'survey' and literature 'review' were described. The discussion then dealt with the main purposes of a literature survey and how to carry out a search for items relevant to your research by using key words to identify the relevant items in various databases. The two main methods of performing a literature survey were briefly described. The discussion then went on to give guidance on how to record both the process and the results of the search.

Moving on to the literature review, the chapter described how to ensure quality in the review by concentrating on primary literature sources, with less emphasis on secondary sources and warned not to simply accept the work of other researchers, but to evaluate their work. Hints were provided on how to evaluate other research. The actual writing of the review was then discussed, including using the 'funnel' approach to structure the discussion of the literature and the grouping of theories and other themes. Finally, the contents of the introductory and concluding paragraphs were suggested.

In the discussion it was assumed that the literature review forms part of a research proposal or a thesis. When you are writing a journal article, you do not provide a comprehensive literature review. You would only refer to the most important research in your field of research and demonstrate how your research fits into the general body of research. The discussion of the literature in a journal article will also deal with the models, theories or frameworks that have been developed by other researchers that you will be using in your research.

Key terms and concepts

databases: online collections of reference material, including abstracts, articles, theses, etc.
key words: words describing the topic of research that are used in a database search to identify relevant literature
literature survey: an exhaustive survey of the relevant literature for a specific purpose
literature review: a structured discussion from a critical and comparative perspective of the important research relevant to a research topic
model: a mathematical expression or a group of mathematical expressions depicting the relationship between variables
primary reference sources: sources of reference that contain reports of original work and include scholarly books, abstracts, Government publications and statutes
secondary reference sources: sources of reference that provide a level once removed from the original and include books on specific subjects and reviews of research
theory (or theoretical framework): a theory is a group of logical related statements that is presented as an explanation of a phenomenon

Test yourself questions

1. What is meant by the terms 'literature survey' and 'literature review' and how do they differ?
2. Give four purposes for carrying out a literature survey.
3. What are the two main methods used to carry out a literature survey?
4. What is a theory, and how is it developed?
5. What do we mean by 'key words' and how are they used?
6. Why is it important to keep accurate records?
7. Give two ways in which we ensure quality in a literature review.
8. Briefly describe the 'funnel' approach to writing a literature review.
9. What should the introductory and concluding paragraphs of the literature review contain?

Multiple-choice questions

1. Research is seldom completely original and builds on existing knowledge. In relation to this statement, which of the following is true?
   a) The statement is incorrect and a research student must strive for complete originality in his or her thesis.
   b) Reading research that has previously been carried out in the field ensures that your research is similar to earlier research.
   c) A survey of earlier research will help you to position your research within the existing body of knowledge.
   d) Every thesis must contain a historical review of all the earlier research in the field.

2. The terms 'literature survey' and 'literature review' are often used interchangeably. In relation to this statement, which of the following is correct?
   a) The two terms have the same meaning.
   b) A research student only needs to carry out either a literature survey or a literature review.
   c) A literature review is a more comprehensive study of existing literature than a literature survey.
   d) A literature review is a structured discussion of relevant research literature identified in the literature survey.
3. Theories play an important role in research. If this statement is accepted as true, which of the following statements are also true?
   a) It is essential that a research student bases his or her research on an existing theory.
   b) Research can be designed to disprove a theory.
   c) Theories can never be rejected (proved to be incorrect).
   d) Research can be designed to develop a theory.
4. In light of the statement: 'Key words assist a research student to identify earlier research that is relevant to his or her own research project,' which of the following statements is true?
   a) Key words are used to structure the literature review, by identifying themes in the literature.
   b) Initially, key words are formulated to start a database search, but they are usually expanded on as the literature survey progresses.
   c) The more key words are used in a literature search, the more efficient the search will be.
   d) Key words identify the databases that may contain literature sources that are relevant to a student researcher's planned research project.
5. Keeping careful records of the literature survey is essential. This statement is clearly true, but which of the following statements are also true?
   a) It is essential to record both the process that has been followed during the literature survey, as well as the precise details relating to each literature item.
   b) Keeping careful records of the literature survey enables the researcher to retrieve relevant literature.
   c) In writing your literature review, you must also describe the process you followed during your literature survey.
   d) A careful record of the literature survey includes a record of bibliographic details for each literature item.

Activities

Assume that you are interested in the costs small businesses incur in complying with their tax responsibilities and you want to find out what research has been done on the topic. You decide to start with an internet search. Follow the steps set out below:
1. Access the internet using whatever software is available on your computer or a computer in the library.
2. In the 'Google' search box (if there is one), type: http://www.scholar.google.com/
   If there is no 'Google' search box, type this internet address in the search box on the home page of the software program you are using.

3. On the Google Scholar home page select 'articles', deselect 'patents' and in the search box type:
Small business tax compliance costs
Question: How many items were identified in the search? Scan the first two pages – how many items did you find that were possibly relevant to your topic of interest? Can you see how inefficient from a time point of view it would be to scan without reading every item to see whether it appears to be relevant to your topic of interest?
3. Return to the Google Scholar home page and in the search box type: 'small business tax compliance costs'
Question: How many items were identified? How many of the items on the first page appear to be relevant to your topic of interest? Do you see how much more efficient the use of parameters/quotation marks has made your search?
4. Now look through the items listed on the page and the next page (or pages), which you access by clicking on the page number at the bottom of the page, and find an item: 'Taxation compliance burden for small business in South Africa.' Click on the item and print it out.
5. Note the following:
    – the details in the table at the top of the page: these are details that you would need in order to provide a reference for your literature review if you use the item
    – the key words: you could use these words to widen your search
    – at the very bottom of the page you have printed out, you will find the internet address that you will use to provide a reference for the item and the date you accessed it.
6. Read the abstract. Note that the citation given at the end of the article agrees with the internet address at the bottom of the page that you have printed out. Do you think that reading the whole thesis will be relevant to your topic of interest and add to your understanding of it?

Case study[30]

Read the following (limited) literature review that formed part of a research proposal submitted by a master's degree student (that had not yet been submitted for approval at the date of printing this book). The provisional title of the thesis is: Value investment strategies: evidence from expected returns in the South African equity market. Evaluate the literature review on the basis of what you have learned in this chapter. The following points may be of assistance:
- Has the master's degree candidate used the 'funnel' method?
- Has he described, discussed and contrasted the main theories, beginning with the seminal work(s)?
- Has his discussion been separated into paragraphs, based on the flow of logic?
- Does his discussion narrow down to the theory he will use in his own research?
- Are you able to decide, having read the proposal, whether he has identified a gap or a niche in the body of knowledge for his own research?
- Has he demonstrated the importance of his research?

Preliminary literature survey

Value investment strategies have been advocated by investors for many years. More than 75 years ago, Graham and Dodd (1934) argued that these strategies yielded returns that outperformed the market. There is also general agreement in the academic community that there is widespread evidence that value investment strategies, on average, outperform growth strategies (see for example, Chin, Prevost and Gottesman, 2002; Chan and Lakonishok, 2004 and Phalippou, 2008).

Value strategies favour investment in value shares, which are shares priced modestly relative to their book value, earnings, cash flow, dividends or some other measure of value. The antithesis of a value share, one which is highly valued by the market, is termed a growth share. A value strategy seeks to exploit the higher returns yielded by investing in a portfolio of value shares rather than growth shares. The difference in returns is termed the value premium.

During the last four decades there has been a significant amount of academic research in this field which has generated 'substantial evidence of superior returns from such strategies' (Chin et al, 2002: 422). Arguably, the most significant work was published in the early 1990s. Three seminal studies from this period are Chan, Hamoa and Lakonishok (1991), Fama and French (1992) and Lakonishok, Schleifer and Vishny (1994).

Chan et al (1991) modelled the relationship between four fundamental variables and returns on Tokyo Stock Exchange data. They found a significant positive relationship between returns and two of their independent variables: the book to market ratio (BE/ME), and the cash flow yield (C/P). The implication of this finding is that value shares yielded higher average returns than growth shares.

Fama and French (1992) built on earlier studies of stock market anomalies in the United States (US). They found that a positive relationship between beta (essentially a standardised measure of the covariance (systematic risk) of a security with the market) and average returns, central to the capital asset pricing model (CAPM), did not exist during the period reviewed. They also found that company size and BE/ME were negatively and strongly positively related, respectively, to average returns. Further findings were that the role of leverage in average returns is captured by BE/ME and that the role of earnings yield (E/P) in average returns is absorbed by a combination of company size and BE/ME.

The Fama and French (1992) study is considered to be important as the 'results delivered a stunning blow to the explanatory power of the capital asset pricing model and sparked debate about the "death of beta"' (Chan and Lakonishok, 2004: 71). In a separate finding more relevant to this research proposal, the Fama and French (1992) study also confirmed that value investment strategies yielded returns that outperformed the market.

Lakonishok et al (1994) evaluated the role of BE/ME, C/P, E/P and a five-year average growth rate in sales (G/S) in average returns in US markets. Like Chan et al (1991) and Fama and French (1992), they found 'investment strategies that involve buying out-of-favour (value) stocks have outperformed glamour [growth] strategies over the April 1968 to April 1990 period' (Lakonishok et al, 1994: 1574).

Chan and Lakonishok (2004) updated and expanded the studies of Chan et al (1991), Fama and French (1992) and Lakonishok et al (1994). They found that value investing continued to generate superior returns in the volatile markets of the late 1990s. Other important studies relating to the value investment strategy in the last decade include Zhang (2005), Fama and French (2006, 2007 and 2008), Anderson and Brooks (2006 and 2007), Phalippou (2008) and Garcia-Feijoo and Jorgensen (2010).

The growing interest in international investment opportunities has prompted the question whether this investment strategy could also be successfully applied to markets other than the US and Japan (Chan and Lakonishok, 2004). The studies have been extended to markets as diverse as Europe (Brouwer, van der Put and Veld, 1997 and Bird and Whitaker, 2003), Taiwan (Chou and Johnson, 1990), New Zealand (Chin et al, 2002) and Canada (Athanassakos, 2009). With few exceptions, these studies indicate that on average, value investment strategies outperform strategies favouring growth shares. It is significant that value strategies have been found to be successful in a range of markets representing varying financial reporting standards, statutes and regulations.

Although value strategies have been shown to be successful in a number of different markets, these are, apart from Taiwan, all developed markets (Standard and Poor's Financial Services LLC, 2010). Taiwan aside, there appear to have been no studies which investigate value investment strategies and the value premium in emerging markets such as South Africa.

An additional matter that will be addressed in the proposed research is the question of the reasons that value investment strategies work. Probably the two most important papers on value investment strategies (Fama and French, 1992 and Lakonishok et al, 1994) offered very different explanations in response to this issue.

Fama and French (1992) argued a risk based explanation for the higher average returns of value strategies. They took the position of the efficient market hypothesis, arguing that the higher returns from value strategies could be attributed to higher risk (Chan and Lakonishok, 2004). This rational explanation attributes higher returns from value strategies to smaller companies and those with high BE/ME ratios being fundamentally riskier i.e. value shares are underpriced relative to their risk. Although this study found that CAPM's beta did not fully capture risk, Fama and French (1992) argued that their other two factors, company size and BE/ME are both proxies for a share's risk.

In contrast, Lakonishok et al (1994) argued that the value premium is not related to risk but is rather an opportunity arising from the sub-optimal behaviour of naïve (or noise) investors and limited opportunities for arbitrage. In their essentially behaviourist (irrational investor) explanation, Lakonishok et al (1994) suggested that naïve strategies include extrapolating historical results too far into the future, assuming a trend in earnings and overreacting to company announcements. According to this argument, the variables used to measure and classify value shares are a proxy for mispricing. The resultant demand for growth stocks causes them to become overpriced while value stocks become underpriced.

Source: Permission was granted by the student and the supervisor to use the research proposal.

References

1. Salkind, N.J. 2009. *Exploring research.* 7th ed. New Jersey: Pearson Education. p. 44.
2. Leedy, P.D. & Ormrod, J.E. 2001. *Practical research, planning and design.* 7th ed. New Jersey: Prentice Hall. p. 10.
3. Welman, C. Kruger, F. & Mitchell, B. 3rd ed. 2008. *Research Methodology.* Cape Town: Oxford University Press.
4. Ibid. p. 38.
5. Leedy, P.D. & Ormrod, J.E. 2001. *Practical research, planning and design.* 7th ed. New Jersey: Prentice Hall. p. 155.

6 Welman et al, 2008, p. 12.
7 Ibid. p. 21.
8 Bailey, K.D. 1982. *Methods of social research*. 2nd ed. New York: The Free Press. p. 39.
9 Terre Blanche, M. and Durrheim, K. (Eds.) 2002. *Research in practice: applied methods for the social sciences*. Cape Town: University of Cape Town Press. p. 3.
10 Oberholzer, R. 2007. Unpublished thesis. *Perceptions of taxation: a comparative study of different population groups in South Africa*. Pretoria: University of Pretoria.
11 Welman et al, 2008, p. 39.
12 Leedy, P.D. and Ormrod, J.E. 2001. *Practical research, planning and design*. 7th ed. New Jersey: Prentice Hall. p. 39.
13 Welman et al, 2008, p. 39.
14 Ibid. p. 39.
15 Ibid. p. 41.
16 Hanlon, M. & Heitzman, S. 2010. *Journal of Accounting and Economics*. A review of tax research. (50):127–178. [Online] Available: www.elsevier.com/locate/jae/ [Accessed: 16 October 2011].
17 Shackelford, D.A. & Shevlin, T. 2001. *Journal of Accounting and Economics*. Empirical tax research in accounting. (31):321–387. [Online] Available: www.elsevier.com/locate/econbase/ [Accessed: 16 October 2011].
18 Salkind, N.J. 2009. *Exploring research*. 7th ed. New Jersey: Pearson Education. p. 45.
19 Ibid. p. 49.
20 Leedy, P.D. and Ormrod, J.E. 2001. *Practical research, planning and design*. 7th ed. New Jersey: Prentice Hall. p. 11.
21 Saunders et al in Welman et al, 2008, p. 43.
22 Salkind, N.J. 2009. *Exploring research*. 7th ed. New Jersey: Pearson Education. p. 74.
23 Leedy, P.D. & Ormrod, J.E. 2001. *Practical research, planning and design*. 7th ed. New Jersey: Prentice Hall. p. 86.
24 Hofstee, E. 2009. *Constructing a good dissertation*. Johannesburg: EPE. p. 97.
25 Leedy, P.D. & Ormrod, J.E. 2001. *Practical research, planning and design*. 7th ed. New Jersey: Prentice Hall. p. 85.
26 Hofstee, E. 2009. *Constructing a good dissertation*. Johannesburg: EPE. p. 94.
27 Ibid. p. 94.
28 Welman et al, 2008, p. 40.
29 Delport, C.S.L. & Fouché, C.B. 2005. *The place of theory and the literature review in the qualitative approach to research*. In: De Vos, A.S., Strydom, H., Fouché, C.B. & Delport, C.S.L. (Eds). *Research at grass roots*. 3rd ed. Pretoria: Van Schaik.
30 Permission was granted by the student and the supervisor to use the research proposal.

PART 2

RESEARCH DESIGN

Peet Venter

4

AFTER STUDYING THIS CHAPTER, YOU SHOULD BE ABLE TO:

- Understand what research design entails
- Be able to explain the effect of practical considerations on research design
- Describe and apply the research design process
- Explain the research design options.

> Most media companies have tended to fight illegal file download providers like BitTorrent with legal action and threats of legal action, a course of action that has proved largely unsuccessful in stopping illegal downloading of movies and other content. Rather than following this rather futile strategy, Australian media giant Fairfax saw the opportunity for using file downloading sites as great sources of free market research, and a great way of targeting online customers with legal products of their own.
>
> Techdirt's Glyn Moody argues that file sharing is marketing in its purest form, since everything on file sharing networks comes with an implicit recommendation – the fact that somebody thinks it is worth downloading and watching. The file sharing public also tends to be young tech-savvy individuals, a demographic highly sought after by media companies.
>
> The result is that file sharing sites provide some of the most reliable market research you could hope for, because it is totally unprompted. It is also free, if you take the trouble to gather and analyse it. TorrentFreak reports that:
>
> *At a government broadband conference in Sydney, Fairfax's head of video Ricky Sutton admitted that in a country with one of the highest percentages of BitTorrent users worldwide, his company determines what shows to buy based on the popularity of pirated videos online.*
>
> *"One of our major ways to get content is going to BitTorrent, and other BitTorrent sites, and find what people are illegally downloading to then go to the content owner and say, 'hey, I watched this last night it's going awesome on BitTorrent' and then say 'how about giving it to us?"*
>
> Apart from using this free, almost real-time source of market research to determine tomorrow's big sellers, Fairfax takes it a bit further to advertise to BitTorrent users.
>
> *"We then bring [the video content] over here and we advertise on BitTorrent that it's legally available on our platform, and then pay some revenue share based on it. That's worked quite effectively," Sutton says.*
>
> The value of this approach is that Fairfax catches people when they are considering illegally downloading, and convinces them to become paying customers.[1]
>
> *Source: Adapted from Moody, Glyn, 2012. Making the most of file-sharing: free market research and a captive audience. Techdirt, Available online at: http://www.techdirt.com/blog/?tag=market+research [Accessed 21 January 2012] and Show doing well on BitTorrent? We'll buy it. 2012. Torrentfreak, Available online at http://torrentfreak.com/show-doing-well-on-bittorrent-well-buy-it-121010/, [Accessed 21 January 2012].*

4.1 Introduction

Whether it is for purposes of a business decision (as in our opening vignette) or in the pursuit of academic knowledge, the purpose of research is to help provide answers to difficult questions. In this process, it is imperative to consider *how* the necessary information will be acquired and used. This is the domain of research design.

In this section of the book we address the important issue of **research design**. The research design is described as the "master plan that specifies the methods and procedures for collecting and analyzing the needed information".[2] It is, in other words, a framework or guideline for the research process to be followed by the researcher, and includes the approach, methods and techniques that will be used to carry out the research. The fact that the research design is a plan implies that the researcher has to make certain decisions about the research process, which may involve choosing between alternatives. In this chapter, we review some of these alternatives, which are then discussed in more detail in the following chapters.

Because economic and management research takes place in a complex environment and since there are so many alternatives available to the researcher, as our opening vignette illustrates, it follows that there is never one single best research design, and that the research design is almost always a compromise between what the researcher wants to achieve and other practical considerations and influences. In the following sections, we discuss some of these influences. We also examine the research design process, and the research design options. In the last section, we outline the following chapters in this section of the book and lastly summarise the chapter.

4.2 Practical considerations in research design

Every research project is subject to limitations that influence and constrain the choices that researchers make. These may range from very practical considerations, such as the availability of funds, to more philosophical and complex limitations, such as the paradigmatic influences of a researcher's supervisors or clients. While some of these considerations are apparent by the time the researcher formulates the research purpose, some considerations and their impact may only become clearer later on. Practical considerations have an effect on every step in the research design process.

4.2.1 Limited resources

Every research project is constrained by the available resources (such as time and money) to conduct the research. This may, for example, influence decisions on the geographical scope and methods of data collection. For example, researchers may prefer to do a national study, using personal interviews, but available funds and the lack of time may force them to use an online survey or other alternative designs instead. In the research proposal phase (see Chapter 8), it is accordingly important to plan the research budget and time lines as carefully as possible to ensure that the available time and money is utilised to the best possible effect.

4.2.2 The required scope

The required scope of the research may also be important in this regard. For example, while Master's degree studies require researchers to demonstrate their ability to conduct research independently, PhD studies require researchers to make an original contribution to the body of knowledge. This implies a substantial difference in research scope and has a strong influence on the research design.

4.2.3 Ethical considerations

It is important to consider ethical issues even (perhaps especially) in the planning stages of the research project. In fact, most academic institutions require students and staff to obtain ethical clearance before commencing with a research project. Ethical considerations are not only limited to academic research, but should also be taken into account by research practitioners in general. Therefore, professional bodies such as the Southern African Marketing Research Association (SAMRA) have 'codes of conduct' that they expect their members to follow (see ethics box). While ethical conduct is important to protect both the researcher and the participants, it does place certain constraints on the research design. It is accordingly important for the researcher to be aware of ethics guidelines and policies and to consider these in the research design, and to obtain ethical clearance where appropriate before commencing with the research.

> **Ethical issues**
>
> SAMRA follows the ESOMAR codes of conduct. ESOMAR has various codes of conduct that guide researchers worldwide on ethical practices in different situations. In the example below, a few such ethical and practical guidelines for conducting research using mobile phones are outlined. Many of these guidelines are also applicable to academic research.
> Firstly, research using mobile phones should conform to all core ethical research principles, such as:[3]
> - Informed consent from participants (meaning that participants should know enough about the research to make an informed choice about participation).
> - The private information of participants should be protected.
> - Participants should not be adversely affected by their participation (the 'no harm' rule).
> - Great caution should be exercised in conducting research among children, for example, verifiable and explicit permission to conduct the research should be obtained from parents or legal guardians.
>
> There are also guidelines specific to conducting research using mobile phones. Three examples of these are given below:
> - Where mobile or web-based applications (apps) are used to collect the data, the participant should be made aware of the purpose of the app, be given appropriate mechanisms to give explicit consent and be provided with a channel where they could obtain more information on the relevant privacy policy.
> - Where mobile phones are used to take photographs or make videos, pictures where participants are clearly visible and identifiable should be regarded as personal information and should only be used with the explicit permission of the participant.
>
> continued →

> - The research design should consider that mobile phone contact should typically be short, and should be in suitable form that is compatible with as many different mobile phone models as possible.
>
> Source: adapted from ESOMAR Guideline for conducting mobile market research. Available online at: http://www.esomar.org/uploads/public/knowledge-and-standards/codes-and-guidelines/ESOMAR_Guideline-for-conducting-Mobile-Market-Research.pdf [Accessed 28 October 2012].

4.2.4 Paradigmatic preferences

While it is ideal in our view that the research problem and purpose should primarily drive the research design, there are instances where researchers or their supervisors or clients have preferences for certain research paradigms. For example, it may be hard to convince a supervisor with a positivist world view and a strong preference for quantitative research that a more flexible and qualitative research design is more suitable than a quantitative survey under certain conditions.

4.2.5 Access

In certain research situations, access to participants may be problematic. Let's say, for example, that the research design for a Masters dissertation requires Chief Executive Officers (CEOs) to be interviewed about their organisations' strategies. It is highly unlikely that CEOs will be willing or able to give generously of their time or confidential information to an unknown graduate student. This type of problem occurs often and if it is not considered properly in the planning phase it can seriously impact not only the design but even the viability of an entire research project.

4.2.6 The role of triangulation

The notion of **triangulation** suggests that the use of multiple sources and methods increases the confidence in the research. In other words, triangulation increases the interpretive validity of the research. Some researchers argue that triangulation presupposes a fixed point of reference, which is not true of qualitative research, and accordingly suggest that **crystallisation** may be a better term to use where triangulation in qualitative methods are used. The idea is that the use of multiple methods in qualitative research may help to present the data in more clarity, yet in its full complexity (as a crystal is multifaceted). The most common form of triangulation occurs where researchers combine the use of qualitative and quantitative research methods in one research project and at the same time. This is a so-called mixed methods approach and is referred to as **methodological triangulation**. There are also other forms of triangulation:[4]
- **Data triangulation**, which suggests the use of more than one data source in a research project. For example, researchers may make use of observation, interviews, and document archives to investigate the same phenomenon. This form of triangulation will have an impact on the data collection decisions of the researcher.
- **Investigator triangulation** refers to the use of more than one researcher in a single research project, which provides an opportunity for achieving intersubjective agreement. This form of triangulation is useful where collaborative research projects

- are a possibility, but is not always practically possible, for example, where research is conducted for purposes of attaining a higher degree, collaboration may not be possible.
- **Theory triangulation** occurs where more than one theoretical perspective is used to interpret the research findings.
- When applying triangulation of measures, researchers take more than one measurement of the same phenomenon. This may involve, for example, a survey, combined with a diary or other qualitative methods.

> **Example box**
>
> In a recent doctoral study, the researcher investigated the middle management strategising practices in a South African organisation. The researcher used in-depth interviews with selected middle managers as a means of collecting data, but also used organisational artefacts such as strategic plans and intra-organisational communication (such as email) as a means of data triangulation. In analysing the data, the researcher used a second person (an expert in qualitative research) to also analyse the same set of qualitative data as a form of investigator triangulation. This step assisted in achieving greater intersubjective agreement and greater crystallisation of the findings.

4.3 Basic research approaches

At this point, it is necessary to revisit two concepts introduced in Chapter 1. The purpose of research can generally be classified as **inductive research**, which is more inwardly focused, or **deductive research**, which is more outwardly focused. Research projects can also be a combination of the two approaches, namely a **mixed methods approach**. These basic approaches are discussed in more detail below, along with **non-empirical** research designs.

It is useful at this point to distinguish between these three terms that you will come across in research literature:

- **Mono-method** research refers to research using a single method, for example, a survey or focus group discussions.
- **Multi-methods** research refers to research using different methods for producing data using the same approach (qualitative or quantitative)[5].
- **Mixed methods** research means research that combines qualitative and quantitative research.

The research problem and purpose often already suggest what type of research has to be conducted, but it is ultimately a decision made by the researcher. This section is followed by a section providing an overview of the main types of research designs and their supporting methodologies and techniques.

4.3.1 Non-empirical research designs

By far the most research in the context that we examine in this book and chapter is empirical in nature, meaning that it relies on new data gathered first-hand from the 'real world'. Non-empirical research, on the other hand, relies on data that already exists, and may have been produced for an entirely different purpose. However, there are also other forms of non-empirical research that may find application in business and management research. The danger with non-empirical research is that it is often not regarded as 'real' research, and the decision to use only non-empirical research should accordingly be approached with caution and with due consideration to the requirements of the course that you are doing research for. For this reason, it is important to consider the advantages and disadvantages of non-empirical research using only secondary sources.

On the positive side, research using secondary data is comparatively easy and cheap to conduct, especially since much secondary data is in the public domain and available for free, or very close to it. Researchers may accordingly be able to draw larger samples than if they were conducting empirical research.

On the negative side, the secondary data may not have been collected for the purpose of the research it is being used for. This implies that the researcher needs to be sure exactly how the data was generated, what exactly it measured and described, and whether it is valid to use in the context of the research it is being sourced for.

4.3.1.1 Literature review

Most research projects do contain a non-empirical component in the form of a literature review (see Chapter 3). However, there may be certain instances where the literature review is a study in its own right. A literature review as a study requires the researcher to read widely and to reorganise the data in a novel way. It is never, in other words, just a summary of the existing literature. The literature review can be used, for example, to:
- Classify literature according to a predetermined taxonomy or theoretical framework
- Develop a new taxonomy or theoretical framework
- Identify commonalities and differences in definitions, methodologies and content in a field of study.

Bibliometric analysis (bibliometrics) is a specialised field that relates to the literature review. In bibliometrics, data from citation indexes are analysed to determine the popularity and impact of specific articles, authors, and publications.[6] From a business and management perspective, bibliometrics can assist in determining different schools of thought in a field of study, and the most influential authors and publications.

4.3.1.2 Conceptual studies

Many fields of study originate in a conceptual study that has, as a purpose, the development of a new theoretical framework from extant research. Conceptual studies accordingly engage with a concept or concepts in a critical way in order to develop a new theory or insights. It requires a very thorough knowledge and insight into the field of study, for example by conducting an extensive literature review. Other researchers may then take this new knowledge and build on it by conducting empirical research. A typical conceptual research project may involve the following:[7]
- Determining the concept and the purpose of the study.
- Analysing the concept's range of meanings and developing a definition or meaning that will be used in the study.
- Developing the critical attributes and constructs of the concept from extant literature and from practice.

- Developing an exemplar case (a case that will represent the "ideal" with regard to the concept), as well as additional cases, which may typically involve developing deviant cases or cases that are polar opposites of the exemplar case. The purpose of this stage is to provide illustrative descriptions of the key characteristics of each case example, as well as significant differences between examples.
- Identifying antecedents and consequences of the concept.

Source: Based on the guidelines for conceptual stage model studies by Solli-Sæther, H. and Gottschalk, P. 2010. The Modeling Process for Stage Models, Journal of Organizational Computing and Electronic Commerce, Vol. 20 No. 3, p 284. Reprinted by permission of the publisher (Taylor & Francis Ltd, http://www.tandfonline.com).

Example box

In a study to determine what 'excellent' strategic decision-making is, a researcher may start with reviewing the literature on strategic decision-making and developing a working definition of strategic decision-making. A next step would involve the development of the processes and different constructs that make up strategic decision-making, leading to the development of a 'model case' of what strategic decision-making would look like in an ideal situation. In order to develop the concept further, the researcher might also consider what poor strategic decision-making might look like. The final step might be to develop a model of strategic decision-making with all of the components (such as antecedents and consequences) clearly identified. This may then serve as input into further empirical research to refine and test the conceptual framework.

4.3.1.3 Analysis of existing data

With the advent of the internet and the information age, there is a wealth of information for researchers to utilise. This can take the form of:
- Textual data such as annual reports, blogs and social media contributions that researcher can analyse (e.g. by using content analysis) to develop new insights
- Non-textual data such as pictures, videos and symbols
- Existing numerical data collected for other purposes, that can be reanalysed or used in simulations, e.g. to develop new insights into relationships between constructs.

Example box

The Bureau of Market Research (BMR) at Unisa has several studies, such as the South African Household Wealth Index and the Consumer Financial Vulnerablity Index that may be used by researchers that want to research certain aspects of personal financial management among consumers.

Ethical issues

When using secondary data, researchers may also have to consider the ethical standards that were applied in generating the data. For example, in a study on the personal finances of consumers, what evidence is there that the data was gathered ethically? If this cannot be confirmed (for example by the 'owner' of the data) it may present an ethical issue to the researcher.

4.3.2 Deductive research

Deductive reasoning is the logical process of deriving a conclusion about a specific instance based on a known general premise or something known to be true.[8] It is a top-down approach in the sense that it moves from the general to the specific. Research based on deductive reasoning will, therefore, start with a strong theoretical basis and specific hypotheses. Based on observations, such as survey responses, the hypotheses can be tested and the theory can be supported or rejected. Once the theory is supported, it can be applied to members of the population that were observed, i.e. it can be generalised. It should be mentioned that deductive research is generally dependent on rigorous scientific methods in sampling and observation, and accordingly favours the positivistic or post-positivistic paradigm. Deductive research is generally only possible where the theoretical foundations in the field of study are established and known widely, in other words, where there is already some measure of certainty or at least relatively low levels of ambiguity. The process of deductive research is depicted in Figure 4.1.

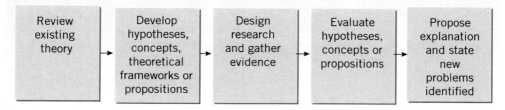

Figure 4.1 Basic deductive research design

The process starts with a review of previous research and existing literature, and the outcome of this review is typically a set of hypotheses, a theoretical framework or concepts, or research propositions. The research is designed in a way that enables the testing or evaluation of hypotheses, concepts or propositions, or the implementation of theoretical frameworks. The purpose is often to generalise the findings of the research to the population in which the research was conducted. This evaluation, and the extent to which findings support hypotheses or propositions (or not), lead to proposed explanations of the findings and the identification of new problems for further investigation. From the preceding explanation, it is clear that deductive research is more suited to fixed, quantitative research designs and testing or supporting theories than to developing new theories, and is accordingly more suited to research seeking to describe populations, or to explain the relationships between variables.

> **Example box**
>
> In 2010, three South African researchers used the well-known SERVQUAL questionnaire (a measure of service quality expectations and perception) to determine the service quality expectation of African retail banking customers. The study involved 4 035 banking customers in ten African countries. The study found that there were significant differences in retail banking service expectations across the different countries. This study is an example of deductive research.[9]

However, not all research deals with describing a population, and the purpose of research is often to explore certain phenomena and to develop new insights or theories. This is the focus of the next section on inductive research.

4.3.3 Inductive research

Inductive reasoning is the logical process of observing particular facts or occurrences and establishing a general proposition on the basis of the empirical observation.[10] It is thus the opposite of deductive research in that it moves from the specific to the general. Where research is inductive, the focus is on observing an object or phenomenon, identifying emerging patterns, and establishing a general proposition (a theory) on the basis of these empirical observations. Inductive research is often used where the theoretical foundations in the field of study are not strongly established and where there is a large degree of uncertainty and ambiguity. It may also be used simply as an alternative to deductive research, where researchers are critical of deductive research or its findings. For example, the current focus on practice-based research in management came about as a result of criticism against the prevailing rational economic perspectives in management research which favours quantification and macro-perspectives of management rather than a human perspective. Inductive research uses mainly flexible research designs, and is strongly associated with the processes of theory building. The process of inductive research is depicted in Figure 4.2.

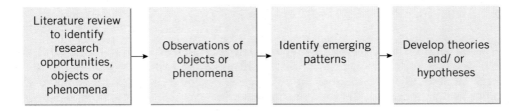

Figure 4.2 Basic inductive research design

Although the observations (using mainly qualitative methods such as interviews) are the starting point of the research process, it is usually preceded by a literature review to identify the research gaps and opportunities. The observations are usually directed at individual actors (rather than at a population) and the purpose is to identify emerging themes or patterns. The identified themes or patterns form the basis for the development of theories and hypotheses. However, the purpose of inductive research is not to confirm or to test the theories, although it should by now be apparent that inductive research may precede or be used in conjunction with deductive research. This, the so-called mixed methods research, is discussed in the following section.

> **Example box**
>
> In a study on internal brand alignment, the researcher found that the extant literature on the topic was very limited, As a result, the researcher opted for a qualitative case study methodology, conducting interviews with senior and middle managers in four organisations as a means to developing a theoretical model for internal brand alignment.[11]

4.3.4 Mixed methods research

Mixed methods research most often refers to research projects where qualitative (inductive designs) are used in conjunction with quantitative (deductive designs) to achieve the research purpose. The approach stems from the philosophical basis of pragmatism ('what works best' for understanding the research problem).[12] The adoption of mixed methods approaches was initially slow because of the traditional philosophical rift between qualitative and quantitative researchers, who regarded the two approaches as fundamentally incompatible. Following the narrowing of this rift, mixed methods designs have become very popular in economic and management research, perhaps because of the inherently pragmatic nature of such research and the inherent benefit of triangulation that is derived as a result. There are four widely recognised ways in which qualitative and quantitative designs may be combined. These four approaches are discussed below.[13]

4.3.4.1 Explanatory mixed methods design

In this mixed methods design, the qualitative research phase is used to develop deeper insights into quantitative findings and to lead to greater clarity and understanding of findings and their implications.

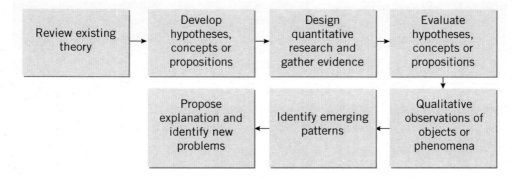

Figure 4.3 Explanatory mixed methods design

After the initial quantitative findings, qualitative observations (such as interviews or focus groups) are used to explore and clarify the findings with selected respondents and to develop a better understanding of their behaviour and characteristics. The subsequent findings should be 'richer' and provide more insights than simply the quantitative findings. This design is relatively simple, and consisting of two discrete steps, it is easy to manage and can accordingly be executed by a single researcher. However, it takes longer and is more expensive than a single-method design.

> **Example box**
>
> In a study on employee commitment and retention using a survey, the researcher could use qualitative interviews with employers and industrial psychologists to identify possible reasons for the survey findings, and also to identify possible solutions to problem areas identified. The qualitative research is thus used to assist in interpreting quantitative findings and provide deeper insights that the quantitative findings could not do on its own.

4.3.4.2 Exploratory mixed methods design

The exploratory mixed methods design is perhaps the most widely used mixed methods design in the economic and management sciences. In this design, the qualitative research phase is used first to explore the research topic. Based on the findings from the qualitative phase, along with the findings from the literature review, the quantitative study is then designed. This type of research is especially appropriate in situations where there is a relatively high level of ambiguity or uncertainty about what needs to be measured. It is also appropriate to use this approach when the qualitative phase is used to build the theory, i.e. to develop the theoretical frameworks or hypotheses, wherefter the quantitative phase is then used to test or support the theory. The basic design for exploratory mixed methods research is depicted in Figure 4.4.

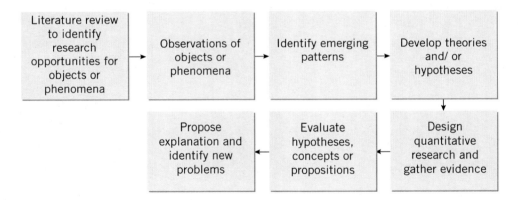

Figure 4.4 Exploratory mixed methods design

The researcher will have greater confidence in the findings; since it is grounded in more than just a literature review. The design is also relatively simple and easy to manage, and can be executed by a single researcher. As in the case of the explanatory research design, it takes longer and is more expensive than a single-method design.

> **Example box**
>
> In a study to determine the drivers of advertising agency retention by their clients, the researcher conducted interviews with advertising industry observers and key role players to ensure the general validity of the theoretical model she developed, and to customise the theoretical framework and research instrument for South African conditions.[14]

4.3.4.3 Triangulation

In this mixed methods design, the qualitative research phase is executed concurrently with the quantitative research phase, as a means of comparing and contrasting findings to arrive at conclusions that have more interpretive validity. As can be expected, it can be very challenging to decide how the actual comparison of findings from the two research streams will take place and how it will be integrated.[15] Because of the concurrent execution of the qualitative and quantitative phases, research projects of this nature may be very difficult for one researcher to manage alone. On the positive side, the concurrent execution means that the project will generally take less time to complete than the explanatory or exploratory mixed methods approaches. Figure 4.5 depicts the triangulation research design.

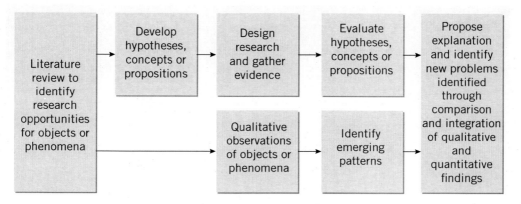

Figure 4.5 Triangulation research design

> **Example box**
>
> In a study examining the innovation orientation of pharmaceutical companies, the researcher plans to conduct two concurrent streams of research. In one stream, the researcher plans to survey pharmaceutical company executives. This is a quantitative stream of research using a structured questionnaire. In the other stream, the researcher plans to interview the customers of pharmaceutical companies, such as physicians and pharmacists, to determine their perceptions of the innovation orientation of pharmaceutical companies. These interviews will be qualitative and semi-structured in nature.

4.3.4.4 Embedded mixed methods design

Embedded mixed methods designs are used where the primary data collection is one type of data, but another type of data (qualitative or quantitative) is used for supplementary purposes. For example, in a case study method (which is primarily qualitative in nature) the researcher may use a questionnaire to gather some data on a specific issue. Conversely, during a quantitative survey, survey questions may be used as a means of gathering supplementary data and to develop a better understanding of the phenomenon being investigated. Since the embedded research design can create some additional complexities for researchers, the purpose of the supplementary research should be very clear and should not detract from the primary research design. In Figures 4.6 and 4.7 the embedded mixed methods design is illustrated.

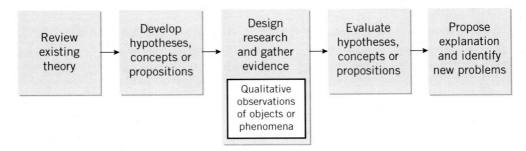

Figure 4.6 Embedded mixed methods in a primarily quantitative research design

Example box

A researcher may decide to include an 'open question' in an otherwise highly structured survey questionnaire. The purpose of such an open question (where respondents may formulate their own answers and are not given structured options) could be to probe certain aspects in more depth. For example, in a questionnaire on customer satisfaction, the organisation may ask its respondents (customers) what actions it could take that will have the biggest effect on improving customer service.

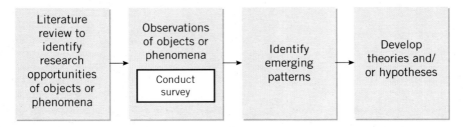

Figure 4.7 Embedded mixed methods in a primarily qualitative research design

Example box

In a predominantly qualitative research project, researchers may request participants to fill in a short structured questionnaire, in order to gather information on a specific aspect in a more structured format. For example, participants in a focus group targeting ICT managers may be given a questionnaire on their work and study background as a means of determining a typical background of ICT managers.

4.4 Types of research designs

Depending on the research problem that has been identified, and the research questions that have been formulated by the researcher, research can be broadly classified as **exploratory**, **descriptive** or **causal**. This categorisation is generally a result of the level of uncertainty associated with the research problem. Each of these categories is described below, along with a brief description of the main types of designs and methods associated with it. A detailed discussion of each design and method is outside of the scope of this chapter, and will be dealt with in more detail in the rest of the chapters in this section.

4.4.1 Exploratory research designs

Every research project has an exploratory phase. The design of the exploratory phase will depend on various practical considerations, and may range from a review of current literature (secondary research) as part of a quantitative study, to an empirical research project of an inductive nature. Most projects with an academic purpose will require a literature review, and this important research element is discussed in more detail in Chapter 3. Under conditions of uncertainty or ambiguity, for example, where little previous research or knowledge exists, exploratory research is used to provide more information and to develop theoretical frameworks, hypotheses or research propositions. These can then be further tested using other research designs. In some instances, the exploratory research may be an end unto itself, where the development of a theory rather than testing or confirming it is the end goal. However, for most research, exploratory research is only the first step. In the sections that follow, we describe the main types of exploratory research briefly, along with some possible applications in economic and management research. The designs, methods and techniques of qualitative and exploratory research is discussed in more detail in Chapter 5.

4.4.1.1 Historical research

The purpose of historical research is to understand the meaning of events that occurred in the past. While historical research does deal with the gathering of historical evidence on such past events, it is much more than simply developing a chronology of events – it is primarily about the interpretation of the events,[16] identifying patterns in the mass of data and making sense of why things happened the way it did. There are lessons to be learned in history, and historical research helps us to uncover those lessons. Historical research is not used very often in economic and management research, but it does offer an interesting approach to better understanding historical economic or business events, as Mark Pendergrast illustrates in his fascinating 'unauthorised' account of the history of Coca Cola, *For God, Country and Coca-Cola: The Definitive History of the Great American Soft Drink and the Company That Makes It*.[17]

4.4.1.2 Phenomenology

Phenomenology originated in philosophy and psychology, and is founded on the perspective that human experiences are inherently subjective and shaped by the context in which people live.[18] The purpose of phenomenology is to understand how human behaviour is shaped by interaction with the physical environment and other people.[19] The key to develop this understanding is hermeneutics, the identification of text passages (hermeneutic units) from interviews that links with key themes in the researcher's interpretation.[20] With the practice turn in management research, phenomenology is increasingly becoming an important tool for understanding, for example, how individuals in the workplace interact with their work environment and how it shapes their behaviour and identity.

4.4.1.3 Ethnography

As the name suggests, ethnography stems from anthropological research. It requires the researcher to become immersed in a situation and to become part of it, in the hope that the subjects of study will, over time act more naturally around the researcher and reveal more about themselves and their practices than they would in a formal research setting. This approach mirrors research in anthropology that required anthropologists to live with tribes or within subcultures for long periods as observers, suggesting that participant observation is one of the key data collection techniques of ethnography. Ethnography is a suitable approach to studying, for example, organisational culture[21] or subcultures within an organisation.

4.4.1.4 Grounded theory

Grounded theory is a research design that seeks to specifically develop theory inductively from the research. It is suitable especially to situations where no or little previous research exists (or where previous research is inadequate). It begins with data collection immediately, and is very suited to studying processes. Data collection could be done using a variety of data collection methods, as long as it focuses on the process being studied and contains the perspectives of the people being studied.[22] Grounded theory is not used very often in economic and management research, but can certainly play a role in theory development in fields where the extant theory is inadequate.

4.4.1.5 Case research

The case research method is one of the most popular exploratory methodologies used in economic and management research. In a case study design, a unit of analysis (such as an individual, an organisation, an event) is studied in-depth for a defined period of time. This type of study could range from a single case to a selection of cases (multiple case studies).[23] The purpose of case study research is to learn more about a poorly understood aspect. In many case study research projects, the organisation or a subunit of an organisation is the focus of a case study approach.

4.4.1.6 Action research

Action research is a strategy of enquiry that attempts to find a solution to a local problem in a local setting,[24] which means that the focus could be on a problem in a single organisation or community. It is a form of applied research that is cyclical and participatory in nature, as the results of the various steps are implemented and become part of the next step in the process. Participants in the research become co-researchers as they contribute to the development of solutions. Action research is an interactive form of knowledge development. Given the pragmatic and interactive nature of action research, it is a research design that can be used to great effect in organisational settings to find solutions to business problems or to develop suitable interventions.

The exploratory research designs are generally more exploratory and qualitative in nature, and the more prevalent types are discussed in more detail in Chapter 5.

4.4.2 Descriptive research designs

Descriptive research is used where the focus of research is to describe a situation, a phenomenon, a person or groups of people or an environment in some detail. It is survey-based research, and aims to answer questions about the *who, what, where, when* and *how* of the phenomenon or object being researched.[25] Descriptive research is quantitative in nature, and as a result uses quantitative surveys as a methodology. The purpose is often to generalise findings to a population, and so it should rely on sampling that ensures that the population is properly represented, and data collection and analysis methods that ensure a relatively high level of accuracy. There are four types of descriptive research designs,[26] which are discussed below.

4.4.2.1 Observation studies

Unlike observation in qualitative research, which is more unstructured and open to the researcher's interpretation, observational studies in descriptive research are much more structured and focused in an attempt to establish objectivity. The researcher observes certain specific occurrences, in specific time frames, either directly or indirectly (by video recording for example) and records the findings meticulously. The observations should yield quantifiable data about the behaviour or phenomenon being recorded that can be generalised to the population being studied. There are many instances in economic and management research where observation might be a suitable research method, for example the behaviours of customers in a retail setting.

4.4.2.2 Developmental designs[27]

Developmental designs have the purpose of establishing how people and their characteristics and behaviour change over time. There are two basic designs in developmental designs:
- Cross-sectional studies will sample respondents from the different developmental groups to measure and compare. Let's say that we want to establish how the perceptions of employees towards labour unions change as they move up the organisational ladder. In a cross-sectional design, we will sample employees at all levels of the organisation – low level employees, junior managers, middle managers and senior managers to compare. While cross-sectional studies are relatively easy and quick to conduct, not all the participants may have been exposed to the same organisational factors, which means that their opinions may differ for reasons other than their development in the organisation, which may raise issues with regard to the validity in the research.
- Longitudinal studies will use the same group of individuals and track them over months or even years. While this type of design ensures that the individuals are exposed to more or less the same environmental conditions, the downside includes the long time it takes to execute the study, and the fact that the respondents may be lost to the study as they leave the organisation for any reason.

4.4.2.3 Descriptive surveys

Rather than describing any form of quantitative and descriptive research, Leedy and Ormrod assign a very specific meaning to descriptive surveys. They describe it as surveys with the purpose of acquiring information about one or more groups of people, by asking them questions and tabulating their answers.[28] The ultimate purpose is to learn something about a population, i.e. to generalise the findings.

Some applications of descriptive research in economic and a management research may include the following:

- Economic and demographic research such as the research on household and business spending patterns conducted by various organisations such as Statistics South Africa and the Bureau of Market Research at the University of South Africa. The typical purpose of this type of research is to provide a detailed picture of the behaviour and characteristics of a population or a relatively broad slice of the population, such as for a province.
- Describing a segment of consumers, customers or employees in more detail. For example, a bank may want to know more about its 'high net worth' clients – their demographic characteristics, what they think about certain key issues, and their financial and other purchasing behaviour.
- Descriptive research may also be used for diagnostic analyses.[29] For example, if enrolments on an MBA programme are declining, descriptive research may help to determine the perceptions of prospective students about the business school in general and the MBA programme in particular.

4.4.3 Causal research designs

The purpose of causal research is to establish cause-and-effect relationships between two or more variables, which can also be described as dependent variables (the effect) and independent variables (the cause). Before examining the types of research, it is useful to define what we mean by causality:

- Having a proper time order of events is the first criterion for causality. In other words, the cause must occur before the effect. This is known as temporal sequence.
- For causality to exist, a change in one variable will also mean a change in the other variable or variables. For example, if testing whether advertising expenditure leads to greater awareness of a product, both advertising expenditure and product awareness must change. If this does not occur (for instance there is no change in advertising expenditure), causality simply cannot exist. This is known as systematic variation, or concomitant variation.
- Sometimes concomitant variation is incorrectly ascribed to causality. This is known as a spurious association. Let's use our example of advertising and product awareness again, and say that advertising expenditure increases, and product awareness increases. However, at the same time there was a newspaper article on the negative health effects of the product. Ascribing the increase in awareness to an increase in advertising may then be spurious, since the negative publicity may have increased awareness as well. It is accordingly important to ensure that a nonspurious association between the variables as a precondition to claiming causality.[30]

As the preceding paragraphs may suggest, causal research requires rather rigorously scientific research designs, such as experimental research designs, to ensure that the findings can be used to test for causality. Control over variables is an important aspect of experimental designs during the observation (the measurement) and the treatment (the interventions or occurrences that the researcher is interested in). There are three types of experimental designs, namely pre-experimental designs, true experimental designs and quasi-experimental designs. As pre-experimental design is in essence an exploratory research design, it was included in that section.

4.4.3.1 True experimental designs

In true experimental designs, there are four important general conditions:
- The use of control groups to compare with the group receiving the treatment
- The assignment of subjects to control and treatment groups has to be random
- Pre-testing is administered to establish baseline measurement
- The researcher controls for possible confounding variables.

If we consider the nature of economic and management research, it is clear that it is often very difficult to assign subjects to control and treatment groups in a completely random fashion, making it very difficult to meet this condition. It is, however, just about impossible to control confounding variables, as the subjects and context of economic and management research are always influenced and exposed to a great variety of stimuli and influences that simply cannot be controlled completely by the researcher. In addition, people are by nature diverse and cannot be forced to disregard their personality and background in the research process.

For example, a researcher wants to determine whether a management training programme achieved the intended causal effect on the participants (e.g. enhancing their management performance). There are three key components of an experimental design:
- **The pre-post test design**. This requires collecting data on managers' level of performance before the intervention took place, and after the intervention took place (i.e. pre- and post-).
- **Treatment and control groups**. Making use of a treatment and a control group allows the researcher to effectively determine the true effects of the programme or intervention under investigation. The treatment group receives the intervention (the training), while the control group does not participate in the intervention (they keep on working as usual). By studying both a group receiving the intervention and another group that does not, you are able to control for the possibility that other factors not related to the intervention (e.g. a participant getting accustomed to a test, or some saturation over the intervening time) are responsible for the difference between the pre-test and post-test results. Both the treatment group and the control group should be of adequate size in order to determine whether an effect took place or not. The sample size should be determined by the specific technique, but, as rule of thumb, each group should consist of at least 30 participants.
- **Random allocation of the participants.** The methodology relies on random assignment and strict controls over confounding factors to ensure the most valid, reliable results. Although no two groups can ever be exactly alike, the two groups should be statistically similar. For this reason, participants are randomly allocated to each of the two groups. Therefore, any difference between the two groups is purely due to chance and not due to selection bias. The methodology does not require a random sample, but it does require random allocation to each of the two groups.

While experimental studies produce the strongest, most valid results, it is not always practical in the social, education or management sciences because researchers cannot exercise laboratory controls in natural-world settings or be able to randomly allocate subjects. For example, while the experimental group is undergoing the training, a member of the control group may read a book on management that influences his behaviour.

The experimental group undergoes the treatment, programme or intervention of interest and the researcher then measures the differences between the two groups based on a particular outcome. For example, an experimental-research study in management could examine the impact of a new marketing strategy on consumer spending between two consumer groups. One group could be exposed to the marketing techniques. The researchers would then measure consumer spending by the two groups to see if the two differ significantly, analysing the results to determine the extent to which the marketing strategy caused consumers in the experimental group to boost their spending.

The greatest strength of an experimental-research design is the high level of certainty with which changes in the outcome of interest (i.e. consumer spending) can be attributed to the independent variable or 'treatment' – in this case, a marketing strategy. By controlling the study bias through random assignment, it is more likely that differences in consumer spending can be attributed to the effects of the marketing strategy rather than other variables that affect differences in spending, such as income. In addition, research studies using an experimental design can be replicated more than once, using different groups of subjects.

The most significant drawback of experimental design is the artificiality of the setting because the effects that occur in an experiment under research controls might not take place in more natural settings. A new marketing strategy may increase consumer spending among a group of research subjects, but may not have the same effects among consumers nationwide. The difficulty in imposing laboratory controls in a natural setting leads many researchers in business, education and social sciences to rely on quasi-experimental designs, which do not randomly assign subjects.

4.4.3.2 Quasi-experimental designs

In quasi-experimental research, randomness is not a condition (for example, treatment and control groups can be 'non-equivalent') and researchers do not control for all confounding variables.[31] The influences of such variables can accordingly not be ruled out completely, and in quasi-experimental research the case for causal relationships is, as a result, much weaker than in true experimental designs. Quasi-experiments are also referred to as natural experiments because membership in the treatment level is determined by conditions beyond the control of the researcher.

However, from an economic and management perspective quasi-experimental research designs are much more practical and possible than true experimental research.

> **Example box**
>
> If we revert back to our example above of management development training, it may not be possible to assign the groups randomly due to working conditions and operational requirements of the business. Once it is impossible to assign the participants randomly to control and experimental groups, the study can only be a quasi-experimental study.

Both true and quasi-experimental research designs are characterised by one characteristic: manipulation of the independent variable, a characteristic it shares with no other research design. Two other forms of quantitative research, which are not experimental due to lack of manipulation, are ex post facto (sometimes called causal-comparative) and correlational. Often both of these types are grouped into what researchers call non-experimental research or simply correlational research. Thus, correlational research can be understood to include both of the types below; namely ex post facto and correlational. For our purposes, we will make a distinction between these two types.

> **Ethical issues**
>
> Given the manipulation of research subjects in experimental research, what are the implications for the researcher with regard to ethicality and disclosure?

4.4.3.3 Ex post facto studies

In ex post facto studies, groups are compared but there is no manipulation of the independent variable. With ex post facto research, the difference between groups on the independent variable occurs independently from the research. For example, suppose a researcher contacts a business unit and requests two managers who employ different management styles. The goal is to compare the employees' performances based on specific criteria. The key here is that the researcher does not manipulate the independent variable. The researcher does not determine which manager or unit will employ which style but merely includes them in the sample and then selects the groups for comparisons.

Therefore the focus of an ex post facto study is group comparisons and non-manipulated independent variables. Groups may be randomly formed in ex post facto research, such as through random sampling of males and females, but randomly formed groups alone are not enough for an ex post facto study to be regarded as an experimental study.

4.4.3.4 Correlational research

The purpose of correlational research is to measure the linear relationship between variables without establishing causality. It simply measures whether there is a relationship (either positive or negative) between the variables. The higher the correlation, the higher the degree of relatedness between the variables.[32] Correlational research is used quite often in economic and management research, for example, to determine the antecedents of a phenomenon, such as customer retention or employee satisfaction. A predictive study is done simply to learn which, among a set, of variables best predicts the dependent variable. The goal here is simply to maximise prediction. A second type of study may be to understand, as best as possible, those variables that are theoretically related to a dependent variable. With this type of study, researchers are interested in testing and confirming theories or hypotheses concerning relationships among variables.

4.5 Chapter outline for this section

In this chapter, we introduced the basic research design options available to researchers. In the following three chapters in this section, we will explore the specific designs in more detail.

In **Chapter 5** we explore the exploratory research designs in more depth. This includes the basic designs, and also the specific sampling, data collection and data analysis options available to researchers in exploratory and qualitative research designs.

Chapter 6 focuses more specifically on as research strategy.

In **Chapter 7,** we look at quantitative data analysis techniques.

4.6 Summary

Research is ultimately about making choices to suit the research problem and the circumstances of the researcher. In this chapter, we introduced the basic research designs as a first step in assisting researchers in making the right choices.

We reviewed the three basic approaches of inductive, deductive or mixed methods research, followed by a review of the three basic research design categories of exploratory, descriptive and causal research. We also introduced the notion of non-empirical research.

In exploratory research, we identified seven research designs that have potentially useful applications in economic and management research, namely historical research, phenomenology, ethnography, grounded theory, case studies, action research and exploratory surveys.

We identified three basic types of descriptive research, namely observation studies, developmental designs and descriptive surveys. When we considered experimental research designs we found that true experimental designs are virtually impossible in economic and management research and subsequently focused only on quasi-experimental research designs. Following our discussion of experimental designs (both true and quasi) we also examine correlational designs (namely ex post facto and correlational designs) as a means of determining causality.

We trust that this chapter offers a first step in assisting researchers to choose the right designs for the right reasons, and that the subsequent chapter will assist in making the right choices to ensure that the overall design is consistent and offers the best possible research solution in the situation.

Key terms and concepts

causal research: to establish cause-and-effect relationships between two or more variables

crystallisation: can be used as an alternative term for triagulation in quantitative research; the underlying idea being that the use of multiple methods in quantitative research may help to present the data in more clarity

deductive research: outwardly focused and aims to make generalisations about the phenomena it is studying, in the population(s) included in the study

descriptive research: the focus of research is to describe a situation, a phenomenon, a person or groups of people or an environment in some detail

experimental research: a research design characterised by the manipulation of respondents into control, and experimental groups based on the independent variable

exploratory research: relies on inductive research (such as qualitative research) to develop hypotheses, theoretical frameworks, concepts or propositions

inductive research: inwardly focused and aims to learn more about specific phenomena in its context

mixed methods research: the use of inductive and deductive methods in combination

non-empirical research: a type of research that uses secondary (rather than empirical) data

research design: a framework or guideline for the research process to be followed by the researcher, and includes the approach, methods and techniques that will be used to carry out the research

triangulation: the use of multiple sources and methods to increase the confidence in the research

Questions for review and critical thinking

1. Assuming you are a Masters student who has to complete a research dissertation in two years, identify possible limitations and influences that will dictate your research design.
2. Compile a table comparing inductive, deductive and mixed methods approaches on their comparative strengths and weaknesses.
3. Compare and contrast the four different descriptive research designs.
4. Explain under what conditions quasi-experimental research will be used.
5. Compare and contrast experimental and non-experimental research in studies to determine causal relationships.

Research activities

Use an online library or Google Scholar to find a research dissertation (such as a Masters or Doctoral dissertation) or research article in a topic that you are interested in. Critically evaluate the research design and identify its strengths and limitations.

Case study[33]

Nkomo's shoe trade

Shepherd Nkomo has been manufacturing and trading shoes from home since 2000. He manufactures and sells two shoe brands, namely MOOs (targeted at adults) and MEs (targeted at children). One of the main problems he currently experiences is the limited space available at home to stock large quantities of shoes. This has largely forced him to only manufacture and sell from home on demand. Looking at the past sales figures of the business (which Shepherd records monthly in hard-copy file format), his home business in Meadowland (with a total of 80 000 households) has flourished since 2003. All houses in Meadowland are demarcated into formal residential zones with clearly marked stand numbers and street names. Based on households' average annual income levels, Meadowland was recently referred to in the local newspaper as a 'middle-income region' (households earning an average of between R7 500 and R5 000 per month). The annual sales figures for the shoe brands sold by Shepherd from 2000 to 2007 are as follows:

2000	MOOs (1 130), MEs (1 085)
2001	MOOs (1 135), MEs (1 095)
2002	MOOs (1 140), MEs (1 105)
2003	MOOs (2 265), MEs (1 815)
2004	MOOs (3 175), MEs (2 145)
2005	MOOs (4 205), MEs (3 155)
2006	MOOs (5 230), MEs (5 160)
2007	MOOs (6 255), MEs (7 175)

Since Shepherd started his business in 2000, he has recorded the name, landline telephone number and residential address of each person who purchased shoes in hard-copy format. This practice was followed to support his monthly promotion campaign of 'buy a pair and win a pair', which is still in place. In fact, the majority of customers buying shoes directly from Shepherd were or are still local residents. These exclude the 50 pairs of children's shoes per month, which Shepherd has, since 2006, distributed to five general dealers located in a small village called Cowville. Shepherd's cousin, Jabu, acts as distribution agent between Meadowland and Cowville and delivers the shoes free of cost to the general dealers. However, for his effort, Shepherd pays him in kind by giving him free pairs of shoes on occasion. Cowville is a poor community (35 000 households) whose residents purchase MOOs and MEs from the general traders at 20% discount. Shepherd regards this approach as an important 'corporate social responsibility strategy' aimed at serving the needs of the poor and specifically children. People in Cowville reside in informal houses (shacks) with no street names or stand numbers. The contact details (name, address, landline telephone and facsimile) of the owners of the general traders are also filed in hard-copy format in Shepherd's filing cabinet.

Jabu, who is a business property developer, recently convinced Shepherd that his shoe business is sustainable enough to consider alternative business options and solutions. Jabu also shares Shepherd's excitement about plans to introduce shoes made from ostrich leather. Based on Jabu's advice, Shepherd is considering moving his home-based business to the newly developed shopping mall complex (Meadow Centre), which opened at the start of 2007. The new shopping complex is a 30-minute drive from Meadowland and is located in Ostrichville, an area famous for its ostrich farming and where 120 000 households reside. This area is classified as a 'middle- to high-income area' (average income of above R15 000 per month) with all households located in formal demarcated residential areas with street/stand names and numbers. Meadow Centre has developed as a popular mall attracting many residents residing in Ostrichville due to the variety of stores (clothing, shoe, hardware, health and grocery stores), parking facilities, entertainment, etc.

Jabu has advised Shepherd that he should carefully consider alternative business options and expansion and should not make any final decisions before conducting some research.

Source: Tustin, D.H. 2012. Practice makes perfect – simplify your marketing research skills. Unpublished. p. 5-6. Bureau of Market Research (BMR), Unisa. Reprinted by permission of Prof. D H Tustin, Bureau of Market Research (BMR), Unisa.

Questions
1. Identify a research problem statement for the research project.
2. Identify an inductive, deductive and mixed methods approach to addressing the research problem.
3. Which one of the above designs would you select and why?

References

1. Adapted from Moody, Glyn, 2012. Making the most of file-sharing: free market research and a captive audience. Techdirt, Available online at: http://www.techdirt.com/blog/?tag=market+research [Accessed 21 January 2012] and Show doing well on BitTorrent? We'll buy it. 2012. Torrentfreak, Available online at http://torrentfreak.com/show-doing-well-on-bittorrent-well-buy-it-121010/, [Accessed 21 January 2012].
2. Zikmund, W.G., Babin, B.J., Carr, J.C. and Griffin, M. 2010. *Business Research Methods*. 8th ed. Canada: South-Western Cengage Learning, p. 66.
3. Adapted from ESOMAR Guideline for conducting mobile market research. Available online at: http://www.esomar.org/uploads/public/knowledge-and-standards/codes-and-guidelines/ESOMAR_Guideline-for-conducting-Mobile-Market-Research.pdf [Accessed 28 October 2012].
4. De Vos, A.S. 2004. Combined qualitative and quantitative approach. In: de Vos, A.S., Strydom, H., Fouché, C.B. and Delport, C.S.L. (eds). 2004. *Research at grass roots*. 3rd ed. Hatfield: Van Schaik.
5. The definitions of multi-methods and mixed methods research are from Creswell's chapter in the 2nd edition of the *Handbook of Mixed Methods Research* (p. 273).
6. De Bellis, N (2009). *Bibliometrics and citation analysis: from the Science citation index to cybermetrics*. Lanham MD: Scarecrow Press. p. 417.
7. Based on the guidelines for concept studies provided by Bear, M. and Moody, L. 1990. Formulating researchable questions or hypotheses. In: Moody, L. (ed). *Advancing nursing science through research*. Newbury Park: Sage.

8   Zikmund et al p. 44.
9   Bick, G., Abratt, R. & Möller, D. 2010. Customer service expectations in retail banking in Africa. *South African Journal of Business Management*, 41(2): 13-27.
10 Zikmund et al (2010).
11 McCoy, S.P. 2012. *Brand Alignment: Developing a model for competitive advantage through a study of selected South African companies*. Unpublished DBL thesis, University of South Africa, Pretoria.
12 Ivankova, N.V., Cresswell, J.W. and Plano Clark, V.L. 2007. Chapter 15: Foundations and approaches to mixed methods research. In: Maree, K. (ed). *First steps in research*. Hatfield, Van Schaik. p. 14.
13 Ibid, pp. 263-268.
14 Jansen van Rensburg, M. 2009. *Antecedents of advertising agency retention*. Unpublished D.Com. thesis, University of South Africa, Pretoria.
15 Ivankova et al (2007), p. 267.
16 Leedy, P.D. and Ormrod, J.E. 2004. *Practical research: planning and design*. 8th ed. (International Edition). Upper Saddle River, N.J.: Pearson Education. p. 161
17 Pendergrast, M. 2000. *For God, Country, and Coca-Cola: The Definitive History of the Great American Soft Drink and the Company That Makes It*. New York, NY: Basic Books.
18 Zikmund et al, p. 55.
19 Ibid, p. 117.
20 Ibid.
21 Ibid.
22 Leedy, P.D. and Ormrod, J.E. 2004. *Practical research: planning and design*. 8th ed. (International Edition). Upper Saddle River, N.J.: Pearson Education. pp. 140-141.
23 Ibid. p. 135.
24 Ibid.
25 Zikmund et al. p. 55.
26 Leedy and Ormrod. 2004. p. 179.
27 The discussion is based on a section in Leedy and Ormorod (2005), pp. 182-183. However, these authors focus specifically on age group comparisons, an idea that was extended to include other categories of development.
28 Leedy and Ormrod, 2005, p. 183.
29 Ibid, p. 55.
30 Zikmund et al, p 58-59.
31 Leedy and Ormrod. 2005. p. 227.
32 Salkind, N.J. 2012. *Exploring research*. 8th edition. Upper Saddle River, N.J.: Pearson Education.
33 Tustin, D.H. 2012. *Practice makes perfect – simplify your marketing research skills*. Unpublished. pp. 5-6.

QUALITATIVE RESEARCH DESIGNS

Peet Venter

5

AFTER STUDYING THIS CHAPTER, YOU SHOULD BE ABLE TO:

- Understand what qualitative research entails and when it is used
- Point out the advantages and disadvantages of qualitative research
- Explain the main qualitative research designs suited to economic and management research
- Make qualitative research design choices in line with the research problem statement
- Make choices with regard to the methods of qualitative research in line with overall qualitative research design choices.

> When famous primate researcher, Jane Goodall, decided to study chimpanzees, she knew that engaging with these animals in their natural habitat was the most likely method of truly understanding their behaviour. By comparison, studying chimpanzees in laboratories or in controlled man-made environments would not yield nearly the same level of understanding. As a result of this decision, Ms Goodall lived among wild Tanzanian chimpanzees for several years, and produced her doctoral thesis, numerous articles and five major books as a result of her field research. Although she was criticised as being manipulative for attributing human behaviours and names to chimpanzees, her fieldwork led to new insights into chimpanzee behaviour. She is credited, for example, with the first recorded observations of chimpanzees eating meat, and making and using tools.[1]
>
> *Sources: adapted from Jane Goodall's biography. Available online at http://www.biography.com/people/jane-goodall-9542363?page=2 [Accessed 7 March 2013]; http://www.janegoodall.org/wp-content/uploads/the-Jane-Goodall-Institute_JaneGoodall_LongBio.pdf [Accessed 6 October 2016]*

5.1 Introduction

Qualitative research designs focus on generating and analysing non-numeric data such as written documents, behaviour and images or verbal data, such as interviews. Qualitative research designs can be used when the purpose of the research is to develop a deeper understanding of a phenomenon or to develop a theory (see for example our opening vignette), or in support of quantitative research as part of a mixed methods approach (see Chapter 4 for an overview of mixed methods designs). In keeping with the adoption of a pragmatic stance in this book, we do not argue that qualitative research is inherently superior or inferior to quantitative research. We rather argue that in some instances, given the research problem and purpose, qualitative research will be more useful than quantitative research while in other cases the opposite may be true. There are also many instances, as the rapid growth of mixed methods designs attest, where the two approaches can easily and successfully co-exist in the same research project.

Qualitative research can generate rich descriptions of complex phenomena that can help researchers to develop deeper and more nuanced insights than would normally be possible with quantitative research, and is accordingly most useful in the following instances:[2]

- When the research objectives or hypotheses are not clear, even after an extensive literature review, qualitative research can help to develop hypotheses or theoretical frameworks, or to clarify research objectives.
- When the purpose of the research is to examine a phenomenon in great depth and detail, qualitative research will provide a means of gathering rich and complex data.
- When the purpose of the research is to examine a phenomenon or object in its natural setting, qualitative research will generally be more useful than survey research.
- Where quantitative research has yielded less than satisfactory results, qualitative research may provide a different perspective offering new insights.
- As part of a mixed methods design, qualitative research may offer a means of methodological triangulation, offering deeper insights and higher validity than quantitative research may offer on its own.

Qualitative research differs from quantitative research in a number of important ways (see Table 5.1 for a comparison of qualitative and quantitative research). For example, qualitative research is generally more suited to exploratory research and theory-building, while quantitative research is typically used for descriptive, confirmatory and causal research. It generates mostly unstructured visual or textual data, while quantitative research relies on surveys to generate highly structured numerical data. Qualitative research relies heavily on the researcher to interpret responses and findings, while quantitative research is highly dependent upon respondents to interpret the survey questions and provide answers. Because of the central role of the researcher in the research process and the subjective nature of interpretation, it may be hard to replicate qualitative studies with different researchers.[3] At the same time, qualitative research relies upon interpretation of data by the researcher, and can accordingly be seen as inherently subjective, as opposed to quantitative research which relies on statistical analysis and is generally seen as more objective. Findings generated by qualitative research cannot usually be generalised to populations, as it does not rely on representative sampling methods. However, qualitative research does offer the opportunity to generate new theoretical propositions, and for that reason, qualitative research should ideally not be purely descriptive, but should also be explanatory.

Table 5.1 Qualitative and quantitative research compared

	Quantitative research	Qualitative research
Scientific roots	Hard science	Soft science
Focus	Concise and narrow	Complex and broad
Researcher perspective	Objective	Subjective

Research approach	Logical, deductive	Dialectic, inductive
Type of research	Descriptive, confirmatory, causal	Exploratory
Role in theory development	Tests theory	Develops theory
Measurement approach	Instruments	Communication, observation
Elements of analysis	Numbers	Words, behaviours, artifacts
Methods of analysis	Statistical analysis	Individual interpretation
Purpose	Generalisation to a population	Uniqueness, rich descriptions

In our exploration of qualitative research in this chapter, we first examine the different paradigmatic perspectives that support qualitative research, followed by an overview of the main types of qualitative research. We then focus on the qualitative research methods and techniques for sampling, data collection, data analysis and the presentation of data.

5.2 Perspectives on qualitative research

Considering the range of research paradigms, it follows that different perspectives also exist within the qualitative research domain. There are four broad qualitative research perspectives, namely interpretivism, critical theory, post-modernism and post-positivism. The four perspectives are not always clearly separable, and overlap in many instances.[4] Interpretivism is the most commonly used perspective in economics and business research, while the critical theory perspective is a niche area of economics and business research. Two additional views were added here. Critical realism presents a perspective that is rooted in post-positivism and post-modernism and is increasingly being adopted in many disciplines, including management. The practice turn in management has led to an increasing focus on what managers actually do (rather than what they are supposed to do). While it is not a paradigm in its own right, it is increasingly being used in business and management studies to address complex research problems.

5.2.1 Interpretivism

Interpretivism is founded in the perspective that phenomena can only be understood by way of the meanings that people assign to them. In other words, if we want to study a phenomenon using an interpretivist perspective, we need to make use of social constructions such as language or symbols.

From an interpretivist perspective we accept that reality cannot be determined by objective observation. It is complex and socially constructed, and because it is socially constructed, there are multiple realities.[5] We cannot, in other words, claim that there is only one objective 'truth'; there are many different socially constructed versions of the 'truth'.

If we want to develop a better understanding of the phenomena, we need to develop an understanding of the reality from the perspective of the people involved. In order to do this, we would need to examine the means by which people socially construct their reality, such as language, symbols, shared meanings and behaviours. In analysing these social constructions, there is a realisation and acknowledgement that researchers themselves are subjective and subject to their own social reality.

The ultimate aim of an interpretivist approach is to provide a rich description of a phenomenon and how people interpret and perceive their involvement in it.

> **Example box**
>
> If we want to examine how employees perceive a newly introduced performance management system using an interpretivist perspective, we could interview employees and managers about their perceptions of and experiences with the system. We could also examine the products of the performance management system (such as documents) to develop a deeper understanding of how employees perceive it – in other words, how they socially construct the reality of a performance management system.

5.2.2 Critical theory

The goal of the **critical theory** perspective is to examine the current discourses in a particular context or society at large in order to identify the power relationships in a system and its structures. In this way, the oppressive nature of the system can be exposed.[6] The power exerted by those in power in a particular system often has its roots in ideology, for example, around race, class and gender; and the role of the critical theory researcher is to expose the ideological underbelly of the system. In the process, the role of the critical researcher is to produce critique of systems in order to address 'false consciousnesses' and 'bourgeois ideology'. At the same time, it falls within the purview of critical theorists to expose the often unconscious needs and struggles of people in the system.[7] The ultimate aim is to provide a basis for removing the roots of oppression in a system.

> **Example box**
>
> If we approach our analysis of the newly introduced performance management system (as outlined in the previous example box) from a critical theory perspective, the discourses (i.e. the talk) around the performance management system can be analysed to identify any possible ideological sources of oppression in the system. For example, universities are often accused that increasing 'managerialism' creates divisions between managers and academics, and is a source of oppression.

5.2.3 Critical realism

Critical realism accepts that there are two dimensions to the world. There is the 'real world' (the intransitive reality), and the concepts and theories that are formulated to explain it (the transitive reality).[8] These attempts at explanation are, however, just approximations of the intransitive reality, as human limitations prevent us from gaining certain or objective knowledge of the world and the phenomena in it. As a result, attempts to explain phenomena are fallible, and will, over time, be replaced by superior theories or explanations. There could also be more than one theory or explanation addressing the same phenomenon. In order to explain observed phenomena or events, critical realists will also frequently use existing theories or explanations as interpretive frameworks to be applied to the phenomena under investigation to potentially explain events.

In the context of critical realism, knowledge production (such as research) is a social practice that is influenced by the conditions, social relations and language in which it is produced. Awareness of these influences is important in evaluating knowledge. It is also central to the critical realist paradigm to be critical of the objects being studied in order to better understand them.[9]

> **Example box**[10]
>
> If we approach our analysis of the newly introduced performance management system (as outlined in the previous example boxes) from a critical realist perspective, we can use extant frameworks (such as performance management theories) as a basis to conduct an in-depth analysis of what is happening and why it is happening. Since the roots of critical realism are in causality and explanation, the research question must be in the form of "What caused the events (e.g. the design of the performance management system) to occur".

5.2.4 The practice turn in management research

Management research is increasingly engaging with the practice turn in the broader social sciences. Whereas traditional business and management research often focused on producing generalisations from normative guidelines (such as widely accepted management frameworks and models), management-as-practice focuses on what people actually do (their practices).[11] These practices do not occur in isolation; they are linked to the social and organisational realities that the actors are rooted in; hence the view here is that management is a situated human activity. The practice turn in social sciences and management has led to the emergence of significant streams of research in subfields of management, such as strategy-as-practice[12] and marketing-as-practice.[13]

> **Example box**
>
> A practice perspective on the newly introduced performance management system (as outlined in the previous example boxes) can assist us in understanding what the participants in the system actually do, how they do it, and why they do it. For example, one research focus area can be on how performance planning and performance assessment meetings are actually conducted by line managers.

5.3 Qualitative research designs

In this section, we review five qualitative research designs that have potential application in economic and management sciences, namely **phenomenology**, **ethnography**, grounded theory, case studies, and action research. We do not have the space to offer a comprehensive overview of each of these methodologies here, and the purpose of this section is to offer some indications of what methodologies could be used under what circumstances. It should be noted that there may be some overlap between different designs, such as between ethnography and case studies, and different designs may be used in combination, but for purposes of clarity, the five designs are treated here separately.

5.3.1 Phenomenology

Phenomenology is an interpretivist research design that is interested in understanding a phenomenon from the perspective of the people involved in it. It seeks to explore the relationship of people with their environment, objects, situations and other people.[14] This approach acknowledges that reality is socially constructed, and the approach of phenomenology is accordingly used to obtain a deeper understanding of a phenomenon by obtaining detailed descriptions of their 'lived experience'.

The purpose of phenomenological research is to develop an understanding of the relationship of people with a phenomenon or phenomena, typically in the form of their perceptions and experiences with it.

Phenomenology relies heavily on the honest, personal accounts of people involved with or exposed to the phenomenon being investigated. In-depth, unstructured interviews where people tell more about themselves and their experiences are accordingly used often in phenomenological studies to gather the detailed descriptions required to develop an understanding of the social reality being investigated. The unit of analysis is, therefore, the individual, and one of the key challenges in phenomenology is to ensure that the individuals being studied feel comfortable enough to be open and honest about their experiences. This can be achieved by, for example, gaining the trust of the individuals by becoming a participant observer, or by guaranteeing anonymity. The method of analysis typically used in phenomenology is hermeneutics.[15]

Hermeneutics rely on the analysis of the text produced as a result of the data collection process, such as interviews in their transcribed form. The basis of hermeneutics is to link the observations (in the form of a section of text, such as a paragraph) to a key theme in the analysis. Content analysis (which includes hermeneutics) is a key method for data analysis in exploratory research, and is discussed in more detail in section 5.4.6.

> **Example box**[16]
>
> Servant leadership is a term that is often used nowadays in the context of organisational leadership. However, it is often not clear what exactly servant leadership entails in an organisational context, and how servant leaders motivate their followers. In an attempt to understand what servant leadership means to leaders and their organisation, two researchers gathered lived experiences of 15 organisational leaders who practice the servant leadership philosophy, and explored how business leaders link their servant leadership practices to their organisation's effectiveness. The researchers were also interested in what organisational barriers exist that prevent effective servant leadership.
>
> The qualitative responses obtained during the interviews with the leaders indicated that the perceived organisational barriers that prevent the servant leadership practices are the organisation's culture, the fear of change, and the lack of knowledge regarding the servant leadership philosophy. This study also gained insight into the impact that these organisational barriers have on one's ability to practice servant leadership, how 'servant leaders' act in organisations and how it affects their organisation's performance.
>
> Source: Savage-Austin, Amy R.; Honeycutt, Andrew. Servant Leadership: A Phenomenological Study Of Practices, Experiences, Organizational Effectiveness, And Barriers. Journal of Business & Economics Research (JBER), [S.l.], v. 9, n. 1, Jan. 2011. ISSN 2157-8893. Available at: http://www.cluteinstitute.com/ojs/index.php/JBER/article/view/939>. Date accessed: 16 aug. 2016. doi:http://dx.doi.org/10.19030/jber.v9i1.939

5.3.2 Ethnography

As the name suggests, ethnography stems from anthropological research and the study of different ethnic groups. It requires the researcher to become immersed in a situation and to become part of it, in the hope that the subjects of study will, over time, act more naturally around the researcher and reveal more about themselves and their practices than they would in a formal research setting. This approach mirrors research in anthropology that required anthropologists to live with tribes or within subcultures for long periods as observers, suggesting that **participant observation** is one of the key data collection techniques of ethnography. Ethnography is a suitable approach to studying, for example, organisational culture, subcultures within an organisation, and consumer behaviour. It should be noted that pure observation may not always be practical or possible in business and management research, and it will typically be combined with textual data such as interviews and documents, as well as artefacts such as brochures and posters.

Because ethnography requires observation as a key method, video recordings may be very useful as a method of data collection, although it may not always be practical or even ethical to use.

> **Example box[17]**
>
> Anthropology is not a field of study normally associated with business, yet ethnography is one of the big trends in business research. ICT companies especially seem to be embracing it, and as a result anthropologists have been appointed in many companies to use their skills in ethnographic research. Ken Anderson is an ethnographer at Intel. He contends that ethnography can help companies to define market needs, which in turn will drive innovation. At Microsoft, ethnographers are used when developing software, such as operating systems. Ethnography in ICT is used to understand how users use and interact with technology in their natural environment (such as the home or office), in order to understand emerging ICT trends.
>
> *Source: Partly based on: Fitzgerald, M. 2005. Corporate Ethnography. MIT Technology Review. Available at: https://www.technologyreview.com/s/404920/corporate-ethnography/ [Accessed 19 August 2016].*

5.3.3 Grounded theory

Grounded theory is a purely inductive research design that seeks to specifically develop theory from the research data. It is suitable especially to situations where no or little previous research exists (or where previous research is inadequate). It begins with immediate data collection, and is very suited to studying processes. Data collection could be done using a variety of data collection methods, as long as it focuses on the process or phenomenon being studied and contains the perspectives of the people being studied.[18] Grounded theory is not used very often in economic and management research, but can certainly play a role in theory development in fields where the extant theory is inadequate. Because grounded theory does not start with any theoretical propositions, the analysis of the data will typically be from the bottom up, in other words by doing initial coding of data and then grouping data until a theory is derived from the data. This process of theorising (creating theory through the data analysis process) is integral to grounded theory. In the process of theorising, the researcher should constantly ask two key questions:[19]
- What is happening here?
- How is it different?

Because grounded theory does not use a mechanistic approach to theory building and is highly iterative and creative, it is important to keep records of the process. Software packages like Atlas.ti make it relatively easy to keep accurate records of the definitions of codes, grouping of codes and theoretical relationships between constructs.

Because the term grounded theory is often misused or incorrectly understood, it is worthwhile to revisit what grounded theory is not:[20]

- Using a grounded theory design is not an excuse to ignore, avoid or postpone reading the existing literature.
- Grounded theory is not about presenting raw data, but should rather present data at a conceptual level that supports new theoretical insights.
- It is not about theory testing, word counts or confirmation of theories. In other words, setting and testing hypotheses and research propositions do not have a place in grounded theory.
- It is not about the mechanistic application of data analysis routines, but it is instead a highly creative interpretive process.
- It is not a perfect approach. On the contrary, it is messy and requires a very deep knowledge and 'feel' for the data collected.
- It is not an easy alternative.

> **Example box**
>
> While we intuitively know that project management has some relationship to strategy implementation, we do not know how project management is used in organisations for strategy implementation. Literature on this topic is rather scant, and a grounded theory approach would be useful in helping us to develop a theoretical framework on this topic. Using grounded theory means that we would first collect data (e.g. through in-depth interviews with project managers and strategic planners or managers), and through our analysis of the data we could then develop a theoretical framework.

5.3.4 Case research

The **case research** method (also referred to as case studies or **case study research**) is one of the most popular exploratory methodologies used in economic and management research. In a case research design, a unit of analysis (such as an individual, organisation, process or event) is studied in-depth for a defined period of time. This type of study could range from a single case to a selection of cases (multiple case studies).[21] The purpose of case research is to learn more about a poorly understood aspect in its natural context. Case research is most appropriate when the phenomenon being studied cannot easily be observed outside of its natural setting, and where it is so complex that it cannot be quantified.[22] This statement already suggests that context is critically important in case research and that context cannot be separated from the phenomenon being studied. In case research projects, the organisation as a whole can be studied (this is referred to as a holistic case study); or the focus can be on subunit(s) of an organisation (this is known as an embedded case study).[23]

Case studies in academic research should almost never be purely descriptive, but should also attempt to address the 'why' question, in other words it should strive to add value by providing some explanation for the 'what' and 'how'. Case research typically also makes use of a variety of methods (such as interviews, focus groups, document analysis, and even surveys) in an effort to develop a deep understanding of the context, as well as the processes and practices. The use of mixed and multiple methods are important to achieve triangulation[24], which is a valuable tool to ensure validity and trustworthiness of the collected data. It is also important to ensure that data collection is done in a way that allows for sufficient depth, breadth and diversity of participants and data sources to ensure trustworthiness of the data.

One of the biggest decisions in case research is whether to use a single case or multiple cases. In the next sections we examine these two approaches in more detail.

5.3.4.1 Single case study

In business and management research, the use of a single case study is very prevalent, unfortunately often for the wrong reasons. Single case studies should never be selected simply because it is convenient (as it so often happens). Single case studies could be selected because they represent critical, extreme or unique case examples. Alternatively, the case may present you with a typical case and the opportunity to study a poorly understood phenomenon in its natural setting.[25] This would suggest that the selection of the case is key, and should again not simply be done for the sake of convenience (e.g. good access to the case organisation because the researcher works there).

Siggelkow suggests that case research serves three possible purposes:[26]

1. **Motivation:** Cases are often a useful way to motivate a research question, by offering evidence in support of the importance of the research question, or counter to generally accepted theoretical principles.
2. **Inspiration:** Cases may serve as inspiration for new ideas and new insights into theory and application.
3. **Illustration:** Pure conceptual arguments may be rather abstract, and cases may provide concrete examples of what the constructs actually look like in real life.

Geoff Easton argues that single case research studies are too often justified only in terms of the interesting results they yield, rather than from a philosophical (ontological and epistemological) perspective. He offers such philosophical support for the use of single cases, suggesting that a critical realist approach involves developing a research question that identifies a complex research phenomenon of interest, in terms of discernible events, and asks what causes these events to happen.[27]

What is important is that researchers opting for a single case study should outline clear and convincing reasons for doing so, and should ensure that it addresses the research questions adequately.

> **Example box**[28]
>
> In their study of market segmentation in a South African ICT company, three researchers found that market segmentation in the case was rather complex and did not always conform to theoretical guidelines for market segmentation. Four sets of market segmentation actions were identified, namely establishing legitimacy, theory embodiment, contextualising and maintaining the process. The single case was used as market segmentation implementation as a situated activity, and it presented an opportunity to study a complex phenomenon (market segmentation implementation) in its natural setting (an organisation). The phenomenon was investigated using participant observation, in-depth interviews, and analysis of documents and artefacts.
>
> Source: http://www.informaworld.com Venter, P., Wright, A. and Dibb, S. 2015. Performing market segmentation: a performative perspective. *Journal of Marketing Management*, 31 (1-2): 62-83. Copyright © Westburn Publishers Limited, reprinted by permission of Taylor & Francis Ltd, www.tandfonline.com on behalf of Westburn Publishers Limited.

5.3.4.2 Multiple case studies

The need for multiple case studies most often relies on the need to establish whether findings from one case holds true across other cases, and as a result offers the opportunity to generalise the findings. Multiple cases are, therefore, used as a means of developing theory. There are very few guidelines with regard to how many cases would be sufficient. One anecdotal view is that four to eight cases could be sufficient, while Eisenhardt also argues that the selected cases should suit the requirements and purpose of the study.[29] Eisenhardt's proposed process[30] for using multiple cases to generate theory is as follows:

1. Get started by identifying the research question and identifying some possible theoretical constructs that will offer more focus and better grounding. At this stage, there should ideally be little focus on theory and hypotheses, in order to retain theoretical flexibility.
2. Select cases from a specified population (e.g. an industry). Cases should not be selected randomly, but rather on the basis of their ability to contribute to a better understanding of the constructs being investigated.
3. Instruments and data collection protocols should be crafted in a way that allows for mixed methods, and where possible, multiple investigators to offer triangulation, diversity of opinion and as a result, better theoretical grounding of findings.
4. Data collection should then take place, while starting data analysis at the same time. The researchers should also be aware of any unplanned opportunities for data collection (such as interviews or meetings) that may assist in developing a better understanding of the unique properties of the case.
5. Data analysis takes place at two levels. Within-case analysis allows the researcher to become familiar with the case and the data, while cross-case analysis (using divergent methods) allows the researcher to look at the data through new lenses and to discover patterns in the data.
6. Shaping hypotheses by understanding the data supporting each construct, and searching for evidence to explain the 'why' behind each relationship.
7. The researcher then reviews the literature to examine both conflicting literature and literature with similar findings in an effort to improve theoretical grounding and to sharpen the constructs. This will offer more possibilities for generalisation of the findings.

8. The project reaches closure with saturation, the point when the marginal benefit of additional analysis becomes small.

While Eisenhardts' process has been criticised for being too positivistic in its approach[31], it does offer one example of how a case research process using multiple cases can be implemented.

> **Example box**[32]
>
> In a study on corporate branding processes and practices, a doctoral researcher decided to follow a multiple case study approach. In the four selected cases, the student investigated the extent to which brand is being adopted as a mechanism to align with corporate strategy, internal culture and organisational performance using semi-structured interviews and document analysis. The research identified some key similarities and differences explaining why certain organisations appeared to do better in their corporate branding efforts than others.
>
> Source: McCoy, Sean Patrick. 2012. Brand alignment: developing a model for competitive advantage through a study of selected South African companies Unpublished DBL thesis, University of South Africa, Pretoria.

5.3.5 Action research

Action research is a strategy of enquiry that attempts to find a solution to a local problem in a local setting,[33] which means that the focus could be on a problem in a single organisation or community. It is a form of applied research that is cyclical and participatory in nature. The results of the various steps are implemented and become part of the next step in the process. Participants in the research become co-researchers as they contribute to the development of plans and solutions. Action research is an interactive form of knowledge development. Given the pragmatic and interactive nature of action research, it is a research design that can be used to great effect in organisational settings to find solutions to business problems or to develop suitable interventions. Action research differs from conventional research in its integration (rather than separation) of research and action, and in that it involves those being studied in the research project rather than treating them as research subjects. Like case research, it can utilise a variety of methods, even quantitative surveys.

A typical action research process is depicted in Figure 5.1. Although there are many different conceptualisations of action research, the process is almost always described as cyclical or a 'spiral', containing a planning phase, an action phase, an observation phase, and a reflection phase, which then leads to replanning and the cycle starting over. In Figure 5.1, the following steps are evident:

1. The first step in the process is to identify the problem, and to develop a deeper understanding of the problem. In the example below (see example box), the application of an empowerment questionnaire helped to develop a better understanding of the low levels of empowerment, and an initial interview helped to identify the needs and problems.
2. The planning process then addresses the problem by developing a first version of a solution. In the example, the facilitator (who also was a researcher in the form of a participant observer) and other researchers developed a strategic plan for the intervention.

3. In the third phase (the action phase), the solution is implemented. In Figure 5.1 this is described as 'trial ways to solve the problem', which suggest that researchers may experiment with different solutions to the problem. In the example, this involved the execution of the strategic plan for the intervention with a group of participants.
4. Following action, there should be an observation phase where the researcher looks back at what happened. This is again a phase where data collection should be done. In the example, this involved participant observation, informal interviews and the application of a questionnaire.
5. The reflection phase requires the researcher and participants to reflect on what happened, and why.
6. In the next phase, the initial planning can now be updated with the data gathered during observation, and with the insights gained during reflection. This may lead to different perspectives on the problem, and different ways of trying to solve the problem.
7. It is important for learning in general to share the findings with others, such as colleagues and participants. From an academic perspective, the publication of results in articles, books and conference papers could be a useful way of sharing the results and insights with the broader scientific community.

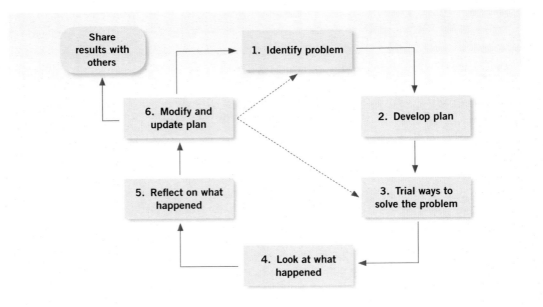

Figure 5.1 The action research cycle[34]

> **Example box**[35]
>
> Researchers used a participatory action research (PAR) process to develop an entrepreneurial development programme in Darling in the Western Cape province of South Africa. Participants voluntarily attended the Snowflake Bake for Profit course. The research process followed the typical cyclical PAR process of plan, act, observe and reflect, and participants and researchers/facilitators jointly identified problems, sought solutions, and developed action plans for next phases of the intervention.
>
> Data was collected using quantitative survey questionnaires, participant observation of the PAR process and informal interviews.
>
> Source: From Journal of Family Ecology and Consumer Sciences Source: Botha, MJ, Van der Merwe, ME, Bester, AB & Albertyn, R. 2007. Entrepreneurial skill development: Participatory action research in a rural community. Journal of Family Ecology and Consumer Sciences, 35: 9-15. Reprinted by permission of the authors

Action research is not a suitable research strategy in every situation, and should be considered with some caution. While it holds considerable benefits for the organisation or community where it is implemented, due to its practical and interactive nature, it does have some negative aspects to consider, such as the fact that it is a very time-consuming and intense process.

In this section we examined five qualitative research strategies. In the next section we examine the methods and techniques of qualitative research in more depth.

5.4 Qualitative research methods

In this section, we discuss the research methods and techniques of qualitative research.

5.4.1 The role of the researcher in qualitative research

In qualitative research, the researcher is typically very close to the study, often as participant observer and even to the extent of working for the organisation where the research is situated. This subjectivity and direct influence on the study is an aspect that cannot be avoided, as the researcher is the primary research instrument. For this reason, the researcher should do everything possible to ensure the trustworthiness of the research. Trustworthiness is described by Lincoln and Guba as consisting of credibility, applicability, dependability and confirmability,[36] while Yin values transparency, being methodical and adherence to evidence as key elements of credibility and trustworthiness.[37] The trustworthiness of qualitative research can be improved by:
- Ensuring, even before the data collection commences, that the research methods to be used will generate the type of data required and that the data collection instruments will yield the data needed to address the research question.
- Ensuring that all data collection efforts are properly recorded and available. In the event of interviews and verbal data, this will include recording and transcribing interviews, rather than just taking notes, that are 'filtered' by the interviewer and may lead to gross inaccuracies in the recall and interpretation of data.

- Keeping notes and records of the research process, for example in the form of 'field notes' to ensure that the process and all key research decisions are recorded and are as confirmable as possible.
- Using multiple sources of data (triangulation); this approach is generally assumed to improve the trustworthiness of data.
- Using more than one researcher to collect and analyse the data may ensure confirmability, and lead to stronger findings and conclusions. At critical stages, input from peers or stakeholders can help to validate the process or data collected.
- The research process, while systematic, should leave room for discovery and adapting to unforeseen events, even to extent of modifying data already collected if conflicting data is uncovered.
- While qualitative data collection does not require sampling in the same sense as quantitative research, it is increasingly important that qualitative research addresses the breadth, depth and diversity of large and complex organisations.[38] This requires researchers to think carefully about the data collection tools, processes and participants.

In the same way that quantitative researchers would describe how they attempted to improve the validity and reliability of their data, qualitative researchers should describe the actions they took to improve the trustworthiness of their data. In the example box below we can see how one researcher described her efforts in this regard.

Example box

Transparency – the research process was documented in the proposal and depicted in a flow chart. Input from the supervisor and peers were gathered at each stage. Notes were made of telephonic conversations with the participants, email communication was recorded and stored and all interviews were digitally recorded. The field notes are also stored and available for scrutiny.

Being methodical – when the participants were identified, a contingency list was generated. This list comprised of additional participants that meet the inclusion criteria. Also, a reflexive diary was created and contains field notes of all communication with the participants and the researcher's own account of the actual interviews, including observation notes.

Adherence to evidence – all interviews were digitally recorded and transcribed verbatim. The explanations given by the participants were recorded as it was given and supplemented with the field notes.

5.4.2 Sampling

In this section, we examine some of the key techniques for selecting case and participants in the research (the sampling strategy) and on the number of participants to be selected (the sample size).

5.4.2.1 Sampling strategies

Qualitative researchers will tend to use non-probability sampling that suits their chosen research strategy. In many cases, researchers may make use of a combination of sampling strategies.

Purposive sampling occurs when the researcher chooses cases or participants according to pre-specified criteria based on the characteristics of the population. This is sometimes also referred to as criterion sampling (sampling according to specified criteria, such as gender, managerial level, age and so on).[39]

Theoretical sampling is often used in grounded theory approaches to select cases or participants that will contribute most to the development of the theory or to fill theoretical voids or gaps.

Deviant case sampling[40] occurs when the researcher purposely selects cases that are different or the opposite of other cases, in the hope of gaining new insights into the phenomenon. Eisenhardt, for example, suggests that in some cases 'polarisation' in the selection of cases (i.e. selecting cases that are polar opposites in respect of the phenomenon being investigated) can contribute to better theoretical insights.[41]

Snowball sampling (a.k.a. chain referral sampling)[42] is often used in cases where participants cannot readily be identified or may be 'hidden'. Participants may be asked to refer the researcher to other members of the population. For example, in a study of online gamers there may not be a ready list of potential participants. So, if an online gamer is identified and interviewed, he or she may refer the researcher to people that they know that also participate in online gaming.

5.4.2.2 Sample size in qualitative data

This seemingly simple question can have a deceptively complex answer in the context of qualitative research, and most guidelines provided are based on anecdote or experience, rather than on hard and fast guidelines. The purpose of the study should guide the number of cases or participants selected, and even then the researcher should be flexible and willing to gather additional data in order to gather sufficient data to address the research question. In essence, the study should continue until saturation is reached. This process is depicted in Figure 5.2. As a practical measure, researchers may decide to do a certain number of interviews (say 10), and will then re-evaluate their position once the interviews have been completed.

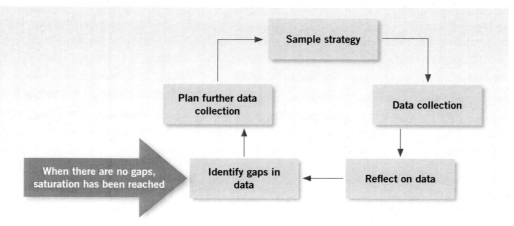

Figure 5.2. Data collection in qualitative research[43]

> **Example box**[44]
>
> In a study on how Chartered Accountants in the mining industry use strategic analysis tools, a researcher initially interviewed two participants through purposive sampling. Snowball sampling was then used to identify seven more interviewees, at which point theoretical saturation was reached.
>
> *Source: Grebe, Lindie. 2014. The use of strategy tools by chartered accountants in the South African mining industry. University of South Africa: Unpublished Master's dissertation. M. Phil. (Accounting Sciences) University of South Africa. 2014. Reprinted by permission of the author.*

5.4.3 Data production

Qualitative researchers can draw on a wide range of data sources. Many qualitative research projects will make use of more than one of the sources discussed below. Most of the data sources we describe below yield verbal data that results in text. In the research planning phases, researchers should already plan on how to record the data. Data recording should be done in a way that will be as unobtrusive as possible and will have the least possible influence on the research process, yet will assist in increasing the trustworthiness of the data. We will return to this point several times in the discussions that follow.

5.4.3.1 Interviews

The use of interviews is very prevalent in business and management research. Interviews can be conducted with one participant at a time, or in groups (**focus groups**).

One-on-one interviews

Interviews attempt to get participants to talk about their experiences, emotions, processes and practices in relation to a phenomenon being investigated. Interviews can be open-ended, structured or semi-structured.[45]

Open-ended interviews are conversations with participants on a specific topic. As the name suggests there is little structure, and the interviewer will guide the participant on specific issues of interest arising from the interview.

Semi-structured interviews start off with a set of broad questions, but as the interview progresses the interviewer may probe specific issues of interest. The advantage of a semi-structured interview is that the interviewer can ensure that certain topics are covered, while still leaving sufficient freedom to explore other ideas.

Structured interviews may contain a lot of detail and follow a structured set of questions similar to a questionnaire. While it may be useful to make data capturing easier, it also limits probing and may accordingly result in important data potentially not being uncovered.

Interviewing is a technique that will improve with use and experience. Some guidelines for successful interviews are:
- Every interview should start with an introduction to set the participants at ease. The more comfortable the participants are, the more likely they are to communicate freely. The choice of venue for the interview can also play a role here.
- In line with ethical guidelines, participants should be informed of their rights and give their explicit informed consent for the interview.

- The interviewer should talk as little as possible, and should rather play the role of an active listener to encourage the participant to talk as much as possible.
- Ask questions that require 'rich' responses. Do not ask questions that can be merely answered with a "yes" or "no". Questions can cover a wide range of aspects, including:[46]
  - Experience and behaviour
  - Opinions and values
  - Emotions
  - Knowledge.
- Use probing questions to get more insight or data on specific aspects. Probing can take the form of asking respondents to give more detail, to clarify by giving examples, or to confirm that you have correctly understood what they are saying.
- Be aware of nonverbal communication (body language) – for example, maintain eye contact and use body language (such as nodding and smiling) as a means of showing that you are listening.
- The interview should be audio- or video recorded, so as to provide an accurate record of verbal and nonverbal communication. The interviewer can additionally take notes, which will serve as input into field notes to be compiled after the interview.
- Interviews should not be too long, so as not to lose the concentration and co-operation of participants – typically a maximum of one hour should be allocated per interview.
- Field notes should be written as soon as possible after the interview and should contain the overall impressions.

Where interviewing takes place in a group it is known as focus group interviews and we discuss this technique in the next section.

5.4.3.2 Focus groups

Focus groups are in essence group discussions facilitated by a moderator (as interviewer). Focus groups are typically groups of between 5 and 12 participants[47] brought together to discuss a specific topic of interest to the researcher. Focus groups would typically be relatively homogeneous in terms of the phenomenon or topic being investigated, and can be open-ended or semi structured. In most cases, more than one focus group should be conducted to accommodate different groups. While focus groups are relatively easy to arrange, it does require certain specialist skills with regard to moderation, and it could be said that the success of focus group discussions depend to a great deal on the skills of the moderator. The role of the moderator is to ensure that participants are at ease; that all participants get to speak and share their views, to keep the discussion focused on the topic, and to avoid group think (which may involve handling dominant participants in a diplomatic way).

The moderator will typically use a discussion guideline that will serve to guide the broader discussion, although the style of the focus group discussion should be informal and conversational. Probing should be used to clarify, confirm or illustrate points made by the participants. Moderators should also be careful not to impose (consciously or unconsciously) their views on the focus group.

Focus groups have several advantages:[48]
- They are relatively quick and easy to arrange.
- The interaction between group members can spur on ideas and creativity and may accordingly produce ideas or insights that may not be otherwise produced. This benefit is referred to as 'piggybacking'.[49]

- It provides the perspectives of several participants at the same time.
- It is subject to scrutiny, since it is recorded, and can (in some instances) be observed from behind a one-way mirror.
- It is flexible, since the moderator has the freedom to probe and elicit more information as required.

However, there are also some disadvantages:
- Each individual in the group has a relatively small potential contribution.
- Certain individuals may dominate the thinking of the group, and lead to group think.
- Focus groups that address sensitive issues must be handled with caution, as participants may be reluctant to respond to sensitive or controversial issues about themselves.
- Depending on the study, it may not be easy to find suitable venues (e.g. venues with one-way mirrors, venues where recording equipment can be set up and so on).
- It may be relatively costly, since there may be payments required if professional moderators are used, payments for venues, and provision of refreshments for participants.
- Given that participants may have to travel and spend their time on participating in a focus group, there may be some expectation of reward, or at least reimbursement that will have to be managed.
- Focus groups are difficult to manage alone, since it requires setting up a room, setting up the recording, moderating, observing and making notes. For that reason it may be quite personnel-intensive.

A typical focus group interview will progress over five stages:[50]
1. The focus group will typically kick off with a welcome and introduction. The moderator and participants introduce themselves.
2. The next step is an icebreaker that will require some broad response from the participants. Techniques such as writing down their views on a broad question may be used during this phase. The icebreaker phase is more important for setting participants at ease than for gathering data.
3. The interview may now become much more specific with questions dealing with the detail being asked. Moderation plays an important role here, as moderators will have to ask probing questions where necessary, or will have to assess whether a topic has been covered in enough depth before moving on. Good moderators will allow the conversation to play out to the extent where certain questions do not need to be asked, as they have been covered sufficiently in the general conversation.
4. If there is a specific objective for the focus group discussion, this question should be asked last. For example, the purpose of the focus group discussion may be to understand what specific actions the organisation can do to improve their customer service. The question: "What specifically can organisation X do in your view to improve their customer service?" should then be asked at the end of the interview.
5. The last phase of the interview is the debriefing, where participants are typically informed of the purpose of the focus group discussion, and given an opportunity for last questions or comments.

It is important for the researcher to carefully plan the focus group interview in order to ensure that the focus group objectives are achieved.

As with interviews, focus groups should always be audio- or video recorded to ensure accurate records for analysis and confirmability. Other researchers (or clients) may observe from an unobtrusive positon, such as an observation room behind a one-way mirror and may make additional notes.

5.4.4 Alternative methods for producing data

Modern technology has enabled alternative ways of eliciting response from participants, such as telephone, email, video telephony, online and mobile discussion forums, blogs, vlogs, apps and so one. These technologies are obviously quite easy and convenient for researchers and participants to use to conduct interviews and focus groups, but researchers should also be aware that these technologies have certain shortcomings that may limit their usefulness under certain conditions. For example, most online technologies do not allow the researcher to observe nonverbal communication, which may be a crucial aspect of certain studies. Because of the asynchronous nature of some interactions (such as email) it may be difficult to probe or clarify interesting ideas or comments immediately.

Apart from the different technologies that may be used, there are also techniques other than direct interviewing that researchers may be able to use to collect data:

- **Diaries** are typically used where events or phenomena are tracked over time (longitudinally). With diaries, respondents record their own responses ('self-reports') repeatedly over time, on paper or electronically (e.g. using blogs or apps). Diaries may be highly structured (as in questionnaires) or may be completely open-ended, although they typically fall in between, similar to semi-structured interviews.[51]
- **Writing about the self**, such as writing a life story (autobiography) or a letter, are also means of gathering self-recorded, rich responses by participants.
- The **Delphi technique** is an iterative process of data collection where experts on a topic are requested to respond to a specific question or set of questions. The responses are then collated and sent back to the same respondents for a next round of responses. In that way, the variances in the answers are reduced and the responses move towards consensus.
- The **nominal group technique** allows participants to record their contributions in silence on their own, and then to share their views, typically one idea at a time, one respondent at a time in a round robin format. In other words, all participants contribute. In most instances, no debates are allowed at this point. When all the ideas have been recorded, and duplicates have been eliminated, discussion is allowed to clarify the ideas captured, and to combine ideas or generate new ideas. Participants are then required to prioritise the items (e.g. by voting) with regard to the original question.[52]
- **Projective techniques** can be used to project beliefs and feelings onto a picture, a third party, an inanimate object or a task situation.[53] The purpose of this technique is that participants are more likely to attribute their own deeper feelings and beliefs to a third party or object. In the same vein, a **thematic apperception test** may be used to present respondents with a picture, that they have to interpret in terms of what is happening in the picture and what is going to happen next. In TAT, the picture used should be interesting enough to elicit a response, but at the same time it should hide the true purpose of the study.
- There are also several techniques that allow participants to produce nonverbal responses. For example, by using rich pictures to describe a concept, participants

individually or in a group can use a complex drawing or set of drawings to describe a concept or idea. As can be expected, the drawings may be complex, diverse and quite difficult to interpret.

There are many different techniques which cannot all be discussed here. However, it is important for researchers to realise that there is a wide array of tools, techniques and methods to choose from. The design should, however, ultimately not be based only on what is convenient to the researcher and participants. Researchers have to ensure that the design fits the problem statement and the purpose of the research and for that reason should carefully weigh the advantages and disadvantages of each component of the design.

5.4.4.1 Participant observation

Participant observation is a data collection technique that is most often associated with ethnography and is often used in business and management studies in conjunction with other data collection methods, especially in case research. Participant observation requires the researcher to be immersed in the research context (e.g. the organisation in the event of a case research strategy) in order to observe the natural experiences of the respondents. Ideally, participant observers will participate in the daily life of the organisation or community they are studying and will endeavour to record their experiences using various data collection techniques, such as field notes, interviews, and the collection of documents and artefacts. Since participant observers may spend a long time in their research setting, it may be difficult to remain objective, and clear steps have to be taken to ensure the trustworthiness of the data collected. In business and management research, a typical participant observation approach can be described as follows:[54]

- The first step is to develop a clear research problem and research question, as objectively and as well founded as possible. In other words, the researcher's judgement should not be clouded by the research context (such as the organisation he or she is working in).
- Selecting the research setting (i.e. delineating the field) may take some thought. Usually researchers in business and management studies will want to do such a study in the organisations that they work for, but, while convenient, this may not always be the best choice.
- Gaining permission to enter the field is generally not only a requirement for participant observation, but also for the ethical research procedures required by most universities. In practice, this may require the researcher to obtain written permission from a duly authorised official of the organisation.
- Bargaining for a research role may already be addressed to some extent when obtaining permission (for example, by stipulating what the research entails). However, when bargaining for a research role other aspects have to be considered. For example, what meetings will the researcher be allowed to attend? Who may he or she interview? What documents will be accessible? The purpose of this phase is to set clear boundaries to the satisfaction of the researcher and the organisation.
- It is important to maintain good relationships with all members of the community. This will not only generally improve access to information, but could occasionally yield opportunities for data collection (such as impromptu discussion on key issues) that may yield new insights.
- Data gathering will involve the use of a variety of data collection tools. It is especially important to, during the data-gathering phase, write up daily (or at least regular) field notes that summarise the observations. In addition to field notes, data collection may

also include more conventional means of data collection, such as surveys, interviews, documents and artefacts, and respondent-generated data such as diaries.
- When the data gathering is completed, the researcher should leave the field in a way that does not leave a void, and that allows the researcher to continue good relationships with the participants. In participant observation, the respondents should never become reliant on the researcher.
- Report writing is the final phase, where the researcher analyses the data collected and writes a report. It may be difficult for researchers to remain unbiased, but all possible steps should be taken to be as unbiased as possible and to maintain the trustworthiness of the data.

5.4.4.2 Direct observation

In contrast to participant observation, which requires immersion in a research environment, direct observation occurs when a researcher observes a phenomenon as unobtrusively as possible. For example, if a researcher is interested in observing the influence of children on the in-store buying behaviour of mothers, direct observation may be a useful approach. Direct observation will often be useful in conjunction with other methods, such as interviewing. While it may be useful to record the observations (e.g. by using a video camera) this may not always be possible and may even, in some instances, be unethical. If we think of our example before, video recording mothers and their children in a store is a sure way of getting in trouble – not only with the subjects, but also with the law! For these reasons, researcher may have to rely on notes or tick-boxes when using observation as a technique in qualitative research.

5.4.4.3 Documents

Documents are the texts produced by the participants or the context that the researcher is studying. Documents may include those that are for public consumption and are in the public domain, such as annual reports and press releases, as well as internal documents aimed at internal audiences, such as strategic plans, company policies, emails and memos. It is important for researchers to ensure that they have clearance to use internal company documents. Documents will rarely be used on their own in research, but are often used as a means of achieving triangulation, along with primary data collection methods. In selecting and evaluating documents, the following criteria should be considered:[55]
- What type of document is it? (primary or secondary, personal or company document, official or unofficial)
- When was it produced?
- Is it based on empirical data (such as market research reports) or is it anecdotal or opinion-based? If empirical, what methodology was used?
- Why was it produced?
- What are the main points, and how does it relate to your study?

5.4.4.4 Artefacts

Artefacts are the physical manifestations of the context and the phenomenon that the researcher is studying. In business and management research, this addresses a wide range of possible data sources, from physical spaces (such as office space), dress, technology used, posters and brochures. Artefacts are generally used in conjunction with other methods of data collection, but can often paint a telling picture of some aspects of the phenomenon being studied. For example, by observing how employees dress or what their office looks like, some aspects of their organisational culture can be inferred.

From our preceding discussion we have seen that there are many different sources of data in qualitative research, most of which will yield textual data. In the next section, we examine the data analysis process in qualitative research.

> **Example box**[56]
>
> In a study on Official Development Aid (ODA) practices in South Africa, the researcher used four data collection methods:
> - Semi-structured interviews
> - Nano narratives, a neologism based on narrative analysis created for this study; to bring confirmability to the main research story, as well as to encourage reflexivity (postcard artefacts)
> - Participant observation which was written up as participant nano narratives
> - Document review which was used to establish the trustworthiness of the research problem and was a secondary focus in terms of the substance of the question
>
> The example illustrates how researchers can use innovative research designs to address their research problem and achieve their research goals.
>
> Source: Williamson, C.M. 2013. *"Strategy in the Skin": An exploration of the strategic practices of South Africa's Official Development Assistance.* University of South Africa: Unpublished DBL thesis. Reprinted by permission of Charmaine Williamson.

5.4.5 Qualitative data analysis and interpretation

Data analysis in qualitative research is perhaps one of the most difficult aspects for researchers to master, as it requires the researcher to assign meaning to the data. Unlike quantitative research, which is normally conducted according to predefined theoretical constructs, qualitative research often requires the researcher to generate the theoretical constructs as part of the theory-building process. Data analysis in qualitative research is also time consuming, as it requires familiarity with the data and a constant interaction between the researcher and the data. In the next section, we examine the different types of qualitative data analysis, as well as the process for analysing qualitative data.

5.4.5.1 Deductive and inductive approaches to qualitative data analysis

Where researchers use existing theories to formulate the research questions and data collection instruments, the qualitative data analysis may be structured according to the research propositions generated by the literature review.[57] This process is described as a deductive approach to qualitative data analysis and is depicted in Figure 5.3. However, this approach runs somewhat counter to the purpose of qualitative research and may result in premature conclusions and important findings being excluded, as data collection and data analysis will be guided by a predetermined theoretical framework. In other words, it supports a more positivistic approach to qualitative research.

The inductive approach to data analysis is a bottom-up approach to theory building, starting with the raw data and from there striving to develop theory (see Figure 5.3); typically used in grounded theory. The first step in this process is to do open coding or first level coding, which involves a line-by-line analysis of the data and the naming of useful concepts in the context of the study. These initial codes are the building blocks of theory.

The next step is to group the initial codes together into meaningful groups. This process is known as selective coding, and it is achieved by integration of categories to produce a theory, which may consist of layers of constructs. The inductive approach also requires the researcher to examine possible relationships between groups and themes; a process known as axial coding. Constant comparison is important, along with negative case analysis which looks for cases that do not confirm the model. These steps are repeated until a theory emerges. From this description it becomes clear how grounded theory is a bottom-up or inductive approach to theory building.

> **Example box**
>
> Inductive data analysis using the Atlas.ti software involves doing a first level coding, and then grouping the first level codes together in 'coding families'. This is the process referred to as selective coding. Coding families can then be grouped together as 'themes', which typically describe the main constructs of the theory. Atlas.ti also has a function for exploring the relationships between coding families and themes, i.e. axial coding.

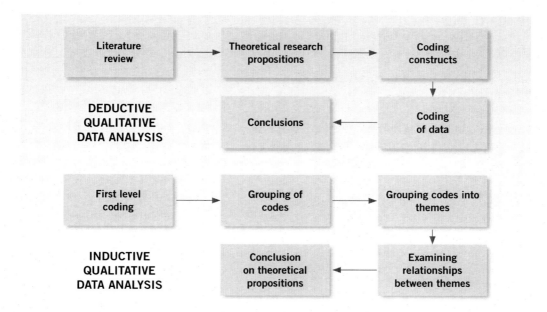

Figure 5.3 Two approaches to qualitative data analysis

In the next section we explore the different types of qualitative data analysis.

5.4.5.2 Types of qualitative data analysis

In this section, we explore the most common approaches to qualitative data analysis, namely **content analysis**, conversation analysis, discourse analysis and narrative analysis.

5.4.5.2.1 Content analysis

Content analysis is typically used to examine textual data such as documents and interview transcripts. The purpose of content analysis is to analyse texts for meaning. There are three main types of content analysis, namely conventional content analysis, directed content analysis and summative content analysis:[58]

- Conventional content analysis is typically used to develop theory and is the inductive process of qualitative data analysis. Where the purpose of the content analysis is to develop theory, the analysis of content may rely on hermeneutics, a process in which a text is broken down into smaller chunks, in order to achieve a greater understanding of the whole.[59] The researcher continuously moves back and forth between the data (hermeneutic units) and the text, in an effort to construct meaning and to develop and refine a theory. This type of analysis is generally the most complex form of content analysis, since it requires the researcher to control the entire process of assigning meaning to the data and to construct theory.
- Directed content analysis is typically used as a means of inductive qualitative data analysis, where codes are developed before (and sometimes during coding) and where the purpose of the analysis is to prove or disprove a theory.
- Summative content analysis is a technique to determine the frequencies of certain terms or words in a set of documents. It should be cautioned that mere quantitative summaries of the use of words of phrases will, on its own, add very little value or meaning to a qualitative research project. For this reason, it should be used in conjunction with other techniques to determine, for example, when and by whom certain phrases or words are used.

5.4.5.3 Conversation analysis

Conversation analysis is the study of verbal and nonverbal interaction and has the purpose of understanding how research participants construct meaning.[60] While conversation analysis initially focused on casual conversations, it has evolved to the study of verbal and nonverbal communication in informal and formal settings (such as company meetings).

5.4.5.4 Discourse analysis

Discourse analysis is concerned with the study of how language is used to construct and change aspects of the world. From a critical discourse perspective, researchers will typically be interested in how underlying ideologies (such as colonialism) or belief systems (such as Christianity) are challenged or reproduced by individuals.[61] Discourse analysis typically involves the analysis of texts, which can be obtained by a wide variety of methods, ranging from secondary data (such as brochures or annual reports) to primary data (such as interview transcripts). Discourse analysis is a contentious technique that is likely to elicit some debate, and requires a great measure of experience before a researcher may feel comfortable with the process.[62]

5.4.5.5 Narrative analysis

Narrative analysis focuses on the analysis of a narrative (such as a story) in order to determine the linkages, relationships and socially constructed explanations that naturally occur within narrative accounts.[63] Narratives can be analysed to determine:[64]

- Narrative strings – commonalities running through and across texts
- Narrative threads – major emerging themes
- Temporal themes – past, present and future contexts presented in the narratives.

In addition to the analysis of the narrative in itself, the text produced by narrative can also be analysed using content analysis or discourse analysis.

5.4.6 The process for analysing qualitative data

In this section, we assume that the recording of data has taken place and that the researcher has a qualitative data set to work with, such as interview or focus group transcripts. The process then starts with the preparation of data for analysis.[65]

5.4.6.1 Preparing data for analysis

The data in its transcribed form may contain some transcription errors. The first step in preparation of the data is accordingly to 'clean' the data, meaning that errors are corrected (for example, where transcribers misheard certain terms). The purpose of cleaning the data is not to edit the data for language and grammar – the transcripts should be exactly as the interview took place. A second aspect of data cleaning is to 'anonymise' the data, meaning that it is cleansed of all aspects that may lead to the recognition of participants.

In addition to cleaning the data, the data should also be properly organised. This may include:

- Ensuring that accessible copies of all data (including field notes) are available
- Saving the data with descriptive file names that are allocated systematically and logically and make it easy to find
- Developing a coding system that makes it easy to reference verbatim quotes, as well as tracing the raw data if needed
- Making backups of data.

Even where data are electronically generated, it should be subject to the same data preparation procedures.

5.4.6.2 Becoming familiar with the data

The process of becoming familiar with the data is a very important step, and involves reading and re-reading the data until the researcher has a good 'feel' for the data and what it contains. This process may be time consuming, but will make the coding and interpretation of data much easier and more meaningful. Writing memos and notes on transcriptions will assist with the process of becoming familiar with the data.

5.4.6.3 Coding and theorising

The approach to the coding and development of theory depends on the analytical process used by the researcher. There are two basic approaches, which have been discussed in previous sections.

In the first approach, the researcher develops *a priori* codes by identifying categories and themes from literature and/or by immersion in the data. In other words, the researcher develops a coding template that is then populated with data. Codes can be amended as data is collected, or new codes can be added.

The second approach is a more grounded approach following a bottom up direction. This process is described in more detail in section 5.4.5.1.

5.4.6.4 Evaluating emergent understandings

When the process of coding and theory development is well under way, the researcher needs to evaluate the emerging theories and findings in two ways:
- Are the findings useful and plausible?
- Are there alternative explanations for the findings, and sufficient evidence that the emerging explanation is the most plausible one?

The need for evaluating findings requires researchers to constantly go back to and re-examine the data for supporting and conflicting evidence and explanations, so that the most plausible and useful explanations can be offered.

The last aspect of data analysis is to write up the findings. We discuss this aspect in more detail in the next section.

5.4.7 Presentation of qualitative data

Writing up qualitative data is generally quite difficult, as there is generally a lot of data, and unlike quantitative data, it cannot always be summarised. It may be useful to review the key mistakes made in reporting qualitative research, as pointed out by the editors of the *Academy of Management Journal*:[66]

1. It is problematic when researchers rely too heavily on their own descriptions of the data, and do not provide sufficient supporting evidence in the form of data (such as verbatim quotes). In other words, they are telling about data and not showing it. The problem is that there is no clear evidence on how the researchers moved from data to findings.
2. On the opposite side of the scale, researchers can present too much data, but not enough of their interpretation and insights. Where data and findings are presented without explaining how it leads to new theoretical insights, the researcher is probably too descriptive.
3. Using terms associated with deductive research to describe qualitative research can lead to misrepresentation of one's research. For example, to state that a 'random sample was selected to achieve representation' does not fit the qualitative research paradigm and might affect credibility.
4. Researchers should avoid quantifying qualitative data, unless there is a clear and convincing rationale for it, and it is justified. However, a statement like 'over half of the respondents ...' in a sample of ten is clearly nonsensical. It may lead to misleading findings, and does not do justice to the rich descriptions that are central to most qualitative research.

As we can see from these common errors, they address two broader areas. Establishing a balance between theory and data is difficult and requires some thought from the researcher. Trying to make qualitative data appear more quantitative (even to the extent of mixing methods inappropriately) is a common error, especially for novice qualitative researchers. In this regard, the researcher can perhaps bear the following aspects in mind:
- Creating a narrative (a story) around the data can be a very useful way to create an interesting presentation of qualitative data. For example, "each theme can be thought of as a character in a story. Who is the central character or protagonist? What obstacles does the protagonist face?"[67]
- Figures and tables can be very useful as a means to organise and present qualitative data, especially when it shows the progression from data to findings.

- Choose the verbatim quotes that are used in the report carefully. Good quotes will be relatively short, but powerful enough to illustrate the point clearly.

Perhaps more than anything else, the challenge to qualitative researchers is to present qualitative data in ways that are interesting to read yet makes it clear what the findings and theoretical implications are and how the researcher got to them. This skill requires experience and practice, and perhaps more than anything else, a deep understanding of the data.

5.5 Summary

Qualitative analysis is most useful when it is used for in-depth explorations of complex phenomena in order to develop new theoretical insights. For this reason, there are certain approaches and philosophies that suit qualitative research better. These approaches were discussed in section 5.3. As we can see in Figure 5.4, the paradigms exert an influence on the type of research problems and questions that researchers may pursue, and may also determine to some extent the strategies of enquiry to be followed.

It also became apparent in our discussion that qualitative research offers many different research strategies and designs, with a multitude of methods, tools and techniques that can be used in isolation or in combination by the researcher. These strategies and methods were discussed in section 5.3 and 5.4, and are summarised in Figure 5.4. It should be noted that researchers are not restricted to a single design for sampling, data collection, and data analysis, but will most likely choose a suitable selection of methods that will fit the research questions to be answered.

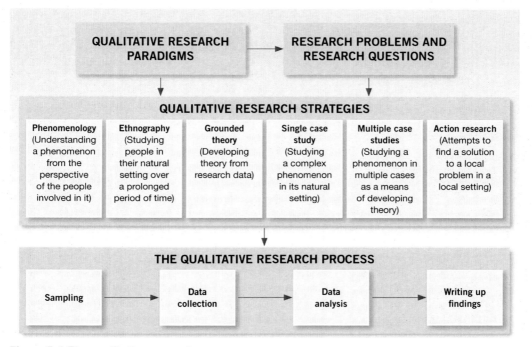

Figure 5.4 The qualitative research process

It may also be useful to review what constitutes good qualitative research. There are nine guidelines for determining what constitutes good qualitative research (see Table 5.2).

Table 5.2 The characteristics of good qualitative research[68]

Characteristic	Description
Purposeful	The methods to collect and analyse data are determined by the research problem and research question.
Explicit	This refers to the principle of transparency, as all assumptions, biases, and other aspects that may influence the research are clearly identified and communicated.
Rigorous	This refers to the aspect of a methodical approach, as the researcher is required to follow a rigorous, methodical process and takes all possible steps to ensure the trustworthiness of the data.
Open-minded	The researcher demonstrates willingness to modify findings when new data emerges that conflict with previously collected data. In other words, the research process is truly iterative.
Complete	The researcher describes and understands the phenomenon in all its complexity and provides a multifaceted, nuanced picture of the phenomenon.
Coherent	The research tells a coherent story, and all aspects of the research 'hang together'. All conflicts in the data are reconciled and explained.
Persuasive	Logical arguments are presented, and one interpretation emerges to the conclusion of others.
Consensual	Other scholars, participants in the research and other stakeholders agree with the researcher's interpretations and explanations.
Useful	The findings and conclusions yield a better understanding of the phenomenon, and may lead to more accurate predictions about future events or lead to interventions for the betterment of society.

Key terms and concepts

action research: a strategy of enquiry attempting to find a solution to a local problem in a local setting
case research (or case study research): a strategy of enquiry to investigate a complex phenomenon in its natural setting
content analysis: an analysis technique for examining textual data such as documents and interview transcripts
critical realism: knowledge production (such as research) is a social practice that is influenced by the conditions, social relations and language in which it is produced
critical theory: to examine the current discourses in a particular context or society at large in order to identify the power relationships in a system and its structures
ethnography: studying people in their natural setting over a prolonged period of time

focus groups: group discussions facilitated by a moderator (as interviewer)
grounded theory: a strategy of enquiry to develop theory from research data
interpretivism: founded in the perspective that phenomena can only be understood by way of the meanings that people assign to them
participant observation: a data collection technique that requires the researcher to be immersed in the research context (e.g. the organisation in the event of a case research strategy) in order to observe the natural experiences of the respondents
phenomenology: understanding a phenomenon from the perspective of the people involved in it

Questions for review and critical thinking

1. Compile a table comparing the major qualitative research strategies in terms of their comparative strengths and weaknesses.
2. Compare and contrast the use of interviews, focus groups and online data collection methods in terms of when they can be used, and their respective strengths and weaknesses.
3. Explain how the use of qualitative analysis software can contribute to the quality of qualitative research.
4. Describe the role of the researcher in qualitative research. How does that differ from the role of the researcher in quantitative research?

Research activities

Visit the Atlas.ti website and watch the video on the product features of Atlas.ti. Take notes on how Atlas.ti (and for that matter all qualitative analysis software) can help to increase the trustworthiness of your data (http://atlasti.com/product/product-videos/).

Case study

Innovation is important for all organisations, and while we know a lot about innovation in general, relatively little is known about how innovation actually occurs in organisations, and why certain organisations are more innovative than others.

You decide that you want to investigate this research problem, and given the complexity of innovation, you feel that a qualitative approach would be best suited to the investigation.

Questions
1. Identify a research problem and a main research question suited to the problem.
2. What possible qualitative research paradigms could apply to the research question and how?
3. Develop a suitable research design based on a research strategy (or combination of strategies) and a method (or collection of methods) for executing the research project. Provide a clear rationale for each of your research decisions.

References

1. Adapted from Jane Goodall's biography. Available online at http://www.biography.com/people/jane-goodall-9542363?page=2 [Accessed 7 March 2013]
2. Adapted from Zikmund, W.G., Babin, B.J., Carr, J.C. & Griffin, M. 2010. *Business Research Methods*. (8th ed.) Canada: South-Western, Cengage Learning, pp.133–134.
3. Zikmund et al (2010: 135)
4. Nieuwenhuis, J. 2007. Introducing qualitative research. In: Maree, K. (Ed). *First steps in research*. Pretoria: Van Schaik.
5. Ibid. pp. 59.
6. Ibid. p. 62.
7. Ibid. p. 62.
8. O'Mahoney, J. & Vincent, S. (2014). *"Critical Realism as an Empirical Project: A Beginner's Guide"*, in Edwards, P., O'Mahoney, J. & Vincent, S. (eds.), *Studying Organisations Using Critical Realism*. 1st ed. Oxford University Press, Oxford. pp. 1–20.
9. Sayer, A. (1992). *Method in social science: A realist approach*. (2nd ed.) London: Routledge.
10. Easton, G. Critical realism in case study research. *Industrial Marketing Management*, 39(2010): 118–128. p. 123.
11. Whittington, R. 2006. Completing the Practice Turn in Strategy Research. *Organization Studies*, 27(5): 613–634.
12. Ibid.
13. For example Järventie-Thesleff, R, Moisander J. and Laine P.M. (2011). Organizational Dynamics and Complexities of Corporate Brand Building – A Practice Perspective. *Scandinavian Journal of Management*, 27(2): 196–204.
14. Zikmund et al. p. 137
15. Ibid. p. 138.
16. Savage-Austin, A.R. & Honeycutt, A.E. 2011. Servant Leadership: A Phenomenological Study Of Practices, Experiences, Organizational Effectiveness, and Barriers. *Journal of Business & Economics Research* 9 (1): 49–54.
17. Fitzgerald, M. 2005. Corporate Ethnography. MIT Technology Review. Available at: https://www.technologyreview.com/s/404920/corporate-ethnography/ [Accessed 19 August 2016].
18. Leedy, P.D. & Ormrod, J.E. 2005. *Practical research: planning and design*. 8th ed. (International ed.) Upper Saddle River, N.J.: Pearson Education. pp. 140–141.
19. Zikmund et al. p. 139.
20. Suddaby, R. 2006. From the editors: what grounded theory is not. *Academy of Management Journal*, 49(4): 633-642.
21. Leedy, P.D. & Ormrod, J.E. 2005. *Practical research: planning and design*. 8th ed. (International Edition). Upper Saddle River, N.J.: Pearson Education. p. 135.
22. Bonoma, T.V. (1985). Case research in marketing: Opportunities, problems and a process. *Journal of Marketing Research*, 22(2), 199–208.
23. Yin, R.K. 2003. *Case Study Research: Design and Method*. 3rd ed. London: Sage.
24. Saunders, M., Lewis, P. & Thornhill, A. 2009. *Research Methods for Business Students*. (5th ed.) Essex: Pearson Education.
25. Ibid.

26 Siggelkow, N. 2007. Persuasion with case studies. *Academy of Management Journal*, 50(1): 20–24.
27 Easton, G. 2010. Critical realism in case study research. *Industrial Marketing Management*, 39(2010): 118–128.
28 Venter, P, Wright, A & Dibb, S. 2015. Performing market segmentation: a performative perspective. *Journal of Marketing Management*, 31(1–2): 62–83.
29 Eisenhardt K.M. 1989. Building Theories from Case Study Research. *Academy of Management Review*, 14(4): 532–550.
30 Ibid.
31 Easton, G. Critical realism in case study research. *Industrial Marketing Management*, 39(2010): 118–128.
32 McCoy, SP. 2012. Brand alignment: developing a model for competitive advantage through a study of selected South African companies, Unpublished DBL thesis, University of South Africa, Pretoria.
33 Leedy, P.D. & Ormrod, J.E. 2005. *Practical research: planning and design*. 8th ed. (International Ed.) Upper Saddle River, N.J.: Pearson Education.
34 Adapted from Honan, E. *Using action research to improve literacy*. The University of Queensland.
35 Botha, M.J., Van der Merwe, M.E., Bester, A.B. & Albertyn, R. 2007. Entrepreneurial skill development: Participatory action research in a rural community. *Journal of Family Ecology and Consumer Sciences*, 35: 9–15.
36 Lincoln, Y.S. & Guba, E.G. 1985. *Naturalistic inquiry*. Beverly Hills, CA: Sage.
37 Yin, R.K. 2003. *Case Study Research: Design and Method*. 3rd ed. London: Sage.
38 Balogun, J., Huff, A.S. & Johnson, P. 2003. Three Responses to the Methodological Challenges of Studying Strategizing. *Journal of Management Studies*, 40(1): 197–224.
39 Nieuwenhuis, J. 2007. Qualitative research designs and data gathering techniques. In: Maree, K. (Ed.). *First steps in research*. Pretoria: Van Schaik.
40 Strydom, H. & Delport, C.S.L. 2005. Sampling and pilot study in qualitative research. In: De Vos, A., Strydom, H., Fouché, C.B. & Delport, C.S.L. (Eds.). *Research at Grass Roots*. 2005. Pretoria: Van Schaik.
41 Eisenhardt K.M. 1989. Building Theories from Case Study Research. *Academy of Management Review*, 14(4): 532–550.
42 Nieuwenhuis, J. 2007. Qualitative research designs and data gathering techniques. In: Maree, K. (Ed.). *First steps in research*. Pretoria: Van Schaik.
43 Adapted from Nieuwenhuis, J. 2007. Qualitative research designs and data gathering techniques. In: Maree, K. (Ed.). *First steps in research*. Pretoria: Van Schaik. p. 82.
44 Grebe, L. 2014. The use of strategy tools by chartered accountants in the South African mining industry. University of South Africa: Unpublished Master's dissertation.
45 Nieuwenhuis, J. 2007. Qualitative research designs and data gathering techniques. In: Maree, K. (Ed.). *First steps in research*. Pretoria: Van Schaik. p. 82.
46 Ibid.
47 Authors differ slightly about these parameters, but 5–12 seems to be a generally acceptable guideline.
48 Adapted from Zikmund et al.
49 Zikmund et al. p. 143.
50 Ibid. p. 147.

51 Sheble, L. & Wildemuth, B. (2009). Research diaries. In B. Wildemuth (Ed.). Applications of social research methods to questions in information and library science (pp. 211–221) Santa Barbara, CA: Libraries Unlimited. Adapted from Leedy, P.D. & Ormrod, J.E. 2005. *Practical research: planning and design*. 8th ed. (International ed.) Upper Saddle River, N.J.: Pearson Education.
52 Delbecq, A.L., VandeVen, A.H. (1971). "A Group Process Model for Problem Identification and Program Planning". *Journal of Applied Behavioral Science*. 7: 466–91
53 Zikmund et al. p 153.
54 Adapted from: Strydom, H. 2005. Information collection: Participant observation. In: De Vos, A., Strydom, H., Fouché, C.B. & Delport, C.S.L. (Eds.). *Research at Grass Roots*. 2005. Pretoria: Van Schaik.
55 Nieuwenhuis, J. 2007. Qualitative research designs and data gathering techniques. In: Maree, K. (Ed.). *First steps in research*. Pretoria: Van Schaik.
56 Williamson, C.M. 2013. "Strategy in the Skin": An exploration of the strategic practices of South Africa's Official Development Assistance. University of South Africa: Unpublished DBL thesis.
57 Saunders, Lewis & Thornhill. p. 489.
58 Hiseh, H.F. & Shannon, S.E. 2005. Three Approaches to Qualitative Content Analysis. *Qualitative Health Research*, 15 (9): 1277–1288.
59 Nieuwenhuis, J. 2007. Analysing qualitative data. In: Maree, K. (Ed.). *First steps in research*. Pretoria: Van Schaik.
60 Ibid.
61 Saunders, Lewis & Thornhill. p. 511–512.
62 Ibid. p. 513.
63 Ibid. p. 514.
64 Nieuwenhuis, J. 2007. Analysing qualitative data. In: Maree, K. (Ed.). *First steps in research*. Pretoria: Van Schaik. p. 103
65 This section is based on Nieuwenhuis, J. 2007. Analysing qualitative data. In: Maree, K. (Ed.). *First steps in research*. Pretoria: Van Schaik. p. 103 and Saunders, Lewis & Thornhill. p. 511–512.
66 Pratt, Michael G. 2009. From the editors For the lack of a boilerplate: tips on writing up (and reviewing) qualitative research. *Academy of Management Journal*, 52(5): 856–862.
67 Ibid. p. 860.
68 Adapted from Leedy & Ormrod (2005).

SURVEYS AS RESEARCH STRATEGY

6

Dion van Zyl
René Pellissier

AFTER STUDYING THIS CHAPTER, YOU SHOULD BE ABLE TO:

- Recognise a survey as a research strategy employed for collecting quantitative data
- Take cognisance of the various characteristics associated with the survey strategy
- Explain the practical considerations as part of designing a survey
- Understand the various elements underlying the design of a questionnaire
- Recognise the various sources of error in surveys.

Valencia needs to conduct a research study as part of completing her postgraduate degree in business management. The aim of her study is to investigate the relationship between job satisfaction and employee retention within medium-sized private firms. Upon discussing the research study further with her supervisor, several questions arise relating to the research design and strategy to employ. What is the purpose of this research – exploratory, descriptive or explanatory? What specific research designs could be adopted? Can quantitative data be collected to answer the research questions and address the research objectives or will qualitative data provide better insight and be more suitable, given the topic and aims?

Valencia notes that various researchers in the past have employed a survey strategy yielding quantitative data. Next the supervisor asked some additional questions that Valencia needed to consider in planning her study. Can she provide definitions for constructs such as 'job satisfaction' and 'employee retention'? How could these constructs be measured quantitatively? Do existing scales[1] exist that she can use? What assumptions will she have to make regarding the methods and tools used to gather the data and measure the variables/constructs under investigation? Can a questionnaire serve as a data gathering instrument? Who should participate in the research? How will she gain access to the participants? What about reliability and validity of the data?

All these questions, Valencia realised, are critical in conducting research. Planning and executing a survey requires a lot of planning!

6.1 Introduction

In Chapter 5, it was noted that the purpose of research is to help provide answers to difficult questions. In doing so, consideration is given, firstly, to *what* information is needed to answer these difficult questions. Part of this consideration involves determining if the information needed must be in the form of quantitative data or qualitative data or even both. Here the research questions and objectives should guide us. Secondly, when we have clarity around what information is needed, the next consideration centres on *how* the information should be acquired (collecting of reliable and valid data) and used (systematically interpreted and disseminated as information).

Employing a survey strategy is a popular and common strategy in management and business-related research. It is quite frequently used to answer questions relating to who, what, where, how much and how many.[1] It allows for the collection of substantial amounts of data and is used typically for exploratory and descriptive research.

A **survey** can be described as a strategy for "acquiring information about one or more groups of people – perhaps about their characteristics, opinions, attitudes, or previous experiences – by asking questions and tabulating the answers."[2] A survey can also be described as a process where a sample of individuals from a selected population is presented with a series of questions in the form of a structured questionnaire.[3] The answers (responses) from each respondent are transformed into numerical format (i.e. quantitative data), which are captured and analysed further using statistical techniques in order to identify underlying patterns and relationships between questions, variables and homogenous groups of respondents.

However, the use of interviews (and a questionnaire) is not the only data collection technique/tool that can be used as part of the survey strategy.[4] Another technique a researcher might consider, involves the use of structured observation and an observation schedule, where the aim is to systematically observe and record the behaviour and actions of survey subjects, be it actual people or other entities, like businesses.

In this chapter, we look towards planning and executing a survey. Employing this strategy involves numerous considerations and choosing the appropriate methods and tools are not always obvious decisions for the researcher.[5] Research projects rarely have similar research questions and objectives. As a result, each project warrants employing different methods as part of the survey strategy. What works for one, might not be suitable for the other. Being familiar with the typical steps and choices available in designing a survey, can help a researcher make informed decisions along the way in ensuring that the research yields reliable and valid measures.[6]

The next section discusses a number of characteristics associated with surveys.

6.2 Characteristics of surveys

It is evident from the definitions presented that surveys are associated with a number of key characteristics. Five key characteristics are listed and briefly discussed below.
- A survey is regarded as a research strategy and not a research method. Different methods can be employed as part of the survey strategy. Methods include, amongst others, interviews, administering of questionnaires and structured observation.
- A survey consists of several interconnected steps. This includes defining the purpose and research objectives clearly and precisely; selecting a survey frame and employing sample design; designing the questionnaire or survey instrument; collecting and analysing data; and lastly, disseminating the results and findings. These steps constitute the life of a survey, consisting of the planning phase, followed by the design phase, and then the implementation phase.

- Surveys are associated with the deductive approach. In other words, we assume that prior to the design of a study, the researcher has a sufficient understanding of the underlying theory (or theories) underpinning the problem statement. A literature review provides the foundation for this understanding on which the research will be built.[7] This gives rise to the formulation of hypotheses that identify the constructs, variables and relationships that will be empirically measured and tested.
- Surveys are associated with the collection of quantitative data. As such, the purpose statement, objectives and hypotheses are specific and well demarcated with a strong emphasis on testing existing theories. Data collected can be analysed using statistical techniques, ranging from producing very basic summary statistics to more advanced procedures such as structural equation modelling.
- A survey enables us to collect large amounts of data about variables, such as people's lifestyles, attitudes, demographics and motives.

In the next section, the various steps in the design of a survey that provide a systematic approach to operationalise a survey study are presented.

6.3 Steps in the design of a survey

There are seven steps in the design of a survey.

6.3.1 Step 1: Translating the problem statement into a set of research objectives

This is the starting point for any research study, irrespective of the methods that will be employed as part of the survey strategy. A management problem (or opportunity) is translated into a set of relevant and manageable research objectives by the researcher. These objectives outline the information needs, as well as the operational definitions that will apply during the research. This determines what is to be included and what is to be excluded.

Having clarity with regards to the aims and scope of the research, the researcher turns towards how and from which subjects or entities the required information must be obtained. In essence, this involves moving from a theoretical understanding of the relationships between concepts/hypothetical constructs to 'operationalising' the research so that empirical evidence can be obtained. In other words, the researcher must translate ('operationalise') the concepts/hypothetical constructs of a theory into variables and the propositions of the theory into hypotheses.

The researcher next considers various choices and research paths as more than one method can yield information (data) relevant to the research objectives and questions. Methodological choices must therefore be made so that the researcher can argue in favour of the scientific rigour of the design chosen. This aspect cannot be emphasised enough. At the end of the project, the scientific community will evaluate the research, firstly, by the processes that were followed and secondly, against the knowledge contribution and the extent to which the research objectives were addressed and the research questions were answered.

> **Example box**
>
> A researcher wanted to investigate the extent to which strategic planning and implementation principles are used within medium-sized, owner-managed businesses in South Africa. The researcher had to determine how empirical evidence could be obtained to address the research objective. The researcher considered the various research designs, as well as the type of data needed. After a review of the literature, a survey was chosen as research strategy and a semi-structured questionnaire was to serve as data gathering instrument. While the focus fell on medium-sized businesses (**unit of analysis**), the researcher also had to decide who within the business would be best suited to answer the questions contained in the questionnaire. The decisions made by the researcher had to be clearly motivated in order to justify the rigour of the design.

6.3.2 Step 2: Sample design

Sampling is rightfully acknowledged to be nowhere more critical than in survey research.[8] Careful consideration of the sampling process is paramount to the claims eventually made about the results and the relevance thereof to a larger population.

In some contexts, a researcher may deal with a small enough population that makes it possible to collect data from every possible member. Such a survey is referred to as a census. However, for a large population it is not always financially viable and practical to target each and every member, which forces the researcher to draw a sample.

> **Example box**
>
> Many students are required to conduct research as part of their studies. The focus of their research frequently falls on improving the understanding of particular business or management problems within the organisations they work in, both for applied and basic research reasons. However, depending on who the repondents are going to be, these organisations might not be large in terms of number of staff (maybe less than 100). This makes it viable to rather conduct a survey amongst all staff members, than drawing a sample. However, if the organisation is large (e.g. more than 2 000 staff members), it would be more practical and financially viable to focus on collecting data from a sample.

The sampling design starts with the identification of a suitable sampling frame. A sampling frame constitutes the list of elements (e.g. potential respondents) from which the sample could be selected and must be consistent with the population the researcher wishes to study. That is, the researcher begins with a population in mind for the study. Practically, however, existing sampling frames often define the study population rather than the other way around. This is often the case in management and business surveys, where information about the whole population may not be readily available. The researcher searches for possible sampling frames and upon evaluating the available frames, a decision is made in terms of which frame presents a study population most appropriate for the study. Researchers are warned to be careful to not select samples from a given sampling frame and then to make assertions about a population similar to, but not identical, to the population defined by the sampling frame.[9]

In the case that no sampling frame exists, the researcher must provide a clear description of the desired respondent. This will assist in the identification and selection of respondents.

Two main sampling techniques can be distinguished, namely probability sampling and non-probability sampling. In the case of probability sampling, every element in the population has a known non-zero probability of being selected, which is the same for every unit of the population, whilst in the case of non-probability sampling, every element does not have a known probability of being selected. In non-probability sampling, members are selected from the population in some non-random manner.

For a finite population, like the number of undergraduate students in a particular academic year, it is possible to select in such a way that every student has a known probability of being selected. This is because the probability of being selected is equal to the number of times a student can be selected divided by the total number in the (finite) population. When the elements of the population are not known or when the number in the population is not known or is infinite, we can only administer non-probability sampling. Therefore, depending on the characteristics of the population and the desired outcomes and techniques the researcher wants, either of the sampling techniques can be employed.

Probability sampling methods include simple random sampling, systematic sampling, stratified random sampling, and cluster sampling. Non-probability sampling methods include convenience sampling, judgment sampling, quota sampling, and snowball sampling.

6.3.2.1 Probability sampling methods

- **Random sampling** is the purest form of probability sampling. Each member of the population has an equal and known probability of being selected. When there are very large populations, it is rarely possible to identify every member of the population, so the pool of available subjects becomes biased.
- **Systematic sampling** is often used instead of random sampling. It is also called an Nth name selection technique. After the required sample size has been calculated, every Nth record is selected from a list of population members. As long as the list does not contain any hidden order, this sampling method is as good as the random sampling method. Its only advantage over the random sampling technique is simplicity.
- **Stratified sampling** is a commonly used probability method that is superior to random sampling because it reduces sampling error. A stratum is a subset of the population that shares at least one common characteristic. Examples of strata might be males and females, or managers and non-managers. The researcher firstly identifies the relevant strata and their actual representation in the population. Random sampling is then used to select a sufficient number of subjects from each stratum. 'Sufficient' refers to a sample size large enough for us to be reasonably confident that the stratum represents the population. Stratified sampling is frequently used when one or more of the strata in the population have a low incidence relative to the other stratums. Also, stratification is preferred when the elements of the population are heterogeneous and can be classified into logical groupings each carrying its own characteristic. In stratifying the population first and then drawing a random sampling across all of the strata, a higher level of significance (or a higher accuracy is produced than without the stratification). Put differently, stratification (i.e. where the population elements can be grouped into logical subgroups) can get away with a smaller size sample and still achieve the same level of

accuracy as random sampling with a bigger sample. From a sampling perspective and noting the costs involved in sampling elements from the population, this is good news indeed.
- **Cluster sampling** may be used when it is either impossible or impractical to compile an exhaustive list of the elements that make up the target population. However, the population elements are already grouped into subpopulations where every subpopulation (or cluster) looks like a baby population, and lists of those subpopulations already exist or can be created. For example, let us say the target population in a study was church members in South Africa. There is no list of all church members in the country. The researcher could, however, create a list of churches in South Africa, choose a sample of churches, and then obtain lists of members from those churches. To conduct a cluster sample, the researcher first selects groups or clusters and then from each cluster, selects the individual subjects either by simple random sampling or systematic random sampling. If the cluster is small enough, the researcher may choose to include the entire cluster in the final sample rather than a subset from it.

6.3.2.2 Non-probability sampling methods
- **Convenience sampling** involves the selection of sample units that are easiest to obtain. This method is used by researchers due to its simplicity. Bias can, however, easily be introduced into the sample.
- **Judgment sampling** enables the researcher to include those cases into the sample that is judged to be best suited and able to provide information required to address the research objectives. This sampling technique works well when dealing with very small samples, such as in case study research.
- **Quota sampling** is the non-probability equivalent of stratified sampling. Like stratified sampling, the researcher first identifies the stratums and their proportions as they are represented in the population. Then convenience or judgment sampling is used to select the required number of subjects from each stratum. This differs from stratified sampling, where the stratums are filled by random sampling.
- **Snowball sampling** is a special non-probability method used when the desired sample characteristic is rare. It may be extremely difficult or cost prohibitive to locate respondents in these situations. Snowball sampling relies on referrals from initial subjects to generate additional subjects. While this technique can dramatically lower search costs, it comes at the expense of introducing bias because the technique itself reduces the likelihood that the sample will represent a good cross section from the population.

Having considered the sampling design, the next step in the survey design process turns towards data collection.

6.3.3 Step 3: Data collection

This step involves the physical collection of the data. In preparation for the fieldwork, a fieldwork plan is required. This plan outlines the manner in which the data will be collected, in other words, if an interview will be used or if a self-administered questionnaire will be distributed. The manner of distribution is also specified (i.e. if it will be physical or electronic). A time schedule also forms part of the fieldwork plan and if relevant, a physical plan of the survey area should be included. The responsibilities of the interviewers, fieldworkers and coordinators are clearly specified.

If interviewers are used to assist in the collection of data, briefing and training sessions must be scheduled. Here the focus falls on the principles of interviewing, respondent selection, question instructions, recording of answers, probing and prompting and closing of interviews. The aim of this is to ensure that the same procedure is followed across all interviews in order to minimise bias. The recruitment and training of competent interviewers are essential to the data collection phase. Interviewers must be able to listen well; have the skills to deal with emotional respondents while maintaining objectivity; and maintaining a positive attitude despite being 'rejected' when requesting an interview.

Fieldwork coordinators must also know how to supervise and manage the fieldwork team. These coordinators not only coordinate, but are also responsible for in-field quality control of the interview and data collection process. This involves ensuring compliance with sampling requirements; completeness of questions; relevance of the answers; clarity of the respondent's handwriting, as well as inconsistencies. Fieldwork coordinators are responsible for ensuring the smooth and consistent implementation of the fieldwork plan.

Other administrative aspects must also be addressed. For example, if a physical questionnaire will be distributed or used, it needs to be printed and checked for completeness. Introductory letters must be designed and if relevant, reply-paid envelopes should be supplied.

A variety of methods and tools can be used to collect numerical data. Some of the more common and popular methods are discussed next.

6.3.3.1 Interview-based surveys

Two main methods of interview-based surveys include personal face-to-face interviews and telephone interviews.

6.3.3.1.1 Personal face-to-face interviews

Face-to-face interviews are conducted by interviewers that work systematically through a questionnaire or checklist by asking the respondent questions and recording the responses. Interviews are conducted at various locations, including going door-to-door in communities, at premises of businesses or by intercepting potential respondents at malls. Face-to-face interviews can also be conducted on a one-to-one basis or in groups. Technology allows increasingly for interviewers to use tools such as laptops and tablets to guide interviews and capture responses.

Advantages
- There is a potentially high response rate dependent on accessibility, availability and willingness of respondents to participate.
- Interviewers can motivate respondents to participate.
- They can also establish some sort of immediate relationship with the respondent. This can help the interviewer in handling complex questions or clarifying questions from respondents.
- The process also allows for interviewers to probe certain responses.
- Interviewers can observe and note nonverbal behaviour and reactions.
- In addition to asking questions, this type of interview provides the opportunity to use visual aids, such as show cards, photographs or product samples.

- Some control can be exercised by the interviewer over the interview process and who is present.
- Lastly, respondents do not have to be literate.

Disadvantages/Limitations
- Personal face-to-face interviews are relatively expensive and require highly skilled interviewers. The geographical area that must sometimes be covered to reach respondents can add to resource constraints. This also results in the data collection process not being as fast as in some of the other methods.
- Asking of sensitive questions can be problematic for some respondents.
- Some respondents might be more inclined to give answers, which they think would be more acceptable in the presence of the interviewer. That can lead to social desirability bias. Interviewers themselves can also introduce bias by not asking questions in a similar way from one interview to the next.[10]

6.3.3.1.2 Telephone interviews

As the name indicates, this type of interview is conducted by telephone and/or cellular phone. This means no face-to-face contact between interviewer and respondent. These types of interviews are increasingly being used in business survey studies. The use of technology such as Computer Aided Telephone Interview (CATI) systems can aid interviewers in the process. With CATI, the interviewer conducts a telephone interview but is guided by a script generated by a survey software program. This process speeds up the data collection and editing process, as responses collected are entered directly into a database. An additional advantage offered by CATI is the ability of the software program to interactively direct the flow of the survey based on the answers provided, as well as information already known about the respondent.

Advantages
- Data gathering can take place relatively quickly over a short period of time.
- The average cost per interview is typically lower compared to personal interviews.
- Interviewers can be supervised directly.
- Interviewers can answer questions from respondents.
- Respondents do not have to be literate as the interview process is guided by the interviewer.
- Various technological advances offer assistance to interviewers, allowing for immediate capturing of responses and in some instances real-time analysis and reporting of preliminary results while data gathering takes place.
- Interviews can take place anywhere and are not location-dependent.

Disadvantages/Limitations
- Data collection is restricted to those respondents that have access to a telephone or cellular phone.
- Respondent's nonverbal behaviour cannot be observed.
- Interviews are typically shorter and contain less complex questions than personal face-to-face interviews.

6.3.3.2 Questionnaire-based surveys

There are three main methods of questionnaire-based surveys, namely mail/postal surveys, web-based surveys and systematic observation.

6.3.3.2.1 Mail/postal surveys

This data collection method involves sending self-completion questionnaires to individuals in the sample. The questionnaire is mailed with an introductory letter noting the purpose of the study and instructions for completion and return. A date is specified by when the completed questionnaire should be returned. A prepaid mail-return envelope is usually included.

Advantages
- Can target a large sample that is geographically widespread.
- No trained interviewers required.
- Responses are free of interviewer bias.
- Lower cost per respondent.
- Can standardise responses.
- Some visual aids can be included, but limited.
- Considered as a suitable method for sensitive topics.

Disadvantages/Limitations
- While traditionally less costly, printing and postage fees could result in significant cost given a large sample.
- Data collection typically takes longer than some of the other methods.
- No control over who answers the questionnaire.
- Dependence on an efficient and effective mail delivery infrastructure within a country.
- Asking of follow-up questions not possible. This also limits asking more complex questions.

6.3.3.2.2 Web-based surveys

Web-based surveys are regarded as a more technologically advanced version of the mail survey and have become an increasingly popular method to collect data in business-related survey research. An invitation is sent to a respondent via email to participate in the survey. Various methods and tools are used to facilitate the data collection process. This includes the questionnaire as an attachment to the e-mail. Alternatively, the questionnaire is published via an online data collection platform such as SurveyMonkey™ or Qualtrics™ with a link sent to the respondent providing access to the online questionnaire. As the questionnaire is aimed at self-completion, clear instructions need to be provided.

Advantages
- Responses are captured into a database in real time resulting in reduced data editing and cleaning up before analysis starts.
- Less costly than mail surveys.
- Allows for relatively fast data collection.
- Suited for targeted samples.

Disadvantages/Limitations
- As in the case with mail surveys, the researcher has no control over who answers the questionnaire.
- Acquiring a representative sample is rarely possible due to the 'convenience' nature of the data-gathering process.
- Asking of follow-up questions is not possible.
- Response rates are often very low.

6.3.3.2.3 Systematic observation

The collection of data through structured observation is less common than the other methods described above. As part of a survey strategy, behaviours being studied are quantified in some way. An observation schedule is normally used as data gathering tool and contains a checklist of the behaviours of interest.[11] Throughout the data collection process, the researcher aims to remain as objective as possible. Five strategies that researchers can employ in order to remain objective are noted, namely:[12]

1. Define the behaviour being studied precisely and concretely so that it can be easily recognised when it occurs.
2. Divide the observation period into small and manageable segments and record whether the behaviour does or does not occur in each segment.
3. Develop and use a specific coding system that facilitates the recording of behaviours observed.
4. Make use of two or three people to rate the behaviours independently, without knowledge of each other.
5. Train the observers to use specific criteria when counting or evaluating the behaviours; continue training until consistent observations are obtained for any single occurrence of the behaviour.

> **Example box**
>
> A well-known example of systematic observation that featured in survey research was that of work done by Stephens, Ledbetter, Mitra and Ford in the early nineties.[13] These researchers focused on the newly emerging role of the chief information officer (CIO), questioning how it has evolved with the changing needs of business. However, the researchers also contemplated the research method that would be most appropriate for answering this question. They acknowledged that simply asking a manager what he or she does would not necessarily relate to what they actually do if they were to be observed.
> The method of data gathering therefore reverted to systematic observation and built on earlier work of Mintzberg (1975) and Ives and Olson (1981). The researchers observed the CIOs of five different companies over time and recorded, in a systematic manner, the behaviour and actions of these CIOs. Prior research was first reviewed to establish a framework that formed the basis of behaviours and actions to be observed. They argued that structured observation can provide richness of understanding while simultaneously providing a quantitative basis for comparison with other studies.

6.3.4 Step 4: Design of a questionnaire and other data collection instruments

A primary goal of a survey is to collect information (data) from respondents by asking them a set of well-directed questions. These questions are often contained in a questionnaire that directs the flow and structure of the questioning and serves as a data collection tool.

The design of a questionnaire is, however, considered by many more an art than a science. Researchers must therefore take note of the important elements forming key aspects of the development process. Heeding the warning of DeVellis (2003), such an endeavour must not be the mere 'assembly', 'throw[ing] together' or 'dredge[ing] up' of questions, but must constitute a systematic and careful process of questionnaire development where the questions share a common cause and consequence, namely that of offering researchers a means of collecting reliable and valid data that will allow them to draw relevant conclusions.[14]

In the subsections that follow, some of the key aspects that a researcher should consider as part of the design of a questionnaire are briefly discussed.

6.3.4.1 Types of variables (i.e. attributes, behaviour, opinion)

Typically questions included in a questionnaire aim to capture three types of responses: opinion, behaviour and attribute.

Opinion

These questions aim to capture how respondents feel or think about something, as well as their preferences. In many cases, this is centred on perceptions and attitudes. It is important to realise that an opinion is just that, a personal belief or judgement that is not founded on proof or certainty.

> **Example box**
>
> Indicate to what extent you agree or disagree with the following statement (where 1 = Strongly disagree; 2 = Disagree; 3 = Neither agree nor disagree; 4 = Agree; 5 = Strongly agree).
>
> *I enjoy shopping at XYZ store.*

Behaviour

These questions aim to capture behaviours exhibited by respondents (or the unit of analysis they report on). In other words, behavioural variables capture data on what respondents did in the past, do now or will do in the future. Researchers must take note of the fact that surveys rely greatly on respondents' ability to recall specific past behaviour and this might differ from actual behaviour exhibited when observed.

> **Example box**
>
> Did you purchase anything during your last visit to XYZ store?
> Yes
> No

Attribute

These questions aim to capture the characteristics of respondents (or the unit of analysis). Typical attributes in the case of an individual would be gender, age, education and income. However, researchers should think carefully about the attributes measured so that it is not done without a clear sense of where it fits into the study. In other words, data should have a link to a specific research objective.

> **Example box**
>
> What is your gender?
> Female
> Male

With the development and formulation of each question, it is critical to ascertain whether the question should capture opinion, behaviour or attribute.

6.3.4.2 Types of questions

The types of questions included in a data collection instrument such as a questionnaire or checklist is determined by the data needed to address the research objectives. The structure and wording of questions are therefore important considerations in order to provide reliable and valid measures.

Various strategies can be followed by researchers in designing a data collection instrument such as a questionnaire.[15] These strategies include adopting complete survey instruments or question sets that were used in past studies, or if good reason exists, adapting some questions. Alternatively, the researcher must develop a set of totally new questions.

Each one of these strategies holds some advantages and potential pitfalls/limitations. If a researcher wishes to replicate a study, either to gather data under a new context for comparison reasons, or to verify previous results, adopting an existing survey instrument of a particular question set might be an appropriate strategy. With this comes the responsibility to ascertain that the original questions offer measures that can yield data that are of acceptable reliability and validity.

Adapting questions are also a consideration for researchers. Circumstances and contexts change, new classifications emerge or certain words might be more appropriate within a certain culture that warrants the adapting of a question. An existing question type might even lend itself to being adapted to measure something new. Irrespective, the researcher must be mindful about what should be measured within the context of the study and the research objectives. It happens quite often that a researcher would change a question's wording while assuming that the same measurement is applied as in the original study. This false assumption will impact on drawing reliable and valid comparisons.

Always carefully consider the wording of questions, as well as flow of the questionnaire, as it will contribute towards the validity of the questionnaire (refer to section 6.3.4.5). It is therefore always advisable to pilot test the data gathering instrument (refer to section 6.3.4.6).

Let's review some of the most common and popular types of questions that researchers can use.

List

The respondent is offered a list of items (or categories/choices). In some cases, the selection of only one listed item is required and is referred to as a single answer response. Alternatively, the respondent is allowed to select more than one listed item irrespective of order (referred to as a multiple response or checklist). Some researchers allow for the inclusion of an item choice that reads 'Other', in order to cover possible items not listed. It is advised that the respondent also specifies what the 'Other' choice is, so that it can be interpreted.

Requirements for answering such a question, depends on the question wording and instruction. The list of items presented are therefore determined by the information sought from the respondent, and could be in the form of an attribute, opinion or behaviour type variable.

> **Example box**
>
> *Single response*
> What is the highest level of education you have completed?
> No schooling
> Some primary schooling
> Primary school completed
> Some high school
> Matric (Grade 12)
> Post-matric certificate/diploma
> University degree
>
> *Multiple response*
> Which of the following coffee drinks are you familiar with?
> Americano
> Café Latte
> Cappuccino
> Espresso
> Mochachino

Ranking

The respondent is offered a list of items and asked to place them in order based on some criteria.

> **Example box**
>
> Rank the following employee benefits in order of importance to you (where 1 = Most important; 2 = Second most important; 3 = Third most important; 4 = Fourth most important).
> Annual leave of 30 working days
> Flexible working hours
> Medical aid
> Pension fund

Rating

The respondent is offered items or statements (even objects) and asked to rate them given a specific discrete categorical response format. One of the most frequently used response formats is the Likert-scale. Respondents are asked to indicate the extent or degree of favourable or unfavourable attitude towards an item, often expressed in the form of a statement. Many different forms of this response format exist aiming to capture different levels of attitudes and opinions of respondents towards a particular aspect, some in the form of a dichotomous scoring, others on a four, five, seven or 10-point scale.[16] A distinction is also made in terms of a balanced and unbalanced response format scale. If an odd numbered balanced Likert-type scale is used, the selection of a relevant middle value/label must take place with great consideration. Each version or format has its own merits and limitations in terms of measurement.

> **Example box**
>
> Indicate your level of knowledge regarding the rules of the following sport (where 1 = Poor; 2 = Fair; 3 = Good; 4 = Very good; 5 = Excellent).
> Basketball
> Cricket
> Hockey
> Rugby

Quantity

Here respondents are required to provide a number indicating quantity.

> **Example box**
>
> How old are you (in completed years)?

6.3.4.3 Types of data

Four levels of measurement can typically be distinguished, namely nominal, ordinal, interval and ratio. The next chapter will consider these types of data more in detail, in particular the types of statistical analysis that can be applied. Here the aim is to briefly introduce them.

Nominal data

This measurement classifies data into distinct categories (exhaustive and mutually exclusive), but no specific ordering/ranking of categories applies. Nominal data merely offer names or labels assigned to categories or characteristics without taking cognisance of any underlying ordering. In fact, the word *nominal* comes from the Latin *nomen*, meaning 'name'.

Examples include gender, home language, province and ethnic group. The categories of 'female' and 'male' offer two mutually exclusive labels that represent nominal data.

Ordinal data

This measurement also classifies data into distinct categories, but here logical rank ordering of categories applies. In other words, the rank order determines differences between categories, suggesting relatively more or less (higher or lower) of the variable. Despite the ordering or ranking, ordinal data do not provide an indication of the extent of how the measurements differ.

One of the most simplistic examples of ordinal data comes from rating questions, where respondents are asked to rate a particular item or statement using a five-point response format such as: 1 = Strongly disagree; 2 = Disagree; 3 = Neither agree nor disagree; 4 = Agree; 5 = Strongly agree. A response of 'Strongly agree' can be regarded as more positive than responses associated with those coded as 1, 2, 3 and 4. While producing measurement data, the only aspect that can really be inferred is the rank order.

Other examples include level of education, grouped age categories and income categories.

Interval data

Interval data offers standard and equal units of measurement. While the numbers reflect difference in degree or amount, the numbers provide an indication of how much it differs. However, with interval data a value of zero is not necessarily reflective of the absence or complete lack of the characteristic being measured.

For example, measuring temperature produces interval data. We know that the difference between 20 and 30 degrees Celsius is the same as the difference between 40 and 50 degrees. But we also know that 40 degrees Celsius is not twice as hot as 20 degrees as 'zero' degrees does not really indicate the total absence or lack of heat. The 'zero'-point is totally arbitrary.

Ratio data

This level of measurement allows for ordered scaling where the difference between two measurements involves a true zero point. The numbers reflect equal intervals between values, but a 'zero'-value is indicative of the total absence or lack of the characteristic being measured.

Examples include measuring variables such as age, money (like income) and weight.

6.3.4.4 Scales as proxy measures for hypothetical constructs

In many survey studies, researchers deal with various theoretical and hypothetical constructs that have varied meanings and definitions. These constructs can also not always be observed by direct means. For example, researchers might be interested in measuring levels of 'quality of life'. This construct might at first seem quite straightforward, but a researcher in management sciences might conceptualise or define 'quality of life' very differently than a researcher interested in measuring 'quality of life' from a health sciences perspective.

Operationalising the quantitative measurement of a construct such as quality of life, or others like self-esteem, job satisfaction, stress, anxiety or business maturity just to name a few, is therefore not always easy. Various strategies and specific techniques have therefore been developed over time to facilitate the measuring of hypothetical constructs. One such strategy commonly used by survey researchers are scales. A typical scale in business and organisational-related survey studies consists of a set of items or statements that respondents evaluate or rate in terms of their extent or degree of favourable or unfavourable attitude towards the item (or statement). The majority of scales used in business-related survey studies are reflective in nature. In other words, respondents would rate a specific item or statement as an outcome (or trait) of the hypothetical construct. These items or statements therefore share a common relationship (correlation) between one another thus constituting a scale.

Several response formats could be used but a favourite is presented in the form of discrete categories, e.g. 1 = Strongly disagree; 2 = Disagree; 3 = Neither agree nor disagree; 4 = Agree; 5 = Strongly agree. By combining the responses over the set of items or statements on a case-by-case basis, a composite score is calculated that now provides a proxy measure for the hypothetical construct.

When faced with the challenge of measuring a specific construct, it is always advised to first review the existing literature. There are literally thousands of validated scales that have been used successfully in past research studies. Some reports and journal articles provide the actual items and statements that make up the scales. Take note that some scales are copyright protected – contact the publisher and enquire about permission (and possible cost) to use the scale. If you decide to develop your own scale, make sure you read up extensively on the process and principles of scale development.

Lastly, when incorporating scales into a questionnaire, it is important to consider the reliability and validity of the scales. See more on reliability and validity in section 6.3.4.6. Chapter 8 also looks at the statistics that can be calculated to evaluate internal consistency and reliability of scales.

> **Example box**
>
> A study was conducted in 2000 investigating the relationship between perceived retail crowding and shopping satisfaction.[17] In order to operationalise the quantitative measurement of the construct of 'shopping satisfaction', a four-item scale was used. Respondents had to indicate their level of agreement with each item based on a seven-point response format.
>
> continued →

1. "I enjoyed shopping at the store."
2. "I was satisfied with my shopping experience at the store."
3. "Given a choice, I would probably not go back to the store." (reverse coded)
4. "I would recommend the store to other people."

It would seem on face value that these items all 'hang' together. In other words, if a respondent would be satisfied with his (or her) shopping experience, then he (or she) would probably agree (to some extent) with items 1, 2 and 4, but disagree with item 3 (which was negatively worded). These items therefore provide an indication of the outcome or effect of being satisfied with the shopping experience (i.e. they are reflective).

By summing the agreement ratings of the four items (having reversed scored item 3 first) and dividing it by the number of items (i.e. four), a basic measure is calculated for the scale. The scale measure ranges from 1 to 7, and if, for example, a rating of 1 would have indicated 'Total disagreement' and 7 'Total agreement', then higher scale values would be reflective of higher levels of satisfaction. Thus, a scale of four items was used to obtain a proxy measure for the construct of 'shopper satisfaction'.

6.3.4.5 Question wording and layout of the questionnaire

Questionnaire design is certainly not easy and involves significant skill. The researcher must be very critical when it comes to question formulation and use of wording. Each word and meaning must be carefully considered to ascertain that valid data can be collected to address the research objectives. Below are some common mistakes that are made when formulating questions.

Questions	Example
Leading questions	"I assume you would agree that teachers do a great job in educating our children?"
Double-barrelled questions	"Do you think government should impose taxes on cigarettes and sugary soft drinks?"
Emotionally loaded words as part of question construction	"What should be done about murderous terrorists who threaten the freedom of good citizens?"
Questions that may embarrass the respondent	"Have you ever cheated on your tax return?"
Overly complex questions	"How well do you think Narayanaswamy's model of self-regulatory control of emotional state explains your own attitudes?"
Questions that contain double negatives creating confusion	"It is not a good idea to not turn in an important document at work."

In addition, questions that contain unnecessary technical terms, jargon and acronyms or words with a double meaning can confuse respondents. Lastly, do not use overly complicated language. Respondents might not know what you are talking about and might be too embarrassed to ask.

The construction of a questionnaire also involves considering the order and flow of questions. Just as the type of variables and questions influence the reliability and validity of the data being gathered, so does the layout, order and flow of questions. Therefore, the logic thereof to the respondent and interviewer should be carefully considered.

Where relevant, include clear instructions that will guide the respondent (and interviewer if relevant) through the questionnaire. Take special note of skip and filter questions and how it would influence the flow and logic. Also remember to include a covering letter or introduction to the questionnaire, explaining the purpose and ethical declarations.

The layout should be attractive and inviting. Colours and font types should be scrutinised. Many survey design software such as SurveyMonkey™ and Qualtrics™ offer various templates that can assist in producing a professional-looking questionnaire.

6.3.4.6 Reliability and validity

Reliability and validity are not the same thing.

Reliability

The term 'reliability' refers in the abstract sense to the stability of the measurement. It ensures that you measure the same thing in the same way in repeated tests (or surveys). In other words, if another researcher were to conduct the same study in the same way, there is a strong likelihood that the findings will be similar.

Reliability has to do with the quality of measurement. In its everyday sense, reliability is the 'consistency' or 'repeatability' of the research measures and outcomes. Before we can define reliability precisely, we have to discuss some fundamentals. Firstly, you have to learn about the foundation of reliability, the true score theory of measurement. Along with that, you need to understand the different types of measurement error because errors in measures play a key role in degrading reliability. With this foundation, you can consider the basic theory of reliability, including a precise definition of reliability. We cannot calculate reliability – we can only estimate it.[18] In the end, it is important to integrate the idea of reliability with the other major criterion for the quality of measurement (validity) and develop an understanding of the relationships between reliability and validity in measurement.

There are several reliability measures, of which four are discussed below.
- **Inter-rater reliability** assesses the degree to which test scores are consistent when measurements are taken by different respondents using the same methods.
- **Test-retest reliability** assesses the degree to which test scores are consistent from one test administration to the next. Measurements are gathered from a single rater who uses the same methods or instruments and the same testing conditions. This includes intra-rater reliability.
- **Inter-method reliability** assesses the degree to which test scores are consistent when there is a variation in the methods or instruments used. This allows inter-rater reliability to be ruled out. When dealing with forms, it may be termed parallel-forms reliability.
- **Internal consistency reliability** assesses the consistency of results across items within a test.

Reliability does not imply validity. That is, a reliable measure that is measuring something consistently, may still not be measuring what you want to be measuring. For example, while there are many reliable tests of specific abilities, not all of them would be valid for predicting job performance. In terms of accuracy and precision, reliability is analogous to precision, while validity is analogous to accuracy.

> **Example box**
>
> Below the basic aspects of accuracy and precision explained graphically using the idea of a hitting a target as example.

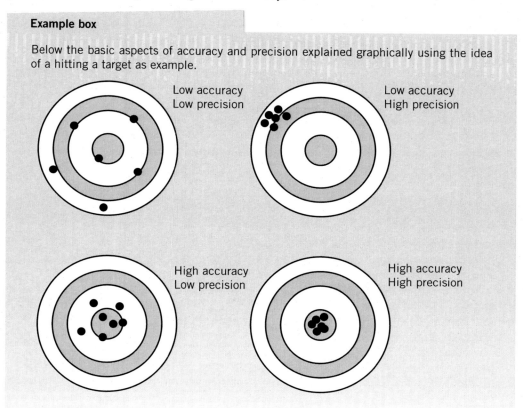

While reliability does not imply validity, a lack of reliability does place a limit on the overall validity of a test. A test that is not perfectly reliable cannot be perfectly valid either as a means of measuring attributes of a person or as a means of predicting scores on a criterion. While a reliable test may provide useful valid information, a test that is not reliable cannot possibly be valid. An example frequently used to illustrate the difference between reliability and validity in the experimental sciences involves a common bathroom scale. If someone who weighs 86 kilograms steps on a scale 10 times and gets readings of 15, 90, 74, 96, etc., the scale is not reliable. If the scale consistently reads '78', then it is reliable, but not valid, since it is consistent but not accurate. If it reads '86' each time, then the measurement is both reliable and valid.[19]

Validity

Does the methodology and methods employed actually allow the researcher to measure what it is supposed to? Validity considers the extent to which an assessment (or a question or a scale) measures what the researcher wants it to measure. There are several forms of validity of which we will look at three, namely construct validity, face validity and content validity.

- **Construct validity** is probably the most well-known form of validity and needs special attention. Construct validity refers to the degree to which inferences can legitimately be made from the operationalisations in the study (such as the measuring instruments) to the theoretical constructs on which those operationalisations were based. Construct validity is related to generalising and involves generalising from your measures to the concept of your measures.

    Construct validity refers to how well an assessment, or topics within an assessment, measure the constructs that the assessment was designed to measure. For example, if the construct to be measured is 'sales knowledge and skills', then the assessment designed to measure this construct should show evidence of actually measuring this 'sales knowledge and skills' construct.

    Regardless of how construct validity is defined, there is no single best way to study it. In most cases, construct validity should be looked at from a number of viewpoints. Hence, the more strategies used to demonstrate the validity of an assessment, the more confidence researchers have in the construct validity of that assessment, but only if the evidence provided by those strategies is convincing.

    In short, the construct validity of a questionnaire should be demonstrated by an accumulation of evidence. For example, taking the unified definition of construct validity, we could demonstrate it using content analysis, correlation coefficients, factor analysis, ANOVA studies demonstrating differences between differential groups or pretest-posttest intervention studies, multi-trait/multi-method studies, etc. Naturally, doing all of the above would be a tremendous amount of work. So, the amount of work a group of test developers is willing to put into demonstrating the construct validity of their test is directly related to the number of such demonstrations they can provide. Smart test developers will stop when they feel they have provided a convincing set of validity arguments.

- **Face validity** checks whether the contents of the assessment or the procedure look like (on face value) they are measuring what they are supposed to measure. It is the validity of an assessment at face value. In other words, an assessment can be said to have face validity if it 'looks like' it is going to measure what it is supposed to measure.

- **Content validity** (or logical validity) refers to whether the content of the assessment or procedure adequately represents all that is required for validity, or the extent to which the measure represents all facets of a given construct. Content validity includes any validity strategies that focus on the content of the assessment. To demonstrate content validity, researchers investigate the degree to which an assessment is a representative sample of the content of whatever objectives or specifications the assessment was originally designed to measure. One strategy that researchers employ to assess content validity, is to ask people who are knowledgeable about the content area, also referred to as experts, to review the question pool and confirm if it covers all potential dimensions.[20]

6.3.4.7 Importance of pilot testing to assess reliability and validity

Before commencing with data gathering, it is best to conduct a pilot test of the questionnaire to assist in refining the questionnaire so that the data gathered meet acceptable levels of validity and to some extent reliability. Any problems in the survey process, as well as measurement should be identified during the pilot test.

The pilot test can involve people that are considered knowledgeable and experts in the subject area, as well as potential respondents to review the question set to determine if there are any omissions of key topic areas. Experts can check question formulation and if the instrument meets the requirements for validity. Potential respondents can be involved to provide insight into establishing if all the words are understood by respondents and if all questions are interpreted similarly by all respondents. This step is referred to as cognitive interviewing.[21] Lastly, it might also be a good idea for a survey statistician to check and evaluate the questionnaire against the data analysis plan developed by the researcher.

There are also other advantages of conducting a pilot test, which are discussed below.
- Getting a sense of how long the questionnaire will take to complete.
- Confirming clarity of instructions, in both the case of face-to-face and questionnaire-based interviews.
- Ensuring that lists of items and categories are mutually exclusive and exhaustive.
- Testing whether any questions are unclear or ambiguous. This also relates to confirming whether certain words used actually mean what the researcher intended.
- Testing the assumption that respondents will be able to recall past behaviour if covered in the question set.
- Testing the assumption that respondents have a presumed knowledge of a particular subject area if covered in the question set.
- Ensuring that the researcher has the same understanding of the wording as the respondents.
- Checking for the use of uncomplicated and clear language.
- Determining which, if any, questions respondents feels uneasy to answer.
- Checking whether the layout is clear and attractive.
- Checking where a response category such as 'Don't know' or 'Not applicable' must be included, if validity in measurement can be maintained. A pilot test involving 30 to 50 respondents can provide preliminary data allowing for some basic statistical analysis and getting a 'feel' for the variation in the data, as well as for checking that the proposed analyses will work.
- Verifying if visual aids are effective or if visual aids should be used in the case of personal interviews.
- Anticipating and sorting out any technical problems that could occur when technology is involved in the survey process.
- Checking if problems are experienced in the recording and capturing of responses.
- Ascertaining if questions are really necessary, or just interesting (which should be avoided). Each question should be linked with or mapped to a specific research objective, question or hypothesis to be tested.

6.3.5 Step 5: Data capturing, coding and editing (including imputation)

Following the collection of the data, it is captured into a database that can be further interrogated and analysed. MS Excel or more specialised statistical programs like IBM SPSS can be used to assist in this process. Quality control is critical during the process of data capturing and data capturing errors must be avoided at all times. Editing must therefore take place to identify missing, invalid or inconsistent entries. These entries can then be corrected or rejected before analysis of the data starts.

6.3.6 Step 6: Data analysis

This step involves the analysis of the data in order to make sense of the variation in the data. In essence, it is about summarising the data so it can be interpreted and provide answers to the research questions and address the research questions. Many researchers regard this step as the heart of the study, since the correct analysis of the data and interpretation of results are critical to the success of the study.

Chapter 8 deals with the statistical analysis of data more in detail.

6.3.7 Step 7: Data dissemination and documentation

At this step, the researcher provides a detailed and complete account of the survey process and the findings that emanate from it. Decisions that were made and the rigour of the design should be argued in order to support the reliability and validity of the survey. The researcher must also, after reflecting, highlight any possible limitations, as well as imperatives for future research.

6.4 Sources of errors in surveys

Surveys, in general, are subject to errors. If a researcher is ignorant of these errors and they make their way into a survey, it can produce results that are meaningless. Errors must therefore be anticipated and the necessary effort made during the design and implementation phases to minimise survey errors.

A survey is essentially subject to two types of errors, namely sampling error and non-sampling error. Sampling error is introduced into the survey as a result of measuring only a portion of the population rather than the entire population, i.e. due to the sampling process. Census surveys therefore do not exhibit any sampling errors. By increasing the sample size, the sampling error usually reduces. Researchers must also consider the sample design as some designs are more favourable to smaller error (e.g. probability sampling).

Two main sources of errors seen in survey research relate to measurement errors and data processing errors.

Measurement errors may result from:
- Incomplete sampling frame (missing entries, incorrect entries or duplications)
- Poor design of data collection instrument (e.g. questionnaire)
- Employing unreliable or inconsistent data collection method (including observer bias)
- Respondent or interviewer bias resulting in incorrect responses given and recorded.

This might be the result of misunderstanding on the part of the respondent or interviewer, originating from:
- use of technical jargon
- lack of concept clarification
- poorly worded questions and/or instructions given for question completion
- inadequate interviewer training
- false information given by respondent due to inability to recall past behaviour or memory
- language barrier
- inconsistent translation when several languages are used.
• Missing data for some respondents
• Applying incorrect imputation methods to provide substitutes for missing values.

Data processing errors may result from:
• Inconsistent data coding and coder bias
• Poorly trained and inexperienced data capturers leading to incorrect and/or inconsistent data capturing.

6.5 Summary

As was noted in Chapter 5, research is about making choices to suit the research problem and the circumstances of the researcher. This is true in the case of planning and executing a survey as research strategy for collecting quantitative data.

This chapter first looked that the most common characteristics associated with a survey. In particular, it was noted that a survey is regarded as a research strategy and not a research method. Different methods can be employed as part of the survey strategy.

Next, the various steps in the design of a survey were reviewed. Aspects of the process included sampling, data collection, data handling, data analysis and reporting. None of these steps stand in isolation and the researcher must decide how they can contribute to addressing the research objectives. Particular emphasis was given to data collection methods and the design of a questionnaire.

Lastly, sources of error in surveys were briefly discussed.

Moving from conceptualising to operationalising research takes careful planning and constant reflection. We hope that this chapter can contribute towards your endeavours to conduct a successful survey.

Key terms and concepts

survey: a research strategy associated with the collection of quantitative data by means of interviews, administering of questionnaires and structured observation

unit of analysis: the subjects or entities being studied and reported on; differs from unit of observation

unit of observation: in business research, the unit of analysis might be the business entity being studied, with data about the business being collected from the owner. The latter constitute the unit of observation

Questions for review and critical thinking

1. What are the specific characteristics associated with a survey strategy?
2. There are a number of steps in the design of a survey. Name and briefly discuss these steps by referring to the various underlying elements in each step.
3. Suppose you are a post-graduate student that must complete a research study as part of completing your course. Compare and contrast the different data collection methods.
4. Discuss the various considerations when designing a questionnaire.
5. How can a pilot study contribute towards establishing acceptable reliability and validity of the survey questionnaire?

Research activities

Use an online library or Google Scholar to find a research dissertation (such as a Masters or Doctoral dissertation) or research article that used a survey strategy as part of the research design. Critically evaluate the justification of the strategy that was used.

Case study

Richard is a marketing research manager in a telecommunications company, and he is extremely worried. His boss has asked him what their company's market share in the business market is, and he did not have an answer. His boss was clearly not impressed, and Richard went searching for information on the internet and in their company library, with little success. He is wondering if it would be possible to determine the market share by doing a survey and to get on a better footing with his boss. He decides to have a discussion about the matter with his team. After the discussion, Richard feels a bit more at ease. His team has assured him that a survey could help to address the question. However, they have warned him that it will most likely require a substantial amount of time and money, two resources that he does not have a lot of. But, he muses, there is no use procrastinating, it is time to sit down and do some planning. After all, successful surveys depend on proper planning.

Questions
1. Identify the problem statement and research objectives for the study.
2. What are the definitions of the key constructs in the study?
3. What are your recommendations with regard to a sample design? Why?
4. How would you recommend the data be collected? Why?
5. Design a one page questionnaire that will address your research questions.

References

1. Saunders, M., Lewis, P. & Thornhill, A. 2009. *Research methods for business students*. 5th ed. UK: Pearson Education.
2. Leedy, P.D. & Ormrod, J.E. 2010. *Practical research: Planning and design*. 9th Ed. New

Jersey: Pearson Education.
3   Skinner, J., Edwards, A. & Corbett, B. 2015. *Research methods for sport management.* New York: Routledge.
4   Saunders, M., Lewis, P. & Thornhill, A. 2009. *Research methods for business students.* 5th ed. UK: Pearson Education.
5   Wiid, J. & Diggines, C. 2009. *Marketing Research.* Cape Town: Juta.
6   Ibid.
7   Ellis, T.J. & Levy, Y. 2008. Framework of problem-based research: A guide for novice researchers on the development of a research-worthy problem. Informing Science: *International Journal of an Emerging Transdiscipline,* 11:17–33.
8   Leedy, P.D. & Ormrod, J.E. 2010. *Practical research: Planning and design.* 9th ed. New Jersey: Pearson Education.
9   Babbie, E. 2016. *The practice of social research.* 14th ed. USA: Cengage Learning.
10 Skinner, J., Edwards, A. & Corbett, B. 2015. *Research methods for sport management.* New York: Routledge.
11 Du Plooy, G.M. 2009. *Communication research: Techniques, methods and applications.* 2nd ed. Cape Town: Juta.
12 Leedy, P.D. & Ormrod, J.E. 2010. *Practical research: Planning and design.* 9th ed. New Jersey: Pearson Education.
13 Stephens, C.S., Ledbetter, W.N., Mitra, A. & Ford, F.N. 1992. Executive or Functional Manager? The Nature of the CIO's Job. *MIS Quarterly,* 16(4): 449–467.
14 DeVellis, R.F. 2003. *Scale development: Theory and applications.* UK: Sage Publications.
15 Saunders, M., Lewis, P. & Thornhill, A. 2009. *Research methods for business students.* 5th ed. UK: Pearson Education.
16 A lot of discourse can be found in the literature on the use of dichotomous scoring vs. four vs. five vs. seven or 10-point rating scales. This chapter doesn't address this aspect but it is advised that the various applications, contexts and measurements be considered.
17 Machleit, K.A., Eroglu, S.A. & Mantel, S.P. 2000. Perceived Retail Crowding and Shopping Satisfaction: What Modifies This Relationship? *Journal of Consumer Psychology,* 9(1): 29–42.
18 Several approaches can be followed and various statistics calculated to evaluate the reliability of our data when working with surveys. Irrespective of the approaches and statistics we use and calculate, it is important to realise that we can never prove 100% that our data is perfectly reliable. Rather we offer evidence through the statistics we calculate (as estimates of some aspect of reliability, e.g. internal consistency when working with scales) that our data is of **acceptable** reliability. More about the approaches and statistics we calculate in Chapter 8.
19 In this example we must also realise that if we would have used a common bathroom scale (mechanical or electronic), the scale itself serves only as measuring tool and at best only provides a proxy measure for the construct of 'weight'.
20 DeVellis, R.F. 2003. *Scale development: Theory and applications.* UK: Sage Publications.
21 Barry, A.E., Chaney, E.H., Stellefson, M.L. and Chaney, J. 2011. So you want to develop a survey: practical recommendations for scale development. *American Journal of Health Studies,* 26(2): 97–105.

QUANTITATIVE DATA ANALYSIS TECHNIQUES IN RESEARCH

7

Dion van Zyl
René Pellissier

AFTER STUDYING THIS CHAPTER, YOU SHOULD BE ABLE TO:
- Recognise the main steps in analysing quantitative data
- Assess the reliability of scales measuring underlying constructs
- Select appropriate statistics to describe individual variables
- Select appropriate tests and statistics to examine relationships between variables and identify difference between groups.

Daisy is staring at the dataset containing all the captured responses from the questionnaires that were completed as part of her academic studies. It feels as if the numbers are swimming in front of her on the screen.

"Where do I start, I am not a statistician?" "How can I make sense of my data?" These are questions that many students and researchers ask when it comes to analysing their data. Conducting statistical analysis is for many a daunting (and frightening) task and I am sure has caused many sleepless nights, including for Daisy. However, as with the other phases in the research processes, a systematic approach is also required for the data analysis. Daisy decides to take a piece of paper and write down the various steps that she needs to follow to first ensure that the data have no data capturing errors. Secondly, she will try and assess the reliability of the scales she included in her questionnaire. After that, she will conduct some preliminary analysis to help her determine the main responses obtained per question. Lastly, she will decide on the most appropriate statistics and tests to use in order to address her research objectives.

7.1 Introduction

In this chapter, we want to offer you a systematic and stepwise approach to analysing your data. Despite many textbooks discussing and explaining how to calculate and conduct statistical analysis, it doesn't always give us guidance on where to start. The approach presented in this chapter has formed the blueprint for many researchers and students over the years and helped them stay focussed on addressing the specific research objectives of their studies. Each research study is unique, but we can identify some common steps and phases in the research process, including that of analysing our data. I have found that when students take a step-by-step approach it helps them gain confidence in their ability to understand what they are busy with, as well as gaining insight into the variation in the data. The latter is ultimately what we as researchers are interested in, as it will help us in support of the findings and conclusions we present.

Having depicted our intentions with the data analysis when we developed our research proposal, it is seldom specific up to the point when we actually engage with the data. This chapter therefore aims to provide you with a systematic process in guiding you through the data analysis.

But before we continue, let's just take a moment to think what it is that we want to accomplish with our data analysis. Having devoted time and effort in gathering data, it is mostly in a raw form. As such, it is basically meaningless. Furthermore, it resides in either electronic format or it might even still be in paper format, where responses were captured onto the survey instrument. Irrespective, the aim of the data analysis is to give meaning to the data so that you, as researcher, can draw appropriate and justifiable conclusions. Quantitative data analysis techniques such as calculation of statistics, constructing of summary tables, creating graphs and employing advanced statistical analysis techniques will help us to explore, describe, present and examine relationships and trends within our data.[1]

Although many of the statistics we produce will be interesting, the question must always be asked "so what?" At the end, the data must, firstly, provide evidence or insight into addressing the research objectives. That is, research deals not only with data gathering and data analysis, but more importantly, with interpretation. Secondly, it can alert the researcher to new insights that might not have been thought of initially, but can add value in understanding the phenomenon being studied.

Two main types of statistics help us achieve the goals of making our data meaningful, namely descriptive and inferential statistics. The aforementioned intend to describe the data with summary statistics, such as percentages, means, medians and charts, but do not attempt to draw conclusions about the population from which the sample was taken. Conversely, with inferential statistics, the aim is to produce statistics that can be used to test a hypothesis and draw conclusions about the population your sample was drawn from. Having said this, many studies use non-probability sampling techniques as part of data collection. This does not restrict hypothesis testing, but caution must be given by the researcher when generalising the original study population, as a non-probability sampling process might have produced a sample that is not representative anymore of the original population defined.

The next section discusses the various steps that can guide a researcher in analysing quantitative data.

7.2 A step-wise approach to analysing your data and reporting the results

This section provides a roadmap or systematic approach to analysing your data. Figure 7.1 presents this step-wise process.

PREPARE YOUT DATA FOR ANALYSIS (Section 7.2.1)

- Selecting a suitable statistical program
- Data coding and code book
- Database design and capturing
- Data cleaning (checking for errors and assessing missing values)

ASSESSING SCALE RELIABILITY (Section 7.2.2)

CONDUCTING PRELIMINARY DATA ANALSYSIS (Section 7.2.3)

- Univariate vs. bi-variate variables
- Categorical and continuous data
- Modifying variables for further analysis

Exploring relationships amongst variables (**Section 7.2.4**)
- Correlation analysis
- Regression analysis
- Exploratory factor analysis
- Confirmatory factor analysis
- Structural equation modelling

Comparing groups (**Section 7.2.5**)
- Chi-square test of independence
- Two independent samples test
- Paired samples test
- Multiple independent samples test

Figure 7.1 Roadmap to analysing data

The first step we will look at is that of preparing your data for analysis.

7.2.1 Step 1: Preparing your data for analysis

In preparing your data for analysis, the researcher must address four main activities, namely choosing a suitable statistical software package as tool to analyse the data, coding the responses, designing the database and capturing the responses and, lastly, checking the database for any errors. These activities are discussed next.

7.2.1.1 Selecting a suitable statistical program to analyse your data

One of the first decisions that you as researcher will have to take is what software package to use. A package like MS Excel® is convenient and provides a user-friendly option for data entry. With Excel certain conditional formatting can also be set to guide data capturing, for example, to highlight cells that fall outside certain parameters (e.g. a code 3 would be invalid if code 1 and 2 are the only valid response options). It furthermore provides options for calculating basic **descriptive statistics**, constructing pivot tables and running some limited statistical analysis such as correlation analysis and hypothesis testing (through the Data Analysis Toolpak).

More advanced statistical analysis packages like IBM SPSS, SAS/STAT and Stata are all part of an abundance of options available to researchers. When reviewing academic articles, the researchers typically indicate what software they have used and this can guide the decision-making process. There are also plenty of free statistical packages available from the internet. More advanced statistical packages that are used for specific types of analysis must also be evaluated. The recommendation to researchers has always been to first establish if the institution they work for or are enrolled at does not provide such software to students. Consulting with a statistician in some instances is also a good idea.

Practical questions you therefore need to ask are what packages are available to you and how much time and money can you invest to learn how to use these packages and the statistical techniques? It is crucial to remember that the statistical package is just the tool and does not make decisions relating to what statistics to calculate. This will depend on your current statistical background, as well as your experience in the specific type of analysis required to address your research questions. Ask your academic institution what training and support they provide to students to assist in conducting statistical analysis. Platforms like statistics.com and Coursera are two of the platforms that also offer statistical training, paid and free. In many instances, it is not about the package, as most of them have very similar algorithms driving the analysis, but about the statistical technique. Even a source like YouTube.com can provide valuable hands-on guidance and videos are regularly uploaded from leading academic institutions. But let's be realistic, to be fluent in statistical analysis takes time and plenty of guiding and exercising to understand what is the right statistic or technique to use. Critically, it is not just running analysis, but more importantly how to interpret and report the results. Justifying the choice of technique and statistic in the context of your research objectives are vital to establish rigour and credibility.

7.2.1.2 Data coding

Before entering data into the selected database, such as MS Excel® or IBM SPSS®, a **code book** must be prepared. This code book provides guidelines on the definitions of each of the variables and how they should be labelled. It also indicates how codes, typically in number format, are assigned to the possible responses. A statistical package like IBM SPSS allows for both variable labels and response codes (also called value labels) to be entered into the database to make statistical output more understandable and user-friendly. Other statistical packages might just require numerical codes to analyse the data.

When preparing a code book, it is also useful to distinguish between the different types of data. That is categorical (i.e. nominal and ordinal) and continuous (i.e. interval and ratio) data (see Chapter 6). In a package like IBM SPSS, the type of data must be specified (nominal, ordinal or continuous).

The coding process is sometimes different when working with categorical or continuous data. For example, some data are inherently numerical (continuous), such as age or distance. These values can be entered directly into the database and do not need to be coded. However, when conducting statistical analysis, the researcher might decide to create logical ordinal categories from these variables (i.e. **binning**). The decisions relating to the deriving of categories are often only taken after the frequency distribution of the data was inspected and a rationale presented for binning. The rationale might be related to sample size (i.e. deriving three equal-sized groups with sufficient subsamples), or based on certain logical ranges (i.e. lower and upper cut-points) relevant to the variable that you are studying. The latter might be guided by logic or theory.

Variables that are categorical, such as gender or province, can be easily quantified by assigning codes to the various response categories, e.g. male = 1 and female = 2. Two important decisions must be taken by the researcher. Firstly, when variables will serve as dummy variables for some statistical analysis procedure, such as linear regression, then it is better to assign binary codes to the response options (e.g. no = 0 and yes = 1). This aids, for example, in the interpretation of coefficients and making sense of how the data behaves. Secondly, the researcher must ascertain that all responses are assigned a unique code. Similarly, as in the case of creating logical groups when working with continuous data, decisions relating to the collapsing of groups are often only taken after the frequency distribution of the responses were inspected and a rationale was presented for collapsing of groups.[2]

Example box

The table shows an example of a code book.

Variable	SPSS variable name	Coding instructions	Type of data
ID number	ID	Unique number assigned to each case	-
Gender	Q1_gender	1 = Male 2 = Female	Nominal
Age	Q2_age	Age in years	Ratio
Highest level of education	Q3_edcuation	1 = No schooling 2 = Some primary schooling 3 = Primary school completed 4 = Some high school 5 = Matric (Grade 12) 6 = Post-matric certificate/diploma 7 = University degree	Ordinal
Perceived Stress Scale	Stress1 Stress2 Stress3 Stress4 Stress5 Stress6 Stress7 Stress8 Stress9 Stress10	1 = Never 2 = Almost never 3 = Sometimes 4 = Fairly often 5 = Very often Items to be reversed coded: 4, 5, 7 and 8 Scale construction: Summate items Range of scale: 10 to 50 Interpretation: Higher values indicating higher levels of perceived stress	Ordinal

Researchers that are working with scales (or indexes), like the Perceived Stress Scale[3] (Stress1 to Stress10), must also include in their code book the operations to derive the measure associated with the scale (or index). That is, what should be done by the researcher to operationalise the measurement? Can item responses just be added together to create a summated scale? Or should certain weights be applied to items before scale measures can be calculated? Are there any items that must be reversed coded? For example, the Perceived Stress Scale items 4, 5, 7 and 8 must be reversed coded and then added with items 1, 2, 3, 6, 9 and 10. The range of the scale is 10 to 50 with higher values indicating higher levels of perceived stress.

Example box

Another example of a scale is the SAARF LSM. The living standard measure (LSM) was developed by the South African Audience Research Foundation (SAARF) with the aim of providing a scale measure that could distinguish living standards.[4] By asking certain questions to respondents (i.e. if they own or have access to a specific item in the household), coding these responses and applying a certain weighting, positive or negative, a single LSM scale measure is calculated for each respondent by means of plugging in the weights and response codes into an equation. This scale measure therefore provides an index value placing respondents on a continuum in terms of the degree of living standard. Higher values are associated with higher degrees of living standard and lower values with lower degrees. Furthermore, guidelines are provided based on cut-points how to convert the continuous scale measures into more homogenous groups or segments. These instructions must preferably be included in the code book as it constitutes an existing scale.

Variable number	Attribute	Weight
1	Hot running water from a geyser	0.185224
2	Computer – Desktop/Laptop	0.311118
3	Electric stove	0.163220
4	No domestic workers or household helpers in household	–0.301327
5	0 or 1 radio set in household	–0.245001
6	Flush toilet in/outside house	0.113306
7	Motor vehicle in household	0.167310
8	Washing machine	0.149009
9	Refrigerator or combined fridge/freezer	0.134133
10	Vacuum cleaner/floor polisher	0.164736
11	Pay TV (M-Net/DStv) subscription	0.127360
12	Dishwashing machine	0.212562
13	Three or more cellphones in household	0.184676
14	Two cellphones in household	0.124007
15	Home security service	0.151623

continued →

16	Deep freezer – free standing	0.116673
17	Microwave oven	0.126409
18	Rural resident (excluding Western Cape and Gauteng rural)	-0.129361
19	House/cluster house/town house	0.113907
20	DVD player/Blue Ray Player	0.096070
21	Tumble drier	0.166056
22	Home theatre system	0.096072
23	Home telephone (excluding cellphone)	0.104531
24	Swimming pool	0.166031
25	Tap water in house/on plot	0.123015
26	Built-in kitchen sink	0.132822
27	TV set	0.120814
28	Air conditioner (excluding fans)	0.178044
29	Metropolitan dweller (250 000+)	0.079321

The weights are summated for those variables with which the respondent complies. A constant of –0.810519 is added, and based on the total summated weights; a respondent is then grouped into one of the 10 LSM segments, depending on the defined ranges.

LSM Group	Total weight
1	Less than –1.390140
2	–1.390140 to –1.242001
3	–1.242000 to –1.011801
4	–1.011800 to –0.691001
5	–0.691000 to –0.278001
6	–0.278000 to 0.381999
7	0.382000 to 0.800999
8	0.801000 to 1.168999
9	1.169000 to 1.744999
10	More than 1.744999

Source: South African Advertising Research Foundation. 2009. *The SAARF AMPS Living Standards Measure (LSM)*. [Online] Available from: http://www.saarf.co.za/AMPS/technicalreport-2009A/data%20files/Technical/21+22.pdf Reprinted by permission of SAARF.

The coding of responses obtained from open-ended questions is a bit more complicated. Take, for example, a question that probes employees across selective corporate companies in terms of major sources of work stress: What is the major source of stress in your working environment? The approach of coding typically starts with reviewing the responses and identifying common themes. These themes might be subjective to the researcher or might be guided by past research and/or theory. Decisions relating to the granularity or detail of the themes and subthemes must be made and these used as a guide in coding responses. For example, codes can be: unrealistic deadlines and expectations = 1, technology overload = 2; being understaffed = 3; isolation at work = 4; bullying and harassment = 5; and so on. Codes 1 to 3 can, however, also represent a theme like 'job overload' and codes 4 and 5 a theme like 'work relationships'. It all depends on the detail required during coding. It is also important to add another numerical code for responses that did not fall into these listed categories (e.g. other = 99).

Even though the code book must be specific to guide the initial process of data base design and capturing (or data importing), it is best to allow for as much granularity as possible in the data. It is therefore better to capture the age of respondents in years (if possible during the data collection phase) and then later on decide how best to categorise them meaningfully for analysis purposes. However, if the data are coded into relatively few categories and you are not allowing for the capturing of the original data, there will be no way to recreate the original detail during analysis.

7.2.1.3 Database design and capturing

Next, the process of designing the actual database can commence. Each variable must be created and where details are required it must be specified. Variables are typically assigned to columns and cases to rows. The software you will be using will, however, provide the specifics. The code book provides the guidelines for creating the database in relation to the variables and measurements. In some instances, online data collection platforms such as SurveyMonkey™ or Qualtrics™ provide options for exporting data into formats compatible with MS Excel or IBM SPSS. Similarly, when dealing with secondary data being extracted from an existing database, options for data export formats would be provided. Nonetheless, the database and variables need to be checked in relation to the code book.

> **Example box**
>
> Below is an extract of the layout of a database. Rows are used for respondents and columns for variables. In this example only the codes were captured, e.g. "1" for male and "2" for female.
>
> | id | Q1_gender | Q2_age | Q3_education | Stress1 | Stress2 | Stress3 | Stress4 | Stress5 | Stress6 | Stress7 | Stress8 | Stress9 | Stress10 |
> |---|---|---|---|---|---|---|---|---|---|---|---|---|---|
> | 1 | 1 | 37 | 6 | 4 | 4 | 5 | 2 | 1 | 4 | 3 | 2 | 5 | 5 |
> | 2 | 1 | 27 | 4 | 4 | 3 | 3 | 5 | 3 | 3 | 4 | 4 | 5 | 1 |
> | 3 | 1 | 31 | 3 | 4 | 3 | 4 | 3 | 3 | 3 | 3 | 3 | 4 | 4 |
> | 4 | 2 | 52 | 6 | 3 | 2 | 3 | 4 | 3 | 2 | 4 | 4 | 3 | 2 |
> | 5 | 2 | 64 | 6 | 3 | 2 | 3 | 4 | 3 | 2 | 5 | 4 | 2 | 1 |
> | 6 | 1 | 35 | 3 | 3 | 3 | 3 | 3 | 2 | 3 | 3 | 2 | 4 | 2 |
> | 7 | 1 | 22 | 3 | 3 | 3 | 4 | 3 | 1 | 3 | 2 | 2 | 4 | 4 |
> | 8 | 2 | 23 | 3 | 2 | 2 | 2 | 4 | 4 | 2 | 4 | 4 | 3 | 2 |
> | 9 | 2 | 56 | 6 | 3 | 3 | 3 | 4 | 4 | 3 | 3 | 4 | 3 | 2 |
> | 10 | 2 | 24 | 4 | 2 | 3 | 3 | 4 | 3 | 3 | 4 | 2 | 2 | 2 |
> | 11 | 2 | 36 | 5 | 2 | 2 | 2 | 4 | 4 | 2 | 4 | 4 | 3 | 2 |
> | 12 | 2 | 37 | 5 | 3 | 4 | 3 | 4 | 4 | 5 | 4 | 4 | 3 | 2 |
> | 13 | 2 | 50 | 5 | 2 | 3 | 3 | 4 | 4 | 3 | 4 | 4 | 3 | 2 |
> | 14 | | 37 | 3 | 4 | 5 | 5 | 4 | 5 | 5 | 3 | 4 | 5 | 5 |
> | 15 | 1 | 40 | 5 | 2 | 2 | 3 | 4 | 5 | 2 | 3 | 4 | 2 | 1 |
> | 16 | 1 | 27 | 4 | 2 | 4 | 5 | 3 | 3 | 2 | 4 | 3 | 3 | 1 |
> | 17 | 1 | 51 | 4 | 3 | 3 | 4 | 4 | 2 | 3 | 2 | 3 | 4 | 4 |
> | 18 | 2 | 23 | 4 | 3 | 5 | 2 | 5 | 5 | 2 | 4 | 5 | 2 | 2 |
> | 19 | 1 | 37 | 2 | 3 | 2 | 3 | 4 | 3 | 3 | 4 | 4 | 2 | 2 |
> | 20 | 1 | 19 | 2 | 4 | 4 | 4 | 2 | 1 | 4 | 2 | 2 | 4 | 4 |
> | 21 | 2 | 48 | 6 | 3 | 2 | 4 | 4 | 4 | 3 | 3 | 4 | 3 | 2 |
>
> If the response labels were captured in the database it would appear as follow:
>
> continued →

| id | Q1_gender | Q2_age | Q3_education | Stress level ||||||||||
				1	2	3	4	5	6	7	8	9	10
1	Male	37	Post matric certificate/ diploma	FO	FO	VO	AN	N	FO	S	AN	VO	VO
2	Male	27	Some high school	FO	S	S	VO	S	S	FO	FO	VO	N
3	Male	31	Primary school completed	FO	S	FO	S	S	S	S	S	FO	FO
4	Female	52	Post matric certificate/ diploma	S	AN	S	FO	S/AN	AN	FO	FO	S	AN
5	Female	64	Post matric certificate/diploma	S	AN	S	FO	S	AN	VO	FO	AN	N
6	Male	35	Primary school completed	S	S	S	S	AN	S	S	AN	FO	AN
7	Male	22	Primary school completed	S	S	FO	S	N	S	AN	AN	FO	FO
8	Female	23	Primary school completed	AN	AN	AN	FO	FO	AN	FO	FO	S	AN
9	Female	54	Post matric certificate/diploma	S	S	S	FO	FO	S	S	FO	S	AN
10	Female	24	Some high school	AN	S	S	FO	S	S	FO	AN	AN	AN
11	Female	36	Matric (Grade 12)	AN	AN	AN	FO	FO	AN	FO		S	AN
12	Female	37	Matric (Grade 12)	S	FO	S	FO	FO	VO	FO	FO	S	AN
13	Female	50	Matric (Grade 12)	AN	S	S	FO	FO	S	FO	FO	S	AN
14	Male	57	Primary school completed	FO	VO	VO	FO	VO	VO	S	FO	VO	VO
15	Male	40	Matric (Grade 12)	AN	AN	S	FO	VO	AN	S	FO	AN	N
16	Male	27	Some high school	AN	FO	VO	S	S	AN	FO	S	S	N
17	Female	51	Some high school	S	S	FO	FO	AN	S	AN	S	FO	FO
18	Male	23	Some high school	N	VO	AN	VO	VO	AN	FO	VO	AN	AN
19	Male	37	Some primary schooling	S	AN	S	FO	S	S	FO	FO	AN	AN
20	Male	19	Some primary schooling	FO	FO	FO	AN	N	FO	AN	AN	FO	FO
21	Female	48	Post matric certificate/diploma	N	AN	FO	FO	FO	S	S	FO	S	AN

KEY: N = Never | AN = Almost never | S = Sometimes | FO = Fairly often | VO = Very often

7.2.1.4 Data cleaning

The analysis of your data and subsequent results produced will be misleading if there are data capturing errors. Before starting with data analysis, it is therefore essential to check for any data capturing or other errors. For example, if a value of 55 was entered instead of the correct value of 5, it can provide seriously distorted statistics. This needs to be identified and if the original questionnaire or data capturing sheet is available it must be checked, verified and corrected. Do not neglect this initial process of checking for mistakes, as it would not only be embarrassing later on to confess that obvious errors were overseen, but it might be impossible to correct the data and subsequent analysis.

Obviously the initial phase of checking for errors will mostly be to scan the database visually. The preliminary analysis phase will also assist in the cleaning up of the dataset. By running frequency tables or calculating summary statistics (e.g. means, medians, minimum and maximum values) it can alert the researcher to possible errors and outliers.

The question that many students ask is what to do when the original questionnaire or data-capturing sheet shows an invalid response. In other words, the data was captured correctly but the response provided by the respondent was invalid. Similarly, if the database is assessed for missing values and it was found that a response was never obtained from the respondent. These scenarios do pose a problem as it asks questions about the control exerted during data collection and fieldwork. What supervision and quality control measures were enforced during the fieldwork phase? Why was the error or omission not identified at an earlier stage? Many studies are conducted under ethical guidelines of the academic institution and this requires anonymity of respondents. Going back to respondents is therefore not a possibility. Even if it was possible, time and money might restrict this corrective action.

The researcher should never just 'guess' what the response would have been. The only action to take is to exclude the value from the database and the variable will contain a missing value (either empty cell or assigned a specific code such as 'Missing value/ No information provided' = 999). The number of missing values should then be assessed in terms of the completeness of the dataset and the conclusions that can be drawn from the available data. Hopefully, the missing values will be limited and randomly distributed given a large sample size and therefore not impact the statistics produced. Some advanced statistical analyses do require data with no missing values. Careful consideration should be given to missing value imputation and should always be approached with caution. Statistical packages like IBM SPSS provide options for excluding missing values from the database. Two common approaches are listwise and pairwise deletion of cases. Listwise deletion excludes all cases from the analysis if a missing value is found in at least one specified variable. Pairwise deletion occurs when the statistical procedure does not exclude cases with missing values but only uses the available data on a variable-by-variable basis. Irrespective, the researcher should never just select the default settings in good faith without understanding what data are lost as it can result in seriously biased results!

In step 2 we will be looking at assessing the reliability of scales.

7.2.2 Step 2: Assessing scale reliability (internal consistency reliability)

When including a scale as part of measurement (e.g. Perceived Stress Scale[5]), it is important to assess the reliability of the scale. Two common indicators of scale reliability are test-retest reliability and internal consistency.[6] The aforementioned approach involves administering a scale to the same group of people on two different occasions and comparing the test-retest correlation between them. Higher levels of correlation are indicative of the scale being more reliable. But be aware that this approach might not be the best use for some scales. A scale that aims to measure levels of stress is not likely to remain stable over time. The statistics might therefore indicate low test-retest reliability, and this might be wrongly interpreted as poor scale reliability.

Internal consistency is the other aspect of reliability, and one that is more commonly addressed by researchers. When items in a scale are all measuring the same underlying construct, it is said to be internally consistent reliable.

This type of reliability can be measured in a number of ways, but calculating and assessing the Cronbach's alpha coefficient is the more frequent approach used. Values for the alpha statistic range from 0 to 1, with higher values indicating greater internal consistency reliability. A recommended minimum value for alpha is 0,7.[7] However, this recommended value needs to be used with caution as alpha values are dependent on the number of items in the scale (less than 10). Therefore researchers need to also calculate and report the mean correlation between items (i.e. inter-item correlation). Ideally the mean inter-item correlation values should fall between 0,2 to 0,5.

7.2.3 Step 3: Conducting preliminary analysis (univariate)

Once the database has been cleaned and the reliability of scales assessed (if included as part of the measurement), the process of conducting preliminary analysis can begin. The aim of this preliminary analysis is mainly to gain a 'feel' for the variation in the data. That is, to inspect the distribution of responses obtained, making decisions regarding the most appropriate statistic to report, if certain categories need to be collapsed, if variables meet the assumptions of the statistical techniques that you will use or if the data require some form of transformation. All of this contributes towards planning for conducting specific statistical analyses to address your research objectives. The preliminary analysis can always still alert us to data errors that might have been missed during the initial steps or outliers that can skew our results.

When dealing with statistics, being aware of the type of data you work with can greatly help you in choosing the correct statistic to calculate and statistical technique to use. For example, when working with categorical data (nominal and ordinal) it is appropriate to examine the distribution of frequencies by categories.

Example box

The table below reports the frequency distribution for the categorical (nominal) variable 'Gender'. It is important to inspect both the actual number of responses (reported in the column labelled 'n') and the frequency distribution (reported in the column labelled '%'). Also, take note of groups that might be over- or under-represented in relation to the population (if known of course). Matching sample characteristics with that of the population can contribute towards assessing external validity.

Category	n	%
Male	136	42,9%
Female	181	57,1%
Total	317	100,0%

When working with continuous data several descriptive statistics can be calculated. These include amongst other:
- mean, median and mode (measures of central tendency)
- minimum and maximum values, range, standard deviation and variance (measures of central dispersion)
- skewness and kurtosis (measures of shape).

The following are definitions for the various descriptive statistics:

If the values of each case for a continuous variable are added and divided by the number of cases then it represents **the mean value** (i.e. the 'average' value). The mean value is one of the most basic statistical models that researchers report and is an indicator of central tendency.

The median value on the other hand represents the middle value when all the values of a variable are arranged in rank order (i.e. the 'average' case). This statistic is often more appropriate to report (and representative of central tendency) when a distribution is **skewed** due to the effect of significant outliers.

The mode represents the value of a variable that occurs most frequently. Be aware of distributions where more than one mode value is evident. A distribution with two or more different modes is referred to as a multimodal distribution.

If the mean, median and mode have the same value and the data are equally distributed either side of the mode then the distribution is symmetrical (see Figure 7.2 for an illustration of this concept).

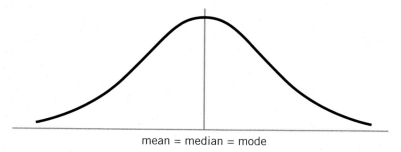
Figure 7.2 Symmetrical shape distribution

A special form of the symmetric distribution, where the data can be plotted as a bell-shaped curve (i.e. the distribution looks the same on both sides) is known as the **normal distribution** (see Figure 7.3). Around 68% of the observations lie within 1 standard deviation from the mean, around 95% of the observations lie within 2 standard deviations from the mean and around 99% lie within 3 standard deviations from the mean. Numerous continuous phenomena follow this shape. If, for example, we were to collect data from the whole population, the resulting distribution would closely resemble the normal distribution. Lastly, a normal distribution can be used to approximate various other distributions if the sample size becomes large enough.

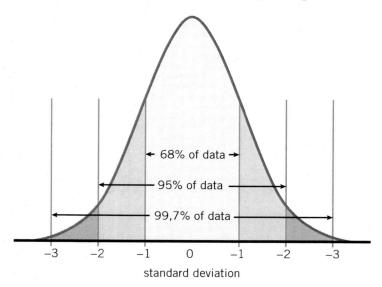
Figure 7.3 Normal distribution

The **minimum value** denotes the smallest value.

The **maximum value** denotes the largest value.

Range is the difference between the highest (maximum) and the lowest (minimum) values for a variable.

The **standard deviation** is a statistic that describes the extent of spread of data values around the mean for a variable containing numerical data.

The **variance** provides an estimate of the average variability of the data. Smaller variances are indicative of individual data values that are closer to the mean. The variance is equal to the square root of the standard deviation.

Skewness statistic gives an indication of the symmetry of the distribution. Perfectly normal distributions have a skewness of 0. If the statistic is positive (> 0), the distribution has values clustered to the left at lower value (with a tail to the right of the histogram), such as in Figure 7.4. If the statistic is negative (< 0), the distribution has values clustered to the right at lower value (with a tail to the left of the histogram), as in Figure 7.5.

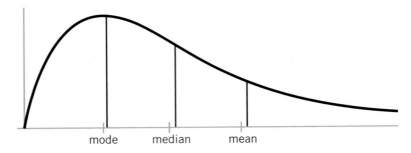

Figure 7.4 Distribution that is positively skewed

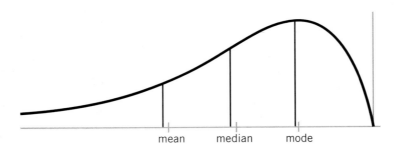

Figure 7.5 Distribution that is negatively skewed

Kurtosis provides information about the 'peakedness' of the distribution. Perfectly normal distributions have a kurtosis of 0 (also referred to as mesokurtic). If the kurtosis statistic is positive (> 0), then the distribution is rather peaked (also referred to as leptokurtic), with values clustered in the centre. If the statistic is negative (< 0), then the distribution is rather flat, with values more spread over the range (also referred to platykurtic). The different types of kurtosis are depicted in Figure 7.6.

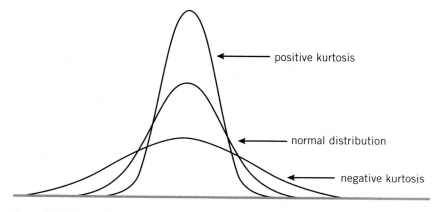

Figure 7.6 Types of kurtosis

Example box

The table below reports descriptive statistics for the continuous variable 'Age'. It is always important to take note of the number of cases and if any missing values are evident. Check each value and ask questions such as: Do the values make sense? What does it tell about the data and the sample? Is the mean close to the median and the mode? What about the kurtosis and skewness, are they different from the expected normal distribution values? Are the minimum and maximum values within the range of possible scores on that variable? Is the standard deviation small or large? What does it say about the accuracy, precision and extent of variation in the data?

Statistic	Value
N	317
Missing	0
Mean	45,38
Median	46,00
Mode	45
Std. Deviation	10,018
Variance	100,351
Skewness	0,080
Kurtosis	−0,149
Minimum	18
Maximum	73

A visual inspection of the distribution can equally contribute towards understanding the variation in the data. Below, the histogram of the data is presented. IBM SPSS, like some other statistical packages, also plots the expected normal curve given the parameters of the actual data. This helps to assess violations from normality.

continued →

It is evident from the statistics and the histogram that the mean, median and mode (measures of central tendency) are almost the same (i.e. very similar or identical) – in other words they are near the same point on the graph. The skewness statistic (measure of symmetry), although positive, is very close to zero. The kurtosis ('peakedness') is negative and is indicative of a distribution that is slightly less flat than what it is peaked (platykurtic). The minimum and maximum values (measures of central dispersion) are within range of what is expected for a variable such as 'Age'. Standard deviation and variation do not suggest excessive deviation from the mean. These statistics and the visual inspection therefore provide indication (and support) of a symmetrical shape that is very similar to what a normal distribution looks like.

It should be noted that though many statistical tests rely on the assumption of normality, it is not referring to the sample distribution alone, but also to the sampling distribution. Think of this distribution as the distribution of all possible means calculated from the population through infinite repetitive samples. Past statisticians have, for example, shown that as samples get big (usually defined as greater than 30) the sampling distribution has a normal distribution.[8] So, despite the sample distribution not being perfectly normally distributed, if the sample is sufficiently large, we can assume the sampling distribution will be approximately normally distributed (also referred to as the central limit theorem).

This allows us to proceed with certain statistical techniques requiring the assumption of normality of data. But my recommendation to students has always been to familiarise themselves with the assumptions and offer reasons why certain assumptions are adopted rather than just stating the assumptions being adopted.

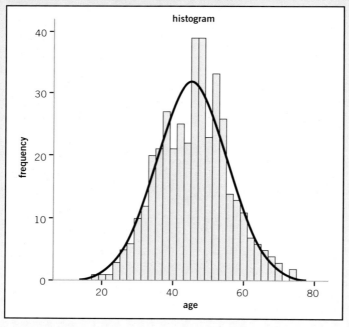

When samples are small (fewer than 30) the sampling distribution has a shape known as a t-distribution. T-tests therefore provide results that are often robust under conditions of small samples. In addition, procedures like bootstrapping and exact test also allow researchers to conduct selective statistical tests when samples might be small, sparse or unbalanced or if assumptions of normality are violated. Be sure to ask your statistician about these procedures.

Many researchers think of ordinal data like Likert-type response categories as purely categorical and do not regard the calculation of these types of descriptive statistics as valid. These statistics can contribute toward assessing the variation in the data. In other words, it is treated almost in a crude manner as interval-like data. But I have never just calculated these statistics without having visually inspected the frequency distribution of the variables (using a bar graph and not a histogram!). These two approaches together have often brought me great insight into the behaviour of the data, allowing me to draw meaningful conclusions.

Reflection

Did you know that the terms nominal, ordinal, interval and ratio were coined in the early 1940s by the Harvard psychologist Stevens? His idea was to provide a description of measurement scales used in psychophysics and to relate them to statistical procedures for which they were permissible. In the years that followed, this hierarchy or classification was adopted by many scholarly research and statistical textbooks and has become common reference points for research practitioners engaged in quantitative data analysis. Over time though, many statisticians have criticised this taxonomy, arguing that it restricts or bounds statistical analysis due its absoluteness. In other words, calculating descriptive statistics would not be appropriate when working with ordinal data.

However, in 1951 Stevens dismissed this idea, admitting that "As a matter of fact, most of the scales used widely and effectively by psychologists are ordinal scales. In the strictest propriety the ordinary statistics involving means and standard deviations ought not to be used with these scales … On the other hand, … there can be invoked a kind of pragmatic sanction: in numerous instances it leads to fruitful results."[9]

Source: Velleman, P. & Wilkinson, L. 1993. Nominal, Ordinal, Interval, and Ratio Typologies are Misleading. The American Statistician, 47(1): 65-72. Page 65, reprinted by permission of the publisher (Taylor & Francis Ltd, http://www.tandfonline.com).

Example box

When working with ordinal data we often treat it as interval-like data. That is, we calculate descriptive statistics to help us assess central tendency, dispersion and shape. But a visual assessment of the distribution of frequencies can often more quickly reveal interesting behaviour in the data.

The two frequency distributions below show very different variation in the data. Yet, two of the statistics dealing with measures of central tendency are similar (i.e. the mean and median = 3) as well as skewness (= 0,000). The differences only become apparent when examining the other statistics like the mode, the standard deviation and kurtosis! Therefore, researchers should look at all the descriptive statistics, and better still also inspect it visually.

continued →

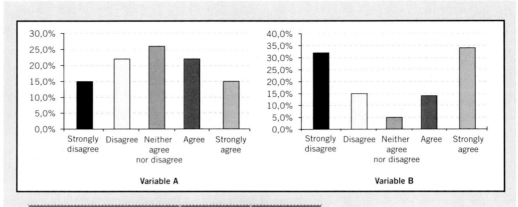

Statistic	Var A	Var B
n	100	100
Missing	0	0
Mean	3,00	3,00
Median	3,00	3,00
Mode	3	1 & 5
Std. Deviation	1,005	1,621
Variance	1,010	2,626
Skewness	0,000	0,000
Kurtosis	−0,022	−1,643
Minimum	1	1
Maximum	5	5

7.2.4 Step 4: Exploring relationships among variables and comparing groups (bivariate and multivariate)

The previous step in the process, namely conducting preliminary analysis, has mainly focused on constructing frequency distributions and calculating descriptive statistics for single variables (i.e. univariate analysis). For many studies, these statistics provide a lot of insight and assist to address some of our research objectives. But as researchers, we are also interested in more than just these top-level results. We ask questions such as:
- How are some variables related to others?
- Can the variation in one variable help explain the variation in another?
- Does the data show a positive linear relationship between variable A and variable B as postulated in the literature or theory?
- Can we predict the outcome of an event based on a specific set of variables?
- Can we identify the variables most likely to predict an outcome of an event?
- Is there a difference in the average measurements of two (or more) independent groups?
- Does one group measure higher (or lower) than another group for a specific variable?
- Is there a difference in the average score of a variable before or after an intervention?

These are but some of the very basic questions we ask, and they are primarily rooted in the purpose of our research, namely to describe a certain phenomenon we are interested in; to explore relationships or to explain causality between variables. The questions that some researchers ask can be very complicated at times. Whatever the reason, this will demand us to move beyond univariate analysis, and to conduct **bivariate** and **multivariate analysis**. Some of these statistical techniques are easy to understand, while others might require substantial reading, training and practice.

The sections that follow will look at some of the statistical techniques used for exploring relationships among variables and comparing groups. The idea is certainly not to present all the technical aspects of a technique or to derive and explain every formula and equation underlying the technique. There are quite a number of excellent textbooks that focus purely on the mathematics underpinning the statistical analysis, some general and others very specific to a particular technique. The idea is to introduce the technique here, what it typically is used for, the questions it tries to address, the data requirements and what the results tells us. Some basic examples will illustrate the application of the technique. This will hopefully broaden your awareness of some of the common techniques we use in business studies.

The next section considers if we need to explore relationships among variables.

7.2.4.1 Exploring relationships among variables

This section focusses on five analysis techniques researchers use to explore relationships among variables. These techniques are discussed superficially here, with the purpose of outlining the options available to researchers. For more extensive information, specialist sources should be consulted. It should be noted that techniques often have very specific data requirements, which researchers should ideally be aware of even before commencing with data collection. For example, Structural Equation Modelling may require large samples, which should inform the data collection process.

7.2.4.1.1 Correlation analysis

Correlation analysis is used to measure the direction and strength of the association between two numerical variables (called bi-variate correlation). The indication of which variable is the dependent and which is the independent is usually argued from a theoretical perspective and understanding of the phenomenon being studied.

One of the most useful techniques for gaining insight into the relationship between the two variables is a scatter plot. By visually examining the pattern, an assessment can be made if the two variables are correlated and if a specific trend is presented.

In addition to presenting the relationship visually, several statistics can be calculated to provide a measure of the direction and strength of the linear relationship. The type of statistic depends on the level of measurement. Two commonly used correlation statistics are the Pearson's product moment correlation coefficient and the Spearman's rank correlation coefficient. The aforementioned (Pearson) works if both the variables are interval and/or ratio data (continuous), but is also used if one variable is continuous and the other dichotomous (e.g. male and female or yes and no). The latter (Spearman) works with ordinal or ranked data, in particular if data is highly skewed.

The correlation coefficients (represented by r) range between −1 and +1. The sign (+ or −) indicates whether there is a positive correlation (an increase in one variable is met with an increase in the other) or a negative correlation (an increase in one variable is met with a decrease in the other). A coefficient of 0 is indicative of no linear relationship between the two variables. The higher the absolute value of the coefficient, the stronger the linear relationship. Coefficients with absolute values 0,10 to 0,29 are often classified as small, values 0,30 to 0,49 classified as medium and values 0,50 to 1 as large.[10]

It is important to realise that the Pearson and Spearman coefficients are measures of linear strength. Not all relationships are linear however. Curvilinear or nonlinear relationship can also exist. Outliers can also have an influence on the coefficients. It is therefore important to first inspect the relationship visually by means of a scatter plot.

Examples of scatter plots are presented below.

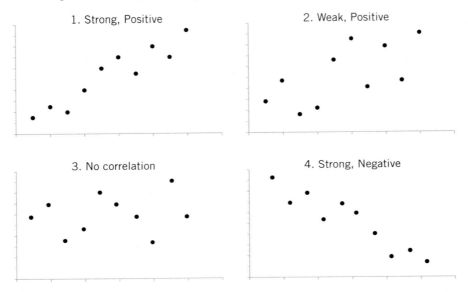

7.2.4.1.2 Regression analysis

Building on the principals of correlation analysis, researchers can apply regression analysis to help predict an outcome variable based on a set of predictor variables. Regression analysis has different applications. In some studies it is used as exploratory technique to identify variables that best explain variation in the outcome variable. In other studies, it is used to test theory, where prior knowledge exists of the phenomenon, and a specific set of variables are hypothesised to predict the outcome variable. The results from the regression analysis in the form of regression coefficients and an equation can also indicate which predictor variables contribute more in explaining variation in the outcome variable.

A variety of regression techniques exist, including multiple linear regression, logistic regression, ordinal regression and nonlinear regression, depending on the characteristics of the data to be analysed.

Example box

In 1973, Anscombe presented four datasets with nearly similar statistical properties.[11] In fact, if linear regression lines are fitted they appear almost similar. That is they have the same intercepts and the same slopes. However, a visual inspection of the scatterplots reveals a different story in terms of the variation in the data. Anscombe wanted to demonstrate the importance of graphing and visually inspecting the variation in the data before analysing it as well as the effect of outliers on statistical properties. This example is referred to as Anscombe's quartet.

continued →

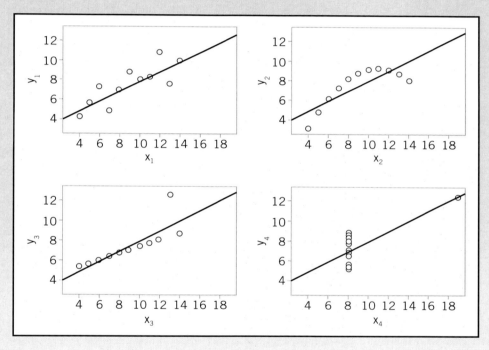

Source: Anscombe, F.J. 1973. Graphs in Statistical Analysis. American Statistician 27(1):17-21, reprinted by permission of the American Statistical Association, www.amstat.org and the publisher publisher (Taylor & Francis Ltd, http://www.tandfonline.com).

7.2.4.1.3 Exploratory factor analysis

Exploratory factor analysis is used to identify hypothetical constructs that might underlie a set of observed variables. The technique analyses the correlations (interrelationships) between a set of observed variables with the aim of reducing the original set of variables into a smaller set of common underlying factors or dimensions. Variables that have high correlations amongst one another are grouped together. The smaller number of components should therefore account for the variability found in the original set of observed variables.

> **Example box**
>
> In a study on perceived customer value in the automotive industry supply chain, exploratory factor analysis was employed to identify the hypothetical construct factors underlying the data. The scale of 16 items was included in the factor analysis and the four identified factors explained a cumulative 72% of variance in the scale response. The extracted four factors represent product delivery and quality (F1), personal interaction (F2), product development support (F3), and improving time-to-market (F4) (see table below).
>
> Product delivery and quality (F1) comprises those items that relate to the technical performance of the supplier, such as product quality, reliability and delivery performance. Personal interaction (F2) relates to the personal relationship that the supplier has with the buyer, and includes aspects like information sharing and how the client is treated. The next factor (product development support, F3) encompasses the extent to which the supplier assists the buyers in developing their products, while improving time-to-market (F4) relates to the extent to which the supplier assists the buyers in getting their products to market quicker.
>
> The mean of the item means can now be used as a proxy measure of the construct and can be used in further analysis, such as structural equation modelling.

7.2.4.1.4 Confirmatory factor analysis

Confirmatory factor analysis (CFA) is used by researchers to test how well a set of observed variables represent a specified number of constructs (i.e. latent variables). In other words, it is used to assess and confirm if data collected fits a particular factor structure or hypothesised measurement model. The model is usually specified based on knowledge of theory and the postulated relationships that exist between constructs. The analysis therefore allows the researcher to test the **hypotheses** statistically.

7.2.4.1.5 Structural equation modelling

Structural equation modelling (SEM) is used by researchers to test complex relationships between observed (measured) and unobserved constructs (**latent variables**). It applies a diverse set of statistical models, methods and algorithms to test how well sets of observed variables define constructs and how these constructs are related to each other. CFA is therefore also regarded as a case of SEM. Another application of SEM is path analysis, which only deals with observed variables.

> **Example box**
>
> Researchers that are interested in a particular construct, for example job satisfaction, might collect quantitative data by asking respondents to rate or evaluate a large number of items that specifically have reference to the particular phenomenon being studied. Using EFA, the researcher can identify sets of items that are highly correlated. By assessing the content of these items that 'hang together' it might point towards several underlying hypothetical subconstructs that can be labelled as promotion, fringe benefits, nature of work and supervision. However, this analysis may not tell us enough about the underlying relationships between these variables, and using correlation analysis, regression analysis

continued →

and/or Structural Equation Modelling, researchers may then explore the relationships between the four factors and job satisfaction. A typical outcome of such an analysis is depicted in the diagram below. In our hypothetical example, we see that supervision and nature of work are the two dimensions with the most direct influence on job satisfaction, with supervision having the biggest impact. However, supervision is impacted, in turn, by promotion and fringe benefits (and especially promotion). What this (hypothetical) finding tells us is that the promotion opportunities and fringe benefits have a significant influence on the perception of supervision, which in turn has a significant impact on job satisfaction.

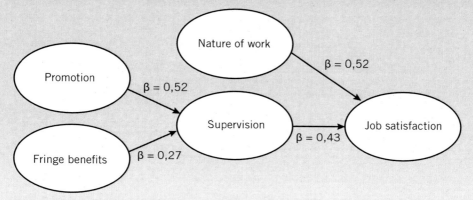

Once the relationships are understood, a further step may include comparative analysis of the findings. For example, how do different employment categories, age or gender groups compare on their levels of job satisfaction or its dimensions? This aspect is discussed in more detail in the next section.

7.2.4.2 Comparing groups

Several statistical techniques and tests exist that enable researchers to compare groups.

7.2.4.2.1 Chi-square test for independence

Researchers that are interested to explore the relationship between two categorical variables can conduct a Chi-square test for independence. The variables can have more than two categories. In essence, the test allows the researcher to assess how likely it is that the two variables are associated. This is done in relation to a null-hypothesis that states that the two variables are independent of each other. When conducting any hypothesis testing, the null-hypothesis is typically the one stipulating no statistical significant difference or relationship between variables or groups. An important notion of testing any hypothesis is that it is not one that is formulated post data collection. A hypothesis is the operationalising of a theoretical postulation originating from theory. Data are then collected to empirically test if there are evidence in the data given the hypothesis stated by the researcher.

Most advanced statistical software packages can conduct Chi-square tests and produces as an output a probability value (p-value). This p-value is indicative of the odds of collecting data from repetitive samples from the same population that will yield results more extreme than what is stated by the null-hypothesis. A researcher compares the p-value to a certain cut-point to assess if the null-hypothesis can be supported by the data. A cut-point of 0,05 is widely used by researchers. If the p-value is less than 0,05, the null hypothesis cannot be rejected.

7.2.4.2.2 Two independent-samples test

The independent-samples test is used when you want to assess if two independent groups are different in relation to a particular numerical measurement. The null-hypothesis states that the two groups are not statistically significant different and any difference that exists between the two groups can be attributed to chance variation alone.

Two main test types can be distinguished, namely **parametric** and **non-parametric tests**. The choice of test depends on the assumptions that are made about the population from which the sample was drawn and the data type. Parametric tests assume a large sample (n > 30), normality of the data and measurement to be on an interval level. Non-parametric tests make fewer assumptions and are useful in cases where your data violate the assumptions of parametric data (i.e. smaller sample, non-normal data and measurement at the ordinal level).

The independent samples t-test is the parametric version and compares the mean scores of two different groups. The non-parametric alternative is the Mann-Whitney U Test. Where the t-test compares the means of the two groups, the Mann-Whitney U Test compares medians.

7.2.4.2.3 Paired-samples test

Multiple measurements are often taken for a single group of respondents. This would mean that we have data for two numerical variables but it measures the same construct but under different conditions, either after an event or to investigate the impact of an intervention. The data are therefore paired for the same respondent. Then a paired-samples test is appropriate to examine if differences between measures are appropriate.

If assumptions of normality are met, a large sample is present and the data is measured at the interval level then a paired samples t-test could be used. The non-parametric version is the Wilcoxon Signed Rank Test.

7.2.4.2.4 Multiple independent samples test

The independent samples test examines if statistically significant differences exist between two independent groups for the same measure. If multiple independent groups are evident (three and more) then a different test is used. The parametric version of the test is the ANOVA test (analysis of variance test), while a frequently non-parametric test used is the Kruskal-Wallis test.

> **Example box**
>
> A study was conducted amongst a group of respondents and the researcher was interested to determine if the marital status of respondents were related (i.e. associated) to their level of education. First, a cross tabulation was constructed where the proportional distributions of marital status are reported for the two groups of respondents, namely those with a matric certificate and those with a university degree. Inspection of percentages shows that very similar distributions are presented for the two groups.
>
> continued →

Marital status * Level of education Crosstabulation

			Level of education Matric	Level of education Degree	Total
Marital status	Single	Count	50%	24%	74%
		% within Level of education	30,9%	35,3%	32,2%
		% of Total	21,7	10,4	32,2
	Married	Count	89	39	128
		% within Level of education	54,9%	57,4%	55,7%
		% of Total	38,7%	17,0%	55,7%
	Divorced/ Widow(er)	Count	23	5	28
		% within Level of education	14,2%	7,4%	12,2%
		% of Total	10,0%	2,2%	12,2%
Total		Count	162	68	230
		% within Level of education	100,0%	100,0%	100,0%
		% of Total	70,4%	29,6%	100,0%

To test if the two variables are statistically associated, the researcher checks the p-value calculated by the statistical package (in this instance IBM SPSS was used). A p-value of 0,335 is reported in the column labelled 'Asymptotic Significance (2-sided)'. A significant relationship is evident if the p-value is less than 0,05. In this case the value is not and the researcher concludes that no statistically significant association exists between the two variables.

Chi-Square Tests

	Value	df	Asymptotic Significance (2-sides)
Pearson Chi-Square	2,185[a]	2	,335
Likelihood Ratio	2,368	2	,306
Linear-by-Linear Association	1,502	1	,220
N of Valid Cases	230		

a. 0 cells (0,0%) have expected count less than 5. The minimum expected count is 8,28.

7.3 Summary

This chapter aimed to provide the researcher with a roadmap to analysing quantitative data. This is certainly not the only approach to use and many textbooks might suggest different approaches. The researcher should always be guided by the research objectives and the purpose of the study.

Many of the techniques discussed here certainly warrant chapters on their own. Textbooks and other resources are plentiful and as researchers we never stop learning. The different studies we engage in and the data we work with keeps us on a continuous knowledge journey. Never stop reading and playing with data. Some techniques are quite complex and excellent work is done throughout the scientific community to develop new algorithms and software to assist us.

Key terms and concepts

binning: process of creating new variables based on grouping contiguous values of existing variables into a limited number of distinct categories
bivariate analysis: analysis of two variables with the aim of assessing the empirical relationship between them
code book: complete document specifying all the variables and measurements contained in your database. It also indicates any instructions for calculating derived variables such as indices and scale measures.
descriptive statistics: statistics that are calculated to describe variables
hypothesis: a theory-based proposition about the relationship between two or more variables or some characteristic that may or may not be true
kurtosis: a statistic that provides information about the 'peakedness' of a distribution
latent variable: a variable that is not directly observed but inferred from other observed variables
multivariate analysis: analysis of multiple variables simultaneously with the aim of assessing the empirical relationship between them
non-parametric test: test designed to be used when data do not meet assumptions of normality
normal distribution: a special form of the symmetric distribution, where the data can be plotted as a bell-shaped curve (i.e. the distribution looks the same on both sides)
parametric test: test designed to be used when data meet assumptions of normality
skewness: statistic giving an indication of the symmetry of the distribution of a variable
univariate analysis: analysis of a single variable

Questions for review and critical thinking

1. Identify the main steps that researchers can take to analyse quantitative data.
2. Why is it important to assess both the validity and reliability of scales?
3. The ability of a researcher to calculate and interpret descriptive statistics is an important skill. List the common statistics that researchers calculate to describe a continuous variable. How should these statistics be interpreted?
4. Researchers can conduct advanced statistical analysis to determine relationships between variables and/or differences between groups. Describe some techniques they frequently use.

Research activities

Use an online library or Google Scholar to find a research dissertation (such as a Masters or Doctoral dissertation) or research article that collected quantitative data. Identify the various statistical tests used to analyse the data and how the results were reported. Also assess how the statistics were used to address and support the research objectives. Were any specific hypotheses stated? Which statistics were calculated to address these hypotheses?

Case study

You are conducting a study on strategy implementation in JSE listed organisations. After a thorough literature review, you develop a questionnaire (see below) addressing what you feel are the salient aspects of strategy implementation.

	Strongly disagree	Disagree	Neither agree nor disagree	Agree	Strongly agree
1. We almost always achieve our long-term objectives.	1	2	3	4	5
2. Our organisation is focused on a few key performance indicators to track our progress with implementation.	1	2	3	4	5
3. The leadership of our organisation is visibly committed to successfully implementing our strategy.	1	2	3	4	5
4. The culture in our organisation strongly supports our strategic direction.	1	2	3	4	5
5. Our internal organisation structure supports strategy implementation.	1	2	3	4	5
6. Our internal operating environment processes and policies support strategy implementation.	1	2	3	4	5
7. We have the right technology in place to successfully implement our strategy.	1	2	3	4	5
8. We have the right competencies in place to successfully implement our strategy,	1	2	3	4	5
9. Strategy implementation is a very important function in our organisation.	1	2	3	4	5
10. We have a clear long-term strategy.	1	2	3	4	5
11. Our organisation's strategy is clearly understood by most people in the organisation.	1	2	3	4	5
12. We are constantly measuring our progress with strategy implementation.	1	2	3	4	5

Following your data collection efforts, you have 115 responses from CEOs or top managers of companies listed on the JSE. As a first step in data analysis, you obtain the descriptive statistics for each scale item. An example of the results is given below.

Example of statistical outputs

Descriptive statistics	Question 3
Mean	3.682
Standard Error	0.070
Median	3.800
Mode	3.900
Standard Deviation	0.352
Sample Variance	0.124
Kurtosis	−0.652
Skewness	−0.817
Range	1.200
Minimum	2.900
Maximum	4.100
Sum	92.039
Count	25.000
Largest(1)	4.100
Smallest(1)	2.900

Questions
1. What processes should you follow before starting the analysis of the data?
2. Examine the table with the results for Question 3. What does this tell you about the data gathered by that question?
3. Describe what you would do with the data in the analysis phase. What possible techniques would you use and why?

References

1. Saunders, M., Lewis, P. & Thornhill, A. 2009. *Research methods for business students.* 5th ed. UK: Pearson Education.
2. Babbie, E. 2016. *The practice of social research.* 14th ed. USA: Cengage Learning.
3. Cohen, S., Kamarck, T. & Mermelstein, R. 1983. A global measure of perceived stress. *Journal of Health and Social Behavior,* 24(2), 385–396.
4. South African Advertising Research Foundation. 2009. *The SAARF AMPS Living Standards Measure* (LSM). [Online] Available from: http://www.saarf.co.za/AMPS/technicalreport-2009A/data%20files/Technical/21+22.pdf.
5. Cohen, S., Kamarck, T. & Mermelstein, R. 1983. A global measure of perceived stress. *Journal of Health and Social Behavior,* 24(2), 385–396.

6. Pallant, J. 2010. *SPSS Survival Manual*. 4th ed. UK: McGraw-Hill.
7. Field, A. 2009. *Discovering statistics using SPSS*. 3rd ed. UK: SAGE Publications Inc.
8. Field, A. 2009. *Discovering statistics using SPSS*. 3rd ed. UK: SAGE Publications Inc.
9. Velleman, P. & Wilkinson, L. 1993. Nominal, Ordinal, Interval, and Ratio Typologies are Misleading. *The American Statistician*, 47(1): 65–72.
10. Cohen, J.W. 1988. *Statistical power analysis for the behavioral sciences*. 2nd ed. Hillsdale, NJ: L. Erlbaum Associates.
11. Anscombe, F.J. 1973. Graphs in Statistical Analysis. *American Statistician* 27(1): 17–21.

PART 3

WRITING A RESEARCH PROPOSAL

8

Elizabeth Stack

AFTER STUDYING THIS CHAPTER, YOU SHOULD BE ABLE TO:

- Understand what a research proposal is
- Explain the purpose of a research proposal
- Know what a research proposal comprises
- Understand how to write a research proposal
- Understand how a research proposal will be judged and recognise common errors found in research proposals.

We last encountered Maria in Chapter 2, where she was just starting out on her research journey. Maria has now carried out her literature survey and has refined her broad idea for a topic into a research question. She has also attended the course on research methodology presented by the university. Her supervisor, Professor Ntuli, has now approved her topic and her research question. Armed with her literature survey and her new knowledge of research methodology, she schedules a meeting with Professor Ntuli to discuss what she needs to do next. His reply is: "Write your research proposal."

Now Maria is once again at sea. What is a research proposal? The only proposal that she knows about is a marriage proposal and she is sure that has nothing to do with what Professor Ntuli is talking about. She plucks up the courage to ask her supervisor what a research proposal is. He hands her a booklet prepared by the university setting out the requirements for a research proposal and tells her to read it and submit the first draft of her proposal in six weeks' time. She looks down at the booklet. It seems to be very thin. Will it tell her how to perform a task that will take her six weeks to carry out?

Maria returns to her study, where she looks up the meaning of 'proposal' in the South African Concise Oxford Dictionary[1] on her desk. She finds that it gives the following meaning for 'propose': "To put forward (an idea or plan) for consideration by others", and for 'proposal': "a plan or suggestion". This seems to suggest that a research proposal must be something that sets out the plan for her research. She settles down to read the research methodology booklet.

Sources: The Shorter Oxford English Dictionary on Historical Principles prepared by William Little, H. W. Fowler & Rev. J. Coulson; edited by C. T. Onions. Third edition (1973:1689). By permission of Oxford University Press

8.1 Introduction

Consulting her dictionary has certainly helped Maria to grasp the basic idea of what a research proposal is. You, like Maria, have completed your literature survey and the next step for you is to write your research proposal. This can be a daunting task. Your research proposal is one of the most important documents you will ever have to write. It is your introduction to the community of scholars and your first excursion into academic writing. Chapter 8 will attempt to prepare you for this important step and make the task less difficult.

Where does the research proposal fit into the whole process of carrying out your research and writing your thesis? The diagram below illustrates this.

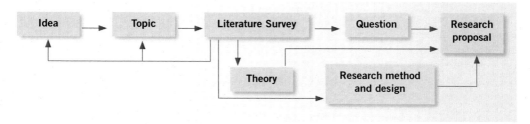

Figure 8.1 Place of the research proposal in the process

The diagram above illustrates that the literature survey has assisted you to narrow down your broad idea to a topic and then to a research question or hypothesis (or questions or hypotheses). It also shows that this is not a linear process. The literature survey has enabled you to identify a theory, framework or model that you will use for your research and that you will have to describe in your research proposal. The line extending from the literature survey block to the research method and design block indicates that the literature survey may have given you ideas about the research method you will use to design your research. You will also describe your proposed research method and design in your research proposal. You will need to study Chapters 3 to 7, dealing with research methodology and design, before you can fully describe the research method and the design you will use for your research. The literature survey will also provide the basis for the literature review in your research proposal.

Only once you have written the research proposal and it has been approved by the research committee or a similar body, can you can start with the hard work of collecting your data, analysing and interpreting it and, finally, writing your thesis.

Universities have different requirements for research proposals. Some require the minimum – a topic and an outline of chapters; others require a detailed document including a full literature review and a full bibliography; many fall somewhere in the middle. This chapter will assume that the research proposal falls somewhere in the middle. At certain universities, a topic statement and an outline of the chapters are approved by a research committee before the student may commence with writing the research proposal, at others only the proposal is approved.

With the increasing importance of ethical research, most universities will also require their students to obtain ethical clearance before they eventually proceed with the research. The research proposal is a very important document in this process, as it is one of the key documents that the ethical committee will consider before granting or denying ethical clearance.

8.2 What is a research proposal?

For the purposes of this chapter, a research proposal is a document approved by your supervisor (and possibly the head of the department in which you are pursuing your studies) that is submitted to a research committee or a colloquium at your university for approval, before you can start your actual research. Leedy and Ormrod refer to it as "the key that unlocks the door to the research endeavor".[2]

Hofstee refers to it as a vital document which "defines to you and your supervisor exactly what you are going to do and how you are going to go about doing it"[3] and states that "[t]he proposal is about getting the concepts approved".[4] Leedy and Ormrod compare it to an architect's plan for a building, emphasising that "each question must be addressed before a pound of dirt is excavated".[5] They refer to the two components – the plan and the approval of the plan.

A research proposal is a very formal structured document that must be presented in the format prescribed by the university and must contain the prescribed information. You are using this document to 'sell' your proposal to a research committee, which may include academics who are not experts in your field of research or even your discipline. You must set out your plan clearly and explain fully, so that the readers are left with no unanswered questions.

Hofstee[6] and Leedy and Ormrod[7] compare a research proposal to a legal contract and Hofstee states that "you are effectively making promises to your university and supervisor; you are listing your obligations in terms of the 'contract'".[8]

A research proposal is therefore a document to be taken seriously and not "a few, hastily written pages".[9]

> **Example box**
>
> Essentially, therefore, a *research proposal* is a document in the prescribed format clearly setting out your plan of action for your research, in which you describe your proposed topic, question and research plan and which you submit to certain persons and bodies for approval. It represents a very important step in the research process and is used to 'sell' your research idea to your supervisor and the committee or structure that approves it.

8.3 The purpose of a research proposal

In defining the research proposal above, the purpose must also be made clear. The research proposal must answer any questions the reader may have about the research project. Welman, Kruger and Mitchell identify the main objective of a research proposal as follows: "to convey the plan in terms of which our proposed research is going to be carried out clearly and unambiguously".[10] Welman et al refer to the two main questions to be addressed in the proposal: Which problem is going to be investigated? How is this problem going to be investigated? Leedy and Ormrod state that the "proposal provides a chance to show with ultimate clarity and detail [that] the researcher can state a problem, delineate the treatment of the data, and establish the logical validity of a conclusion."[11]

Among the functions of the research proposal, the following are the most important.
- It provides *you* with your plan of action – how you are going to proceed with your research. Welman et al express the view that it helps you to clarify and organise your

ideas.[12] It also informs your supervisor of your plan and enables him or her to judge whether your research is relevant and achievable. In the words of Welman et al, it establishes that the research is "practically possible".[13]
- It is required for approval of the research and for ethical clearance before you can start the research process. It enables you to convince the committee that you have an appropriate research project and plan and that you are competent to carry it out.
- It is the written contract between you, the university and your supervisor. The approval of the committee is usually recorded in the minutes of the meeting and often serves before the Senate of the university. At certain universities, registration for the degree is provisional and only confirmed when a research proposal has been approved.
- It opens your lines of communication with the wider body of scholars. Welman et al state that the function of the proposal is to "convince the audience" of the relevance, value and appropriate scope of your proposed research.[14] From them, you will receive ideas, advice and criticism that are invaluable for the success of your thesis.
- It is possibly your first experience of formal academic writing and is an important learning experience on the road to writing your thesis.
- As you will see later, it also contains much of what will be included in your thesis.
- It may also be used to apply for funding for your research project – either from your university or an outside funding body.

8.4 Preparing to write your proposal

You have carried out your literature survey and have received approval from your supervisor for your research **topic** and research **question** and you now need to start writing your proposal. As with anything that you do, proper *planning* will make your task much easier. The first step in your planning is to find out exactly what a research proposal comprises and what the formal requirements for the proposal itself and its approval are at your university. Another aspect that is emphasised by Salkind is to plan for the time it will take you to carry out each individual activity.[15] Hofstee warns of the necessity of getting pre-approvals in writing at every critical juncture.[16] You need to plan *in advance* for a number of other things as well.

- **Gaining access to your data:** The data for your research may consist of documents, pen-and-paper tests, observations, interviews, questionnaire responses or the results of an experiment. You need to ensure in advance that you will be able to gain access to the data. Documents may be confidential, private or of historical significance. You will need to get written permission, in advance, to use these documents. There are many instances of students having to abandon their studies because of documents not being available, people refusing to be observed or interviewed, or permission not being granted to carry out research using certain participants such as, for example, employees, prison inmates, patients in mental hospitals or minors. Where permission is required to use documents or people for your research, this permission must be obtained in writing.
- **Complying with the ethical requirements:** There are a number of ethical requirements to be complied with, particularly where living beings or confidential documents are the units of analysis. Ethical requirements must be taken into consideration when planning your research. How you will address these issues, must be reflected in your research proposal and therefore you must plan this in advance of writing the proposal. Ethical

considerations that you should address include the following:
- Protection from harm: most research involving living beings will carry some measure of risk for potential harm or distress. Steps will have to be taken to protect participants from harm. This is especially important where the objects of the study are vulnerable, such as young children or the aged.
- Informed consent: participants in any research project must be clearly informed about the nature of the research, the potential for harm, how the raw data will be used and how it will be protected from third parties. Participants must give their written consent (or the consent of parents or guardians must be obtained). The use of deception in carrying out research is only permissible under very limited circumstances and only when the study cannot be conducted meaningfully without it. Consent forms must be drawn up and submitted for approval to the ethics committee or other bodies dealing with ethical approval for research to be carried out.
- Ethics committees or internal review boards assessing research proposals will ensure that the ethical requirements have been complied with. Permission must be gained in advance from these bodies. In many disciplines, such as medicine and psychology, ethical codes are prescribed.

An ethical dilemma

Many researchers in academia are carrying out educational research using questionnaires administered to first-year students or using student data from the university's data base, without getting ethical clearance for this. Some of these students are under the age of eighteen. Any research involving minors (someone under the age of eighteen) requires the permission of their parents or guardians. A student's personal information (provided on the registration form, for example) may not be used unless the student (or the parent or guardian of the student) gives his or her written consent, after having been fully informed about the research project, what the data will be used for, the confidentiality of the data and their personal anonymity.

- **Ensuring the availability of the resources required:** When designing your research, you must decide what resources you will need. This may include equipment such as computers, tape recorders, computer software, etc. You may need to appoint research assistants to help with interviews, administering questionnaires or gathering other data. You may have to consider travelling and accommodation costs. You may need to attend training courses to equip you with the skills to carry out the research. All of this requires funding and you will have to decide where the funding will come from. Where funding will be required for your research, this must be arranged in advance and the research proposal must provide information concerning the source(s) of funding.
- **How the proposal will be evaluated:** In order to write a good research proposal, you need to know how it will be evaluated or judged. This is where an early consultation with your supervisor is essential. Not only will they be able to tell you about and possibly provide documentation on the prescribed form and contents of the proposal, but will also give you valuable advice, based on experience, of where the research committee places its emphasis in judging proposals and what their 'pet hates' are. You may need to present and defend your proposal in person and your supervisor will be able to give you valuable advice on how to prepare for this.

8.5 The structure and content of the research proposal

In broad terms, your research proposal must explain **WHY** you are undertaking your research, **WHAT** your research aims to achieve and **HOW** you plan to carry out your research.[17] Hofstee also explains that the proposal defines exactly what you are going to do, how you are going to do it and why it makes sense to do it.[18]

Babbie and Mouton provide a very brief discussion of the content of a research proposal, including the following points:[19]

- The proposal must set out the motivation or rationale for the study, including the reasons for the study, where it fills a gap in the literature and that it represents a practical and urgent problem.
- The problem or objective (what you want to achieve), the unit of analysis and the practical significance of the research, must be discussed.
- A preliminary literature review must be presented, including the work of other scholars and alternative theories.
- The research design must provide details about:
    - the subjects, including how they will be protected from harm
    - the conceptualisation and measurement methods
    - a definition of the variables
    - how the variables will be measured
    - how the data will be collected
    - how the data will be analysed – the purpose and logic.
- A time frame and budget.

8.5.1 Guidelines for a research proposal

Writers on research methodology and universities give different guidelines for what a research proposal should include. The following example highlights the most common requirements. Each component reflected in this model outline is discussed in more detail below.

> **Example box: outline of a research proposal**[20]
>
> - Title page
> - Introduction
>   - Background to the problem
>   - Statement of the research problem
>   - Statement of the research subproblems
>   - Purpose of the study, or research question
>   - Objectives of the study
>   - Rationale for the study
>   - Scope of the study
> - Literature review
> - The proposed research methods
>   - Research philosophy
>   - Research design
>   - Data sources
>   - Sampling

- Data collection techniques
- Data analysis and interpretation
- Ensuring reliability and validity
- Ethical considerations
* The student's personal work plan (what will be done when)
* A provisional outline of the chapters of the thesis
* References

8.5.1.1 Title page

The title page reflects:
- **The provisional title:** Crafting a good title is very important. The discussion of a literature search in Chapter 2 referred to databases of previous research. Here you would have looked at the titles of journal articles or other research items to decide whether they seemed to be relevant to your research and whether you wanted to follow up on them. This indicates how important it is that the title describes your proposed research clearly. The title should not be too long and should ideally encapsulate the research question. 'Clever' titles should be avoided and titles should not be in the form of a question. A bad (imaginary) title would be: "The banking industry in Europe – *quo vadis*?" Welman et al state that the title must concisely, yet unambiguously, identify the exact topic of the research – not the general field of study.[21]
- **The name of the candidate:** The full name of the candidate and (usually) the student number) appears on the title page.
- **The degree for which the thesis is presented:** The degree designation is written out in full, for example, Master's Degree in Commerce.
- **The department in which the candidate is enrolled:** You may be presenting your degree in, for example, the Department of Economics and this must appear on the title page.
- **The name of the supervisor:** Supervisors for each candidate are approved by the university and the full name and title of both the supervisor and co-supervisor, where relevant, are reflected on the title page.
- **The approval of the proposal by the supervisor and/or the head of the department:** Students may not submit their proposals to the research committee (or other structure) without the consent of their supervisors and, at certain universities, the head of the department in which they are registered.

8.5.1.2 Introduction

The introduction usually describes the broad field of research, sets out the problem statement and the rationale for the research, as well as the purpose of the research – **why** the research is being carried out. Definitions of key terms may be included in the introductory paragraph. Welman et al state that the background information should include reference to relevant research literature and motivations as to the importance of the proposed research.[22] The review of the research literature may be in a separate paragraph, depending on the university's requirements. Salkind includes in the introductory paragraph the problem statement, the rationale for the research (including a statement of the research objectives), the hypothesis and definitions of the terms used in the research.[23]

Leedy and Ormrod set out the following requirements for the introduction to a research proposal:[24]
- the problem and subproblems must be clearly stated and the hypotheses or problems clearly articulated
- all relevant terms must be defined
- delimitations must be set out clearly
- the reason for conducting the research (why it is important) must be explained.

8.5.1.3 Review of the literature

In this section, a literature review is presented. The requirements of universities differ. Some require a comprehensive review of all the relevant literature, others require a limited or preliminary review, sufficient to describe the main theories or theoretical frameworks and a discussion of the most important research carried out on the topic, narrowing down from a broader perspective to the particular theory or framework to be used in the present research. Welman et al express the view that the research proposal should include "only a meaningful summary of the literature that is directly relevant to the proposed research and will enhance understanding of the formulation of the objectives of the research project".[25]

Refer to Chapter 3 for a discussion and an example of a limited literature review.

8.5.1.4 The research question or hypothesis

According to Welman et al, all research questions or hypotheses must be stated and the rationale for each must be clarified as established by the concise literature survey.[26] The placing of the research question or hypothesis differs from university to university. In some cases, the introduction, literature review and research question are combined in one paragraph, possibly entitled 'context'.[27] In others, the question is reflected separately. Certain authors recommend (and certain universities prescribe) that the research question should be stated right at the beginning of the proposal and others that it should be stated at the end of the literature review. Wherever it is placed, it is a critical element of the proposal and must be placed in such a way that the readers are easily able to identify it. The type of research also influences the content of this section. For example, in the case of exploratory research hypotheses, very specific research objectives may not be appropriate, and the research proposal may accordingly have only research questions.

The research question(s) and hypothesis(es) are often discussed as *alternate* ways of articulating the research problem, depending on whether the research is qualitative or empirical. In empirical research, the research question(s) will usually be stated and then translated into one or more hypotheses which capture all the elements of the question, while in qualitative research projects, hypotheses will not be stated.

8.5.1.5 The purpose and goals of the research

The purpose of the research must be clearly stated. This differs from the research question and the goals of the research. It articulates **WHY** you are carrying out the research. You will have identified exactly what the problem is and expressed this in the form of a research question or hypothesis. The purpose will be to carry out research in order to provide an answer to the research question. Your description of the purpose of your research will also help to substantiate the importance of the research.

The goals of the research set out **WHAT** you plan to do to provide an answer to the research question(s). The goals must clearly set out the steps you will take in order to address the research question. The goals must also cover all the aspects of the research question and all variables that will be tested in the research.

If you look at the research proposal that forms the basis of the case study at the end of this chapter, you will note that the research questions are not set out at the end the contextual section, but as part of the general discussion. The research is in the field of finance and deals with the performance of shares on the stock market. The essence of the questions appears to be included in these extracts:

> Although value strategies have been shown to be successful in a number of different markets, these are, apart from Taiwan, all developed markets (Standard and Poor's Financial Services LLC, 2010). Taiwan aside, there appear to have been no studies which investigate value investment strategies and the value premium in emerging markets such as South Africa.
>
> An additional matter that will be addressed in the proposed research is the question of the reasons that value investment strategies work. Probably the two most important papers on value investment strategies (Fama and French, 1992 and Lakonishok et al, 1994) offered very different explanations in response to this issue.

The goals of the research are set out as follows:

> This research has two goals. Firstly, the research will set out to establish whether there is evidence in support of the relative effectiveness of value investment strategies in the South African equity market. In other words, the research aims to establish whether a value premium exists in a South African context.
>
> Secondly, the possible reasons (both rational and behaviourist) for the relative success of value strategies will be examined. In doing this, the research aims to establish whether the South African equity market data provides evidence for one side or the other of the rational/irrational debate.

If you look carefully at the two goals, you will see that the highlighted text appears to be stating the *purpose* of the research, while the text that is not highlighted sets out the goals of the research.

In its *Higher Degrees Guide* under the heading "The goals of the research" Rhodes University states that:[28]

> [t]his section should either set out the specific question(s) to which the candidate hopes to find an answer, or, in the case of open-ended topics in the humanities, outline the subject/area/field to be critically investigated. It should indicate clearly what the research intends to achieve and what the intended final deliverable is.

From this extract, it is clear that this section includes the research question, the purpose of the research and the intended final outcome. The goals as stated in the research proposal that forms the basis of the case study at the end of the chapter (quoted above) therefore meet these requirements. Different universities situate the question, the purpose and the goals in different sections of the proposal, but all of these aspects must be addressed in the proposal.

8.5.1.6 The research method and design

This section must describe in detail **HOW** you are going to carry out your proposed research. Welman et al state that the "proposed method [and] procedures should be scientifically well founded".[29] The section must set out clearly:

- The population from which the participants will be drawn, the number of participants (the whole population or a sample) and how they will be selected (randomly or non-randomly and what particular selection strategy will be applied), as well as the number of groups and how they will be formed
- How the data will be collected (questionnaires, observation schedules, interviews, pen-and-paper tests, experiments, etc.)
- The variables and how they will be measured
- How that data will be analysed and interpreted.

Welman et al also advise that if new or modified methods are proposed, their use should be justified.[30] The reader of the proposal should be satisfied that the proposed methods are the most appropriate. The Rhodes University *Higher Degrees Guide* notes that "where methods used are well-recognised in the discipline, they need only be briefly mentioned. Where they are not standard, or are innovative, a more detailed description is required, so that their viability can be assessed".[31]

The Rhodes University *Higher Degrees Guide* also sets out the following requirements for this section:[32]

> This section should contain a description of the "subjects" or research participants where appropriate, details of the sample size, a description of the study site if appropriate, the intended data analysis methods/techniques, the proposed time schedule for the research and ethical issues.

Leedy and Ormrod are of the view that the interpretation of the data is the most challenging part of the task of proposal-writing – every detail of the procedure must be spelt out and choices must be supported with a rationale based solidly on accepted research methodology and analytical thinking.[33]

In your description of the research method and design in the research proposal, it should not be necessary to enter into a philosophical discussion of the research paradigm into which your research fits and why you have positioned your research in this way. This would form part of the research methodology chapter in your thesis.

What is absolutely essential is that the title of the thesis, the research question, the research hypotheses, the purpose and goals of the research and the research methods and design are all in alignment. Welman et al refer to the overall 'fit' of the proposal and that it must demonstrate that the methods flow from the research questions which arise from the literature review.[34]

8.5.1.7 Ethical clearance

As explained in the section dealing with planning to write a research proposal earlier in this chapter, researchers need to plan for the ethical issues. The research proposal must make it clear what ethical considerations arise in the planned research and how they have been addressed. If ethical clearance was required from the ethics committee of the university or the faculty, this must be appended to the proposal. Any consent form that participants would need to sign must also be appended. Where the research creates the potential for distress or harm, the research proposal must explain how this will be dealt with, possibly by debriefing or counselling. A research project that includes asking participants in interviews about whether they have or would consider evading tax is an example of how a research project may cause embarrassment or distress to participants.

8.5.1.8 Other aspects of the proposal

Definitions of terms must be set out in the proposal. These may simply be terminology that is relevant to the research, but may be definitions that you have developed to explain a concept or concepts that you will test or analyse in your research. You may make certain assumptions in designing your research and these assumptions need to be clearly stated, together with the impact that they will have on the design of your research, the results and your conclusions. Limitations of the scope of the research and the impact these will have on the research also need to be clearly explained.

Leedy and Ormrod explain the importance of setting out the resources available to carry out the research, including the qualifications of the researcher, the availability of the data, the means by which the data will be secured, other required facilities and the limitations of the study.[35]

8.5.1.9 Provisional outline of the chapters of the thesis

Certain universities require a brief outline of the proposed chapters of the thesis. Even where it is not a specific requirement, this is a valuable exercise for the researcher, as it clarifies his or her planned research. Comparing this with the goals of the research, will ensure that all the goals will be adequately met.

8.5.1.10 References

Certain universities require a full bibliography, other universities simply a list of the works that were actually cited in the proposal. This list must be complete, accurate and set out in terms of the university's prescribed referencing method. There are many different referencing methods and some methods that are in common use in commercial research are the Harvard method, the APA (American Psychological Association) method and the EndNote method. Referencing is discussed in Chapter 10.

8.5.2 Concluding remarks

The research proposal is usually submitted to a research committee or colloquium for approval. Students are often required to defend their research proposal before the committee. Whether you are presenting it in person or only the written document, a well written proposal should leave the readers with no unanswered questions. Your research proposal should be such that it convinces the committee and readers of the proposal of the quality, relevance and achievability of your proposed research and your ability to carry it out. Welman et al refer to the 'value' of a research proposal and state that it "entails demonstrating a measure of research competence or problem-solving ability and, to a lesser degree, adding to the body of knowledge in a field of science."[36]

8.6 How to write a reseach proposal

Welman et al state that a research proposal must be such that "all questions that may possibly occur to the potential reader should be anticipated and dealt with".[37] Leedy and Ormrod discuss the attributes of a proposal as follows:
- The proposal must demonstrate whether the writer possesses the ability to think clearly without confusion, that is, logically and systematically.
- The proposal must be a straightforward document – no waffle – which separates the essential from the irrelevant.
- The first sentence must capture the reader's interest.
- It is not a literary production; the language must be clear, sharp and precise.
- It must be properly structured, with headings and subheadings in logical sequence.[38]

What follows are a number of practical hints that may assist you in writing your proposal.
- Remember that you are writing your proposal to be read by non-expert readers. Explain your research problem, question and theoretical underpinning, as well as the research method and design in such a way that they will understand clearly what you are saying. You are not writing for your supervisor whom you assume understands what you are trying to say. Welman et al state that the proposal should be formulated in such a way that "someone else should be able to execute the proposed research without having to consult its compiler".[39] Leedy and Ormrod advise you to assume that your readers know nothing about your topic and warn against assuming that readers are aware of critical pieces of information.[40]
- Salkind emphasises the importance of the appearance of a proposal – "the medium is the message".[41] Leedy and Ormrod discuss the need for the proposal to be clearly organised by the proper use of headings and subheadings and express the opinion that "[t]hey hint at an orderly and disciplined mind".[42] Leedy and Ormrod advise using appendices to present details that are not central to the discussion to avoid them interfering with the flow of writing.[43] Appendices may include ethical approvals, written permission to use certain data, draft questionnaires, interview schedules or observation checklists and possibly long quotations from statutes or other documents. Certain universities impose constraints on the length of a proposal, which may limit or preclude the addition of appendices.
- You must accept that you will probably have to write many drafts before you are able to satisfy your supervisor. Salkind stresses that all written material must be proofread twice: once for content and once for spelling and grammar.[44] The need to edit your document is also stressed by Hofstee.[45] If your language skills are not as good as they could be, you may need to make use of an editor. Leedy and Ormrod provide hints on revising a proposal. They recommend that students set it aside for a few days so that this can be approached with a fresh eye. In the process of revising, they advise students to look for disorganised thoughts and illogical thinking and for ambiguous phrases and sentences where the meaning is not clear. They also advise students to seek feedback from others who will read it objectively and provide constructive criticism.[46]
- A useful way of making sure that your discussion does not wander away into interesting but irrelevant byways is to print out your research question and goals in big letters and stick it on the wall in front of your desk. In that way you constantly keep the 'goalpost' in sight.

> **Tips on writing a research proposal**
>
> - Your proposal must be written in such a way that it captures the attention of the reader.
> - Check that the title, the question, the goals and the methodology are aligned.
> - Make sure that any questions the reader of your proposal may have are answered in your proposal – particularly how you plan to carry out your research.
> - Language and grammar are important; a poorly written proposal creates the impression that the researcher will not have the ability to carry out the research.
> - The literature survey must be presented in the form of a critical comparative analysis that supports the research question and demonstrates the contribution the research will make.
> - Keep the proposal brief and to the point – don't wander off into interesting byways.

8.7 Judging the proposal

The research proposal will be judged on the basis of the requirements prescribed by the particular university. This section of the chapter will summarise the requirements of a research proposal based on the writings of the authors of textbooks on research methodology, documents made available by four South African universities (the University of Johannesburg, Pretoria University, Stellenbosch University and Rhodes University) prescribing their requirements for a research proposal, and my own experience as a supervisor. Weaknesses that I have observed in research proposals will also be discussed in this section of the chapter, to assist you in avoiding these mistakes.

Welman et al comment that the evaluation is done exclusively on the basis of the proposal and not "in terms of its good intentions".[47] Included in the evaluation criteria they discuss, is that "the overall 'fit' of the proposal should be indicated, showing that the methods flow from the research questions, which arise from the literature" and that "possible flaws in procedural design and an estimate of their effects upon the research findings should be reported".[48] Therefore, the research committee will look for an alignment between the title, the goals and the method, including the theory used, and will expect you to identify any threats to the validity of the research.

Welman et al state two further criteria: feasibility of the research, which includes availability of data, the particular research design, the time and technical skills required and the financial support; and the value of the research in demonstrating the researcher's competence and whether it adds to the body of knowledge.[49] Leedy and Ormrod, in discussing common weaknesses, quote from George N. Eaves in *Grants* Magazine as follows:

> " the single most important qualification [in competing for a grant] ... is the demonstrated ability to think clearly and logically, to express logical thought concisely and cogently, to discriminate between the significant and the inconsequential, to display technical prowess, to handle abstract thought, to analyse data objectively and accurately, and to interpret results confidently and conservatively ...[50] "
>
> Source: Eaves, G. N. (1984:151). Preparation of the research-grant application: Opportunities and pitfalls. *Grants Magazine, 7, 151-157.*

This, undoubtedly, encapsulates what the evaluators of your research proposal and, eventually, the examiners of your thesis will be looking for.

8.7.1 Requirements of a research proposal

From an analysis of the documents provided by the four universities referred to above, it is clear that the frameworks they prescribe for their proposals are very similar and include all of the information discussed in section 5, dealing with the content and structure of a research proposal, but under separate headings or sections. A few differences have become clear from the available documents. Some universities require a full bibliography, which would mean that the student would have to carry out an extensive literature survey before writing the proposal. One university requires the submission of a topic statement for approval, containing some of the information normally included in a research proposal, prior to the submission of the full proposal. Most of the universities require a chapter outline while at some others it is optional. The prescribed length of the proposal differs from university to university – some universities prescribe a minimum number of words and others a maximum number of pages.

The example below provides a detailed description of exactly what a research proposal should contain and the basis on which it will be judged.

RECOMMENDATIONS FOR AN ACCEPTABLE PROPOSAL

1. Cover page

The cover page must comply with the university/faculty/departmental requirements. All relevant information must be provided.

2. Provisional title

- The provisional title must be brief – usually between 12–15 words.
- It must reflect the nature of the research, the research problem and should include the key words.
- Avoid 'catchy', funny or clever titles.
- It should not be in the form of a question.

[Note: A person carrying out a search of library data bases should be able to decide, based on the title, whether this thesis is relevant for his or her own research.]

3. Background and problem statement

- Describe the background to and context of the study.

[Note: This could be done by means of a limited literature review in order to describe the nature of the problem, or by way of a clear description of the practical, work-related problem giving rise to the research, together with references to literature (where relevant).]

- Formulate the research problem clearly and concisely, but comprehensively.
- State the research hypothesis(es), where relevant, incorporating all research variables.

[Note: This section usually starts with a broad description of the background, narrowing down to the research problem – therefore, from the general to the specific. It must be clear from this section where the present research fits into the broad body of knowledge. The research problem and the goals of the research (next section) must be closely aligned.]

4. Research goals

- State the goals of the research clearly.
- An overarching goal is usually stated, followed by the subgoals required to achieve the broad goal of the research.
- There must be a clear link between the research goals, the title and the research problem.
- Do not confuse the research goals with the research methods.
- Make sure that the goals are realistic and achievable – this relates to the scope of the research.

[Note: The goals set out WHAT you aim to do.]

5. Purpose of the research

- Clearly state the reason why the research will be undertaken – this is based on the research question.

[Note: The purpose of the research may be, for example, to attempt to bring certainty where uncertainty exists in a particular area; to develop a model for future use in solving a problem; to test a theory in a context where it has not been tested; to attempt to solve a practical problem; or to bring a new perspective to a field of research, etc. This section explains WHY you are doing the research.]

6. Significance of the study

- Describe the contribution that the present research will make to the general body of knowledge.
- Do not make the claim that 'this study will make an important contribution …' – you should simply indicate, to the extent necessary to enable the reader to judge its importance, where the research fits into the existing body of knowledge, indicating the gap that it could fill or the practical problem that it could help to solve.

[Note: This section sets out WHY the research is important.]

7. Literature review

- The literature review takes the form of an argument, using relevant literature to support the argument.
- Major landmark studies or classic, seminal studies related to the research problem must be included.
- The most recent research must also be included.
- Predominantly, journal articles should be included in the body of the literature surveyed (books and textbooks are often not up to date or at the cutting edge); internet sources must be used judiciously as the standard of the content varies.
- Contrasting views or research findings must be discussed, compared and critically evaluated.
- The literature review must be set out clearly and systematically. It could be set out in chronological order.
- The literature survey must support the research question, justify the significance of the research and reflect its purpose. Your research is grounded in existing literature and the review should reflect this.
- The literature must be well presented and interpreted.
- Do not present material that may be interesting but not relevant. Focus on the research question.

8. Research methods and design

In describing your research methods and design, you must include the following:
- Describe the data to be used for the research, including the population and how the sample will be selected (where relevant).
- Describe how the data will be obtained and secured – documentary sources, questionnaire or interview, or observations.
- Describe how the data will be measured (where relevant) – for example, by way of a pen-and-paper test.
- Describe how the data will be analysed – qualitative thematic analysis or quantitative statistical analysis, or a combination of both.
- Describe how the results will be interpreted – for example, using existing research, an existing model or theory, etc.
- Justify the research methods you have chosen to use.
- Reflect on potential sources of bias.
- Explain how you will try to ensure the objectivity, reliability and validity of the conclusions (for example, using multiple methods, models, populations, measuring instruments, sources of documentary data, etc.).
- If you are doing empirical research, describe the design of the questionnaire, interview schedule, observation checklist, etc.

9. Definitions, assumptions and limitations of scope

- State the relevant definitions and if you have adopted special definitions for the purpose of your research – these must be clearly explained.
- Set out any assumptions that you will make in designing and carrying out your research.
- Any limitations of scope must be clearly identified – these limitations may apply to the research population, time period, etc.

10. Ethical considerations

- Clearly identify all relevant ethical considerations (which would apply in every case where human beings or animals are the subjects of the research).
- Explain how the ethical considerations will be addressed in order to protect the participants:
  - confidentiality of the responses
  - anonymity of the participants
  - the right of participants to withdraw from the research or the voluntary nature of their participation in a once-off intervention
  - how the participants will be protected from harm (where relevant)
  - the use of a letter of consent and its contents
  - any debriefing that will be carried out (where relevant)
  - compliance with the requirements of ethical committees, panels, etc.
- In certain types of research, the documents used are all in the public domain and ethical considerations seldom arise.

11. Preliminary chapter outline

This could be in the form of a draft list of the contents of the chapters or set out in paragraph form describing what will be covered in each chapter of the thesis.

12. Reference list

- Make sure that you follow the prescribed referencing method TO THE LETTER.
- Make sure that the reference list is accurate and complete.
- At some universities, the research proposal reference list only contains the list of sources actually cited in the proposal; at other universities a full bibliography is required.

(Author's summary)

8.7.2 Defending your proposal

At many universities, candidates are required to defend their research proposals at a meeting of the research committee where it is being presented. You may become really discouraged when the research proposal that you have worked so hard to write is criticised by members of the research committee. You should welcome this criticism, as it will help you to improve your research and prevent problems at a later stage when you are doing the research. You should welcome the chance to share your work with members of the research committee. You can benefit a great deal from their comments. Their questions will indicate where you have not explained concepts clearly enough. They may warn you that the scope of your proposed research is too wide. They may provide you with useful comments and ideas. Your research may even have deviated into the unknown territory of another discipline and may be making claims or assumptions that are not valid.

Hofstee also advises students that they should be grateful for the opportunity to defend their proposals as they may get valuable hints and have problems pointed out. He advises students to start the presentation by "giving a little background information about your topic", then defining the problem and "spend[ing] time on the significance of the problem and the benefits of solving it", emphasising "what it is that you are going to do and how you plan to do it". He also advises students to "weigh all comments carefully before you respond" as "[a]ny potential pitfalls spotted can end up saving you a *lot* of work."[51]

8.7.3 Weaknesses in research proposals

It is my experience that assessing a research proposal is similar to assessing a thesis – it just has a different focus. Some common failings that I have encountered include the following:
- The title usually has to be changed as it does not reflect the tenor of the research, including the main key words.
- The introductory or context paragraph(s) do not set out the logical development of the research problem or question. Research identified in the literature survey is simply documented, with no attempt to use the literature to present an argument by comparing and contrasting earlier findings in order to demonstrate where the research fits in – the gap that it fills. Therefore the literature survey does not contribute to identifying the research problem.
- Instead of allowing the reader to judge the relevance and importance of the proposed research from the presentation of the argument leading up to the formulation of their research problem, students often make ambitious claims about the importance of their particular research and its contribution to the body of knowledge.
- Many students fail to recognise that they are writing the proposal to be read by a person who is an informed reader, but not an expert on the topic. The discussion is not sufficiently explanatory. Terms and concepts are often not fully explained or defined.
- The section in which the goals of the research are set out is usually one of the weakest sections of the proposal. Ideally, an overall goal or research question should be presented, followed by all the subgoals that need to be achieved in order to achieve the main goal.
- Students frequently confuse the goals with the contextual discussion (particularly the contribution to be made to the field of study) and, even more frequently, include research methods with the goals. Often, the poor articulation of goals reflects the fact that the student has a broad idea of what he or she wants to achieve, but has not done enough reading or thinking in order to present clear goals for the research.

- The description of the research methods and design is almost invariably the most poorly written section of the research proposal, the section which attracts the most criticism and where the most input is required from the supervisor. The students do not set out clearly what data will be used, how the data will be obtained, how it will be analysed and interpreted.
- Research goals, the anticipated contribution that the research will make and the contextual discussion are often described, instead of the method.
- Frequently, students do not have any clear plan for how they are going to set about doing the research, and put down some vague ideas. In other instances, the student has extravagant plans for conducting the research including, for example, large samples from a widespread geographical area or large numbers of interviews, clearly not considering the scope of the research and its achievability. Often the student has not made sure that the data will be available before submitting the proposal.
- Many students forget to identify ethical issues that arise and the need for ethical clearance by the appropriate structure in the university.

When assessing a research proposal, in addition to looking for these errors and omissions, I look particularly at:
- The literature survey in the contextual discussion and the reference list appended to the proposal in order to see whether the student has used mainly references from the popular press rather than primary sources such as reputable journal articles, and whether more recent, as well as seminal research, has been discussed.
- The alignment between the goals and the research method and design – whether in carrying out the research in the way the student proposes, he or she will be in a position to achieve the goals.
- The scope of the research – whether the student has taken on too much for a Master's thesis or half thesis, or too little for a Doctoral thesis.

Leedy and Ormrod list the following weaknesses identified in proposals submitted to the National Institute of Health which also apply in your field of research:[52]
- **Weaknesses related to the research problem:** The description of the project is so nebulous and unfocused that the purpose of the research is unclear. The problem is unimportant or unlikely to yield new information. The hypothesis is ill-defined, doubtful or unsound, or it rests on insufficient evidence. The problem is more complex than the investigator realises. The problem is of interest only to a particular, localized group, or in some other way has limited relevance to the field as a whole.
- **Weaknesses related to the research design and methodology:** The description of the design and/or method is so vague and unfocused as to prevent adequate evaluation of its worth. The data the investigator wishes to use are either difficult to obtain or inappropriate for the research problem. The proposed methods, measurement instruments, or procedures are inappropriate for the research problem. Appropriate controls are either lacking or inadequate. The statistical analysis has not received adequate consideration, is too simplistic, or is unlikely to yield accurate and clear-cut results.
- **Weaknesses related to the investigator:** The investigator does not have sufficient training or experience for the proposed research. The investigator appears to be unfamiliar with the literature relevant to the research problem. The investigator has insufficient time to devote to the project.

- **Weaknesses related to resources:** The institutional setting is unfavourable for the proposed research. The proposed use of equipment, support staff, or other resources is unrealistic.

8.8 Summary

After reading this chapter, you may become despondent about the amount of work you need to do to write your research proposal, before you can even begin to collect your data and do the 'real' research. Hofstee notes that writing a proposal represents "maybe not half", but a substantial amount of the required work to be done.[53] Estimating that, on average, it takes two years to complete a thesis, you can plan to spend between eight and ten months getting your research proposal completed and approved.

In addition, you will also have done much of the work needed to write your thesis. Your research proposal usually forms the basis for the first chapter of your thesis and the literature review will form the basis of the literature review chapter in your thesis. Your description of the research method and design will also form the basis of the research methodology chapter of your thesis. It is therefore time well spent. Once you have written your research proposal, you will know exactly what you plan to do and how you are going to set about doing it.

In my experience, in getting to the point where they are able to submit an acceptable research proposal, students often experience certain associated problems, including:

- *When to stop surveying the literature:* Students find difficulty in judging when they have done enough reading in order to write the research proposal. Usually, the research proposal does not require an exhaustive survey of the literature; that is required for the thesis itself. You need to do sufficient reading to be able to explain the context of the research, the nature of the research problem, the niche that your research occupies in the body of knowledge and to demonstrate the contribution it will make to this body of knowledge.
- *Writing skills:* Some students have had very little training in formal academic writing. In many instances, you will need to make use of an editor.
- *Logical reasoning skills:* Students often find it difficult to construct a logical argument. This starts from the internal logic of each sentence, each paragraph, etc. This often manifests as a problem with writing, but has a deeper underlying cause – problems with logical reasoning. It is also reflected in the inability to structure the chapters, headings and subheadings in a logical way to reflect the development of the research argument. Remember that your proposal (and your thesis) is an extended argument, supported by evidence. You must be constantly aware of possible illogicality in all aspects of your research and make sure that every aspect of your proposal is logical.

One of the most pressing questions a supervisor has to face, is how much assistance a student should be given. It is not uncommon for students to have to submit up to five or more drafts of their proposals, before it is suitable for submission to the research committee. Don't hesitate to consult your supervisor regularly, but don't expect him or her to tell you exactly what to do and how to do it. As a researcher, you must be able to work independently.

Not all universities require a formal research proposal. Welman et al express the opinion that "[e]ven if a research proposal is not required ... it remains an essential element in the research process because it represents the blueprint or ground plan for the proposed research."[54] Hofstee concurs and advises that "it is to your and your supervisor's advantage to do a comprehensive proposal anyway."[55]

This chapter has set out to discuss everything that you need to know about writing a research proposal. It has discussed what a research proposal is, identified its purpose and given you guidelines on how to prepare to write the proposal by describing the planning process. It also discussed the structure and elements of a research proposal in detail, gave you hints on how to write a proposal and explained how your proposal will be evaluated by the research committee. Now all you have to do is to start writing.

Key terms and concepts

data: pieces of information yielded by a particular situation under investigation
ethical considerations in research: steps to be taken by a researcher to protect participants from harm or distress and to ensure the confidentiality of responses by participants or of documents used in the research
research proposal: a formal document in the prescribed format setting out a plan for a proposed research project that is presented for approval to a committee or other body
research question: a precisely articulated question that describes all aspects of the problem or issue to be investigated in a research project
research topic: a broadly stated area of research from which a research question will be identified and developed
variables: logical attributes of a particular phenomenon or unit of analysis (for example, the phenomenon 'gender' is explained by the variables 'male' and 'female')

Questions

1. Give a definition of a research proposal.
2. What are the purposes of a research proposal?
3. What steps do you need to follow in preparing to write your research proposal?
4. List the elements that comprise a research proposal.
5. There are five attributes of a good research proposal. Name three.
6. Why do we need to defend our research proposals and what is the benefit of this?

Multiple-choice questions

1. A research proposal is a researcher's 'plan of action', which is formulated following a certain process. Which of the following statements is true?
    a) A research student surveys the literature, develops a research question and submits a literature review and a research question to a research committee for approval.
    b) The writing of a research proposal can be described as a linear process, starting with the identification of a research topic and ending with a statement of the goals of the research.

c) In the process of preparing to write a research proposal, the literature survey assists in identifying a topic and narrowing it down to a research question.
   d) After the research proposal has been written, the researcher decides on the methods to be used to carry out the research.
2. A research proposal serves a number of purposes. Which of the following is a purpose of a research proposal?
   a) It provides a detailed description of how your literature survey will be carried out.
   b) It is used to persuade the research committee of the university that you have a relevant and achievable research project.
   c) In a research proposal, the statement of the goals of the research includes a description of the method by which the goals will be achieved.
   d) The research proposal provides the student researcher with an opportunity to communicate with the wider body of scholars.
3. Proper planning will make the task of writing a research proposal much easier. In light of this statement, which of the following is true?
   a) You cannot plan to write a research proposal, as it is a matter of trial and error.
   b) You can only start planning to write your research proposal when you have identified a topic for your research.
   c) Planning to write your research proposal includes planning to address the ethical requirements of your research.
   d) Planning the collection of your data includes deciding on how many people you will interview.
4. Most research proposals have a very similar structure. Which of the following statements is true?
   a) A research proposal must explain how, why and when you plan to carry out your research.
   b) The research proposal starts with an abstract and then lists key words relevant to your research.
   c) The research proposal consists of a review of relevant literature, the goals of the research and the research method and design.
   d) The research proposal may include an anticipated outline of the chapters of the thesis.
5. When you write your research proposal, you should make sure of certain things. Which of the following considerations are relevant?
   a) You must write the proposal in such a way that a relatively uninformed reader will understand the question, the goals and the methodology.
   b) You must make sure that you answer any of the questions that the reader may have about your planned research.
   c) You must not provide so much detail that another researcher is able to duplicate your research.
   d) You need not be too concerned about language and editing at this stage as the research committee is only interested in the research plan.

Activities

1. A research student has included the following statement in the introductory section of his research proposal:

   > The South African Institute of Chartered Accountants (SAICA) has recently issued a *Competency Framework* describing the competencies required by a Chartered Accountant, comprising both technical and personal competencies (referred to as "pervasive skills"). Included in the pervasive skills are communication skills, interpersonal skills and the willingness to share ideas. One of the ways to develop such skills is by teamwork assignments as part of an academic programme.

   What do you think the topic of the thesis is?

2. The research student (referred to above) has stated his research question as follows:

   > Will a teamwork assignment given to a third-year accounting class, in which small teams of students selected by the lecturer carry out an assignment and evaluate each other's performance, develop their communication and interpersonal skills and their willingness to share ideas?

   Translate this research question into specific goals that the research student must achieve in order to answer the research question.

3. The research student (referred to above) has proposed the following title for his research:
   Competence – a challenge for accountants
   Do you think that this is an appropriate title? Can you suggest a better title?

Case study[56]

The following is an example of a research proposal. You have already seen part of it in Chapter 3, where you were asked to evaluate the limited literature review. You must now evaluate the rest of research proposal, based on the following guidelines:
- Does the title reflect the research questions?
- Has the student stated the research goals clearly and do they reflect all the elements of the research question?
- From his description of the methodology can you understand exactly what he plans to do, or do you have unanswered questions?
- Is there an alignment between the methods he proposes to use and the goals he has stated?
- Does he appear to be referring to primary reference sources and are they fairly recent?
- Is the presentation clear and logical?

```
┌─────────────────────────────────────────────────────────────────┐
│                      **Rhodes University**                      │
│                       **Research proposal**                     │
│ Name of candidate:                                              │
│ Student number:                                                 │
│ Proposed degree:    Master of Commerce                          │
│ Department:         Accounting                                  │
│ Provisional title:  Value investment strategies: Evidence from  │
│                     expected returns in the South African       │
│                     equity market                               │
│ Type of thesis:     Full thesis                                 │
│ Name of supervisor:                                             │
│ Date of submission: September 2011                              │
│                                                                 │
│                                                                 │
│ Approved: _____  _____                           │
│           Head of Department    Date                            │
└─────────────────────────────────────────────────────────────────┘
```

1. **Field of research and provisional title**
   Field of research: Finance
   Provisional title: Value investment strategies: Evidence from expected returns in the South African equity market

2. **Background and problem statements**
   Value investment strategies have been advocated by investors for many years. More than 75 years ago, Graham and Dodd (1934) argued that these strategies yielded returns that outperformed the market. There is also general agreement in the academic community that there is widespread evidence that value investment strategies, on average, outperform growth strategies (see for example, Chin, Prevost & Gottesman, 2002; Chan & Lakonishok, 2004 and Phalippou, 2008).

   Value strategies favour investment in value shares, which are shares priced modestly relative to their book value, earnings, cash flow, dividends or some other measure of value. The antithesis of a value share, one which is highly valued by the market, is termed a growth share. A value strategy seeks to exploit the higher returns yielded by investing in a portfolio of value shares rather than growth shares. The difference in returns is termed the value premium.

   During the last four decades there has been a significant amount of academic research in this field which has generated "substantial evidence of superior returns from such strategies" (Chin et al, 2002:422). Arguably, the most significant work was published in the early 1990s. Three seminal studies from this period are Chan, Hamoa and Lakonishok (1991), Fama and French (1992) and Lakonishok, Schleifer and Vishny (1994).

   Chan et al (1991) modelled the relationship between four fundamental variables and returns on Tokyo Stock Exchange data. They found a significant positive relationship between returns and two of their independent variables: the book to market ratio (BE/ME), and the cash flow yield (C/P). The implication of this finding is that value shares yielded higher average returns than growth shares.

Fama and French (1992) built on earlier studies of stock market anomalies in the United States (US). They found that a positive relationship between beta (essentially a standardised measure of the covariance (systematic risk) of a security with the market) and average returns, central to the capital asset pricing model (CAPM), did not exist during the period reviewed. They also found that company size and BE/ME were negatively and strongly positively related, respectively, to average returns. Further findings were that the role of leverage in average returns is captured by BE/ME and that the role of earnings yield (E/P) in average returns is absorbed by a combination of company size and BE/ME.

The Fama and French (1992) study is considered to be important as the "results delivered a stunning blow to the explanatory power of the capital asset pricing model and sparked debate about the 'death of beta'" (Chan and Lakonishok, 2004:71). In a separate finding more relevant to this research proposal, the Fama and French (1992) study also confirmed that value investment strategies yielded returns that outperformed the market.

Lakonishok et al (1994) evaluated the role of BE/ME, C/P, E/P and a five year average growth rate in sales (G/S) in average returns in US markets. Like Chan et al (1991) and Fama and French (1992), they found "investment strategies that involve buying out-of-favour (value) stocks have outperformed glamour [growth] strategies over the April 1968 to April 1990 period" (Lakonishok et al, 1994:1574).

Chan and Lakonishok (2004) updated and expanded the studies of Chan et al (1991), Fama and French (1992) and Lakonishok et al (1994). They found that value investing continued to generate superior returns in the volatile markets of the late 1990s. Other important studies relating to the value investment strategy in the last decade include Zhang (2005), Fama and French (2006, 2007 and 2008), Anderson and Brooks (2006 and 2007), Phalippou (2008) and Garcia-Feijoo and Jorgensen (2010).

The growing interest in international investment opportunities has prompted the question whether this investment strategy could also be successfully applied to markets other than the US and Japan (Chan and Lakonishok, 2004). The studies have been extended to markets as diverse as Europe (Brouwer, van der Put and Veld, 1997 and Bird and Whitaker, 2003), Taiwan (Chou and Johnson, 1990), New Zealand (Chin et al, 2002) and Canada (Athanassakos, 2009). With few exceptions, these studies indicate that on average, value investment strategies outperform strategies favouring growth shares. It is significant that value strategies have been found to be successful in a range of markets representing varying financial reporting standards, statutes and regulations.

Although value strategies have been shown to be successful in a number of different markets, these are, apart from Taiwan, all developed markets (Standard and Poor's Financial Services LLC, 2010). Taiwan aside, there appear to have been no studies which investigate value investment strategies and the value premium in emerging markets such as South Africa.

An additional matter that will be addressed in the proposed research is the question of the reasons that value investment strategies work. Probably the two most important papers on value investment strategies (Fama and French, 1992 and Lakonishok et al, 1994) offered very different explanations in response to this issue.

Fama and French (1992) argued a risk-based explanation for the higher average returns of value strategies. They took the position of the efficient market hypothesis, arguing that the higher returns from value strategies could be attributed to higher risk (Chan and Lakonishok, 2004). This rational explanation attributes higher returns from value strategies to smaller companies and those with high BE/ME ratios being fundamentally riskier, i.e. value shares are underpriced relative to their risk. Although this study found that CAPM's beta did not fully capture risk, Fama and French (1992) argued that their other two factors, company size and BE/ME are both proxies for a share's risk.

In contrast, Lakonishok et al (1994) argued that the value premium is not related to risk but is rather an opportunity arising from the suboptimal behaviour of naïve (or noise) investors and limited opportunities for arbitrage. In their essentially behaviourist (irrational investor) explanation, Lakonishok et al (1994) suggested that naïve strategies include extrapolating historical results too far into the future, assuming a trend in earnings and overreacting to company announcements. According to this argument, the variables used to measure and classify value shares are a proxy for mispricing. The resultant demand for growth stocks causes them to become overpriced while value stocks become underpriced.

3. Research goals

This research has two goals. Firstly, the research will set out to establish whether there is evidence in support of the relative effectiveness of value investment strategies in the South African equity market. In other words, the research aims to establish whether a value premium exists in a South African context.

Secondly, the possible reasons (both rational and behaviourist) for the relative success of value strategies will be examined. In doing this, the research aims to establish whether the South African equity market data provides evidence for one side or the other of the rational/irrational debate.

4. Methods, procedures and techniques

In order to establish the existence or otherwise of a value premium, the research will follow a methodology derived from Fama and French (1992), Lakonishok et al (1994), Chin et al (2002) and Anderson and Brooks (2006).

The research will study companies listed on the Main Board of JSE Limited (JSE) (previously known as the Johannesburg Stock Exchange). Two categories of data are required for each company: accounting variables and share prices. The four accounting variables, market capitalisation, BE/ME, P/E and C/P, can be extracted from the annual financial statements of the companies and share price data. The annual financial statements and share price data are available in a standardised format on the McGregorBFA online database. The database's standardised and published financial statements start from 1971 and 1988 respectively. However, JSE price data is only available from 1990. As both categories of data are required, the period to be studied will be limited to the 20 year period commencing in 1990.

The accounting variables will be used to allocate companies to value or growth portfolios. Long term differences in returns between the value and growth portfolios will be calculated, in order to establish the size (and direction) of the value premium.

In order to contribute to the academic debate on the comparative plausibilities of the rational and behaviourist narratives, the South African data will be examined for evidence on the relative risks of growth and value portfolios. This line of enquiry is motivated on the basis that, according to the rational argument, value strategies are fundamentally riskier. The risk of each strategy will be determined by calculating the historical betas of each share in each portfolio.

5. References

Anderson, K. & Brooks, C. (2006). 'The Long-Term Price-Earnings Ratio'. *Journal of Business Finance and Accounting*, vol. 33, no. 7–8, pp. 1063–1086.

Anderson, K. & Brooks, C. (2007) 'Extreme Returns from Extreme Value Stocks: Enhancing the Value Premium'. *The Journal of Investing*, vol. 16, no. 1, pp. 69–81.

Athanassakos, G. (2009). 'Value versus Growth Stock Returns and the Value Premium: The Canadian Experience 1985–2005'. *Canadian Journal of Administrative Sciences*, vol. 26, no. 2, pp. 109–121.

Bird, R. & Whitaker, J. (2003). 'The performance of value and momentum investment portfolios: Recent experience in the major European markets'. *Journal of Asset Management*, vol. 4, no. 4, pp. 221–246.

Brouwer, I. , van der Put, J. & Veld, C. (1997). 'Contrarian Investment Strategies in a Eurpoean Context', *Journal of Business Finance and Accounting*, vol. 24, no. 9–10, pp. 1353–1366.

Chan, L. K. C., Hamao, Y. & Lakonishok, J. (1991). 'Fundamentals and Stock Returns in Japan'. *The Journal of Finance*, vol. 46, no. 5, pp. 1739–1764.

Chan, L. K. C. & Lakonishok, J. (2004). 'Value and Growth Investing: Review and Update'. *Financial Analysts Journal*, vol. 60, no. 1, pp. 71–86.

Chin, J. Y. F., Prevost, A. K. & Gottesman, A. A. (2002). 'Contrarian Investing in a Small Capitalization Market: Evidence from New Zealand'. *The Financial Review*, vol. 37, no. 3, pp. 421–446.

Chou, S. R. & Johnson, K. H. (1990). 'An Empirical Analysis of Stock Market Anomalies: Evidence from the Republic of China and Taiwan' in Rhee, S. G. and Chang, R. (Eds.) *Pacific-Basin Capital Markets Research*, North-Holland: Elsevier Science Publishers.

Fama, E. F. & French, K. R. (1992). 'The Cross-Section of Expected Stock Returns'. *The Journal of Finance*, vol. 47, no. 2, pp. 427–466.

Fama, E. F. & French, K. R. (2006). 'The Value Premium and the CAPM'. *The Journal of Finance*, vol. 61, no. 5, pp. 2163–2185.

Fama, E. F. & French, K. R. (2007). 'The Anatomy of Value and Growth Stock Returns'. *Financial Analysts Journal*, vol. 63, no. 6, pp. 44–54.

Fama, E. F. & French, K. R. (2008). 'Disecting Anomalies'. *The Journal of Finance*, vol. 63, no. 4, pp. 1653–1678.

Garcia-Feijoo, L. & Jorgensen, R. D. (2010). 'Can Operating Leverage Be the Cause of the Value Premium?'. *Financial Management,* vol. 39, no. 3, pp. 1127–1153.

Graham, B. & Dodd, D. L. (1934) *Security Analysis*, New York: McGraw Hill.

Lakonishok, J., Schleifer, A. & Vishny, R. (1994). 'Contrarian Investment, Extrapolation, and Risk'. *The Journal of Finance*, vol. 49, no. 5, pp. 1541–1578.

Phalippou, L. (2008). 'Where Is the Value Premium?'. *Financial Analysts Journal,* vol. 64, no. 2, pp. 41–48.

Standard and Poor's Financial Services LLC. (2010). 'S&P Global BMI'. [Online]. Available: http://www2.standardandpoors.com/spf/pdf/index/SP_Global_BMI_Factsheet.pdf [Accessed 08/06/2011].

Zhang, L. (2005). 'The Value Premium'. *The Journal of Finance*, vol. 60, no. 1, pp. 67–103.

References

1   The Shorter Oxford English Dictionary on Historical Principles prepared by William Little, H. W. Fowler & Rev. J. Coulson; edited by C. T. Onions. Third edition (1973:1689). By permission of Oxford University Press.
2   Leedy, P.D. & Ormrod, J.E. 2001. *Practical research, planning and design.* 7th ed. New Jersey: Prentice Hall. p. 122.
3   Hofstee, E. 2009. *Constructing a good dissertation.* Johannesburg: EPE, p. 59.
4   Ibid. p. 60.

5. Leedy, P.D. & Ormrod, J.E. 2001. *Practical research, planning and design*. 7th ed. New Jersey: Prentice Hall. p. 122.
6. Hofstee, E. 2009. *Constructing a good dissertation*. Johannesburg: EPE. p. 61.
7. Leedy, P.D. & Ormrod, J.E. 2001. *Practical research, planning and design*. 7th ed. New Jersey: Prentice Hall. p. 138.
8. Hofstee, E. 2009. *Constructing a good dissertation*. Johannesburg: EPE. p. 61.
9. Leedy, P.D. & Ormrod, J.E. 2001. *Practical research, planning and design*. 7th ed. New Jersey: Prentice Hall. p. 123.
10. Welman, C., Kruger, F. & Mitchell, B. 2008. *Research methodology*. 3rd ed. Cape Town: Oxford University Press. p. 279.
11. Leedy, P.D. & Ormrod, J.E. 2001. *Practical research, planning and design*. 7th ed. New Jersey: Prentice Hall. p. 124.
12. Welman, C., Kruger, F. & Mitchell, B. 2008. *Research methodology*. 3rd ed. Cape Town: Oxford University Press. p. 279.
13. Ibid. p. 280.
14. Ibid. p. 279.
15. Salkind, N.J. 2009. *Exploring research*. 7th ed. New Jersey: Pearson Education. p. 259.
16. Hofstee, E. 2009. *Constructing a good dissertation*. Johannesburg: EPE, p. 60.
17. Rhodes University. 2010. *Higher degrees guide*. Grahamstown: Rhodes University. p. 19.
18. Hofstee, E. 2009. *Constructing a good dissertation*. Johannesburg: EPE. p. 59.
19. Babbie, E. & Mouton, J. 2009. *The practice of social research*. Cape Town: Oxford University Press. p. 103.
20. Based on the structure of a research proposal provided by the department of Business Management at the University of South Africa.
21. Welman, C., Kruger, F. and Mitchell, B. 2008. *Research methodology*. 3rd ed. Cape Town: Oxford University Press. p. 280.
22. Ibid. p. 280.
23. Salkind, N.J. 2009. *Exploring research*. 7th ed. New Jersey: Pearson Education, p. 256.
24. Leedy, P.D. & Ormrod, J.E. 2001. *Practical research, planning and design*. 7th ed. New Jersey: Prentice Hall. p. 123.
25. Welman, C., Kruger, F. and Mitchell, B. 2008. *Research methodology*. 3rd ed. Cape Town: Oxford University Press. p. 280.
26. Ibid. p. 281.
27. Rhodes University. 2010. *Higher degrees guide*. Grahamstown: Rhodes University. p. 11.
28. Ibid. p. 12.
29. Welman, C., Kruger, F. and Mitchell, B. 2008. *Research methodology*. 3rd ed. Cape Town: Oxford University Press. p. 281.
30. Ibid. p. 282.
31. Rhodes University. 2010. *Higher degrees guide*. Grahamstown: Rhodes University. p. 12.
32. Ibid. p. 12.
33. Leedy, P.D. & Ormrod, J.E. 2001. *Practical research, planning and design*. 7th ed. New Jersey: Prentice Hall. p. 133.
34. Welman, C., Kruger, F. & Mitchell, B. 2008. *Research methodology*. 3rd ed. Cape Town: Oxford University Press. p. 284.
35. Leedy, P.D. & Ormrod, J.E. 2001. *Practical research, planning and design*. 7th ed. New Jersey: Prentice Hall. p. 123.

36 Welman, C., Kruger, F. & Mitchell, B. 2008. *Research methodology*. 3rd ed. Cape Town: Oxford University Press. p. 284.
37 Ibid. p. 280.
38 Leedy, P.D. & Ormrod, J.E. 2001. *Practical research, planning and design*. 7th ed. New Jersey: Prentice Hall. p. 124.
39 Welman, C., Kruger, F. & Mitchell, B. 2008. *Research methodology*. 3rd ed. Cape Town: Oxford University Press. p. 280.
40 Leedy, P.D. & Ormrod, J.E. 2001. *Practical research, planning and design*. 7th ed. New Jersey: Prentice Hall. p. 129.
41 Salkind, N.J. 7th ed. 2009. *Exploring research*. New Jersey: Pearson Education. p. 256.
42 Leedy, P.D. & Ormrod, J.E. 2001. *Practical research, planning and design*. 7th ed. New Jersey: Prentice Hall. p. 124, 125.
43 Ibid. p. 129.
44 Salkind, N.J. 2009. *Exploring research*. 7th ed. New Jersey: Pearson Education. p. 56.
45 Hofstee, E. 2009. *Constructing a good dissertation*. Johannesburg: EPE. p. 61.
46 Leedy, P.D. & Ormrod, J.E. 2001. *Practical research, planning and design*. 7th ed. New Jersey: Prentice Hall. p. 129.
47 Welman, C., Kruger, F. & Mitchell, B. 2008. *Research methodology*. 3rd ed. Cape Town: Oxford University Press. p. 279, 280.
48 Ibid. p. 284.
49 Ibid. p. 284.
50 Leedy, P.D. & Ormrod, J.E. 2001. *Practical research, planning and design*. 7th ed. New Jersey: Prentice Hall. p. 135.
51 Hofstee, E. 2009. *Constructing a good dissertation*. Johannesburg: EPE. p. 62.
52 Leedy, P.D. & Ormrod, J.E. 2001. *Practical research, planning and design*. 7th ed. New Jersey: Prentice Hall. p. 137.
53 Hofstee, E. 2009. *Constructing a good dissertation*. Johannesburg: EPE. p. 59.
54 Welman, C., Kruger, F. and Mitchell, B. 2008. *Research methodology*. 3rd ed. Cape Town: Oxford University Press. p. 279, 280.
55 Hofstee, E. 2009. *Constructing a good dissertation*. Johannesburg: EPE. p. 62.
56 Permission was granted by the student and the supervisor to use the research proposal in this chapter.

RESEARCH REPORTING

9

Elizabeth Stack

AFTER STUDYING THIS CHAPTER, YOU SHOULD BE ABLE TO:

- Plan the writing of your report
- Understand the structure and content of a research report
- Appreciate how the report will be evaluated
- Write your report
- Deal with problems that arise during the writing process.

Hope for Alzheimer sufferers
By *Markus Parks*

An early diagnosis for Alzheimer's Disease may be on the horizon.

In a recent study researchers in South Africa attempted to identify certain characteristics (or markers) that indicated the likelihood of a person suffering from Alzheimer's Disease, thus making an early diagnosis possible.

The researchers carried out extensive tests on the brain tissue of deceased patients who suffered from Alzheimer's Disease, as well as on the brain scans of living patients. The study was initiated ten years ago and scans were carried out annually on the brains of the participants, over a period of ten years. The brain scans were performed on two thousand people aged sixty years and older – a thousand who showed no signs of early dementia and a thousand exhibiting various stages of the disease. The participants in each sample included an approximately even number of men and women and a representative range of age and population groups.

Certain changes in the brain structure and tissue of Alzheimer sufferers were identified that were shown to be closely linked with the disease and its onset, which were absent from the brains of non-sufferers. In the research group that initially showed no sign of the disease, certain participants later started to exhibit the early marker symptoms and later the full onset of Alzheimer's Disease developed. The study also indicated that women were more prone to suffer from the disease, as were members of the white population group.

An early diagnosis of the disease and the more likely sufferers therefore seems to be possible.

Source: A hypothetical article in a hypothetical health magazine

9.1 Introduction

You have completed the exciting part of your research – the voyage of discovery. Now you have to tackle the writing of the research report. This is not an impossible task or an insurmountable hurdle, even if this is your first experience of writing an extended report. This chapter will attempt to make the writing process a painless and even enjoyable one.

You may wonder what the extract above has to do with writing your report. Quite a lot really. It is a report on research that has been carried out on the early diagnosis of Alzheimer's Disease. You will note that the extract opens with an attention-grabbing sentence. That is a valuable lesson for the introductory chapter of your report. It also states the issue right at the beginning, not like a detective novel which gives all the clues, but leaves the 'punch line' until the last few pages. This is another excellent hint. Then the report goes on to spell out the research problem and describes the research method used in the experiment. You learn that the study involved 2 000 participants (a large enough sample to make the results fairly **reliable**) and both men and women of varying ages and from all population groups were involved (thus controlling possible variables). The study continued over a period of ten years and involved multiple testing, thus strengthening the results. Finally it reports the results of the study and summarises them in the final paragraph.

> **Example box**
>
> Leedy and Ormrod write that "[t]he research report is a straightforward document that sets forth clearly and precisely what the researcher has done to resolve the research problem."[1] Thus the report describes the research problem and explains exactly how the research student went about solving the problem. It is similar in many ways to a research proposal, except that the proposal presents the research plan and the thesis the execution of the plan.

Leedy and Ormrod refer to the objectives of a research report as follows. It should:[2]
1. give readers a clear understanding of the research problem and why it merited an in-depth investigation;
2. describe exactly how the data was collected in an attempt to resolve the question;
3. present the data completely and precisely ...; the data should substantiate all the interpretations and conclusions the report contains; and
4. interpret the data for the reader and demonstrate exactly how the data resolve the research problem.

There are a number of different types of research report. The extract above is a report in a magazine. This is not what this chapter discusses. A journal article is also a report and in the concluding paragraph of this chapter the writing of a journal article will be discussed briefly. This chapter focuses mainly on the reporting of research in the form of a **thesis**. Some institutions refer to it as a dissertation (in the case of a Master's degree by full thesis) or a treatise (in the case of a half thesis, or mini thesis).

9.2 Planning to write the report

You are probably tired of the word 'planning', but it is the most important element in ensuring your success in carrying out and reporting on your research.

Before starting to write your thesis, you must find out exactly what the institution's requirements are for the submission of a thesis. In Chapter 8 you read that Maria was handed a booklet by her supervisor and told to read it to find out what is required of a research proposal. A booklet (or some other document) issued by *your* university will explain the requirements for a thesis, including what the title page should look like, the font and font size to be used, the size of the margins, how many copies to make and how the thesis should be bound. Familiarise yourself with this information. If the university does not provide this information, speak to your supervisor who will give you the information.

Early on in your research, you would have been told what the prescribed length of a thesis is at your university. Your supervisor would have warned you if the scope of your proposed research was too wide for the type of thesis you would be writing. At Rhodes University, a half thesis at Master's degree level should comprise no more than 30 000 words and a Master's degree thesis no more than 50 000 words. Universities do not normally prescribe a length for doctoral theses. The length of a thesis differs in various disciplines – a doctoral thesis in mathematics may be less than 100 pages, while in history it may be very long. Hofstee writes that a dissertation is "as long as it needs to be."[3]

There may be other administrative directives that you need to comply with. At most universities, candidates are required to give the Registrar notice of intention to submit their thesis. This gives the department in which the candidate is registered enough time to appoint external examiners.

You should also ask your supervisor for a copy of the instructions provided by the university to examiners of your thesis. If you know how examiners are going to assess your work, you will know what to aim for. Examiner's reports are discussed in section 9 below – how the report will be judged.

At this stage of your research, you need to do some very careful planning for the amount of time you need to complete the work. Universities have a final date by which theses must be submitted if candidates wish to graduate at the next graduation ceremony. Your time line should work backwards from that date to where you are in the process now. You need to bear in mind that your supervisor will need a certain amount of time to read the draft of each chapter of the thesis as you submit it. Discuss this with your supervisor and factor it into your planning. Once your supervisor has given you feedback on each chapter, you will need to make the changes he or she recommends. This takes time and you should allow for this. Then your supervisor will want to look at the first full draft of your thesis and give you feedback on it and you will need to make any further changes he or she suggests. This could take a month. Then the thesis needs to be printed and bound – possibly another two days. Once you have calculated this part of your timeline, the rest of the time will be available for the actual writing of the thesis. Don't underestimate the time it will take to check all your references to make sure that they are correct and to double check all cross-references in your thesis.

You should also re-read your research proposal in preparation for starting to write your thesis. Much of what you have written in your research proposal can be incorporated (with amendments and additions) into your thesis. Don't waste time duplicating what you have already done. Finally, go to the library and skim through a few theses in your discipline. Look at their structure and read their **abstracts**, the first chapters and the final chapters.

These are the most important sections of the thesis. Then skim through the rest of the chapters. This will give you a good idea of what your thesis should look like.

9.3 The structure and contents of the report

The structure of theses at most universities and described by many writers of research textbooks is surprisingly similar. This means that examiners of a thesis are also familiar with this structure. Don't strive for originality in the structure of your thesis. Your examiners may not feel comfortable with something they have not seen before. Hofstee refers to this structure as the "classical structure for dissertations" and warns that "substantial deviation from the classic structure is risky." He also states that "[t]he structure of your dissertation is the skeleton that supports your work. It may *not* be weak."[4]

The following example illustrates the usual structure of a thesis.

> **Example box**
>
> The structure of a thesis includes the following sections:
> - Title page
> - Abstract
> - Acknowledgements
> - List of contents, tables, figures and graphs
> - Chapter 1 – Introduction
> - Chapter 2 – Literature review
> - Chapter 3 – Research methodology
> - Chapters 4 onwards – the body of the thesis
> - Final chapter – Conclusion
> - List of references
> - Appendices

Welman and Kruger describe the contents of a thesis as comprising an introduction in which the research problem and the theoretical background and research hypothesis arising from it is described, a description of the procedures and methods followed to investigate the research problem, the results obtained and an interpretation and discussion of the results.[5]

Much of the required content of each of these components is discussed below.

9.3.1 Title page, acknowledgements and list of contents, diagrams, figures and graphs

When you submitted your research proposal for approval, you gave a provisional title for your thesis. Normally this would not change but if it does, you would need to comply with the university regulations relating to changing a title of a thesis. Refer back to Chapter 8, where the title of a thesis was discussed. Salkind describes the title page as "the first thing a reader sees" and that "the title itself should be able to stand alone, convey the importance of the idea, and communicate the content of the manuscript."[6] It should be concise and explanatory.

If you do decide to include acknowledgements in your thesis, this should be placed after the abstract (see 9.3.2 below). Keep it brief and not sentimental. It does not form part of the thesis, but examiners do read it.

The list of contents should reflect chapter numbers and names, headings and subheadings, together with the page numbers on which they appear. A list of tables, figures and graphs must also be given, with their page numbers. When you revise your thesis, as you will do, you must check carefully that the page numbers are still correct. Examiners often refer back to the list of contents and wrong page numbers are very irritating. The last thing you want to do is to irritate your examiner!

9.3.2 The abstract

The abstract is the first thing examiners read and it gives them an initial impression of the relevance and quality of the thesis. Abstracts are *published documents* (as you will remember from the discussion on how to carry out a literature search) and must therefore be very carefully written. The abstract is found on the first page of the thesis (after the title page). Welman et al are of the opinion that "[i]n some respects the abstract is the most important section of the report";[7] future researchers will scan it and only the title and the abstract of a report are stored for retrieval purposes and published in journals of abstracts. The abstract presents a brief, comprehensive summary of the important points covered in your research. It tells the reader in one succinct paragraph what the research is about. The abstract covers the following points:[8]

- What the objective of the study was – the question, problem or hypothesis.
- The *principal* method or methods that were used for the research.
- Who the research participants were, the population that was studied, or what constituted the data being researched.
- What the major results were.
- The primary conclusions and implications flowing from the interpretation and discussion of the results.

The abstract should not include tables, graphs or references. The abstract usually includes a list of **key words** at the end, which relate to the research. This enables librarians to classify the research.

The number of words in an abstract for a thesis is usually limited to 350. A journal article also starts with an abstract, but it is usually shorter than for a thesis –between 100 and 200 words.

Because the abstract has to capture the essence of the whole thesis, you will probably have to rewrite it several times before you are able to say it all within the word limit.

9.3.3 The introductory chapter

The first chapter of your thesis is very important. It sets the scene for your research and in it you must capture the readers' interest and convince them of the relevance and importance of your research. Salkind summarises the purpose of the introductory chapter as follows: it "[p]rovides a framework for the problem that is being studied and a context for the statement of the purpose of the study …"[9] Because of its function and importance, it should be written last, just before the abstract. Welman et al describe the purpose of the first chapter as being to describe the objective of the research, as well as its importance.[10] Leedy and Ormrod refer to "a meeting of minds between the writer and the reader of the report."[11]

Much of what was included in your research proposal, forms the basis of this chapter. This chapter generally begins with a description of the problem area and a statement of the research problem. It then continues by narrowing down the focus of the discussion to a formulation of the research question, generally referring only to the research of selected researchers that relates directly to your research question. The theory or theoretical framework to be used in the research is also dealt with in this chapter, again usually with reference to selected literature. In this chapter, the importance of your research is revealed by indicating the gap or niche that it fills or the contribution that it makes to the body of knowledge.

The chapter then goes on to describe the purpose of the research and sets out the goals and the hypothesis(es) and the relevant definitions. Leedy and Ormrod state that the chapter should include "careful definitions of any key terms ... that may be open to varied interpretation".[12] It concludes with a section describing what the following chapters of the thesis will deal with.

In half theses, the full literature review may form part of the introductory chapter. If this is the case, it will closely resemble the literature review in the research proposal (refer to Chapter 3), but will be expanded to include all the relevant literature.

In half theses, and sometimes even full Master's theses, where the research method and design is standard and uncomplicated, this discussion may also form part of the first chapter.

Many studies in economic and management research are conducted in specific industries, sectors or organisations. In such instances, it may be necessary to include a short chapter on the context of the study, if it cannot be adequately dealt with in Chapter 1. The purpose of the context chapter is to provide the reader with the necessary background to understand the dynamics of the context and why the research will make a useful contribution.

9.3.4 The literature review

Having written the literature review in your research proposal, you will find that you don't need to do very much more to write this chapter. You may have to survey the literature again briefly to bring your review up to date with new research in the field, or you may need to carry out a more extensive literature search. The way in which you write and structure the review of the literature in your thesis is exactly the same as in your proposal (refer to Chapter 2).

Just as is the case with the literature review in the research proposal, this chapter must culminate with the formulation of the research question(s) and hypothesis(es). It must also provide the rationale for the research and indicate its importance. For Doctoral theses, given the extensive nature of the literature review, it may be necessary to include more than one chapter dealing with literature.

9.3.5 The research methodology chapter

Welman et al state that "[t]he purpose of this section relates to the requirements of controllability and replicability, which are part of the scientific method."[13] Salkind echoes this statement.[14] With regard to the content, Welman et al advise that it should "provide enough information on the execution of the project so that readers may be able to evaluate the appropriateness of the methods … and the results obtained eventually".[15] Leedy and Ormrod state that the method must be described "with the utmost precision".[16]

When writing the research method and design section of your research proposal, you will have discussed most of the basic components that you need to include in this chapter. Now that you have done the research you will be able to provide a more comprehensive discussion.

Although it was not necessary for the research methodology section in your research proposal, you will have to discuss the **research paradigm** within which you have positioned your research and defend your choice of this paradigm in your thesis. The research paradigm will dictate the research design (quantitative, qualitative or mixed methods), the methodology and the nature of the 'truth' claims you are able to make in relation to the results of your research. The paradigm, the design, the methodology and the interpretation of the results must all be aligned.

This is a critically important chapter. The research methodology must be described in sufficient detail to enable readers to understand exactly how you carried out your research and allow other researchers to **replicate** the research you have carried out. In addition to a discussion of the research paradigm, your research methodology chapter should contain the information described below, to the extent that it is relevant to your research.

- The **units of analysis** must be described (these may be human beings, documents, events or institutions, etc.).
- The **data** and the way in which it was collected must be described, for example, questionnaires, interviews, observations, the analysis of documents, pen-and-paper tests, or experiments. Questionnaires, interview schedules or observation checklists and the pen-and-paper tests must be included as appendices to the thesis and this chapter must provide a cross-reference to them.
- Where human beings or groups of human beings, such as companies or other institutions, or ethnic or other groups in a particular setting, form the population from which the sample was drawn, this must be described. The size of the sample and how the sample was selected (random or non-random sampling) must be stated. Reporting the response rate is also essential as it assists the reader to judge the validity of the results.
- Where documents or events are the units of analysis, these must be described in detail, as well as how they were selected and obtained.
- If the research is designed as an experiment, the experimental and control groups must be described, as well as how they were selected to **control the variables** involved, such as gender, age, population group, education level, etc. Potential 'nuisance' variables should also be discussed, where these cannot be controlled.
- The way in which the data was **analysed** must be described in detail. This may be by applying certain statistical tests in quantitative research or by the thematic analysis of data in qualitative research. This must be carefully specified. If statistical tests were used, the rationale for using these particular tests must be explained.
- Where specific equipment or **standardised tests** were used, these must be described in detail. Where measuring instruments have been developed specifically for the purpose of the research, the way in which they were developed and tested must also

be described. If research assistants are helping with the research, the way in which they were trained or briefed must be explained.
- **Assumptions** that formed the basis of the research and any limiting factors must be carefully spelled out. Hofstee refers to assumptions as "things that you take to be true without checking whether or not they are true."[17] They can be likened to the premises of deductive logic. Delimitations of the scope of the research should also be set out.
- The **ethical** considerations of your research and how you dealt with them, must be described. Any consent forms that participants have completed must be included as an appendix to your thesis and a cross-reference provided. Refer back to the discussion of the ethical considerations in Chapter 3.

You should also revise the chapters in this textbook that deal with the particular research methodology you will be using.

9.3.6 Chapters dealing with the data collection, measurement, analysis, results and interpretation

The actual collection and measurement of the data, the analysis of the data, the results obtained and interpretation of the results will be dealt with in two or more chapters, depending on the nature of the research. For example, the collection, measurement and analysis of the data and the results may be presented in one chapter and the interpretation in another.

Each of the chapters should start with an introductory paragraph linking it with the previous chapter, set out the particular goal or goals of the research that are addressed in the chapter and briefly describe what the chapter deals with. Each chapter should end with a concluding paragraph where the main findings are briefly summarised and a link to the following chapter is provided. Refer to section 9.5 of this chapter, where instructions on writing the thesis are provided.

Make use of headings and subheadings, as well as brief summaries, where a section includes complex or detailed discussions. Sentences that link sections of the chapter should be included. This enables you to structure your argument and enables the reader to follow the 'golden thread'. This aspect is discussed in more detail in section 9.5.

Summarising data and results in the form of graphs, diagrams and tables enhances the understanding of the readers. Data in this form should not simply be provided and left to the readers to interpret, but must be discussed and interpreted in sufficient detail to reflect your reasoning and conclusions. The data is presented as evidence for your conclusions. Leedy and Ormrod express the opinion that "the *interpretation of the data* is the essence of research."[18]

In discussing the results, Salkind states that:[19]

> the author … is free to explore important relationships between past research, the purpose of the current study, the stated hypothesis, and the results of the current study. Now is the time for an evaluation of what has been done and a 'measuring up' to determine whether the reported results fit the researcher's expectations.

Leedy and Ormrod instruct researchers to restate each subproblem, as it will "keep your reader oriented to the progress of the research as it is being reported" and "focus the reader's attention on the specific aspect of the research problem under discussion".[20]

Matters such as the statistical significance tests that were performed or threats to the reliability and validity of the results should be discussed in this part of the thesis.

> **Example box**
> How you present your findings is very important. You don't want your reader to struggle to make meaning out of a large body of data. If you are doing empirical (quantitative) research, presenting the results poses few challenges. The data and the findings will already have been summarised using statistical methods and their presentation is fairly standardised, usually in the form of a table. If you are using descriptive statistics, you can also use graphs, histograms, scatter plots and various types of charts to present your findings in pictorial form. It is essential, however, that you provide narrative explanations as well. Don't leave it to your reader to interpret the results.
> If you are doing qualitative research, your findings will be presented in narrative form and can be very long and complex. To make the presentation more accessible to the reader, you can start by giving an overview of how the findings will be presented. The findings can be summarised in the body of the report and the full data set included as an appendix. Tables, figures, bulleted lists or other means can be used to present the summarised findings concisely. Tables can be set up in the form of themes and subthemes, trends, patterns or critical events, or even organised in terms of the theoretical framework on which your research was based. It is, however, essential that your summarised findings are backed up with evidence from the data, usually verbatim quotations that illustrate a particular finding (for example, excerpts from interviews). The findings must also be linked with the objectives of the research and the literature review.

9.3.7 The concluding chapter

Like your first chapter, your last chapter is very important. It draws together all the aspects of the research project for the reader. Leedy and Ormrod state that in the concluding chapter "all loose threads should be gathered together ... looking backward [and] ... distilling into a few paragraphs precisely what has been accomplished ..."[21] It therefore sums up your whole thesis and consolidates the readers' impression of the value of your research.

The concluding chapter should re-state the research question and the goals you have set for the research, should summarise what has been dealt with in all the preceding chapters and demonstrate exactly how the goals of the research have been achieved. It must also set out your conclusions clearly and indicate whether the theories you tested or used in your research were confirmed, challenged or extended.

In the course of your research, you may have identified **rival hypotheses** that have challenged your findings or explanations of your findings, or problems may have arisen due to the limiting assumptions you made in your research, or there may have been **'nuisance' variables** that you did not anticipate and were not able to control. Your final chapter should discuss these in full, as well as the possible impact they had on your results.

No research is perfect. You must therefore reflect on inadequacies in the design of your research, sources of **bias** and challenges to the **reliability** and **validity** of your findings. If you don't discuss them, your examiners will, and they will penalise you accordingly.

> **Ethical issues**
>
> These reflections on your own work are the mark of an objective and ethical researcher. Leedy and Ormrod advise that, in the interest of advancing the frontiers of knowledge, "you must be sufficiently objective to admit when your thinking was incorrect and offer reasonable explanations …" and look at "the evidence squarely and without prejudice … report candidly and precisely what the impersonal data affirm."[22]

During the course of your research, you would probably have identified opportunities for further research and these should be pointed out in your final chapter. These research opportunities may have arisen as a result of limitations in the scope of your own research, simplifying assumptions you have made, problems you have experienced in carrying out your research or further gaps in the body of knowledge.

As a final word on what the concluding chapter should achieve, Leedy and Ormrod advise researchers to "see the research endeavour as through the wrong end of a telescope: clearly, minutely and at some distance, with all significant aspects brought together in proper perspective."[23]

9.4 How the report will be judged

As was indicated in section 9.2, dealing with planning to write the thesis, understanding what examiners will look for and how they will assess your work will assist you to write your thesis. This section of the chapter discusses the guidelines provided to examiners by universities, the criteria they stipulate for their assessment and also provides a detailed anecdotal discussion of how a number of examiners approach the task of examining a thesis.

9.4.1 Guidelines and criteria provided to examiners

Universities provide examiners of Master's and Doctoral theses with guidelines on the examination of theses and the basis on which they should be assessed. These guidelines usually differ to a certain extent for a Master's degree by half thesis (or a treatise), a full thesis (or dissertation) at Master's degree level and a Doctoral thesis. What follows is a summary of the guidelines and assessment criteria most frequently used.

9.4.1.1 Guidelines

The guidelines presented below are typical examples of guidelines provided to examiners by most universities. The *Guidelines for Examiners for the Degree of Doctor of Philosophy* issued by Rhodes University states that:[24]

> [t]he thesis must show that the candidate: understands the purpose of the investigation; has read and understood the relevant literature; has developed (or adapted) and used the appropriate methods and techniques; [and] as a result of independent research, has made a substantial and original contribution, the substance of which, in the opinion of the examiners, is worthy of publication in an accredited academic journal.

In the case of a thesis at Master's degree level, Rhodes University (*Internal and External Examiner's Report,* undated: 1) states that:[25]

> [w]hen the award of the degree with distinction is under consideration, examiners are asked to look for evidence of exceptional methodological and conceptual skills, clarity of exposition and argument, sound judgement, originality of approach, and some contribution to knowledge.

The Faculty of Economic and Management Sciences (Potchefstroom Campus) of the North-West University issues *Guidelines for the evaluation of theses, dissertations and mini-dissertations* (undated). These guidelines state that "[the thesis] should provide an indication of the candidate's familiarity with the literature pertinent to the research, provide evidence of research skills and the ability to present the research in a proper report." The thesis should also make an "undeniable contribution to the knowledge of and insight into the subject field." A thesis should also provide evidence of originality, "be it through the uncovering of new facts, or through the practising of independent critical abilities".[26] The candidate should be able to document the research problem and objectives in a systematic, logical and persuasive manner, explain the research method and design and present the results and conclusions in a scientifically correct manner.

9.4.1.2 Assessment criteria

Rhodes University, again because it is typical of the assessment criteria in general use, sets out the criteria for a Master's degree by half thesis, as given in the example box below.

> **Example box**
>
> Assessment criteria for a thesis include the following questions:[27]
> - Has the candidate adequately identified and described the research problem/question and goal within a clearly identified field?
> - Is the candidate sufficiently acquainted with the relevant literature?
> - Is the candidate sufficiently skilled at using appropriate research methods and techniques, as revealed in the analysis and interpretation of data and findings?
> - Has the candidate presented the material in a logical, clear and systematic way?
> - Has the candidate presented the material in a linguistically and stylistically accepted way?
> - Has the candidate provided evidence of critical reflection on the research process?
> - Is there evidence that learning has taken place through the research process? The rationale accompanying the projects should draw attention to this aspect.
> - Do you recommend the candidate be awarded the degree?
> - Do you recommend a distinction?

The guidelines for a Master's degree by full thesis are substantially the same as those listed above. In the case of the degree of Doctor of Philosophy, the criteria include the criteria described above and, in addition, ask two questions. Does it constitute an original contribution? Is the substance of the thesis worthy of publication?[28]

The Faculty of Management Studies at the University of KwaZulu-Natal provides examiners with a document entitled *Information for the Guidance of Examiners of Master's Dissertations* that contains very similar criteria, but where a pass with distinction is considered by an examiner, the criteria are qualified by the use of the words "profound understanding" [of the nature and purpose of the investigation], "exceptional ability" [in evaluating and applying the relevant literature] "in a judicious manner", a "thorough command" [of relevant research techniques], a "full and penetrating" [interpretation of the findings] and a "critical assessment" [of their significance, including any limitations or implications for further research].[29]

9.4.2 How examiners examine a thesis in practice

From discussions with colleagues about how they approach the examination process, it appears that we all follow a fairly standard process and evaluate the components of a thesis in a similar manner. What is significant is that most examiners read the abstract, the first chapter and the last chapter at least twice. This indicates their importance. The following summary explains what your examiners are likely to look for:

- The **title** and the **abstract**. Does the title reflect the nature of the research question? Would researchers surveying the literature be able to use the title and abstract to decide on the relevance of the research for their own research? They will read the abstract carefully and critically – is it in the required format? Are the key words stated and do they reflect the content of the title and the abstract? At their second reading, they will ask whether the abstract accurately and clearly reflects the contents of the thesis.
- The **list of contents** section. They will read this to get an overview of the research.
- The **reference list**. Examiners will scrutinise it and ask the following questions:
    - Has the candidate accessed relevant sources?
    - Are the references predominantly from **primary sources**, such as academic journals, rather than text books, the internet or the popular press?
    - Is the list complete – no important sources omitted?
    - Do the references provide appropriate coverage, from seminal articles to the most recent?
    - Is the referencing method technically correct?
- **Chapter 1**. This is the most important chapter and examiners read this and the final chapter twice, right at the start of the examination process and again at the end to determine whether:
    - the **introduction** describes the research problem and its context, narrowing down to a clearly stated research question or hypothesis and if this is achieved by way of a logical argument supported by evidence from the most important research carried out in the field;
    - the **question or hypothesis** is clearly stated, the **theory** used in the research is clearly described, the **scope** of the study is appropriate and the topic **relevant and interesting**;
    - **definitions**, critical **assumptions** and **limitations of scope** are clearly stated;
    - sufficient information is provided to decide whether or not the study is important; and
    - the **goals** are set out clearly, address all aspects of the research question and are closely aligned with the title of the study.
- The **concluding chapter.** This chapter is also read twice, at the beginning and again at the end to establish whether:
    - the conclusions are clearly aligned with the research goals set out in the first chapter and whether they answer the research question;
    - the conclusions are linked with the theories, frameworks or findings in earlier research;

- limitations, problems and unresolved issues are made explicit, discussed and their impact evaluated; and
- opportunities for further research are identified.
- The chapter dealing with **research methods and design**. Examiners read this to determine whether:
  - the candidate has situated the research within a particular research paradigm and provided a rationale for this and whether this classification appears to be appropriate;
  - the unit(s) of analysis and the data have been clearly described, as well as how the data will be collected;
  - the sample size and selection procedure are appropriate in relation to the goals of the research;
  - where relevant, the way in which the data will be measured has been specified and whether this appears to be appropriate;
  - the way in which the data will be analysed has been described and is appropriate, as well as, where relevant, that the appropriate statistical methods have been applied;
  - the ethical concerns are described, how these will be dealt with and whether this is acceptable; and
  - there is a clear alignment between the research goals and the research methodology.
- Remaining **chapters**. Each chapter is read to decide whether:
  - the introduction to the chapter links it with the previous chapter and describes how it addresses a particular goal of the research; whether it provides an overview of what is covered in the chapter – these aspects constitute the 'golden thread' that must run through the thesis;
  - arguments are clearly developed by means of suitable headings and subheadings and if there is clear 'signposting' by means of summaries of complex arguments and linking sentences to ensure that the reader can follow the argument;
  - the discussion is logical and clear, in terms of the development of the argument;
  - the concluding section briefly summarises the findings in the chapter and provides a link with the next chapter.
- In general, examiners also look at the following:
  - errors: grammatical, language, spelling, punctuation, sentence construction and internal logic of sentences; mathematical errors; instances of incorrect or missing in-text referencing and instances of unsubstantiated assertions.
- The final assessment of the examiner expresses an opinion of the overall academic merit of the thesis.
  - What is the quality of the work?
  - Has the research been duly rigorous?
  - Has the student interpreted the results – not simply documented them, leaving it to readers to form their own conclusions?
  - Does the thesis make a contribution to the body of knowledge?
  - Does the thesis demonstrate aspects of originality in the question, methodology, or interpretation; or does the thesis give a new perspective on established research?
  - Is it publishable (or parts of it)?

Now that you understand what is expected of your thesis, you need to start writing. But writing the report also involves certain skills. This is discussed in the next section.

9.5 Writing the report

One of the first recommendations is that you do not wait until you have completed the research process before you start writing. Write sections of chapters or even paragraphs as you go through the steps in your research process. You can file them electronically in the chapters in which they will appear. These pieces of writing can be sorted and arranged later, but you will have made a valuable start and you are unlikely to forget important things that occurred to you at various stages of the research.

The second suggestion (that was made in Chapter 8 when the writing of the research proposal was discussed) is that you should print out your research question, goals and subgoals and paste them on the wall in front of your desk or computer. This will keep you on track.

9.5.1 Hints on writing

The following hints on academic writing will assist you to achieve quality in your thesis. If you have serious problems with language, grammar and punctuation, however, you may need to employ a professional editor, as it is not your supervisor's duty to correct these aspects of your thesis.

9.5.1.1 Technical aspects

Take great care with your choice of words and expressions. Language use must be clear and correct and no slang terms or jargon should be used. The proposal (and the thesis) should be written in 'academic' style. Avoid the use of emotive words, such as 'huge', 'terrifying', 'shocking', etc. Academic writing appeals to the logic of the reader and not the reader's emotions.

Pay particular attention to punctuation and grammar.
- Use the 'spell check' option, but set it on United Kingdom or South African English. Don't simply rely on it, however, as it does not identify all errors, such as 'bare' when you mean 'bear', 'where' when you mean 'were', 'wait' when you mean 'weight', etc.
- Make sure that you write full sentences. Sentences often start with words such as 'while', 'if', 'although', 'since' or 'because'. These are words that qualify certain clauses in a sentence. Sentences starting with these words are also often incomplete, for example: "As research is a skill that few have mastered and there are few textbooks relevant to researchers in commerce." This is not a sentence.
- Singular and plural are often mixed up, for example: "One class of taxpayers are ...".
- Semi-colons (;) are often used instead of a comma (,). If you feel tempted to use a semi-colon, you probably need to break the sentence into two sentences. In general, use short sentences wherever possible.
- The apostrophe 's is frequently used incorrectly. If you write 'taxpayer's returns', you are saying 'the returns of the taxpayer'. In the plural that would be: taxpayers' returns. Taxpayer's is not the plural of 'taxpayer'.
- Avoid using capital letters, unless absolutely necessary.
- In some disciplines or faculties, it is not permitted to use the first person 'I' (or 'we'). You can use expressions such as "it is submitted ... ", or "it can be concluded ...", rather than "I think" or "I conclude".

- Use the simplest possible language. Some novice researchers believe that in academic writing you should use 'big' words. Unfortunately, they often use them incorrectly. One candidate used words that sound the same, but have a different meanings, like 'confer' instead of 'infer'. Keep your choice of words simple and **consult a dictionary**.
- Abbreviations and acronyms must be used **very sparingly**. Only use an abbreviation or acronym when a particular term is used many times in the thesis (or proposal) and is in common use in this form, for example, 'gross domestic product' is invariably referred to as GDP. Another example that would be acceptable is the South African Revenue Services (referred to as SARS). Excessive use of acronyms and abbreviations is irritating to the reader. Write the expression out in full the first time it is used in **each** chapter and then, in brackets, the abbreviation or acronym. If you are using a number of abbreviations or acronyms, provide a list at the beginning of your thesis, after the list of contents.
- If you include a bulleted list of items following a colon (:), each bulleted item should begin with a lower case letter and end with a semi-colon. If the bulleted items are complete sentences, you should start with a capital letter and end with a full stop.
- Numbers of up to ten must be written out in words; numbers greater than ten are expressed in figures. This rule does not apply when a sentence begins with a number, in which case it must be written out in full. It also does not apply to numbers in tables or in equations or calculations.
- Proofread very carefully. Placing a ruler under the line of type that you are proofreading helps to slow down your eye. It is difficult to proofread directly from the computer screen, so use a hard copy. Reading your work out loud enables you to identify where there is a lack of clarity in your logical reasoning.

9.5.1.2 Referencing

Every statement that you make that is not your own **must** have a reference, whether it is a quotation or simply a paraphrase of something someone else has stated. Statements such as "it is a well-known fact" or "most writers agree" must be backed up by references as authority for these statements. Where the reader of your work would be uncertain whether a statement is your own or that of another writer, make it clear by stating, for example, "it is submitted ...", "it appears that ...", "clearly ...", "therefore ...", or "it can be concluded ...". Another way of doing this, is by saying "in the opinion of the writer ...", but this can become clumsy.

Long quotations are indented and a smaller font is used, without inverted commas. Shorter quotations within a sentence should be placed within inverted commas.

> **Ethical issues**
>
> Failure to provide a reference, even when you are only using the ideas of another and not quoting directly, is plagiarism (often referred to as academic theft). An ethical researcher acknowledges all contributions by others to the thesis.

9.5.1.3 Logical argument

Welman et al refer to a research project as "an extensive exercise in logical reasoning" and advise researchers to "be careful not to get lost in details that disrupt the logical train of thought."[30] Research is therefore, in essence, an **extended argument** in which a hypothesis or question is subjected to testing and interpretation, using sound logic. You should keep referring back to your hypothesis or question and the basis of your argument as you write, letting the logic of the argument run through your paper like a 'golden thread'. To achieve this, each chapter should begin with a brief **introductory paragraph** indicating how the chapter will fit into the argument you are putting forward and also linking the present chapter with the previous one. Each chapter should end with a brief **conclusion** in which you summarise what has been dealt with in the chapter and link it to the following chapter. Hofstee advises that "introductions and conclusions are your most important tools to explain your structure to your reader ... [and] should be used at every opportunity at all levels." Effective use will "fix the logic of your work in their minds".[31]

The structure of your document must follow your line of reasoning. A report, journal article and a thesis are all **extended arguments**. Paragraphs must reflect units of logic (not every sentence a new paragraph, or paragraphs that run over several pages). Headings and subheadings must emphasise the flow of your reasoning. Hofstee states that "[h]eadings are a powerful way to help readers understand your structure and the development of your arguments ..." and advises that they should be short and to the point.[32] Where you have put forward a long involved argument in a section or a paragraph of the chapter, this should briefly be summarised and linked with the new section or paragraph. You must lead the reader through your argument, using 'sign posts' and links. Monitor the internal logic of each sentence very carefully.

It is important to include a sufficiently **detailed explanation** of the background and a definition or explanation of important concepts. You are not writing for your supervisor who understands these concepts, but for other readers (including outside examiners). You should assume that the person reading your work is a reasonably informed, but not an expert reader. To give a few examples: Eugene, who is writing on failure prediction models, has explained what is meant by corporate failure, why it is important to be able to predict corporate failure and has discussed the background to the development of failure prediction models. Blake, who is writing on share valuations, has discussed under what circumstances it is necessary to value shares and has described the various valuation models and their application. Only once you have adequately explained the background and technical aspects of a theory, concept or definition, is your reader able to contextualise and understand the research and follow your argument.

The most important aspect of reporting on your research is maintaining the '**golden thread**' of your argument. On a macro-level, the goals, methodology and the methods used in your research must be logically aligned. At a more detailed level, every sentence, paragraph, heading and subheading must clearly and logically maintain this golden thread.

Finally you must accept that you may have to revise what you have written several times. Leedy and Ormrod warn that it may take "not several days, not several weeks, but several *months* to complete the report-writing process."[33]

9.5.2 Other problems experienced by researchers

Research is often a lonely experience and researchers commonly experience a measure of depression at some stage in the process, manifesting as writer's block, doubts about the worth of their work and feelings of isolation. Often, these symptoms are interlinked. Hofstee refers to them as "dissertation blues" and he is of the opinion that "most often the reasons for lack of submission [of the dissertation] are psychological."[34] He advises researchers to "[b]reak it down into small manageable parts" and that "[c]*onsistent work* ... leads to a dissertation that looks as if it is the product of extremely high-level intellectual work".[35]

9.5.2.1 Writer's block

Leedy and Ormrod speak of becoming "'stuck' indefinitely in the process of writing their final dissertations".[36] Hofstee writes about "over-ambition and perfectionism" which can also lead to writer's block.[37] When you get stuck and feel that you cannot continue, you should put the thesis away for a couple of weeks. When you take it up again, you will probably find that it is quite easy to continue, and if you don't, one way to get started again is to read through what you have written and start editing your work. The creative juices will soon start flowing. Problems seem to sort themselves out in your mind, without you consciously thinking about it.

9.5.2.2 Feelings of worthlessness

At certain stages in their research, most researchers begin to doubt themselves and the value of their research. The cause of this is often that they become so grounded in their research and familiar with their work that it appears to be simplistic or banal. Hofstee writes that research is "a learning process and learning can be uncomfortable".[38] One way to overcome self-doubt is, again, to put the thesis away for a couple of weeks. When you start re-reading what you have done, you will realise that you *have* done good work. Hofstee reminds researchers that "[y]ou wrote a good proposal . . . didn't you?"[39]

9.5.2.3 Loneliness and isolation

Particularly for part-time students, feelings of isolation and loneliness are common. Hofstee believes that this leads to "a sense of alienation ... leads to demotivation, self-doubt, and to questioning the worth of what you are doing".[40] Ask your supervisor to give you contact details of academic support groups or online discussion forums. He or she may also be able to, with their permission, give you the names of your fellow students. You could arrange informal meetings over a meal, perhaps, to talk about your research problems and ideas. You will be amazed at how valuable these conversations are and how much you will be able to help each other with ideas and criticism. If you can't meet in person, internet chat rooms can provide a similar forum for the exchange of ideas.

Whatever your problems are, discuss them with your supervisor. He or she will be able to help. Even if your problems are personal, rather than work-related, do keep your supervisor advised of them, as these problems may delay the dates on which you can submit written work, disrupt your supervisor's work programme and may impact on deadlines that have been set.

9.6 Summary

Leedy and Ormrod conclude that "[t]he research document that you write is a clear reflection of your scholarship as a researcher ...".[41]

This chapter has described the importance of planning before you start to write your report and explained in detail the structure and contents of a typical research report. In order to assist researchers to write good quality reports, this chapter has provided insight into how examiners assess the quality of a research report. To improve the quality of the written report, a number of hints were provided on 'good' academic writing and the chapter has also given advice on how to deal with personal problems that may arise during the process of writing the report.

The chapter has been written on the basis that it was discussing the requirements of a thesis. There are a number of other types of reports that researchers may write, including journal articles. What follows is a brief comparison of a journal article and a thesis:

- Length: the journal to which you intend to submit your article will prescribe the maximum length of the article. This will usually be in the region of 25 pages. From this, it is clear that a journal article presents a very concise form of research report.
- Abstract: the abstract is very similar, except that the length is limited to about 200 words. This also indicates how focused and to the point a journal article must be.
- The literature review: this would be very limited. Only the most important research and research directly connected with the topic of your article should be discussed.
- The methodology: you have no room to present a philosophical discussion of the research paradigm into which your research fits. Despite the need for brevity, the methodology section should enable the reader to understand exactly how you designed and conducted your research.
- The results and their interpretation: this is the core of the journal article and must be presented fully but briefly. Tables, graphs and diagrams often help to summarise the findings in an efficient and space-saving manner.
- Conclusion and recommendations: the article must present these, but in the most concise form possible.
- Style and referencing: the journal to which you submit your article will provide the requirements and you must adhere strictly to them.

Key terms and concepts

abstract: a summary of a thesis in which the problem, research methods used to address the problem and the findings are briefly described

assumptions: basic premises or beliefs that we accept to be true, without subjecting them to testing in our research

bias: any influence, condition or set of conditions that, singly or together, distorts the data and therefore attacks the integrity of the facts

control (controllability): in research we seek to control those variables that we are not testing

data: refer to Chapter 8

key words: refer to Chapter 3

limitations of scope: restrictions that we place on the breadth of coverage of our research, for example, limiting time periods, geographical areas, populations that are the subject of our research, the types of documents, etc.

nuisance variables: those unidentified variables that may have influenced our research results

primary sources: refer to Chapter 3

reliable (reliability): the reliability of the conclusions reached in the research is related to the measuring instruments used and the extent to which observations or measures are consistent or stable

replicate (replicability): research methods should be described is such a way that another researcher is able to carry out research in exactly the same way

research paradigm: a basic belief system based on assumptions relating to the nature of the reality we wish to establish in our research, the relationship between us (the researcher) and what can be known and how the enquirer (researcher) can go about finding out whatever he or she believes can be known

rival hypotheses: alternative explanations for the results achieved in the research

standardised tests: tests that are in common use and have not been developed by us for the purposes of our research

theory: refer to Chapter 8

thesis: a long essay or dissertation involving personal research written for or as part of a university degree

unit of analysis: those people, incidents, perceptions, artefacts, documents, etc. that will be the subject of our research

validity: the degree to which what was observed or measured is the same as what was purported to be observed or measured

variables: refer to Chapter 8

Questions

1. What is the purpose of a research report?
2. Name three planning steps that you should take before starting to write your research report.
3. Outline the components of a research report.
4. What are the most important chapters in a research report? Why?
5. Why should you be concerned about what examiners think about your thesis?
6. What should you do if you experience writer's block?

Mutiple-choice questions

1. A research report, including a thesis, is an extended argument based on evidence. If this statement is true, which of the following are also true?
    a) The thread of the argument must be maintained by means of headings, linking sentences and summaries.
    b) The argument put forward in a thesis simply relates to the research process.
    c) The examiners of a thesis are interested only in the results of the research and not the development of the argument.
    d) The argument presented in a thesis is unique in the sense that only evidence and not logic is acceptable.
2. The goals of the research form the basis of the entire research process. Accepting that

this is true, which of the following statements are also true?
- a) Each chapter must restate all the goals of the research in the introductory section.
- b) Each chapter, excluding the first, must include in the introduction a statement of the particular goals addressed in the chapter.
- c) The final chapter need not restate the goals of the research as they have been set out in detail in the preceding chapters.
- d) There is no need to re-state the goals of the research in each chapter, as the reader of the thesis can refer back to the first chapter.

3. The structure of most research reports, including theses, is very similar. As a result of this, which of the following statements are true?
- a) A thesis differs from other forms of research report only in respect of the need to include a description of the research methodology applied.
- b) A thesis differs from a journal article only in respect of its length.
- c) The title of a thesis must reflect the structure of the report.
- d) Including an abstract in a thesis is optional.

4. In the concluding chapter of a thesis a researcher should reflect on certain aspects of the research. Which of the following statements is therefore correct?
- a) The researcher should reflect on the goals of the research – whether or not they were appropriate.
- b) The researcher should reflect on inadequacies in the design of the research.
- c) The researcher should try to assess the impact of 'nuisance' variables on the results of the research.
- d) The researcher should reflect on opportunities for further research.

5. Universities provide examiners with guidelines on what an examination report should contain. Which of the following statements are true in relation to these guidelines?
- a) Examiners need only 'tick' the relevant box on the guidelines provided and need not include a detailed report.
- b) Examiners of Doctoral theses must report whether or not the thesis has made a substantial and original contribution.
- c) There is no difference between the assessment criteria for a Doctoral and a Master's thesis, except with regard to the length of the thesis.
- d) An examiner should pay particular attention to the student researcher's ability to explain the research method and design.

Application questions

To test your writing ability, the following exercise may be of assistance. Identify the nature of the errors in the following sentences.

1. As South Africa is a country of many cultures with differing values and beliefs that affect the political perceptions of its people.
   There are three methods to calculate free cash flows. Namely the operating perspective, the finance perspective and the migration method.
2. It will make a huge difference to the Gross National Product of South Africa.
   Many taxpayers engage in disgraceful tax evasion schemes, depriving the country of desperately needed tax revenue.

3. I will compare and contrast international methods of energy taxation to South Africa. I will analyse how electricity consumption is taxed in countries around the world.
4. Peter Dingaza who is a South African resident earning his income in the form of remuneration and investments. However, Peter has a hunch that dividends paid by foreign company's will not be taxed as per the income tax act; and wishes to affect huge foreign investments. As a friend informed him that their tax advisor suggested with regards to Section 1 of the act. Peter is terrified that he will be fined; because he is a good citizen and tax avoidance is an evil.

Case study[42]

An abstract forming part of a thesis is replicated below. The title of the thesis is:
- *An analysis of the financing mechanisms proposed for funding national health insurance in South Africa.*

Evaluate this abstract, based on the following guidelines:
- Does the writer state the research question?
- Is the research method used to carry out the research described?
- Does the writer describe the data used in the research?
- Are the major results presented?
- Has the researcher reached a conclusion?
- Do they key words appear to be appropriate?
- Does the title of the thesis reflect the nature of the research as described in the abstract?

ABSTRACT
In the 2011 Budget Speech, the Minister of Finance announced that South Africa would be introducing National Health Insurance. The Minister described the financing mechanisms under consideration for funding National Health Insurance. The Minister also referred to eight countries, namely Japan, South Korea, Taiwan, Chile, Colombia, Mexico, Thailand and Vietnam as examples of countries which had successfully implemented universal health coverage. These countries were selected for the purpose of the present research.

The goal of this study was to analyse the health care financing mechanisms under consideration in South Africa to determine if they were in line with international trends and "best practice" in relation to South Africa's economic profile. To determine whether the economic situation in South Africa is comparable to the eight countries selected for the research, a high-level comparison was made of the economic profile of South Africa and the eight countries, based on certain demographic, macro-economic, health expenditure and health status indicators. The health care financing mechanisms used in the eight countries were also analysed.

International trends suggested that health care should be financed primarily through pre-payment systems, that financing mechanisms should preferably be progressive in nature and that a large share of funding should be from government sources (albeit shared between general tax revenue and specific health care contributions). The financing mechanisms under consideration in South Africa reflect these norms. The health systems in the eight countries analysed all exhibited elements of "good performance" and also complied, to a large extent, with international trends, but the financing models used for funding health care in the eight countries were country-specific and could therefore not be compared directly or used to recommend a system for South Africa.

> Aspects not addressed by this thesis include the implications of a centralised healthcare system, the implications of a single-payer system, the benefit package to be offered and its cost implications, the role of private healthcare providers and how the significant human resource scarcity and infrastructure backlogs will be addressed.
>
> **Key words:** National Health Insurance; taxation; universal health care
>
> *Source: Stevens, Nicol Susan. 2012. Unpublished thesis, Masters M.Com. Faculty of Commerce, Accounting. An analysis of the financing mechanisms proposed for funding national health insurance in South Africa. Grahamstown: Rhodes University. Available [online] http://hdl.handle.net/10962/d1001642*
> *Reprinted by permission of the author.*

References

1. Leedy, P.D. & Ormrod, J.E. 2001. *Practical research, planning and design.* 7th ed. New Jersey: Prentice Hall. p. 285.
2. Ibid. p. 288.
3. Hofstee, E. 2009. *Constructing a good dissertation.* Johannesburg: EPE. p. 38.
4. Ibid. p. 35.
5. Welman, C., Kruger, F. & Mitchell, B. 2008. *Research methodology.* 3rd ed. Cape Town: Oxford University Press. p. 248.
6. Salkind, N.J. 2009. *Exploring research.* 7th ed. New Jersey: Pearson Education. p. 270.
7. Welman, C., Kruger, F. & Mitchell, B. 2008. *Research methodology.* 3rd ed. Cape Town: Oxford University Press. p. 249.
8. Adapted from Leedy, P.D. & Ormrod, J.E. 2001. *Practical research, planning and design.* 7th ed. New Jersey: Prentice Hall. p. 294.
9. Salkind, N.J. 2009. *Exploring research.* 7th ed. New Jersey: Pearson Education. p. 271.
10. Welman, C., Kruger, F. & Mitchell, B. 2008. *Research methodology.* 3rd ed. Cape Town: Oxford University Press. p. 249.
11. Leedy, P.D. & Ormrod, J.E. 2001. *Practical research, planning and design.* 7th ed. New Jersey: Prentice Hall. p. 289.
12. Ibid.
13. Welman, C., Kruger, F. & Mitchell, B. 2008. *Research methodology.* 3rd ed. Cape Town: Oxford University Press. p. 250.
14. Salkind, N.J. 2009. *Exploring research.* 7th ed. New Jersey: Pearson Education. p. 271.
15. Welman, C., Kruger, F. & Mitchell, B. 2008. *Research methodology.* 3rd ed. Cape Town: Oxford University Press. p. 250.
16. Leedy, P.D. & Ormrod, J.E. 2001. *Practical research, planning and design.* 7th ed. New Jersey: Prentice Hall. p. 289.
17. Hofstee, E. 2009. *Constructing a good dissertation.* Johannesburg: EPE. p. 88.
18. Leedy, P.D. & Ormrod, J.E. 2001. *Practical research, planning and design.* 7th ed. New Jersey: Prentice Hall. p. 291.
19. Salkind, N.J. 2009. *Exploring research.* 7th ed. New Jersey: Pearson Education. p. 272.
20. Leedy, P.D. & Ormrod, J.E. 2001. *Practical research, planning and design.* 7th ed. New Jersey: Prentice Hall. p. 290.
21. Ibid. p. 291.

22. Ibid. p. 291.
23. Ibid. p. 291.
24. Rhodes University, 2012, p. 1.
25. Rhodes University Internal and External Examiner's Report, undated, p. 1.
26. The Faculty of Economic and Management Sciences (Potchefstroom Campus) of the North-West University *Guidelines for the evaluation of theses, dissertations and mini-dissertations* (undated).
27. Rhodes University Internal and External Examiner's Report, undated.
28. Rhodes University External Examiner's Report Form, undated, p. 1.
29. Faculty of Management Studies at the University of KwaZulu-Natal provides examiners with a document entitled *Information for the Guidance of Examiners of Master's Dissertations*, undated, p. 1.
30. Welman, C., Kruger, F. & Mitchell, B. 2008. *Research methodology*. 3rd ed. Cape Town: Oxford University Press. p. 248.
31. Hofstee, E. 2009. *Constructing a good dissertation*. Johannesburg: EPE. p. 42.
32. Ibid. p. 41.
33. Leedy, P.D. & Ormrod, J.E. 2001. *Practical research, planning and design*. 7th ed. New Jersey: Prentice Hall. p. 301.
34. Hofstee, E. 2009. *Constructing a good dissertation*. Johannesburg: EPE. p. 71.
35. Ibid. p. 72.
36. Leedy, P.D. & Ormrod, J.E. 2001. *Practical research, planning and design*. 7th ed. New Jersey: Prentice Hall. p. 301.
37. Hofstee, E. 2009. *Constructing a good dissertation*. Johannesburg: EPE. p. 74.
38. Ibid. p. 78.
39. Ibid. p. 75.
40. Ibid. p. 73.
41. Leedy, P.D. & Ormrod, J.E. 2001. *Practical research, planning and design*. 7th ed. New Jersey: Prentice Hall. p. 285.
42. Stevens, N. 2011. Unpublished half thesis. *An analysis of the financing mechanisms proposed for funding national health insurance in South Africa*. Grahamstown: Rhodes University.

ACADEMIC LITERACY

Wilhelm van Rensburg

10

AFTER STUDYING THIS CHAPTER, YOU SHOULD BE ABLE TO:

- Understand the meaning and implication of the concept academic literacy in terms of your own research writing
- Follow the processes suggested in this chapter in order to become fully academically 'literate' by means of critical reading and research writing
- Become part of an academic discourse community which acknowledges other members by referencing authors and avoiding plagiarism
- Find your own scholarly identity manifesting in your academic writing by developing persuasive arguments with your own authorial voice.

> The Faculty of Education at the University of Johannesburg experienced a bottle-neck with the through-put rate of its graduate students who could comfortably manage the course work components of their degrees, but who struggled with the writing of their dissertations and theses. As an experiment, a graduate writing centre was initiated with the express aim of providing these graduate students with academic writing support. Under a director, the centre employed a number of tutors, using the latest technology to assist students with their writing. The tutors were all qualified researchers and experienced writers, and after intensive tutor training, helped students on an individual, face-to-face basis, with their writing. The students provided the subject knowledge of the topics they were researching, and the tutors, the knowledge and skills about **academic writing**. Additional small group writing workshops and training sessions on research methodology were also offered at the centre. After considerable success, the centre launched a subject journal, publishing the findings of many of the students' research projects. In this manner, graduate students were initiated in the **academic discourse community** by developing the necessary literacy which enabled them to become members of that community. The question, however, remains: if you do not have the benefit of a graduate writing centre at your institution of higher learning, what do you do? This chapter focuses on a sensible and effective approach to becoming academically literate in and through your writing.

10.1 Introduction

Having read the preceding chapters on how to prepare a proposal for your research report, thesis or dissertation, and all the aspects one has to keep in mind when thinking about this, leaves one with an important task: actually *writing* the proposal, covering all the concepts succinctly in the required number of words. It is impossible, as you might have realised by now, to leave the writing 'till the end'. You have invariably done quite a bit of writing at this point: making notes of the articles and chapters from books you have read; summarising the main points of the authors; paraphrasing their **arguments**, putting their ideas in your own words; formulating your own ideas about the topic you are researching; theorising or explaining what you anticipate to find in your research, and so on. As you might have realised as well, some of these bits of writing require very specific skills, such as **summarising** and **paraphrasing**, whereas other parts of writing are at a higher cognitive level, such as formulating an argument, expressing new ideas in writing, and linking the various ideas to form a coherent whole. And just when you thought you knew everything about academic writing, you stumble across this type of writing:[1]

> The move from a structuralist account in which capital is understood to structure social relations in relatively homologous ways to a view of hegemony in which power relations are subject to repetition, convergence, and re-articulation brought the question of temporality into the thinking of structure, and marked a shift from Althusserian theory that takes structuralist totalities as theoretical objects to one in which the insights into the contingent possibility of structure inaugurate a renewed conception of hegemony as bound up with the contingent sites and strategies of the re-articulation of power.

The ninety-four word sentence comes from Helen Sword's book, *Stylish Academic Writing*. You will not be wrong if you think this example is everything but 'stylish', let alone comprehensible. You might find it difficult to understand what the author is trying to say. You might, however, have noticed, if you were a linguist, that this sentence is what is known as a complex sentence: two simple sentences joined together (the linking word 'and' appears somewhere in the middle of it), which might help you to decipher the two ideas spliced together in this type of sentence. You might have noticed the use of nominalisation (i.e. turning a verb into a noun) 'repetition', 'convergence', and 're-articulation', and so on. You might have been puzzled by the jargon, or specialist subject vocabulary with which you might not be familiar – 'structuralist', 'hegemony', and so on, or what the French theorist, Louis Althusser, referred to in the sentence. And so, you might rather want to summarise this rather long sentence into a quarter of its original length (i.e. about twenty-five words) or you might want to paraphrase it, putting Butler's ideas in your own words. You might agree that although the example constitutes academic writing, it might be lacking in comprehensibility and hence, it fails to communicate its complex ideas to an attentive reader.

Consider a second, much shorter example of academic writing:

> The presence of trust in human relationships is delicate and required. Building trust is probably the most important component of a solid and healthy relationship. Trust can take a long time to build, but at the same time, can be destroyed by a single action or misconception. Authors have defined trust as the belief or confidence in an individual's integrity, fairness and reliability.

This piece of writing is certainly not as complex as the first one, and yet, it lies on the opposite end of the spectrum of academic writing: albeit simple, it is rather simplistic and flawed in conceptualising and argument and formulating it coherently. What, for example, does the writer mean with 'required' at the end of the first sentence? In addition, the author seems to string together a series of definitions of trust without advancing any position or viewpoint. Despite the fact that the language is simple and the length of the sentence is short, this piece of writing also does not constitute an acceptable form of academic writing. Although there is mention of other authors being acknowledged in this piece of writing, they are not listed by name and simply by regurgitating their definitions, this does not seem persuasive. What, then, does constitute an acceptable form of academic writing? In order to answer the question, one has to understand something about the notion of academic literacy.

10.2 Academic literacy

Academic literacy is commonly defined as the ability to read and write within a particular context such as higher education, but there are other ways of looking at it. It also implies taking on the 'mantle' of academia, reading and writing within that context with the aim of effective communication. Literacy refers to a student's capacity to use written language to perform those functions required by the culture in academia in ways and at a level judged acceptable by the readers. Thus, a student needs to acquire specific vocabularies of different subject areas, or discourses, which would then provide him with the language to advance thought, mainly in and through writing. The example contains such concepts as 'structuralism', 'hegemony', 'Althussarian theory', and so on.

In certain cases, the plural term, academic literacies is used, encompassing the idea of multi-literacies referring to the integrated academic language ability that enables students to cope with the demands of studying in a tertiary academic environment as a whole. This means that students are able to develop an understanding of different academic texts, their structure, type of contents and how language is employed to create this structure and content. Academic literacies also entail how students deal with text and the interpretation and construction of their own pieces of writing using strategies for selecting, arranging and generating information appropriate in argumentation. In their writing, students display their academic literacy proficiency and their familiarity with academic language conventions such as register, style, tone, appropriateness and correctness of language, as well as the use of argumentation in analysing and synthesising the literature.

> **Example box**
>
> **Academic literacy entails:**[2]
>
> 1. Understanding a range of academic vocabulary in context
> 2. Interpreting and using metaphor and idiom, and perceiving connotation, word play and ambiguity in various academic texts
> 3. Understanding relations between different parts of a text, being aware of the logical development of an academic text, via introductions to conclusions and knowing how to use language that serves to make the different parts of a text hang together
> 4. Interpreting different kinds of text type (genre), and showing sensitivity for the meaning that they convey, and the audience that they are aimed at

5. Interpreting information and producing information presented in graphic and visual format
6. Making distinctions between essential and non-essential information, fact and opinion, propositions and arguments, cause and effect, classifying, categorising and handling data that make comparisons
7. Seeing sequence and order, doing simple numerical estimations and computations that are relevant to academic information, that allow comparison to be made, and can be applied for the purposes of an argument
8. Knowing what counts as evidence for an argument, extrapolating from information by making inferences, and applying the information or its implications to other cases than the one at hand
9. Understanding the communicative function of various ways of expression in academic language (such as defining, providing examples, arguing, and so on)
10. Making meaning (e.g. of an academic text) beyond the level of the sentence

Source: Weideman, A. (2003) Academic Literacy: Prepare to Learn. Pretoria; Van Schaik Publishers, p. ix.
Reprinted by permission of Van Schaik Publishers.

Reflection

Ask yourself to what extent you are competent or not yet competent with regard to your own academic writing in terms of each one of these ten criteria of academic literacy. Assess how literate you are academically.

If you are not entirely satisfied with your academic writing skills and if you think you are not literate to 'converse' in the academy at this point, there is plenty that you can do to improve your writing skills. The first step would be to understand that writing is a process and to know what the process entails. If you do this, you would be aware, at a meta-cognitive level, of where you are in your writing and how to advance, or improve and self-correct, or simply to continue writing when you are stuck, or get so-called 'writer's block'. It will also help you to submit a better written product if you have followed the steps in the process outlined below.

10.3 Structuring the writing of a research report

Conventionally, students have been taught somewhere in their schooling careers about writing an introduction, body and conclusion for an essay or an assignment. Sometimes they have also been told about planning or drafting their essay before actually writing it. This culminates into a simple, linear model of writing consisting of three phases: pre-drafting, or planning; drafting, or actually writing a rough, first version of their texts; and then, lastly, re-thinking and or revising their texts (Figure 10.1).

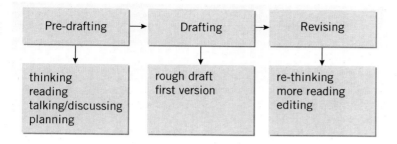

Figure 10.1 Linear model of writing

Source: Author's own material

Although this is good advice in terms of writing, and a workable process to follow, it is a rather simplistic plan. Especially when you realise that writing is an iterative process, one in which you keep doing, or going back to, in order to improve the way in which you communicate your ideas to the reader and in which you share your understanding and insights with the reader in as an intelligent way as possible. This simple process is more of a plan-write-edit model which is merely technical and/or procedural in nature.

I want to suggest a more complex, nuanced model initially developed by Flower and Hayes[3], which captures the cognitive processes students pass through during their writing. See Figure 10.2.

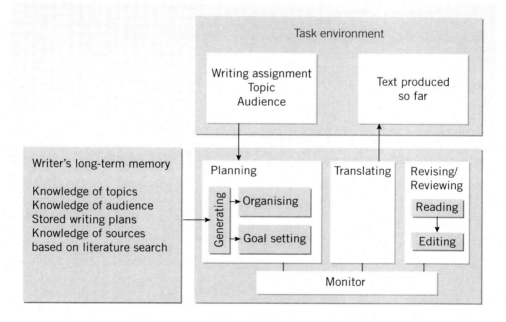

Figure 10.2 Structure of the writing model

Source: L. Flower & J. Hayes, "A Cognitive Process Theory of Writing" Figure 3.1: Structure of the Writing Model in College Composition and Communication, 1981 32 (4) 364–387. Copyright 1981 by the National Council of Teachers of English. Reprinted with permission.

The model illustrated in Figure 10.2 takes into account the task environment, which consists of the writing assignment and the text to be produced, as well as knowledge stored in the student's long-term memory, knowledge about the topic, knowledge of audience, stored writing plans, and knowledge of sources based on literature research. The three cognitive processes that the writer moves through are planning (generating, organising, goal setting), translating, and revising/reviewing. In the planning stage, the writer generates ideas, or in Flower and Hayes's terms, "the act of building an internal representation".[4] Once this is done, the ideas are organised creatively or grouped and arranged in a coherent structure with goal setting in mind. Goal setting is both procedural and substantive and if the student works at defining his/her own rhetorical problem and goal setting, this can assist in developing a good creative writer. Flower and Hayes use the term 'translate' for the subsequent cognitive process during which ideas are written or transcribed into words but drawing on the writer's ability with the use of the English language and all its conventions.[5] With inexperienced writers, and with writers where English is their second language, this process is challenging and requires much effort in drawing on long term memory and the knowledge of the language. The 'reviewing' process draws on evaluating and revising the written product and may act as a springboard to further planning and translating. Underlying all three cognitive processes, is the monitor which works as a regulator or coordinator advising the student when to move to the next process or between processes. This model emphasises the recursive nature of writing with each of the processes occurring at any moment.

Thus, in contrast to the linear model of writing, the multi-draft process with plan-draft-revise cycles could be seen not only as a way of improving writing, but also as a tool for clarifying and extending thinking. It is this iterative process in the development of writing that can contribute to higher reasoning skills and better subject understanding. The **writing process** and the subsequent products of writing correspond to certain powerful learning strategies. Students who do not write regularly and copiously, lose many opportunities for learning. Learning 'through' writing may be developed by means of an iterative process of writing, that incorporates eight stages (Figure 10.3):[6]

- pre-writing
- planning
- drafting
- reflection
- review
- revision
- additional research
- idea regeneration of the final process of editing and proofreading.

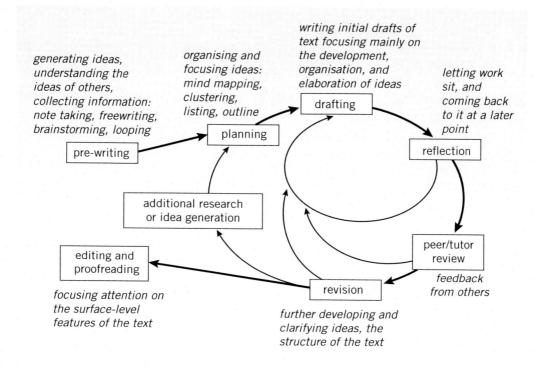

Figure 10.3 The iterative process of writing

Source: Coffin, C., Curry, M.J., Goodman, S., Hewings, A., Lillis,T.M. & Swann, J. Teaching Academic Writing: A toolkit for higher education. Copyright © 2003. London: Routledge p.34. Reproduced by permission of Taylor & Francis Books UK.

This iterative process of writing represents a toolkit to draw on for making meaning in different contexts to gain access to a particular way of using language and thus participating in a specific social and cultural context where a specific discourse is required. This writing process encourages the student to move through various stages of writing such as pre-writing, planning, drafting and reflecting. But this process also allows students to revisit sections of the writing at any stage of the process to reflect and rework them in an iterative manner, until they are ready for the editing, proofreading and polishing stages. In editing and proofreading, the student is able to attend to the mechanics of writing or the lower order concerns such as punctuation, spelling, formatting, referencing and creating footnotes.

A fourth model of academic writing (figure 10.4) was proposed by Sarah Haas contingent on five 'modes' of writing – exploring, **structuring**, polishing and publishing, unloading and incubating – each containing specific aspects of that mode.[7]

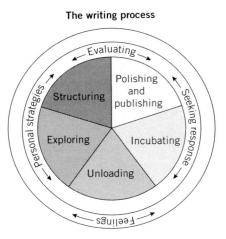

Figure 10.4 The Haas model, 2011

Source: Haas, S. S. (2010). By writers for writers: developing a writer-centred model of the writing process (Doctoral dissertation, Aston University) Copyright © S. Haas sshaas@mac.com. Reprinted by permission of Sarah Haas.

The writing process in this model is represented by five cones, or 'slices' of a pie graph type of diagrammatical representation – the five modes – which fit together to form a circle. The Exploring mode includes aspects such as finding a topic, searching for literature, taking notes, reading, brain storming, listing and finding a focus. Outlining, drafting, revising and editing comprise the Structuring mode which is the second cone. The third cone comprising polishing and publishing, consists of printing out, making graphs and charts, making it look 'pretty', submitting, copy editing and being evaluated. The Uploading mode, where a writer will take the 'chaos' that is in his/her head and attempt to get it out of his/her head includes two interesting words, namely babbling – unmonitored speaking, and scribbling – and unmonitored writing.[8] Finally, the Incubating mode incorporates such action as ruminating which is conscious thought, and steeping – considered unconscious thinking. Haas explains that the arrow in Figure 10.4 represents the random movement of the students between each of the modes illustrating the interlinkedness of each of the processes. Although students begin at one stage and seem to move in a linear way towards a goal, there is constant movement between the modes, with students following different pathways depending on their ways of writing. Haas explains that "the way a writer moves from the start to the finish … is recursive, moving back and forth, and round and round through different modes, inching forward until the piece of writing is as complete as it is going to be."[9]

In reviewing literature on these four models of writing processes, Roz Ivanic suggests recognising that these "can refer to either or both the cognitive and the practical processes" where the cognitive process "might be learned implicitly, while the practical ones are extremely amenable to explicit teaching".[10] Murray also reiterates that understanding of the writing process with feedback stages could facilitate the teaching of writing[11] and is seen as a behavioural dimension which could assist writers in achieving their goals and thus developing self-efficacy.

> **Reflection**
>
> List the advantages and disadvantages of each of the four models. Reflect on which one would work best for your own style of writing.

10.3.1 Using knowledge by making notes

In this section, you will be shown how to gather material for use in your academic writing. The questions you have to ask yourself at this stage are:
- What is the topic about which I need to write?
- How well do I know my subject?
- Do I understand the discipline in which I study?

In other words, you need to have a good idea about the general positioning of what is required of you in your writing. Then you have to ask yourself another set of questions:
- Given that I am writing about a particular topic, what do I know about it?
- What are my own ideas about it?
- What do I want to say about the topic?
- What is my position?
- What point do I want to make about it?
- How do I go about letting the reader understand my viewpoint?

These questions will eventually become the basis of your 'argument'. You may well write down your ideas in a brainstorm type of diagram or representation, with as many links between the ideas as possible. In this manner, you will be able to identify areas of which you know very little, or sections you need to read about in order to fill in the gaps in your knowledge. It is, in fact, a good strategy to have a guiding question when you approach the literature on your topic. Otherwise you may well be consumed by all the information you can possibly get from sources on that topic. It is essential that you do go to a library or information centre in order to gather information about your topic. Books and journals are all very useful sources, as well as electronic texts and websites. You may have good ideas of your own about the topic, and you may even have gotten a couple of ideas from your friends or fellow students about the topic, but this type of 'common knowledge' needs to be verified by authoritative sources, and that is why you need to consult authoritative literature on the topic. You will find this kind of literature in full-length books in the library, as well as in academic subject journals in your disciplines. In addition, there are usually many electronic sources available on the topic, but, be warned, many of these are not verified or trustworthy. Think, for example, how many times you have seen an article on Wikipedia footnoted with the words; "source needed". It is information that often needs research results to verify it and ensure that it is authoritative. Be careful when you consult such sources.

Next, once you have located the texts, what do you do with them? Read them carefully, of course, and then you may want to summarise them, or maybe paraphrase them, or you may want to quote some part of the texts directly, integrating it in your own writing. Critical reading is recommended. This means you are constantly in conversation with the author about what he/she is saying and the points they are making. You are questioning their knowledge but identifying gaps and omissions in their reasoning and their writing, and you are following their arguments carefully, looking for proof and for convincing arguments to persuade you to accept their points.

Let us start with summarising skills. In essence, this writing skill entails extracting the main idea of a section, article, chapter, or even a whole book and expressing it in your own words. A summary is usually about one quarter of the original passage. In terms of a whole book, an author often outlines the main points he/she wants to make in the introduction of the book. They usually use one chapter to advance a complementary idea or put forward another facet of their central argument, dealing with as many comprehensive ideas about the topic as possible in subsequent chapters.

> **Example box**
>
> **Original paragraph**
> "It is accepted fact that governments do not make profits, but do create the environment in which organizations and employees can interact to the advantage and benefit of all concerned. Thus, the well-being of the citizens of any country is inextricably linked to the effectiveness of their organizations. However, for organizations to achieve their goals, they must constantly look for better ways to organize and manage their work."[12]
>
> **Summarised version**
> Although governments create a productive, mutually beneficial economic working environment for organisations, they still have to conduct their work in an effective way.
>
> **Paraphrased version**
> Despite the fact that governments do not aim for profitability, they do enable an interactive working environment mutually beneficial to businesses and workers. This means that there is a linkage between the health of the people of the country and the health of organisations in the country. Organisations therefore have to strive for better organisation and management of their business.
>
> **Plagiarised version**
> It is generally assumed that governments do not make profits, but do create the environment in which organisations and employees can work to the advantage and benefit of everybody. Thus, the well-being of the citizens of any country is directly linked to the effectiveness of their organisations. However, for organisations to reach their aims, they must constantly look for better ways to organise and manage their work.

These examples illustrate the way in which only the essence of an original idea can be summed up in about a quarter or a third of the original. It also demonstrates that paraphrasing entails putting an original idea into one's own words in more or less the same number of words. The skill of paraphrasing is to change the word (e.g. 'workers' for 'employees'), change the word order (e.g. 'linkage' moved from the back of the sentence to the front), and/or change word categories (e.g. the verbs 'organise' and 'manage' become the nouns 'organisation' and 'management').

A third way to reference someone else's ideas in your writing is by means of direct quotation. One might, for example, come across a very succinct piece of writing to which one might be drawn and then feel compelled to quote directly. This is acceptable, as long as you put it in quotation marks and reference it properly (i.e. the author, the year of publication and the page number on which it occurred) but keep in mind that only about 10 per cent of the total of your writing should be directly quoted. For the rest, you need to either summarise or paraphrase. Another way in which one can quote directly is to integrate a short sentence or part of a sentence into your own, provided that you acknowledge the original source of content.

10.3.2 Organising ideas in sentences, paragraphs and sections

Once you have read enough about your topic, and have made sufficient notes about the ideas and theories expressed in the texts and have understood the research results reported in these, you are ready to put together a first draft. Remember, you are not merely stringing together loose ideas about the topic: you have to arrange them in a coherent sequence. This sequencing is called developing an argument. An argument refers to a particular point you are making, backed up with evidence to support the point in a convincing manner. The first sentence of a paragraph, often called the 'topic sentence' contains the main idea of a paragraph. The subsequent sentences are nothing else but back-up evidence qualifying and/or expanding the topic sentence. This can take on many formats. You may supply facts to prove the point you are trying to make. You may supply examples to show that your point is valid and widespread. You may even provide a counter argument to show the strength of your own point. These sentences can be simple in nature, which means that they are usually short and contain only one main verb. Or the sentences may be compound, which means that there are more than one verb in it, usually joined with a linking word such as 'and', 'but', 'however', and so on. Sentences may also be complex, which means that they consist of at least one clause, containing a main verb, and one phrase, which means having part of a verb, such as a participle, for example 'Having read all the relevant texts, the student drafts the essay'. The first part of the sentence is an example of a verb phrase. It has no subject, which is implied in the second part of the sentence (the student, in this example). The second part of the sentence has a full clause, a main verb, namely 'drafts'.

One way to ensure **cohesion** within a paragraph is to see to it that all the sentences are linked in some way or another with one another. In addition, the writer must ensure **coherence** between paragraphs, or sections, and one way to do that is to link paragraphs by using the last word or phrase of one paragraph, and starting the next paragraph with those words, obviously adding another point to your overall argument. In this manner you establish a logical flow of ideas in your sections and between your paragraphs.

Example box: Linking words

When you want to:	Use these words or phrases:
Clarify something	that is, in other words, put another way
Summarise a point or conclude a section	in sum, to summarise, in short, briefly, to conclude
Add a point or example	in addition, furthermore, similarly
Counter argue	on the other hand, in contrast, nevertheless, in spite of
Show cause and effect	as a result of, consequently, subsequently
Sequence items in a list	firstly, secondly, thirdly, lastly, next
Prove a point	since, because
Give an example	for example, for instance, to illustrate

Example box

"High-profile corporate bankruptcies, contentious CEO compensation and the current global financial crisis have highlighted the importance of corporate governance and increased a scholarly interest in the subject. Although an extensive body of knowledge around governance issues exists, it is limited in terms of the methodological approaches followed in gathering empirical samples about the topic.

Extant literature has predominantly used the agency theory approach to focus on the monitoring and control roles of the board. In terms of board leadership, the attention has been on the structure, specifically CEO duality, but the subject of leadership behaviour in the boardroom has been neglected. This void is referred to as the 'black box' of what happens behind the boardroom door. In his review of 127 published articles on board leadership, Hamidi (2012) found that empirical studies have mostly concentrated on large, listed United States corporations with very few studies in small medium enterprises (SMEs).

The small medium enterprise (SME) sector is seen as a significant roleplayer in the economic prosperity of many countries. The South African government has identified the SME sector as a means to achieve accelerated economic growth and it is commonly understood that SMEs are pivotal to South Africa's focus on employment creation. A challenge to this objective is the high failure rate of enterprises in the SME sector in SA.

There has been a call for alternative methodological approaches, empirical samples from different institutional and national contexts and more studies that focus on actual board leadership behaviours to ameliorate the high failure rate among SMEs. This study aims to address this call and will focus on board behaviours in the SME sector in SA. A mixed methodological research approach will be used to develop a competency model for board leadership."

Source: Author

The main idea, or 'topic' of paragraph one is the fact that there seems to exist numerous problems with regard to corporate governance. Paragraph two focuses on one aspect of corporate governance, namely boardroom behaviour. It focuses the topic, in other words, narrowing it down to a specific aspect. Paragraph three redirects the topic on boardroom behaviour to SMEs. And the last paragraph looks at research required to explain the relationship between boardroom behaviour and the high failure rate among SMEs. These four paragraphs constitute the central argument of this introductory section. They are also very coherent in the sense that they build on each other to advance the central argument.

On paragraph level, one can, for example, highlight the way in which cohesion is established in paragraph 3 of the short piece of writing above by saying, for instance, that the main idea of this paragraph is the common perception that SMEs are linked to economic prosperity. In the next sentence, the notion of economic prosperity is defined in terms of growth through employment creation, and the third sentence introduces the notion that many SMEs fail, which might hamper economic growth. So, as you can see, this paragraph has a tight cohesion.

10.3.3 Developing an argument

An argument is usually associated with a verbal expression of some form or another of disagreement about a topic, but in academic writing it takes on another format entirely. An argument in this type of writing entails a process of persuasion rather than disagreement. The author has a point to make, and he/she has to convince the reader of the merits of his point by using a range of techniques. These techniques involve giving reasons for making a claim, and providing evidence for the claim. The claim is usually a contentious, debatable statement that you want the readers to accept. The reasoning entails the logic you are using to convince the reader that your claim is true or desirable; and the evidence is usually the facts, or statistics, or examples, or testimonies that you use to support your reasoning. Argumentation is therefore used to build knowledge through a series of statements. It is therefore useful when you analyse the workings of a phenomenon, or what it means, or why it is important to study. Likewise, arguments serve a critiquing function in the sense that they evaluate someone else's work or writing or opinions.

An argument can be structured by following five steps:
- First, write an Introduction in which you set your argument in a context. Who, for example, may care to read your argument? Why is your problem, or issue, important?
- Secondly, make a claim: formulating a statement with which readers might want to disagree.
- Thirdly, support your claim with evidence, or reasons for its validity. This can take the shape of quoting facts, statistics, or expert opinions that you get from the sources, or literature you have consulted.
- You might then want to express a counterargument, introducing and/or responding to opposing arguments.
- Lastly, you have to restate and expand on your claim by asking the question: Why would readers want to agree with me? The challenge with argumentation is to use other viewpoints to your advantage in order to advance your own argument. It is, however, important to acknowledge your sources, no matter how often and how much you draw from other authors.

This leads us to the next section of academic writing, the practice of referencing.

10.4 Referencing

Referencing is a sure way in which you indicate to your reader that you are familiar with the authoritative writers on the topic on which you are writing. It shows that you are knowledgeable about the most current literature on the topic and are familiar with the current debates and issues in the field. You need to show this, because you want to join the debate and make equally important and valuable points that can only add to the resolution of the debate and/or a way to find solutions to a complex problem. One references in text when you quote somebody else's words directly, or even when you paraphrase or summarise their points, one has to acknowledge the fact that the ideas are not your own. In addition, you have to list these sources in a reference list, or bibliography at the end of your text, assignment, or document. Keep in mind that there is nothing wrong, inferior, or weak about using somebody else's ideas. You are 'original' in the sense that you use their ideas in a new, creative way, or in a novel configuration that has not been done before. In addition, you might even be able to add to or extend their ideas, or even to contract them. In this manner, you become part of a discourse community which engages with the problems of a field of study in a scholarly manner. But, like in every other community, there exist certain rules and conventions about the way in which one does that. The rules of referencing are summarised in the next section which uses fictitious sources as a point of illustration.

TABLE 10.1 RULES OF REFERENCING

The source I am using is a ...	How should I cite the source in my text?	How should I list the source in my bibliography?
Book with one or two authors	In one model of HRM (Adams, 2010), stakeholders fulfill ... Adams (2010) proposes four roles ... Adams's (2010) models hold that ... The Balanced Scorecard (Brown & Cohen, 2011) consists of ... Brown and Cohen (2011) argue that ...	Adams, D. (2010). *Human Resource Management: An advanced course.* New York: New York University Press. Brown, A., & Cohen, B. (2011). *The Balanced Scorecard: Translating strategy into action.* London: Routledge.
Book with three or more authors	The first time: The HR Scorecard compliments the Balanced Scorecard (Dewey, Evans, & Faraday, 2012), or Dewey, Evans and Faraday (2012) argue that ... The second time: The HR Scorecard compliments the balanced Scorecard (Dewey, et al, 2012), or Dewey et al, (2012) argue that ...	Dewey, A., Evans, B. & Faraday, C. (2012). *The HR Scorecard: Linking people, strategy, and performance.* Boston, MA: Harvard Business School Press.
Chapter in a book	Confirmed by empirical research (Groenewald, 2013) it is evident that...	Groenewald, A. (2013). Labour shortages explained. In: A. Adams, B. Brown, & C. Cohen (Eds.), *The Future of Human Resource Management.* (pp. 25-35). New York: Blackwell Publishers.
Journal article	Howie (2013) argues that ...	Howie, S. (2013). Changes in newcomer information seeking and the relationship with psychological contract fulfillment. *Journal of Occupational and Organizational Psychology*, 84 (2), 201-211.
Newspaper article	A recent opinion poll on the reasons why students drop out (Ivan, 2013) holds that ...	Ivan, R. (2013, August 21) Alarming dropout rates among the new generation *The Saturday Star.* Retrieved from http://timesmedia.com

Internet article	Jones, Kaplan & Louw (2012) recommend that students should ...	Jones, A., Kaplan, R. & Louw, U. (2012). Human Resources vs Human Capital: What is in a name? *Human Capital Review*, 2(5). Retrieved from http://www.humancapitalreview.org/Article_ID
Document from an organisation	A recent report (Statistics South Africa, 2013) indicates that ...	Statistics South Africa (2013). *Census 2011: Statistical release – P031.4*. Pretoria: Statistics South Africa.

There are various referencing styles, such as the Harvard method or the American Psycological Association (APA) style. Ensure that you know which referencing method is acceptable for the institution or publication you are writing for.

10.4.1 Plagiarism

Students plagiarise for many reasons. Plagiarising involves the direct lifting of source material of other authors and using it as if the ideas and words are one's own without acknowledging the origin of the sources. Firstly, students may not know what actually constitutes **plagiarism** in academia. They are under the illusion that because knowledge is freely available from books and journals in the library and electronically from internet sources, they are welcome to use these with careless abandon. The main enterprise of a university, however, is creating new knowledge, not reproducing or regurgitating existing knowledge. That is what scholarship is all about, and what grants one membership to an academic discourse community, and that is the most important and powerful skill that you will be taught at a university. Generating new knowledge is often associated with originality.

> **Example box: Original academic writing**
> - You say something no one has said before.
> - You do empirical work that has not been done before.
> - You synthesise things that have not been put together before.
> - You make a new interpretation of someone else's material/ideas.
> - You do something in this country that has only been done elsewhere.
> - You take an existing technique and apply it to a new area.
> - You work across disciplines, using different methodologies.
> - You look at topics that people in your discipline have not looked at.
> - You test existing knowledge in an original way.
> - You add to knowledge in a way that has not been done before.
> - You write down a new piece of information for the first time.
> - You give a good exposition of someone else's work.

Secondly, students often leave writing an assignment too late, and they do not gather information and, more importantly, digest and interrogate sources critically, in order to write a new, creative essay. Thirdly, students view copying as a quick and easy way to

complete a task. In addition, if one wants to explore the reasons as to why students often plagiarise, one can list personal and situational factors as well. Personal factors can be enumerated as including such aspects as low self-esteem, little or no moral integrity, feelings of inadequacy, lack of competent writing skills, and often, pure ignorance about the topic, coupled with fear of failure. Situational factors that can be listed in order to explain the plagiarism phenomenon at universities include:
- the very high pressure on university students to perform and accomplish in a very short period of time
- the very lenient, or even lack of penalties for transgressors
- very generic open-ended topic on which to write, requiring very little higher order thinking, reading and/or writing skills
- and the general laissez-faire attitude of the lecturers and tutors who are often too busy to care about their students.

In addition, lecturers' reluctance to report plagiarism may also play a role in this cycle of perpetual copying on the part of students. Often little or no preventative measures are taken to curb this wide-scale practice among students.

10.5 Structuring requirements of academic research writing

An academic writer is highly aware of the fact that the different functions in any piece of writing are contingent on very specific linguistics forms. The relationship between form and function is called the genre, or structural requirements of academic writing. What, for example, are the genre requirements of the research proposal you are preparing at present? What linguistics structures are you likely to use when you have to introduce your research topic? Or when you have to write the background chapters or sections (e.g. the Literature Review, or the Theoretical Framework) of your proposal, and ultimately of your full dissertation? Or what language does one use when writing about the methodology one is following in gathering data? How does one write about the findings once the data has been analysed? How does one use language in discussing one's findings, or drawing conclusions from one's research? Lastly, what are the linguistic requirements when writing the abstract to one's research? All these sections have very specific genre requirements in terms of the language structures one has to use.
- Examining the typical structure of an Introduction, students are well-advised to follow a fairly standard line of argument, developed by Swales and Feak. They recommend that Introductions consist of three 'moves':[13]
    - establishing a research territory
    - identifying a niche
    - signaling how the topic in question occupies that niche.

10.5.1 Language usage

The importance or centrality of a research topic is usually established through the use of the present tense or the present perfect tense in a sentence, for example, "In these areas, reducing poverty is an important step in empowering the population." and "The charting of water flow is of great interest to engineers and scientists alike." In both instances, the verb 'is', has been used to signal the centrality of the research topic. In addition, such words as 'important' and 'great interest' have also been used to indicate the importance of the research territory. In this way the student can establish his/her research territory by using these simple linguistic structures. Language is extremely important in constructing an argument, because it constitutes the medium in which the message is conveyed.

10.5.2 Establishing a niche within a broader research territory

This is the next 'move' the student has to make in the introduction. The most apt linguistic structures that can be used to establish the niche are those that have the function of indicating a gap in the research; either in terms of the literature, or in terms of the theoretical framework, the methodology followed, or the way in which data have been analysed in previous studies. Specific linguistic structures that indicate this are the following phrases: 'disregard', 'fail to consider', 'ignore', 'is limited to', 'misinterpret', 'neglect to consider', 'overestimate', 'overlook', 'underestimate', and so on. These are all verb phrases. In terms of adjectives, the following words fulfil a similar function of identifying a gap: 'controversial', 'incomplete', 'inconclusive', 'misguided', 'questionable', 'unconvincing', 'unsatisfactory', and so on. Noun phrases functioning as signifiers of 'gaps' in the research include: 'little information/attention/work/data/research'; 'few investigations/researchers/attempts'; 'no studies/data/calculations'; 'none of these studies/findings/calculations', and so on. These phrases are very useful in indicating that a gap exists in the research and the student can use them to structure a convincing argument for the research he/she plans to do.

10.5.3 Linguistic structures

The final 'move' should signal what the student plans to do in the study overall. The linguistic structures that best serve this function are signposting (the typical use of 'In Chapter 1, I plan to ... In Chapter 2, I review the literature ... In Chapter 3, I show the research methods ...', and so on). This move signals the fact that the research will be done systematically and the enumeration testifies to such an approach. Students also often use such words as 'firstly', 'secondly', 'thirdly', and so on to indicate their intentions. Also note the use of active verbs in the present tense in these examples: 'plan', 'review', 'show', and so on.

10.6 Writing the background chapters

The background consists of the literature review and/or the theoretical framework of the study and requires that the student reports on what research has already been done, or what theories actually exist to explain or interpret the phenomenon under study.

> **Example box**
>
> Such reporting verbs are: point out, propose, indicate, maintain, recommend, claim, argue, observe, describe, assert, support, say, identify, believe, think, urge, affirm, state, report, explain, question, challenge, suggest, present, dismiss, and so on.

These verbs form a veritable thesaurus of options for the student to use when reviewing the literature and he/she can easily choose between them to vary the presentation of the review, or the theories.

In addition to the choice of reporting verb, another linguistic form of importance for the background chapters is the choice of tense. The present tense is used when you want to make a generalisation, or when you refer to the state of current knowledge, when you present certain findings. The past tense is used when you refer to a single study, or when you refer to a specific piece of research and its findings. The present perfect tense is used when you refer to a general area of investigation or inquiry, or when you make a general statement about the validity and currency of previous research.

10.7 Linguistic strategies

When writing the methodology section of your research, include very detailed *descriptions* of the way in which you obtained the informants, or participants, or drew your sample; the location/setting of the interviews; the issues and themes covered in the interview; any piloting and/or adjustments made and the reasons for these; and the way any obstacles have been overcome. It also includes a detailed description of the way in which the data are being analysed. The linguistic emphasis, as a result, is on adjectives, and on sequencing the events and describing the methodology, the methods and the materials in as much detail as possible.

10.8 The Results/Findings chapter or section

The function of the Results/Findings chapter/section of your study entails the presentation of meta-textual information, presenting results, and commenting on these results. Meta-textual information is usually presented in linguistic structures dealing with statements and references to previous sections of the study. Presenting results are done by means of statements, backed up by evidence. Commenting on results involves linguistic structures such as comparison, justification, strength limitations and/or generalisability of the study, making claims, and so on. Some of these structures are called hedges and boosters.

> **Example box**
>
> Examples of adverbs and adjectives that signal hedging in which the writer withholds full comment to a proposition, are: seems, appears, perhaps, might, possibly, and so on. Examples of boosters in which the writer emphasises his/her certainty with regard to a proposition, are: in fact, definitely, it is clear that, and so on.

10.9 The conclusion

Writing the conclusion entails a very specific series of functions about which the student has to account: an introductory restatement of aims and research questions; a consolidation of his/her research (e.g. the findings, limitations, and so on); practical applications/implementations; and recommendations for further research. Thompson has this to say about writing conclusions:[14]

> " A [research report,] thesis [or dissertation] is a long text and the restatement of the aims and questions is a necessary reminder to the reader, several chapters [sections] on, of what the starting point of the research was. The concluding chapter is also an evaluation of the whole research project. The evaluation is strategically important as the targeted readers are also evaluating the project, to determine whether the writer is worthy of [the reward of a degree]. In the conclusions chapter, therefore, the task of the writer is to point out what his/her achievements have been, and to forestall criticisms by identifying limitations in the research." "

The conclusion therefore consists typically of three sections: an introductory statement, restating the issue being researched, the work carried out, the purpose of the study, the research questions, and the hypotheses, or working solutions; a second section, the consolidation of the research space in which the methods are summarised and evaluated and the results and claims are also summarised; and a third section, the recommendations and implications, in which future research, practical applications, and limitations of the study are highlighted. The linguistic structures best suited to fulfill these functions are reporting (e.g. 'The present research has indicated that ...'), commenting (e.g. 'There are no examples in the data, but they might exist as, for example, evaluative comments on other work'), and suggesting (e.g. 'Further research in this field would be of great help in the future development of ...').

10.10 Summary

Academic literacy requires a huge amount of responsibility from the student writer. Not only does he/she have to develop a vast range of writing skills (such as summarising, paraphrasing and referencing techniques) but also the student has to have the knowledge about the writing process (such as the various models proposed in terms of writing process at the outset of this chapter) in order to function at a higher order cognitive level and show awareness of writing as a convention and practice as such, not only focusing on the writing itself, expressing understanding and making meaning in and through writing. In addition, the student has to integrate the genre requirements and/or structural formats in his/her writing and exhibit scholarly values and attitudes towards academic writing so that he/she can become a full member of the academic discourse community.

Key terms and concepts

academic discourse community: like-minded intellectuals who share a common value system about their disciplines and whose research practice follow the same rigorous rules and conventions, and is open for peer scrutiny and review
academic literacy: a scholar's academic skills in terms of reading and writing at an advanced level and his/her disposition towards his/her field of study
academic writing: a specific, formal way of writing in academia, with constant previewing and reviewing of any sustained written argument, which is constantly backed up with evidence

argument: a series of claims made in a research report or dissertation which is backed up with evidence based on empirical research and/or the scholarship of other authors in the field

coherence: the explicit links between various sections of a sustained piece of academic writing, established through such means as linking words/devices; the use of pronouns and punctuation; in-text referencing; and the inclusion of headings and subheadings

cohesion: the explicit links between the various sentences within one paragraph, usually established by means of a topic sentence and through such devises as examples elaborating on the topic; the use of pronouns and punctuation; and linking words/devices

paraphrasing: putting another author's ideas in one's own words by, for example, changing the word order, changing the word class, or substituting one word for its synonym

plagiarism: the intentional using of an author's words or concepts without acknowledging its source

referencing: the explicit recording of the source from which an author is quoting or paraphrasing, either in-text, or in an alphabetically arranged list at the end of a research report or dissertation

structuring (a research report): the explicit signposting of the overall structure of a research report, signalling the route in which the author intends on advancing his/her argument, usually divided into some form of introduction, body and conclusion; the introduction typically includes a problem statement, as well as a purpose statement

summarising: reducing the ideas, concepts and claims of an author into about a quarter of the origin, retaining the gist of the argument

writing process: the iterative nature of writing as opposed to the product of writing. Writing goes through various stages of thinking, reading, planning and so on, before a first draft is written and revised, until it is eventually edited for surface errors.

Questions

1. What is academic literacy?
2. What is academic writing?
3. How does one construct an argument?
4. How does one write an introduction?
5. What is the general structure of a research report?
6. Describe the writing process you use when you have to do academic writing.
7. Describe the way in which you go about reading an article critically in order to get information to use in your academic writing.
8. Read three articles about plagiarism and write an essay on the topic.
   Download the following three articles that are easily accessible on the internet:
   - Insley, R. (2011). Managing plagiarism: A preventative approach. *Business Communication Quarterly* 74(2): June 2011: 183–187.
   - Szabo, A., & Underwood, J. (2004). Cybercheats: Is information and communication technology fuelling academic dishonesty? *Active Learning in Higher Education* 5(2), 2004: 180–199.
   - Thomas, A., & De Bruin, G.P. (2012). Student academic dishonesty: What do academics think and do, and what are the barriers to action? *African Journal of*

Business Ethics. 6(1) January – April 2012: 13–24.

9. Write an essay of about two pages in which you explain the phenomenon of plagiarism: why it is so widespread among students, why lecturers are often reluctant to do something about this unethical practice, and how plariarism can be managed by both students and lecturers.
   - Include in your essay a large section in which you summarise the contents of each one of these three articles. Signpost very clearly by writing, for example, "Summarising the main ideas in Article 1, ...". In addition, also paraphrase a couple of the most pertinent points made in each of the articles. Again, you are urged to signpost very clearly by writing, for example, "In other words, ...", or "Putting the main ideas in my own words, it is clear that ..." and so on. Lastly, you are required to quote directly at least ten per cent of the two pages, from any one or more of these three articles. The test is to see whether or not you are able to use the correct method of referencing. At the end of the essay, draw up a list in which you alphabetise the articles, as well as any additional sources you might have used.

10. Writing an abstract to the study is an important skill that students have to develop in addition to all the writing rules and conventions required by thesis and dissertation writing. It entails writing an overview of the study; restating the aim of the study; the reasons for doing the study; the methodology used in the study; and the findings of the study. It is not necessarily a summary of the study. Rather, it is more a distillation of the structure of the whole study. I often compare writing an abstract to squeezing the water out of a soaked sponge. The 'water' or detail is all gone, and the shape of the sponge has virtually shrunk to a small little entity, but the constitutive elements of it are all there. Examine the following example and identify all the elements in this abstract. Decide whether it is an effective abstract or not.

A thorough, sophisticated literature review is the foundation and inspiration of substantial, useful research. The complex nature of academic research demands such thorough, sophisticated reviews. Although graduate development is a key means for improving academic research, the literature has given short shrift of the role and importance of the literature review in dissertation writing. This article suggests criteria to evaluate the quality of dissertation literature reviews and reports a study that examined dissertations at three universities. Acquiring the skills and knowledge required to be academic scholars, able to analyse and synthesize the research in a field of specialization, should be the focal. intergrative activity of pre-dissertation graduate development. Such scholarship is a prerequisite for increasing methodological sophistication and for improving the usefulness of academic research (adapted from: Boote, & Beile, 2005: 3).[15]

Ask yourself the following questions:
- What is the main argument of the article as put forward in this abstract?
- What is the 'gap' in the research as identified by these two authors?
- How do they indicate 'filling the gap'?
- What methodology have they employed?
- What were some of the results on which they report?
- What tense of the verbs has been used in writing this abstract?
- Why are there changes in verb tense?
- Are there any hedges or boosters in this abstract?
- How would you suggest improving this abstract when asked to rewrite it?

Case study

The Graduate School at the University of the Free State has embarked on a novel way of developing academic literacy. The School was afforded a dedicated space in which to develop essential knowledge, skills and attitudes with regard to the professionalisation of not only their academic staff, but also of all their graduate students. Teaching staff are given the opportunity to develop their research skills and harness new methodologies with regard to study supervision, and graduate students are given the opportunity to acquire specialised research skills such as electronic data analysis. In addition, students are introduced to the very important aspect of theory in their studies and theorising their research. They are taught what a Literature review is all about, and what possibilities exist with regard to structuring a suitable methodology for their studies. In terms of academic writing, graduate students have the opportunity to submit drafts of their proposals and drafts of various chapters from their research report for constructive feedback. The students who enroll for short, one- or two-day academic workshops that are offered throughout the academic year, are from various disciplines at the university and, as a result, the emphasis is on research methodology as such and not necessarily on disciplinary subject knowledge. Specialised courses for specific disciplines are, however, often arranged on prior request. The School thus advances the notion of academic literacy into a sophisticated discourse about research and scholarship.

References

1. Judith Butler, quoted in Sword, H. 2012. *Stylish Academic Writing*. Cambridge, MA: Harvard University Press.
2. Weidemann, A. 2003. *Academic Literacy: Prepare to Learn*. Pretoria: Van Schaik, p. ix.
3. Flower, L. & Hayes, J. 1981. A Cognitive Process Theory of Writing. *College composition and Communication*. 32 (4) 364-387.
4. Ibid. 32 (4) 372.
5. Ibid.
6. Coffin, C., Curry, M.J., Goodman, S., Hewings, A., Lillis, T.M. & Swann, J. 2003. *Teaching Academic Writing: A toolkit for higher education*. London: Routledge. p. 34.
7. Haas, S. 2009. Writers Groups for MA ESOL Students: Collaboratively Constructing a Model of the Writing Process. *ELTED Journal*, 12: 23-30.
8. Ibid. 12: 26.
9. Ibid. 12: 28.
10. Ivanic, R. 2004. *Writing and Identity: The Discoursal Construction of Identity in Academic Writing*. London: Routledge, p. 231.
11. Murray, R. 2007. *How to write a thesis*. Buckingham, UK: Open University Press. p. 9.
12. Grobler, P., Bothma, R., Brewster, C., Carey, L., Holland, P. & Warnich, S. 2013. *Contemporary Issues in Human Resource Management*. Cape Town: Oxford University Press Southern Africa. p. 36.
13. Swales, J.M. & Freak, C.B. 1994. *Academic writing for Graduate Students: Essential Tasks and Skills*. Ann Arbor: University of Michigan Press. p. 175.
14. Thompson, P. 2005. Points of focus and position: intertextual reference in PHD theses. *Journal of English for Academic Purposes*. p. 317-318.
15. Judith Butler, quoted in Sword, H. 2012. *Stylish Academic Writing*. Cambridge, MA: Harvard University Press.

Index

A

ABI/INFORM 57
abbreviations 228
abstracts 216, 218, 225, 231, 234–235
academic
 discourse community 237, 255
 literacy 237–258
academic research
 producing 23–24
 writing 237, 251, 252–253, 255
access to participants 77
accounting variables 210
Accounting Standards Board (ASB) 20
accuracy 149
acknowledgements 218
acronyms 148, 228
ACSA *see* Airports Company South Africa
action research 88, 109–111, 126
actors' approach to creating business knowledge 12
administrative directives 216
advertisements and advertising campaigns 2–3
advertising expenditure 90
AECI 20
Africa 33
agency theory approach 248
Agricultural Research Council (ARC) 20
Airports Company South Africa (ACSA) 20
alternate and alternative hypotheses 43
Alzheimer's Disease 214, 215
American Psychological Association (APA) referencing style 251
analytical approach to creating business knowledge 11–12
Anbor 57
Anderson, Ken 105
annual financial statements 210
Annual Reports 34
ANOVA tests and studies 150, 178

Anscombe's quartet 175
anthropology 105
APA referencing style *see* American Psychological Association referencing style
applications (apps), mobile or web-based 76–77
applied business research 22–23, 27
approval of proposal by supervisor and/or head of department 192
apps *see* applications, mobile or web-based
ARC *see* Agricultural Research Council
arguments 202, 238, 249, 256
Armaments Corporation of South Africa (ARMSCOR) 20
ARMSCOR *see* Armaments Corporation of South Africa
artefacts 119–120
ASB *see* Accounting Standards Board
assessment criteria 224–225
association, spurious 90
assumptions 201, 221, 225, 232
Atlas.ti software 121
attributes 142
audience 241, 242
Australia 34, 74
Automobile Association of South Africa 20
average returns of value strategies 69, 70
axial coding 121

B

background
 chapters, writing of 253–254
 to studies 199
bar graphs 171
baseline measurement 91
basic
 business research 22, 27
 research approaches 78–86
behaviour 141–142
behaviourist analysis 70, 194, 210

BE/ME *see* book to market ratio
best practice 234
beta 43, 69, 70, 209, 210
bias 65, 222, 232
bibliographical details 62
bibliographic details, recording of 59
bibliographies, listing of sources in 250–251
bibliometric analysis (bibliometrics) 79
Bidvest 20
binning 159, 180
BitTorrent 74
bivariate
 analysis 180
 correlation 173
BMR *see* Bureau of Market Research *under* University of South Africa
boardroom behaviour 248
book to market ratio (BE/ME) 69, 70, 208, 209
books, referencing of 250
boosters 254
bootstrapping 170
brain scans 214
brand 37, 109
British American Tobacco 20
Budget Speech (2011) 234
business research, philosophy and aims of 2–30

C

Canada 34, 70, 209
capital asset pricing model (CAPM) 69, 70, 209
CAPM *see* capital asset pricing model
carbon taxes 56
case research method 88, 106–109, 126
case studies:
 development of academic literacy by Graduate School at the University of the Free State 258

financing mechanisms proposed for funding national health insurance in South Africa 234–235
impact of leadership practices on service quality in PHE institutions 49
innovation in organisations 127
marketing research 154
Nkomo's shoe trade 96–97
research proposals 207–211
strategy implementation in JSE listed organisations 181–182
value investment strategies 68–70
case study research 106–109, 126
cash flow yield (C/P) 69, 208, 209
categorical variable 177
CATI systems *see* Computer Aided Telephone Interview systems
causal
 -comparative research *see* ex post facto research and studies
 research designs 86, 90, 95
causality 103
CD-ROM databases 57
CEF *see* Central Energy Fund
Central Energy Fund (CEF) 20
Centres of Excellence (CoEs) 34–35
CEOs, research into *see* Chief Executive Officers, research into
CFA *see* confirmatory factor analysis
chain referral sampling *see* snowball sampling
Chapter 1 225
chapters
 in books, referencing of 250
 of theses 221–222, 226
Chief Executive Officers (CEOs), research into 77, 182
chief information officers (CIOs) 140, 250–251
children, caution to be exercised in conducting research among 76

Chile 234
chimpanzee behaviour, research into 99
Chi-square test for independence 177, 179
CIOs *see* chief information officers
citing of sources in texts 56, 196, 201
claims 249
clients, 'high net worth' 90
cluster sampling 136
Coca Cola, history of 87
code book 159, 160, 161–162, 163, 180
codes of conduct 76
coding 123, 152, 160
 families 121
CoEs *see* Centres of Excellence
coherence 126, 247, 256
cohesion 247, 248, 256
Colombia 234
communication, intra-organisational 78
company size 69, 70, 209
Competition Commission 20
completeness 126
Computer Aided Telephone Interview (CATI) systems 139
concepts 202
conceptual studies 79–80
concluding
 chapter 222–223, 225–226
 remarks 196
conclusion 231, 254–255
concomitant variation 90, 95
confirmatory factor analysis (CFA) 176
confounding variables 91
consensual characteristic 126
consent of participants, informed 76, 190
constructivist paradigm 6–7
construct validity 150
Consumer Financial Vulnerability Index 80
content
 analysis 104, 121, 122, 126
 validity 150
context
 paragraphs 202
 of study 199

control groups 91
controllability 231
control of variables 220
convenience sampling 136
conventional content analysis 122
conversation analysis 122
corporate
 branding processes and practices 109
 governance 248
 strategy 109
correlation analysis 173–174, 176–177
correlational research 92–93
counterarguments 249
Coursera 159
courses of action
 evaluating 21–22
 selecting and implementing 21
covariance 69, 209
cover page 199
C/P *see* cash flow yield
critical
 realism 102–103, 126
 theorist/post-modernist paradigm 6
 theory 102, 126
Cronbach's alpha coefficient 165
cross-sectional research and studies 8, 27, 89
crosstabulation 179
crystallisation 77, 95
customer service 86

D

data 205, 220
 alternative methods for producing 117–120
 analysis 78, 80, 152, 157–179, 220, 221–222
 becoming familiar with 123
 capturing 152
 cleaning 164–165
 coding 159–163
 dissemination 152
 gaining access to 189
 production 114–117
 triangulation 77, 78
 types of 144–145, 160
Data Analysis Toolpak 158

database design and capturing 163–164
data collection 78, 105, 106, 136–140, 157, 221
   instruments 141–151
deductive
   and inductive approaches to qualitative data analysis 120–121
   research 8–9, 27, 78, 81–82, 95
defence of proposal 202
definitions 201, 225
degree for which thesis presented 192
Delphi technique 117
demographic research 90
Denel (Pty) Ltd 20
department in which candidate enrolled 192
Department of
   Labour 58
   Trade and Industry 58
depression 230
descriptive
   statistics 157, 158, 169, 171, 180
   surveys 89–90
descriptive research 7–8, 86, 95
   designs 88–90
Desmond Tutu HIV Foundation 20
detailed explanation 229
developmental designs 89
deviant case sampling 113
diagnostic analyses 90
diagrams 218
diaries 117
dictionaries, consulting of 186, 187, 228
direct
   observation 119
   quotation 246–247
directed content analysis 122
discourse analysis 122
dissertation blues 230
Doctor of Philosophy 224
documentation 152
document review 120
documents 102, 119
   from organisations, referencing of 251
drafting 240, 241, 242, 243
drivers of advertising agency retention of clients 84

E

earnings yield (E/P) 69, 209
EBSCO Host 57
ECONLIT 57
editing 152, 242, 243
education, level of 178–179
Education and training 34
efficient market hypothesis 70
E-journals A to Z via SFX 57
electronic databases 52, 56, 66
embedded mixed methods design 85–86
Emerald Full text 57
empirical unfolding of research problems 45
employee commitment and retention 84
engagement levels of employees 37
entrepreneurial development programme 111
E/P see earnings yield
epistemology 6, 27, 107
equity market returns 68–70
errors in
   surveys, sources of 152–153
   theses 226
ESOMAR codes of conduct 76
ethical
   banking 37
   clearance 195–196, 203
   considerations in business research 76–77, 201, 203, 205, 221
   dilemmas 190
   requirements, complying with 189–190
   research 18–19, 27, 187
ethical issues:
   bias and referencing 65
   ESOMAR codes of conduct 76
   ethical standards applied in generating data 80
   manipulation of research subjects in experimental research 93
   objectiveness 223
   plagiarism 228
ethicality of research 40
ethics committees 190
ethnography 88, 105, 126
Europe 33, 70, 209 evaluating the work of others 63

evidence 112, 249
exact test 170
examination by examiners of a thesis in practice 225–226
examiners and examiners' reports, guidelines and criteria provided for 216, 218, 223–225
experimental research 11, 95
explanation 103
explanatory
   mixed methods design 83–84
   research 8, 37, 86
explicit characteristic 126
exploratory
   factor analysis 175–176
   mixed methods design 84
   research and research designs 7, 87, 95
exploring 243–244
ex post facto research and studies 92–93
extended argument 229

F

face validity 150
Fairfax 74
field research 99
figures 218
file sharing 74
financial institutions 2–3
financing mechanisms proposed for funding national health insurance in South Africa 234–235
findings 62
First National Bank (FNB) 2–3
Flower and Hayes' writing model 241–242
FNB see First National Bank
focus groups 86, 114, 115–117, 127
For God, Country and Coca-Cola: The Definitive History of the Great American Soft Drink and the Company That Makes It (Pendergrast) 87
four Ps 34
frequency distribution 159, 160, 166, 171, 172
fringe benefits 177

G

general sources 61
golden thread of argument 229
Goodall, Jane 99
Google Scholar 56, 58
government publications 58
graduate writing centre 237
graphs 218
grounded theory 88, 105–106, 127
groups, comparing of 177–179
growth
   rate in sales (G/S) 69, 209
   shares 69
G/S *see* rate in sales *under* growth
Guidelines for
   the evaluation of theses, dissertations and mini-dissertations (North-West University) 224
   Examiners for the Degree of Doctor of Philosophy 223

H

Haas model 243–244
harm, protection from 190
Harvard method of referencing 251
health care financing mechanisms 234–235
hedges 254
hermeneutics and hermeneutic units 104, 122
Higher Degrees Guide (Rhodes University) 195
higher education institutions 37, 49
histograms 170, 171
historical research 87
HSRC *see* Human Sciences Research Council
Human Sciences Research Council (HSRC) 20
hypotheses 42–44, 48, 146–147, 176, 177, 180, 193, 222, 225, 232
hypothesis testing 157, 177

I

IBM SPSS® 152, 159, 160, 163, 165, 169, 179

ICT
   companies 105, 108
   managers 86
idea regeneration 242, 243
ideological sources of oppression 102
illegal file download providers 74
illustration 107
implementation principles 134
imputation 152
incubating 243–244
independent variables 92–93
inductive
   approaches to qualitative data analysis 120–121
   research 9–10, 27, 78, 82–83
inferential
   approach to research 11
   statistics 157
Information brokerage 34
Information for the Guidance of Examiners of Master's Dissertations (University of KwaZulu-Natal) 224–225
information from literature items, extracting of 60
informed consent of participants 76, 190
innovation
   in organisations 127
   orientation of pharmaceutical companies 85
inspiration 107
interest 225
inter-method reliability 148
internal
   brand alignment 83
   consistency reliability 148, 165
   culture 109
   review boards 190
Internal and External Examiner's Report (Rhodes University) 224
international investment opportunities 70
internet 52–53, 56, 58, 59, 80
   articles, referencing of 251
interpretation 221–222, 231
interpretivism 101–102, 127
interpretivist/constructivist paradigm 6

inter-rater reliability 148
interval
   data 145
   -like data 171
interview-based surveys 137–138
interviewees 114
interviews 78, 84, 102, 104, 109, 111, 114–115, 120
intransitive reality 102
introduction 225, 249, 252
introductory
   chapter 218–219, 229
   paragraphs 202
investigators, weaknesses related to 203
investigator triangulation 77–78
Islamic banking 37
isolation, feelings of 230
iterative process of writing 242–243

J

Japan 70, 209, 234
job satisfaction 177
Johannesburg Stock Exchange *see* JSE Limited
Journal of Accounting and Economics 58
journal articles, referencing of 250
JSE *see* JSE Limited
JSE Limited (JSE)
   listed organisations 181–182
judgment sampling 136

K

key words 56–57, 66, 218, 231
King III, new 34
knowledge 12–13, 17, 34, 202, 245–247, 251
Kruskal-Wallis test 178
kurtosis 166, 168–169, 170, 171, 180

L

language usage 252–253
latent variables 176, 180
leadership
   behaviour in the boardroom 248

practices, impact of on service quality in PHE institutions 49
legal action 74
length of journal articles and theses 74, 231
leptokurtic distribution 168
LexisNexis 57
library catalogues 57
Likert-type response categories 171
limitations of scope 201
linear
   model of writing 240–241
   regression lines 175
linguistic
   strategies 254
   structures 253
linking words 247
list of contents 218, 225
lists 143
literature
   reviews 27, 53, 60–65, 66, 79, 193, 200, 219, 231
   surveys 52–71, 186, 187, 202, 203, 204
literature items
   evaluating the quality of 61–62
   extracting of information from 60
living standards measure (LSM) 161, 162
logical
   arguments 229
   reasoning skills 204
   validity see validity under content
loneliness, feelings of 230
longitudinal research and studies 8, 27, 89
LoveLife South Africa 20
LSM *see* living standard measure

M

mail surveys 139
management development training 92
manipulation
   lack of 92
   of research subjects in experimental research 93
Mann-Whitney U Test 178
market
   research 74
   segmentation 108
marketing 74
Master's degree 16, 31, 49, 53, 64, 68, 76, 114, 192, 203, 215, 216, 223, 224
maximum values 166, 168
MBA programmes 90
McGregorBFA online database 210
mean value 166, 167
measurement
   of data 221–222
   scales 171
measure of symmetry 170
measures
   shape 166, 171
   triangulation of 78, 85, 95
measures of central
   dispersion 166, 170, 171 see also maximum values; minimum values; range; standard deviation; variance
   tendency 166, 170, 171 see also mean value; median value; mode
media companies 74
Media Institute of Southern Africa 20
median value 166
memory, writer's long-term 241, 242
mesokurtic distribution 168
methodical approach 112, 126
methodological
   approaches and research designs 11–14
   triangulation 77, 100
methodology 62
Mexico 234
Microsoft 105
   Internet Explorer 58
middle management strategising practices 78
minimum values 166, 168
mining industry 114
Minister of Finance 234
mixed methods research designs 13, 78, 83–86, 95
mobile
   phones, ethical and practical guidelines for conducting research using 76–77
   and web-based applications (apps), ethical use of to collect data 76–77
mode 166, 167, 170, 171
monitoring 241, 242
mono-method research 78
Moody, Glyn 74
motivation 107
MS Excel® 152, 158, 159, 163
multi-methods research 78
multiple
   case studies 108–109
   independent samples test 178
multivariate analysis 180

N

name of
   candidate 192
   supervisor 192
nano narratives 120
narrative analysis 120, 121, 122–123, 124, 210
National
   Gambling Board of South Africa 20
   Research Foundation (NRF) 34
   Treasury 58
national health insurance, financing mechanisms proposed for funding 234–235
Nelson Mandela Children's Fund 20
Netscape Navigator 58
Networking 34
newspaper articles, referencing of 250
New Zealand 70, 209
niches, establishment of within a broader research territory 253
'no harm' rule 76
nominal
   data 145
   group technique 117
   variable 166

non-
  empirical research designs 78–80, 95
  experimental research 92–93
  parametric tests 178, 180
  probability sampling methods 136, 157
  textual data 80
nonspurious association 95
normal
  curve 169
  distribution 167, 170, 180
North-West University. Faculty of Economic and Management Sciences. Potchefstroom Campus 224
notes, using knowledge by making 245–247
NRF see Research Foundation under National
nuisance variables 222, 232
null hypotheses 43, 177, 178
numerical data 80

O

observation studies 89, 99, 111, 119, 120
ODA practices see Official Development Aid practices
Official Development Aid (ODA) practices 120
one-on-one interviews 114–115
online
  customers, targeting of 74
  databases and searches 57, 58
ontology 6, 27, 107
OPAC 57
open-
  ended interviews 114
  mindedness 126
operating systems 105
opinions 141
opportunities, identifying 21–22
ordinal data 145, 171
organisational
  artefacts 78
  barriers 104
  performance 109

organising of ideas
  encountered during literature surveys 63
  in sentences, paragraphs and sections 247–248
outliers 166, 174, 175
overpricing 70

P

paired-samples test 178
paragraphs 202, 247–248
parametric tests 178, 180
paraphrasing 238, 246, 256
Parks, Markus 214
PAR process see participatory action research process
participant observation 88, 95, 105, 111, 118–119, 120, 127
participants, random allocation of 91
participatory action research (PAR) process 111
path analysis 176
Pearson's product moment correlation coefficient 173
Pendergrast, Mark 87
People 34
perceived customer value in the automotive industry supply chain 176
Perceived Stress Scale 160–161, 165
perceptions 85, 102, 104
performance
  good 234
  management systems 102, 103
personal
  face-to-face interviews 137–138
  financial management among consumers 80
  interaction 176
persuasiveness 126
Phenomena 34
phenomenology 87, 104, 127
photographs, ethical use of mobile phones to take 76
pictures and drawings, use of 117–118
pilot testing to assess reliability and validity, importance of 151

plagiarism 18, 27, 246, 251–252, 256
planning
  of research 56–57, 203, 240, 241, 242, 243
  to write reports 216–217
platykurtic distribution 168, 170
polishing 243–244
positivist/post-positivist paradigm 6, 7
postal surveys 139
postcard artefacts 120
practical considerations in research design 75
practice turn in management research 103
pragmatism 7
precision 149
pre-drafting 240, 241
preliminary
  analysis, conducting of 166–172
  chapter outline 201
preparing of data for analysis 158–165
pre-
  post test design 91
  testing 91
  writing 242, 243
primary
  objectives 49
  reference sources 61, 66, 225
probability
  sampling methods 135–136
  value (p-value) 43, 177, 179
product
  awareness 90
  delivery and quality 176
  development support 176
profitability of companies 34
Programmes 34
projective techniques 117
project management 106
promotion opportunities 177
proofreading 242, 243
protection of
  participants from harm 190
  private information of participants 76
provisional
  outline of thesis chapters 196
  title 192, 199

INDEX

publishing 243–244
purposefulness 126
purposive sampling 113, 114
p-value *see* value *under* probability

Q

qualitative
  approach to research 11
  case study methodology 10, 83
qualitative data
  analysis and interpretation 120–123
  presentation of 124–125
qualitative research
  designs 99–130
  methods 84, 85, 86, 111–125
Qualtrics™ 139, 163
quantitative data analysis techniques in research 84, 85, 86, 92–93, 100–101, 111, 156–183
quantity 144
quasi-experimental designs 92–93
questionnaire-based surveys 139–140
questionnaires 85, 86, 111, 134, 141–151, 156, 190
quota sampling 136
quotation, direct 246–247

R

random
  assignment of subjects 91, 95
  sampling 135
range 166, 168, 170
ranking 143–144
rating 144
ratio data 145
rational analysis and narratives 194, 210
reading, when to stop 58
recommendations 231
record-keeping 58–60
references and referencing 56, 65, 196, 201, 225, 228, 231, 249–252, 256
reflection 242, 243
regression analysis 174–175, 176–177

relationship between
  job satisfaction and employee retention within medium-sized private firms 131
  perceived retail crowding and shopping satisfaction 147
relationships among variables, exploring 172–179
relevance to research 60, 62, 225
reliability 148–149, 151, 215, 222, 231
REMGRO 20
replicability 220, 231
reporting
  of research 18
  verbs 253
report writing 119, 229
reproduction 63
research
  additional 242, 243
  approaches 3–10, 27
  design 3, 10–18, 27, 74–98, 195, 201, 203, 226
  frameworks 54
  goals 62, 193–194, 200, 202, 203, 210, 225
  methods 14, 17, 195, 201, 203, 210, 226
  models and model cases 54, 66, 80
  objectives 41–42, 48, 49, 62, 133–134
  paradigms 3, 6, 27, 77, 220, 232
  philosophies 6–7, 27
  problems and problem statements 7, 21–22, 31–51, 133–134, 199, 202, 203, 215, 230
  proposals 24, 27, 186–213, 215
  propositions 48
  purpose 7–8, 14–18, 40–44, 193–194, 200
  questions 33, 40–41, 48, 86, 142–144, 147–148, 189, 193, 205, 225
  reporting 214–236
  reports, structuring the writing of 240–248

  results 221–222, 231
  statements 49
  subproblems 39
  subquestions 41
  techniques 210
  theories 9, 46–47, 54, 66, 225
  topics 4–6, 33, 48, 189, 205, 225, 241, 242, 248
Research/knowledge production 34
research methodology 6, 14, 27, 45–46, 203, 231
  chapter 218–221
resources
  limited 75
  required, ensuring availability of 190
  weaknesses related to 204
Results/Findings chapter or section 254
retail banking service expectations 9
Reunert 20
review of the literature 241, 242, 243
revising 240, 241, 242, 243
Rhodes University
  criteria of for a Master's degree by half thesis 224
  Guidelines for Examiners for the Degree of Doctor of Philosophy 223
  Higher Degrees Guide 195
  Internal and External Examiner's Report 224
  online catalogue 57
rigorous characteristic 126
risk 70, 209, 210
rival hypotheses 222, 232
roadmap to analysing data 157–158
role of
  the researcher in qualitative research 111–112
  theory in problem formulation 46–47
role players 84

S

SAARF *see* Audience Research Foundation *under* South African

Sabinet Online 57
sample
    characteristics 166
    design 134–136
    size in qualitative data 113–114
sampling 112–114
    distribution 166–172
SAMRA see Southern African Marketing Research Association
SAS/STAT 159
saturation, theoretical 114
scale
    measures 161
    reliability, assessing 165
scales as proxy measures for hypothetical constructs 146–147
scatter plots 174, 175
Science Direct 57
scientific methods 27, 81, 95
scope
    limitations of 201, 225, 232
    required 76
    of research 203, 225
Scopus 57
secondary
    objectives 49
    reference sources 61, 66
sections, organising of ideas in 247–248
segment of consumers, customers or employees, detailed description of 90
selecting of a suitable statistical program to analyse data 158–159
selective coding 121
SEM see structural equation modelling
semi-structured
    interviews 85, 109, 114, 120
    questionnaires 134
sentences, organising of ideas in 247–248
servant leadership 104
Service rendering 34–35
SERVQUAL questionnaire 9, 81
share price data 210
significance
    level 43

of studies 200
significant outliers 166
signposting 226
simulation approach to research 11
single case studies 107–108
skewness statistic 166, 168, 170, 171, 180
small medium enterprises (SMEs) 248
SMEs see small medium enterprises
'snowball' method 56
snowball sampling 113, 114, 136
Snowflake Bake for Profit course 111
social construction 102
sources 250–251
    primary, secondary and general 61
sources of
    errors in surveys 152–153
    research items relevant to research 57–58
South African
    Audience Research Foundation (SAARF) 161
    Concise Oxford Dictionary 186
    Department of Labour 21–22
    Household Wealth Index 80
    Revenue Services 58
Southern African Marketing Research Association (SAMRA) 76
South Korea 234
Spearman's rank correlation coefficient 173
spurious association 90
standard deviation 166, 168, 171
standardised tests 220–221, 232
Stata 159
statements of
    overall purpose 40
    research purpose, formulating 40–44
statistical
    analysis 156
    package 169, 179

tests 170
Statistics
    South Africa (Statistics SA) 58, 90
step-wise approach to analysing your data and reporting the results
Stevens, Stanley Smith 171
'Steve' radio campaign 2–3
strategic
    analysis tools 114
    decision making 80
    plans and planning 78, 134
strategies, sampling 113
strategy
    disclosure 34
    implementation 106
stratified sampling 135–136
structural equation modelling (SEM) 173, 176–177
structured interviews 114
structuring of research reports 243–244, 256
Strydom, Johan 62
style 231
subjects, assignment of 91
summarising 238, 246, 256
summative content analysis 122
supervisors and supervision 177, 216
SurveyMonkey™ 139, 163
surveys as research strategy 131–155
Sutton, Ricky 74
symmetrical shape distribution 167
synthesising 63
systematic
    observation 140
    sampling 135
    variation 90
systems approach to creating business knowledge 12–13
style 231

T

Taiwan 70, 209, 234
targeting of online customers 74
task environment 241, 242
TAT see thematic apperception test

tax avoidance, reasons for 55
t-distribution 170
Techdirt 74
technical aspects of writing 227–228
technology 105
telephone interviews 138
temporal
  sequence 90, 95
  themes 122
tense, choice of 254
terms 202
testing theories 81
test-retest reliability 148
textual data 80
Thailand 234
thematic apperception test (TAT) 117
themes 60, 121
theoretical
  frameworks 66
  sampling 113
  saturation 114
theorising 123
theory
  building 27, 82
  triangulation 78
theses 31, 215, 216–217, 223, 231
threats of legal action 74
Tiger Brands 20
time-to-market 176
title page 192, 217
titles 202, 225
Tokyo Stock Exchange data 69, 208
transitive reality 102
translating 241, 242
transparency 112, 126
treatment groups 91
trend in earnings 70
triangulation, role of 77–78, 85, 95
true experimental designs 91–92
t-tests 170, 178
tutors 237
two independent-samples test 178
Type
  I error 43
  II error 43

U

underpricing 70
understandings, evaluating emergent 124
Unisa *see* University of South Africa
United States of America *see* USA
units of
  analysis 33, 48, 134, 153, 220, 232
  observation 153
univariate analysis 166–172, 180
universal health coverage 234–235
universities 18, 23, 24, 27, 58, 102, 118, 143, 160, 178, 186, 187, 188, 189, 190, 191, 192, 193, 194, 195, 196, 197, 198, 199, 201, 202, 203, 205, 216, 217
university libraries 56
University of
  the Free State. Graduate School 258
  Johannesburg. Faculty of Education 237
  KwaZulu-Natal. Faculty of Management Studies 224–225
University of South Africa (Unisa)
  Bureau of Market Research (BMR) 80, 90
  Department of Business Management template for evaluating journal articles 62
unloading 243–244
USA (United States of America) 33, 34, 69, 70, 209, 248
usefulness 126
Utrecht Work Engagement Scale *see* UWES
UWES (Utrecht Work Engagement Scale) 37

V

validity 148, 149, 150, 151, 166, 223, 232
value investment strategies 68–70, 208–211
variables 69, 91, 92–93, 141–142, 160, 167, 172–179, 205, 208, 210, 220, 222, 232
variance 166, 168
verbs, reporting 253
video recordings 105
videos, ethical use of mobile phones to make 76
Vietnam 234

W

Water Research Commission (WRC) 20
weaknesses in research proposals 202–204
Web-based surveys 139–140
weights 162
Wikipedia 58
Wilcoxon Signed Rank Test 178
work, nature of 177
worthlessness, feelings of 230
WRC *see* Water Research Commission
writing 18, 63–65, 117, 186–213, 227–230, 241, 242, 256

Y

YouTube.com 159